O·50
A

48
61
69/70

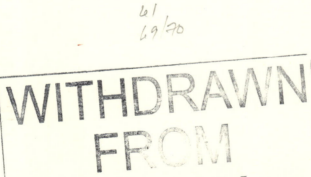

PSYCHOLOGICAL ISSUES

VOL. IX, Nos. 2/3   MONOGRAPH 34/35

FREUD: THE FUSION OF SCIENCE AND HUMANISM

The Intellectual History
of Psychoanalysis

Edited by
JOHN E. GEDO and GEORGE H. POLLOCK

INTERNATIONAL UNIVERSITIES PRESS, INC.
239 Park Avenue South • New York, N.Y. 10003

Library of Congress Cataloging in Publication Data
Main entry under title:

Freud, the fusion of science and humanism.

   (Psychological issues; v. 9, no. 2; Monograph; 34-35)
   CONTENTS: Gedo, J. E. and Wolf, E. S. From the
history of introspective psychology: the humanist strain.
—Trosman, H. Freud's cultural background—Gedo, J. E.
and Wolf, E. S. The "ich" letters. [etc.]—Bibliog-
raphy: (p.   )
   1. Freud, Sigmund, 1856-1939. 2. Psychoanalysis—
History—Addresses, essays, lectures. I. Gedo, John E.
II. Pollock, George H. III. Series. [DNLM: 1. Psy-
choanalysis—History. WI PS572 v. 9 no. 34/35 / WM11.1
F8891
BF173.F85F742   150'.19'52   75-792
ISBN 0-8236-2031-X

PSYCHOLOGICAL ISSUES

HERBERT J. SCHLESINGER, *Editor*

CONTENTS

ACKNOWLEDGMENTS

We acknowledge our gratitude to the following publications for permission to reprint certain material included in this volume:

The Annual of Psychoanalysis and Quadrangle/The New York Times Book Co. (Chapters 2 and 4); *Psyche* (Chapters 3 and 15); *The Journal of the American Psychoanalytic Association* and International Universities Press (Chapters 5, 6, 7, 8, 10, 11, 13, and 14); *The Psychoanalytic Study of the Child* and Quadrangle/The New York Times Book Co. (Chapter 9); *The American Imago* (Chapter 12).

We also express our thanks to Jacqueline Miller and Suzette H. Annin for their careful editorial assistance in the preparation of this volume.

PREFACE

The first half century of the history of psychoanalysis is closely intertwined with the personal biography of Sigmund Freud. Analysis is unique as an intellectual discipline in having been entirely created by one man; critics who attack present-day psychoanalysis by alleging that Freud's inheritors have erected a cult with the founder as hero have simply ignored this unparalleled aspect of the origin of this field of science. As a matter of fact, in the 35 years since the death of Freud, psychoanalysts have, by and large, lost sight of his vision of humanist introspection; the profession of psycho-analysis has become something like a medical specialty, emphasizing therapeutic goals over Freud's primary aim of understanding man's inner life. It is only through historical studies of the development of psychoanalysis that we can hope to recapture the general purport of Freud's work and to escape relegation into narrow clinical pragmatism. This book is one attempt to reverse the trend of putting the cart of Freud's analytic procedure before the horse of his great discovery of the method of scientific self-study.

In putting together this collection of papers on the intellec-tual history of psychoanalysis, we have chosen to begin with a section devoted to the cultural and personal background from which Freud entered his professional life. Gedo and Wolf trace the history of introspective psychology, with special reference to its development in the Renaissance and its subsequent relegation to the province of the humanists with the triumph of the Cartesian revolution which has stamped science with its materialist bias. In Chapter 2, Trosman reviews some of the specific intellectual currents of the nineteenth century which exerted a significant influence on Freud. The next two chapters examine the available productions of Freud's adolescence, demonstrating some of the channels through which the humanist heritage became available to the future creator of psychoanalysis.

We then leave Freud as an 18-year-old medical student. The papers of this collection make no contribution to his biography for the next two decades of his life. We shall focus on his activities once more as of the early 1890's, when he laid the foundations for psychoanalysis in his collaborative work with Josef Breuer. This will be the subject matter of Part III. In the interval, the history of psychoanalysis must, exceptionally, abandon its concentration on Freud's person; it has to turn its attention to the work of three persons without whose participation in the development of the study of emotional disturbances Freud might not have utilized his genius in the service of elucidating psychopathology.

Consequently, Part II consists of two historical studies about these three persons. Miller and his co-authors discuss the influence of the great Parisian neurologist, Jean Martin Charcot, on his Viennese disciple, Sigmund Freud; although their paper describes the relevance for psychoanalysis of Charcot's work on hysteria, it also gives us some glimpses of Freud's personal situation in the mid-1880's. In the next chapter, Pollock illuminates the psychological investigations of Josef Breuer, Freud's principal supporter for 15 years and the essential collaborator with whom he ultimately launched his psychoanalytic enterprise. This paper also considers the personality of Breuer's patient "Anna O.," who devised the cathartic method of psychotherapy under the name of "chimney sweeping." The identity of this fascinating and creative woman, Bertha Pappenheim, was first revealed by Ernest Jones. Since the publication of his Freud biography, further historical research has been performed, among others by Pollock (1971, 1972, 1973), about Frl. Pappenheim's illness as well as her subsequent life. In his papers on this topic, Pollock has summarized the results on these investigations; by studying the possible significance of Frl. Pappenheim's later activities, he has also succeeded in reaching some new insights about the nature of the clinical problem with which Josef Breuer and "Anna O." had been confronted in 1881-1882.

The thread of the narrative continues with the Breuer-Freud collaboration through the early 1890's which culminated in the publication of *Studies on Hysteria* (1893-1895). The personal history of Freud's struggles during these years of financial hardship, expanding family responsibility, and professional transition has been adequately described in previous studies. We have therefore chosen to highlight the scientific issues of his development in this period. Part III traces the evolution of his methodology from the canons of conventional Baconian science toward a unique blend of science with humanism.

In Chapter 7, Gedo and co-workers demonstrate the inner coherence between observational data and Freud's theoretical conclusions up to 1895, as well as the absence of logical connections between evidence and hypotheses in Breuer's portion of *Studies on Hysteria*. The next chapter is an attempt to compare Breuer's psychological work with his publications in the realm of physiology. Schlessinger et al. conclude that the loose reasoning in Breuer's "Theoretical" chapter in the *Studies* was quite atypical of his work as a scientific author; they go on to postulate that such a departure from his customary scientific style must represent the effects of those unconscious conflicts within Breuer which Pollock delineated in Chapter 6. Although Freud also had repressed conflicts which were stirred up by intimate exposure to his patients' transferences, he was able to avoid Breuer's failure as a psychologist through the greatest achievement of his career, that of including his own self within the field of his observations.

Chapter 9 records the turning point in Freud's professional

life, the moment of his alienation from the medical community, his lecture on "The Aetiology of Hysteria" (1896b). Wolf attempts to show that the negative reception of Freud's presentation could hardly have been caused by the content of his lecture; he makes a strong case for the possibility that the audience rejected it because of Freud's *style,* which was permeated with a sense of his own greatness. This lecture therefore stood at the threshold of placing Freud's own psychic life in the scientific spotlight as the proper subject matter of the psychologist's research. His self-analysis followed in short order, and in his subsequent writings he began to utilize the results of his introspective efforts as his prime evidential base. Simultaneously, Freud replaced the cathartic treatment he had inherited from Bertha Pappenheim and Josef Breuer by a technique based on the patient's associations, thereby inaugurating the psychoanalytic method. In Chapter 10, Trosman traces Freud's cryptomnesia about one source of the free-association procedure in some of the favorite reading of his early adolescence, the work of Ludwig Börne.

With the establishment of psychoanalysis as an introspective psychology, supplemented by observing others through empathic participation in their free associations (see Kohut, 1959), Freud had arrived at his mature working methods. Part IV describes several aspects of his activities in the last four decades of his life. Chapter 11, by Sadow et al., shows the interplay between Freud's self-observations and his careful secondary-process revision of hypotheses by tracing the fates of three early psychoanalytic concepts. In the next chapter, Gedo attempts to correlate the sequence of some of Freud's analytic discoveries with the clues available about the themes which emerged in his self-analysis after he ceased to communicate its results to Wilhelm Fliess. In Chapter 13, Trosman discusses one area in which Freud's introspective efforts did not succeed, that of his need to elevate the author of the Shakespearean opus into a personage of higher station than he could attribute to the ordinary man from Stratford. Finally, Wolf and Trosman elucidate the idealization behind Freud's relationship to one of his *Doppelgängern,* the essayist Popper-Lynkeus, as one of the consequences of his own eminence.

The last section of the collection examines Freud's impact on his followers, both past and present. The former are represented by his "Paladin and Grand Vizier," Sándor Ferenczi, whose psychoanalytic writings are reviewed by Gedo in Chapter 15. He demonstrates the continuing influence of Freud on most of Ferenczi's creative efforts, both through direct discussion and correspondence and by way of the internal dialogue within the mind of Ferenczi between his own self and the thoughts and ideals of his teacher and analyst. As for the present, the special problems of studying the life of Freud from the vantage point of those who have identified with his professional activities are discussed in the last chapter by Kohut. This concluding essay reviews the special features of Freud's creative accomplishment which may have necessitated the relationship to Fliess that proved to be central for the success of his introspective efforts. It ends with a proposal for possible future extensions of psychoanalysis into the realm of investigation of the historical process.

In presenting a sampling of work on the history of psycho-analysis produced in Chicago within the past decade, we have tried to unify, through editorial introductions to each paper and a series of editorial footnotes,[1] what may at first glance appear to be a diverse body of work. It is true that a number of these papers were produced as a collaborative effort in a Workshop on the Scientific Methodology of Psychoanalysis organized by the then Director of Research at the Chicago Institute, George H. Pollock. Moreover, the studies carried out individually by Gedo and by Pollock after the cessation of formal activity by the Workshop owe their inspiration to the impetus provided for research in the history of psychoanalysis by this official encouragement. This atmosphere has been perpetuated by a regular forum for work in progress provided by the weekly Research Conference at the Institute.

Thus the formal authorship of each paper in this volume probably fails to tell the whole story of the many helpful influences on its creation. We have made the editorial decision to eliminate the many acknowledgments of help received by

[1] The editorial footnotes are designated by letters (a, b, c...) within each chapter; the authors' own footnotes retain their original numbering.

the authors which were appended to these papers as originally published. In any case, most of these tributes referred to one or another colleague who is also represented by a contribution to this book. (However, a special note is probably due to some of those who generously lent assistance with the translation of the great mass of German source materials upon which most of this research was based. In this regard, Drs. Leslie Gable, Ernest Mond, Gerhart Piers, and Ernest Wolf were given explicit credit by various authors. Dr. Lothar Rubinstein was helpful in gathering evidence concerning the background of Josef Breuer; Pollock's work in that area was supported by the Foundations' Fund for Research in Psychiatry; the study of Popper-Lynkeus was supported by Grant MH 21, 060-06, U.S.P.H.S., and the Anne Pollock Lederer Fund gave generous support for Kohut's work on Chapter 16, and, together with the Fred M. Hellman Publishing Fund, supported the preparation of the manuscript of this entire volume.)

Heinz Kohut, who is represented only by the paper he wrote especially for this volume, is nevertheless no newcomer to our ranks. Not only did his 1966 discussion of a paper by Max Schur at the Chicago Psychoanalytic Society influence some of the essays in this collection; the studies originally published in Germany were commissioned from the actual authors on his recommendation. One of these initiated a collaboration between Gedo and Wolf which produced three of the papers presented here. It also led Wolf into some solo efforts, one of which is included here, and into certain joint projects with Trosman, again represented by one of these papers. Harry Trosman's researches in the history of psychoanalysis began almost 20 years ago, and in many ways he must be regarded as a pioneer for this field of activity in Chicago. For the most part, he has followed an independent intellectual course, one that had a strong impact on the entire psychoanalytic community in Chicago.

At any rate, our own estimate is that the papers we have included in our collection have sufficient unity of style, content, and approach to merit consideration as parts of one whole. We trust that the reader will respond to this volume with the delight of the gourmet when he samples the collection of 16 home-grown vegetables, each in its individual sauce, served in that temple of gastronomy, the Petite Auberge at Novès. Proudly, they call it *un bouquet de notre jardin;* with equal pride, we present this bouquet from ours.

PART I

BACKGROUND

1

FROM THE HISTORY OF INTROSPECTIVE PSYCHOLOGY: THE HUMANIST STRAIN

JOHN E. GEDO and ERNEST S. WOLF

[*The Ancestry of Psychoanalysis*. The psychoanalyst as historian is on familiar ground, as the search for evidence of the past and its interpretation in terms of meaning and significance are the shared methodological tools of both disciplines. Therefore, when we turn our attention to the history of psychoanalysis itself, we do so with the purpose of defining more clearly the very nature of psychoanalysis. As is the case with the person who undergoes an analytic experience in the hope of mastering his self with the aid of greater self-knowledge, so psychoanalysis as a discipline has increasingly devoted itself to self-study in order to maintain the creative impetus it possessed in the period of its gestation within the mind of Sigmund Freud.

The qualities of Freud's genius are so exceptional that they are not likely to be duplicated within the ranks of psychoanalysis in the foreseeable future; these aspects of the origin of psychoanalysis have recently been reviewed in Eissler's book on the Freud-Tausk relationship, *Talent and Genius* (1971b). In the following chapter, Gedo and Wolf address themselves to those aspects which *can* be replicated, namely, the specific characteristics of an introspective psychology. To this end, they have collected evidence concerning the history of this discipline up to the lifetime of Freud, with special reference to the period of the Renaissance. They have found that introspective psychology first flourished in Greece in late classical times and, like so many other intellectual endeavors, flowered again between the fourteenth and the early seventeenth centuries. They go on to describe some of the reasons for its decline between the age of Montaigne (the foremost introspective psychologist of the Renaissance) and that of Freud.

It may be of particular interest that the history of introspective psychology reveals it to have been a specialty of the "humanists." This term refers to a particular type of Renaissance intellectual who, in addition to their classical learning, focused their professional activities within the areas of poetry, history, and moral philosophy. It cannot be a coincidence, then, that Freud drew much of his inspiration for his psychological work from the poets, that he made his clinical activities into an analogue of the work of the archeologist (who shares with the historian the goal of searching for man's past) and applied his insights to manifold problems of history, and that he has been called by at least one eminent social critic, Rieff (1959), the saving moralist of the culture of the West. Many of the later chapters in this collection examine one or another of these aspects of Freud's intellectual life in some detail. Gedo and Wolf suggest that it is of the essence of the nature of the psychoanalyst's activity to engage in self-analytic introspection, to use the tools of poetry and history, and to aim at moral self-improvement.

Another implication of this chapter is that the prevailing intellectual climate of each era is determined by the major developments in philosophy within the age that preceded it. It has been fashionable among psychoanalysts to look upon Freud's discipline as something *sui generis,* created from the void. This attitude has been sanctioned by Freud's repeated comments depreciating the contributions of philosophers. It should be recalled, however, that Freud was merely expressing opposition to metaphysical preoccupations; he was in fact quite expert in epistemology and, of course, a major contributor to the field of ethics. He avoided the writings of the philosophers most germane to his subject matter, Schopenhauer and Nietzsche, in order to preserve an uncontaminated freshness of viewpoint toward his field of study. The very fact that Freud stated this as a conscious policy demonstrates that he did not regard psychoanalysis as an intellectual discipline without antecedents.

We now know that Freud had entertained a very serious intention of obtaining professional training in philosophy during his first years at the University of Vienna. Stanescu (1971) has reviewed the contents of an unpublished correspondence spanning those years which describes the major impact of his professor of philosophy, Franz Brentano, on the adolescent Freud. The connection between Freud and Brentano had been previously noted by Merlan (1945, 1949). Through the courtesy of Dr. Stanescu, we have seen a copy of one of Freud's letters in which he reviewed in detail Brentano's opinions about each of the major modern philosophers discussed in Gedo and Wolf's account of the evolution of epistemology since 1600. It is noteworthy that Brentano stressed the importance of Descartes and Leibniz but minimized that of Kant, and that Freud regarded his teacher as an admirable spokesman for a point of view diametrically opposed to his own. Another interesting revelation of the correspondence in Stanescu's possession is the fact that in 1873 the 17-year-old Freud was quite familiar with what Nietzsche had written up to that point. This does not mean, of course, that he continued to follow the philosopher's output during the later and more significant part of Nietzsche's career; in fact, it is quite probable that his interest in philosophy did not continue after he invested himself with enthusiasm in his physiological researches in Brücke's laboratory. Schur (1972) has revealed that, in a letter of February, 1900, to Wilhelm Fliess, Freud reported having just acquired the works of Nietzsche, "where I hope to find words for much that remains mute within me" (p. 202).

It would be unjustified to draw too many inferences from the evidence thus far made public about Freud on the subject of the intellectual sources of his psychological work. Nevertheless, studies such as this chapter may begin to place psychoanalysis within the context of a coherent tradition in Western culture—Eds.]

Chaque homme porte la forme entiere
de l'humaine condition.
                    Michel de Montaigne

HUMANISM AND INTROSPECTIVE PSYCHOLOGY

Paul Oskar Kristeller, probably the foremost historian of the intellectual currents of the Renaissance, has demonstrated that the humanist strain in Western culture was not, as has been popularly supposed, a reaction to mediaeval scholasticism. In Italy, the country to which the concept of a rebirth of classical learning and ideals is most applicable, these contrasting intellectual movements were actually contemporaneous and by no means always in opposition to each other. Kristeller (1961, 1965) differentiates between them primarily on the basis of professional affiliations: "... the term *Studia humanitatis* ... was taken up by the scholars of the early Italian Renaissance to stress the human value of the fields of study which they cultivated: grammar, rhetoric, poetry, history, and moral philosophy.... Soon the professional teacher of these subjects came to be called *humanista,* a 'humanist' " (1961, p. 121). It was within these fields, in contrast to medicine, law, philosophy, and theology — the strongholds of scholasticism and of the Aristotelian heritage — that the study of the Roman and, somewhat later, of the Greek classics gained momentum, transforming the European intellectual landscape in the course of three centuries.

The first prominent humanist was undoubtedly Petrarch, and the direction in which humanism was to carry Western man may be discerned from the beautiful anecdote about his ascent of Mont Ventoux:

> ...overwhelmed by the marvelous view, he took Augustine's *Confessions* out of his pocket and opened it at random. He found the following passage: "Men go to admire the heights of mountains, the great floods of the sea, the courses of rivers, the shores of the ocean, and the orbits of the stars, and neglect themselves." "I was was stunned," Petrarch continues, "closed the book and was angry at myself since I was still admiring earthly things although I should have learned long ago from

pagan philosophers that nothing is admirable but the soul"
[Kristeller, 1961, p. 125].

In his *Letter to Posterity* and in the posthumously published
Secretum, Petrarch revealed himself as the first great introspective autobiographer since Augustine. The fourteenth-century
humanist was still unable to read Greek and had to rely
exclusively on Latin sources: he called Cicero his father and
Virgil his brother.

Although men have always been concerned with the study of
Man, even when ostensibly absorbed in contemplation of their
God or in meditation on the nature of the world, psychology as a
science separate from other endeavors is an achievement of the
Renaissance. Classical Greece had given birth to great philosophers who were also deeply discerning psychologists, but the
term "psychology" was coined in 1540 by the Lutheran humanist
Melanchthon[1] (born Schwartzerd, "black earth," and helleni-
cized in the spirit of the age). A complete history of introspective
psychology would have to start, at the very least, with the
Platonic Socrates, who embodied the Delphic commandment
gnothi seauton, "Know thyself," and for whom the path to
knowledge was that of systematic introspection. The contributions of Plato, Aristotle, the Cynics, the Stoics, and the
Epicureans deserve to be reviewed in detail (see Zeller, 1883).
The collapse of Greco-Roman civilization around the time of
the death of its last great psychologist, St. Augustine, led to
the eclipse of these aspects of intellectual life, however, and to
systematic denial of the claims of the self until the age of
Petrarch.

Renaissance humanism thus provided psychology with a
new beginning and a name. Its growth was at first slow,
marked for the most part by discourses on the dignity and
excellence of Man, such as those of Gianozzo Manetti and Pico
della Mirandola. A sample of the latter's psychology may
illustrate the progress achieved by 1494: "... many forces
contend within us in deadly intestine war, worse than the civil

---

[1] It is probably no coincidence that a portrait of Melanchthon hangs above the
couch in Freud's consulting room between those of his two greatest teachers,
Charcot and Brücke.

wars of states. . . moral philosophy will halt the unreasoning drives of the many-sided brute, the passionate violence and the anger of the lion within us. . . . After both beasts are felled, like a sacrificed sow, an inviolable covenant of peace between flesh and spirit will have been accomplished" (1494, p. 149).

By the beginning of the sixteenth century, the stage was thus set for the emergence of a scientific introspective psychology, and its manifestations are easily detectable in the works of the major writers of the age, even through a cursory survey. Machiavelli, in his *Discourses* (1512-1527), explains the formation of character on the basis of identifications. Michelangelo, in one of his letters (1496-1563), makes a distinction between his actual self and the projective image of him constructed by the observer. In *Pantagruel,* Rabelais (1532) gives interpretations of two dreams, demonstrating wish fulfillments and the use of symbolic notation; in one instance, he reports an argument about the meaning of the dream which hinges on whether the dream is traumatic or a successful attainment of the wish. Rabelais also describes the suggestibility of patients and their responsiveness to the moods of their physicians. Both Rabelais and Erasmus, the latter in his *Praise of Folly* (1511), are explicitly aware of the significance of slips of the tongue: they make use of pseudo slips to indicate a pretense of innocence when someone wishes to announce an unpalatable truth. Erasmus stresses that the passions are not merely in conflict with reason; they are also needed to fuel every constructive action. Self-love is essential if man is to achieve, to avoid shame and discontent, to have pleasure and thus to become tolerable to others. Erasmus also made use of the quotation from Terence which has become a psychoanalytic motto: ideally, nothing human must be alien to man. Erasmus's friend Juan Luis Vives was almost modern in his emphasis on introspection as a way of gaining understanding of the emotions and of their influence on behavior. He was the first to describe the importance of psychological associations and their ability to evoke apparently long-forgotten memories.

An exhaustive survey of the literature of the sixteenth century is beyond the scope of this study; fortunately, it is not necessary for our purposes, because the introspective psychology of humanism found an encyclopedist in its greatest exponent, Michel de Montaigne. As Kristeller states:

> When we come to the end of the Renaissance, the subjective and personal character of humanist thought finds its most conscious and consummate philosophical expression in the *Essais* of Michel de Montaigne. Montaigne had received a humanist education, he knew Latin before he knew French, and his quotations from ancient authors, especially Plutarch and Seneca, fill many pages of his writings. The essay, in the form which he created and bequeathed to later centuries, is written in the first person, like the humanist letter, and is equally free in its style and structure: we might call the essay a letter written by the author to himself. Montaigne shares with the humanist his exclusive preoccupation with moral questions, his lack of interest in logic and metaphysics and the other learned disciplines, as well as his dislike for the scholastic type of learning. His philosophical position, though flexible, shows the impact of ancient skepticism, and to a lesser extent, of Stoicism.... What all humanists actually felt but did not express in so many words, he states most bluntly and clearly, namely, that he intends to talk primarily about himself and that his own individual self is the chief subject matter of his philosophizing ... By elevating introspection and the observation of actual human conduct to the rank of a conscious method, Montaigne already passes beyond the boundaries of humanist thought and literature, and leads the way toward the psychological study of moods and manners [1965, p. 66].

MICHEL DE MONTAIGNE (1533-1592)

Montaigne transformed the raw materials of his classical humanist education into a higher level of wisdom in his *Essays*. He mentioned or quoted Socrates over one hundred times; Plato, Cicero, and Seneca receive similar attention. The Stoic and Epicurean philosophers are called upon just slightly less frequently. A lover of Latin poetry, Montaigne quotes Horace, Ovid, and Virgil as copiously as he does the philosophers. He did not read Greek, so that the ancients spoke to Montaigne mostly in Latin or through Latin translations of Greek originals. His most important source may have been Plutarch, who became accessible in the middle of the sixteenth century in the form of Amyot's brilliant translation into French. Of all these authors, it seems that Seneca, Plutarch, and Horace were his favorites.

Friedrich (1940) has shown that Montaigne used the classics only after they had become part of himself and had thus been transformed into appropriate representations of aspects of himself. In other words, he did not mouth tradition; tradition spoke through his mouth. It is a facile temptation to claim that others have already said what Montaigne sets before us, but such a statement is erroneous because what he has to tell us is not the same as the original had been. The classics are the place where Montaigne discovered himself. When Montaigne is talking about Man's susceptibility to music or to the dark and wide spaces within a church, he is probing the depths of his soul. In this way, the *Essays* become a portrait of Montaigne, a special and, up to his own time, unique one: by candidly painting the truth of the moment, that of his own reactions to the outer world in their spontaneous flux, from contradiction to contradiction, Montaigne creates an unsurpassed image of inner reality. Sayce (1972) points out his utter candor in revealing his most secret thoughts and actions, his unsparing unveiling of his own limitations, tempered only by humorous self-mockery. Michelet may have been the first to note that the *Essays* provided the earliest exact and minute description of the inner man. As Sayce puts it, in their minute differentiation of successive states of mind, they are without doubt "a conscious piece of self-analysis."

It would be difficult to deny an indirect influence on Freud through the line of Montaigne's successors, the most famous of whom may have been Shakespeare, Cervantes, Sterne, Diderot, Goethe, Flaubert, and Nietzsche (see Chapters 4 and 13). There is no evidence, however, that Freud had read Montaigne before 1915; there are no references to him in Freud's writings. In 1915, a two-volume French edition of the *Essais* was presented to Freud by Lou Andreas-Salomé; these volumes are preserved in Freud's library at Hampstead. Marginalia in these books indicate that Freud read them with interest (Trosman and Simmons, 1972). Thus the intellectual connection by way of Nietzsche was literally brought to Freud's attention by the woman who formed a personal bridge between them.

Montaigne's contribution to psychology has been largely overlooked or misunderstood until recently. Telle (1968) may have been the first to do it justice in stating: "From the point of view of scientific method one can say that Montaigne, in 1580, was three hundred years ahead of his time and that among his contemporaries only some physicians could have had an inkling of his attainment." In the following section, we shall attempt to demonstrate this attainment in some detail.

MONTAIGNE'S PSYCHOLOGICAL "SYSTEM"[2]

1. METHOD

Plato's injunction "Do thy job and know thyself" served as the summary of Montaigne's aims for his philosophy. He added that, in order to do one's job, one must know oneself first, with specific reference to one's motivations. His writings were an attempt to create a self-portrait, as frank as was socially possible at the time, with a view to putting forward

[2] In spite of the massive critical literature on the work of Montaigne, ably classified in Frame's annotated bibliography (1955), no systematic study of his contribution to psychology has come to our attention. Therefore we have undertaken to extract the relevant passages from Montaigne's writings. Fortunately, all of these are available in English translation. In addition to the three books of *Essays*, they include a *Travel Journal* (probably the first record of an *Italienische Reise*) and a score of personal letters. Although extremely revealing about Montaigne as a person, the *Journal* and the correspondence did not prove to be germane to this study.

We read Montaigne's *Essays* in several translations, and noted all passages containing statements of his views on psychological topics. The page references in this chapter refer to the translation by Donald M. Frame, as published by the Stanford University Press (1965) in *The Complete Essays of Montaigne*. These extracts were scrutinized in order to classify them into appropriate topical categories. Twenty categories were developed; in what follows they have been given titles drawn from current psychoanalytic terminology. This is not meant to imply that Montaigne used equivalent categories in any explicit fashion. This schema permitted the classification of every extract without exception, but many extracts had relevance to several of the selected topics.

Montaigne's contribution to each of these 20 topics has been summarized in the following account of his psychological "system."

questions in order to seek the truth. He was explicit in
disclaiming certainty, clearly labeling his statements as opinions based on reasoning, without reliance on faith. He knew
men cannot be judged on the basis of their outward actions; in
order to discover the springs that set them in motion, we must
undertake the arduous, even hazardous, task of probing their
inner world.

Montaigne quoted the dictum of the younger Pliny that
each man could provide a good education for himself were he
able to spy on himself from close up. Before Montaigne, only
rare authors in antiquity had recorded such an attempt to
penetrate the "opaque depths" by following the movements of
the mind. Montaigne devoted many years solely to this self-
study, an enterprise he declared to be both useful and
difficult. He defined his "trade" as the business of *living* and
the practical task as the translation of thoughts into words. He
thought that making his findings public would mitigate the
risk of falling into naïve self-love; Montaigne was keenly aware
of the fact that it would be more difficult to disclose information favorable to himself than to confess his limitations. It
should be recalled that, at the time of publication, his *Essays*
were the first written self-portrait in history.

Montaigne described his method of self-scrutiny as follows:
"As my fancies present themselves, I pile them up; now they
come pressing in a crowd, now dragging single file.... I let
myself go as I am" (p. 297). His conclusions therefore
depended on his capacity to sift the truth about himself. He
declared that one could only penetrate to the essentials of
one's self by enduring and total commitment to its study. If
one then notes all of one's associations, they assume an order
and a purpose. Montaigne made the claim that "no man ever
penetrated more deeply into his material" (p. 611). Although
he found this task most consuming — "we have enough to do at
home" (p. 767) — he did supplement his findings by turning to
biographies which dealt with the inner life, so that he might
be able to generalize his conclusions to all of mankind.
Nonetheless, he expressed skepticism about the reliability of
such borrowed evidence; at bottom, he was convinced, "Let us
only listen, we tell ourselves all we most need" (p. 822). In

other words, he thought that self-study would enable him to learn about the character of others. Nevertheless, to the detriment of his subsequent influence, Montaigne always refused to systematize his findings.

2. GENERALIZATIONS ABOUT HUMAN BEHAVIOR

Montaigne characterized human behavior as unpredictable, diverse, "undulating"; he saw life as "continuous flux." He held the seeking of pleasure and the avoidance of pain to be the most basic human goals. At the same time, he declared that man is born to *act*. He knew that a person cannot be evaluated on the basis of isolated acts, that, to judge a man, one must follow his actions long and carefully, observe his everyday behavior and discount the effects of isolated efforts. Even then, man's behavior may not betray any central goal, especially because outward actions need not accurately reflect man's inner life. Thus actions are meaningful only in the context of a view of the whole man.

Montaigne argued that man and the animals are subject to the same natural laws, i.e., that man's adaptational efforts are just as *natural* as are those of the beasts. He based his conclusions on the further premise that the motivations of all men are essentially the same; the universal self-preservative instincts of animals determine many of these.

His general assessment of the human condition was that man's lot is not so unhappy: he is more worthless than wretched and more stupid than malicious.

3. THE PSYCHIC APPARATUS

In Montaigne's psychology, the main differentiation within the mind is the dichotomy between the passions and reason; this had sometimes been conceptualized before him as man possessing two souls. The balance of forces between these major sets of conflicting functions is capable of alteration; the soul, mistress of man's condition and conduct, may be helped to gain active mastery over his attitudes by means of insight. Indeed, Montaigne thought that this should be the prevailing goal of philosophy.

He differentiated reason from volition, which was defined

as conscious intentionality; behavior was clearly seen not to be controlled by volition at all times. On the other hand, Montaigne also stressed that at a deeper level the soul cannot escape its own scrutiny. His psychology focuses on man's subjective reactions to the meanings of his experiences; in his terms, it is the soul that allots qualities to experience. He equated virtue with the dominance of reason, which leads to deliberation and consistency. Conversely, vice is the unruliness of passively following the appetites or floating between states of mind. However, Montaigne also knew that the soul is never "straight and composed" in anyone; as Lucretius had put it, "error affects all."

The many activities stemming from man's impulses and not subject to his reason are determined by unconscious mentation. As a normal example, Montaigne mentions unself-conscious body language. Although animals also have mental processes, it is reason that differentiates man from the beasts, as it permits the regulation of his behavior on the basis of judgment and volition.

In addition to the appetitive and cognitive (or "consenting") aspects of mental life, Montaigne distinguished a third function of the soul, also unique to man, the "imaginative" one. However, he explicitly cautioned that science divides man into functions and faculties in an artificial manner; such an "imaginary republic" creates the risk of missing the essence of the human condition altogether. St. Augustine had stated that the essence of man is to be found in the relation of the soul to the body; however, nothing is understood about the matter. Lucretius had concluded that the mind is corporeal; Montaigne concurred with this view, citing as evidence the changes in mental functioning brought about by the action of drugs. He concluded that health requires harmony within both body and soul. He understood this not simply as an avoidance of stimulation but believed that the mind needs optimal quanta of stimuli.

Montaigne's over-all metaphor for the functioning of the mind was that of the erection of flood-control devices in order to avoid situations of helplessness.

4. AUTONOMOUS MENTAL FUNCTIONS

According to Montaigne, the most fundamental and certain of mental experiences is the perception of pain. He held many other capacities to be innate, however, such as the acquisition of speech and of other means of communication, the function of basic thought processes, etc. He followed Lucretius in thinking that knowledge has to be acquired through sense perceptions; these are highly unreliable as well as species specific, i.e., by no means an accurate reflection of "reality." Montaigne noted that perceptions are significantly altered by man's passions.

Although he stated that thoughts are necessarily translated into *words*, Montaigne also cautioned against confusing words with the things for which they stand. Another mental function which he discussed is memory; he cited Cicero's opinion that memory is the receptacle of all that concerns the conduct of life. Montaigne noted that man thus acquires *habits* to which he adheres with tenacity. They result from the effects of example and education on both drive dispositions and restraints. Almost any behavioral pattern may become automatized; according to Montaigne, this was the quality of the virtue of Socrates, for example.

5. TRAUMA AND ABREACTION

Montaigne stressed the potential for traumatization. When overwhelmed by events, man is beyond grief, in a bleak and dumb stupor which is overcome only gradually, through a process of mourning. Petrarch and Catullus had noted the possibility of similar traumatization by love, and Seneca had made the same point with regard to any excessive emotion. The need of abreaction was put in terms of the necessity of venting these feelings on some object, even on a part of oneself, if none other is available.

Other psychoeconomic issues were also discussed. Montaigne noted the palling of pleasure as a consequence of gratification and, following Cicero, the need to seek pleasures, either real or remembered, in order to escape the unpleasure of mounting tensions. Conversely, too much pleasure is also fearsome because it is experienced as a threat of being overwhelmed. Horace had noted that excessive pleasure is actually perceived as painful. Montaigne thought that the intensity of passions can be inferred from the degree of defense erected against them. He was aware of the signal function of fear, commenting that its absence implies that the person has been stunned and has lost his capacity for foresight. As for the issue of working through, Montaigne noted that losses of functional capacity are more easily adapted to if they occur gradually.

6. MOTIVATIONAL DYNAMICS AND CONFLICTS

Because he saw man as forever in the grip of hopes and wishes, Montaigne defined the main goal of his inquiry as the elucidation of motivations. In general, he formulated these in terms of conflicts between reason and the passions. The latter are particularly hard to control if their satisfaction has become habitual. Wishes even have the power to interfere with man's judgment about reality. Private wishes tend to be at the expense of others and in the service of personal ambitions for reputation and glory.

Conflicts occur not only at the behest of reason, but also whenever passions offend the conscience. Hence man has always been seen as torn between good and evil. The essential universality of such motivations is stressed by Terence's famous dictum, "Let nothing human be too foreign," a point buttressed by Montaigne's conviction that many impulses are in fact unconscious. He cautioned, however, that in assessing motives it is unbalanced to see only evil. Reason and virtue also carry weight, and many people achieve victory over their disordered appetites and the imperfections of their character.

Nonetheless, Montaigne kept returning to the importance of sexual and aggressive impulses, the universality of malice and sadism, of resistance to authority, even that of one's own burdensome sense of obligations. He carefully differentiated behavior in action from the impulse life. For instance, he expressed doubt that repetitive offenders suffer from guilt conflicts, whatever they may claim about this.

Montaigne also identified internal conflicts stemming from the clash of various motivations with the "ruling pattern" of the person. The latter resists both further educational efforts and even the passions. On the other hand, he believed that narcissistic gratifications help man to endure hardships and conflict. He noted that some conflicts involve the internalization of persecutory "demons" and that the nature of wishes is essentially limitless and ineradicable, e.g., greed and ambition are incapable of moderation. Hence man is perpetually in a state of ambivalence, a condition already described by Petrarch.

7. CHARACTEROLOGY

Montaigne was emphatic about the determining force of man's character upon his fate: "Our good and our ill depend on ourselves alone." Ancient authors such as Sallust and Cornelius Nepos had already made this point. Montaigne discussed the stability of man's habits, especially the rigidity of thought processes, which may impair adaptation. These ideas were sometimes couched in the language of the then current theory of "humors"—e.g., each man must choose the course that best suits his humor: the ambitious should seek glory.

Montaigne referred to Terence as one author who had stressed character in his portrayals, showing the variety of ways in which man may be put together. Cicero had viewed consistency of conduct as optimal but possible only if man has no need to imitate the nature of others. It is this consistency to which Montaigne referred as the "ruling pattern," as it resists external influences. He saw rigidity as a handicap, however, holding variety and adaptability in humors and dispositions to be optimal.

8. CONSCIENCE

Montaigne believed that the laws of the conscience are determined by custom. He thought that its scope might be enlarged by setting children the proper example. He noted the internalization of morality in those evil people who resort to ritualized prayers or expiatory acts, thus showing some conflict over their misdeeds. The power of conscience is also shown by man's frequent willingness to die a martyr to its standards, as well as his tendency to betray, accuse, and fight himself. Montaigne cited such examples of this as asceticism, the seeking of cuckoldry, hatred of the genitals, and compliance with circumstances of lengthy suffering. He knew that conscience may be externalized as a fear of punishment; this is already the work of the conscience, as it is a form of self-punishment in itself. The conscience also causes punishment dreams. On the other hand, it may provide assurance and confidence for the well-intentioned, even in the most extreme of unfavorable environments.

Conscience cannot be inculcated by constraint, and the maintenance of good behavior on the basis of the expectation of external approval is always shaky. In contrast, the satisfaction and pride resulting from the approval of one's conscience is unparalleled, and its disapproval is like an ulcer. True guilt forestalls misdeeds; thus, the repetitive offender betrays a lack of conflict with his conscience. Irrational self-reproaches also do not betoken guilt: we do not repent what lies outside of our powers—we *regret* it.

Montaigne believed that conscience is strengthened by an increase in reason rather than by a decrease in the appetites. Although he recognized that adherence to duty may be difficult for the young, he considered the excessive severity and temperance of some older people not to be the result of an improvement of conscience but to be a new form of vice.

9. OBJECT RELATIONS

Montaigne emphasized man's need for his objects, if only as recipients of the discharge of his emotions. He therefore held the undermining of human bonds through actions such as lying as the worst of vices. Identifications with one's important objects, ambivalence toward them, and various way stations to an optimal relationship, that of friendship in the Platonic sense, were some of the topics he discussed. Montaigne understood that real solitude consists in withdrawing the soul from others, something likely to be successful mostly in mystics who then merge themselves with the deity.

The futility of relationships based on the exercise of power rather than of affection was underscored by the paradox that men often prefer to be subjects rather than masters. The object attachments of animals are often stronger than those of man who, incidentally, has as much need of solitude as of relatedness. Montaigne quoted Seneca to the effect that the capacity to be a friend to others depends on being a friend to oneself.

10. GENETIC FACTORS AND EDUCATION

Plato had taught that vices are established in early childhood, especially if undesirable behavior is condoned by the parents. Hence Montaigne believed that children must receive training to abhor vices, which must not be overlooked in their play activities, which constitute the serious actions of the child. He considered punishment appropriate only for serious matters, not for the trivia with which the children of his day were being tormented. In connection with the finding that the contents of the conscience depend on social customs, Montaigne noted that incest prohibitions had for so long been customary that the impulses themselves had totally disappeared.

Although work and experience have a desirable hardening effect on children, Montaigne cautioned that training by means of sadistic methods is counterproductive and likely to lead to rebellion. He believed it is important to teach children the facts about human psychology instead of inculcating them with magical beliefs. He advocated that undesirable behavior be discouraged by shaming, believing that prohibitions are less effective because they tend to glamorize the forbidden act.

Montaigne held parental affection to be natural and instinctive, almost as fundamental as self-preservation and the avoidance of harm, because one loves one's children as one loves himself. He knew that filial affection is much less regular; as Aristotle had stated, the activity of parents is satisfying to them, but the receptive role of the child is merely one of great convenience. Parents have a much more difficult time with their children's maturation, which arouses competitive ambivalence. Parents who manage through controlling

behavior instead of earning respect by reason and tact forgo
the family affection they will desperately need during the
impotence of old age. Similarly, women cannot be ruled
authoritatively by their husbands. All violence and abuse of
authority produce destructive hostility. Refusal to conform to
the natural succession of generations leads to the same
emotional consequences.

Montaigne noted that the wet nurses regularly employed by
the upper class loved the nurslings more than their own
babies. The latter were customarily turned over for their
feeding to a she-goat. The goat and infant would then form a
couple, and neither would accept a substitute for the other;
such a baby, deprived of its specific she-goat, would die.

Montaigne believed in education by example in order to
mold both the drives and the modes of their restraint. He
warned that the child has need of a set of offered ideals until
he learns to be certain within himself. The brutalizing of small
children is therefore doubly outrageous: it fails as education
and it is an example of vengefulness. Montaigne thought that
a simple upbringing, in the midst of ordinary people, would
be most suitable in providing the proper examples.

The most notable lack in Montaigne's comments about
childhood is the absence of observations about infantile
sexuality. He does, however, quote Horace on the subject of
openly incestuous dreams in children. In contrast, Montaigne
was quite aware of parents' incestuous love for their children
and interpreted the Pygmalion myth as a reflection of this
tendency.

In summary, Montaigne gave special importance to the
study of beginnings, for he believed that at their inception all
things are most manageable.

11. TOPOGRAPHY

Awareness of the unconscious had already been demonstrated by Lucretius, whom Montaigne quotes on the subject.
Cicero had also discussed the fact that information received
does not necessarily penetrate to the depths of the personality.
Impulses in particular are likely to remain unconscious, in
"the opaque depths." In this sense, mental life may rightly be

compared to dreaming. Montaigne's insight into the unconscious is also shown by his descriptions of the process of repression. He made it clear that each person must be held
responsible for his own conduct, however ignorant of his
impulses he may be.

12. DEFENSIVE FUNCTIONS

Montaigne first noted the importance of defenses in terms
of the barriers against the work of mourning. Later he stressed
the escape from unpleasure by means of fantasied gratification, which, however, merely leads to mounting tension. His
concept of defense was not merely an economic one, as shown
by his description of obsessional prolixity with the purpose of
avoiding cogent thoughts, of distracting oneself by various
special passions (such as the search for ultimate causes), or the
attempt to disavow certain matters by means of repeated
negation or argumentation. He saw both the commission of
errors and dreaming as mechanisms for regaining contentment and security; the context does not make it entirely clear
whether he had in mind the formation of delusions. Elsewhere, however, he quoted Seneca: Ignorance is a poor
remedy for ills! Psychotic denial of reality will not cure
anything.

Montaigne was also familiar with the defense of projection,
especially in the form of the tendency to find fault with other
people: "We say things about another that we would more
properly say about ourselves, if we knew how to turn our
attention inward as well as extend it outward" (pp. 286-287).
The temptation to judge others in terms of ourselves is another
projective manifestation he described. He repeatedly stressed
the tendency to disavow flaws and limitations, even by means
of such measures as the use of extreme avoidance, which
Montaigne called "dying to escape the trouble of living well."
He discussed various aspects of magical thinking in the service
of defense, e.g., the "expiatory" actions of unscrupulous and
habitual criminals. He stressed that those who hide their vices
generally also do so from themselves: they disguise them from
their conscience by withdrawing them from awareness. Thus
the sickest is least aware of what ails his soul.

Montaigne even conceptualized a hierarchy of various defenses in the service of avoiding helplessness. He cautioned against misunderstanding mere movement by mistaking it for rational activity, thus sealing the eyes and stunning the understanding in order to deceive ourselves.

13. AFFECTS AND DANGERS

Early in his work, Montaigne gave much emphasis to the dangers of being inundated with affects such as grief or love. He stated that affects cannot be checked without discharge, once they have been aroused. He showed awareness of the chronicity of certain affects, e.g., that of holding on to a grievance. The central danger, in his view, is the experience of pain, which is feared more than death itself.

Montaigne showed the relativeness of actual circumstances with regard to situations of danger by pointing out that men will brave both pain and death if sufficiently motivated by other considerations. Moreover, suffering in itself is not necessarily regarded as threatening, as shown by masochistic proclivities. As an illustration, he cited his own pleasure in disbursing money. He thought that in actuality all feelings are mixtures of pain and pleasure.

Montaigne noted the distorting effect of strong emotions on cognitive functions, e.g., his own relapse into his first language, Latin, on such occasions. One consequence of this is the tendency of many people to be threatened by the arousal of affects, a trait which Montaigne believed to be abnormal. In this connection, he concluded that anxiety about potential developments is often more painful than the occurrence of these events. He also decided that the aim of adaptation must be the seeking of ease, usually in the form of pleasure, the most sought-after form of which is voluptuousness. Montaigne thought that living up to the ideals and standards of the conscience is a gratification superior to that of sexuality, as it is more enduring. He noted the complexities of assessing affect life because of the common tendency to identify with the affective states of others. He quoted Seneca about the possibility of feigned emotions: "This man is inwardly happy. That man's happiness is a veneer" (p. 191).

Montaigne believed that creative accomplishments are pos
sible only when fueled by the passions. In general, however, he
agreed with Plato that moderation in reactions of pleasure
and unpleasure is best. The attainment of wisdom will then
create cheerfulness.

14. DREAMS AND FANTASIES

Montaigne collected many conclusions about dreaming
from ancient writers. Lucretius had noted that unconsciously
man dreams of immortality and that he betrays his evil deeds
in dreams and deliria. He had also observed the occurrence of
dreaming in dogs. St. Augustine had written that being
dominated by "figments of the imagination," i.e., delusion, is
the worst of fates. Cicero had concluded that there exist wish-
fulfilling dreams. Pliny had thought that a dream could cause
bodily illness; Montaigne corrected him, pointing out that the
dream had come about in consequence of the dreamer's
unconscious perception of the somatic change. Horace had
referred to the openly incestuous dreams of children. Both
Accius and Cicero had noted that dreams repeat the dominant
ideation of waking life, i.e., that they make use of day
residues.

Montaigne observed the general occurrence of fancies and
visions, "chimeras and monsters," and he concluded that they
have the purpose of restoring contentment and security, in
spite of the fact that man is so ignorant about himself that he
cannot even manage to fantasy what would really satisfy him.
For instance, many dreams are in fact in the nature of punishment. He also pointed out that there is a continuum between
dreaming and waking mental life, with reveries occupying an
intermediate position; hence Montaigne paid special attention
to his reveries in his effort to study himself. He gave due
weight to the significance of fantasies: "A strong imagination
creates the event" (p. 68). He gave such examples of this as
nocturnal emissions, trances, or the stigmata of St. Francis. In
pathological states, dreamlike ideas gain credence, thus creating delusions. This was Montaigne's explanation of witches,
instead of the theories of evil prevalent in his day.

In summary, Montaigne's position is represented by the

statement: "Dreams are faithful interpreters of our inclinations; but there is an art to sorting and understanding them" (p. 843).

15. THE DRIVES

Montaigne pioneered in ascribing to sexuality its proper place in mental life, pointing out that sexual need has the power to cause diseases. He noted various areas of sexual pathology, e.g., hatred of the genitals and sexuality, impotence, and various guilt conflicts aroused by sexual wishes, such as excessive modesty. He showed some awareness of incestuous conflicts; thus, he calls marital love quasi-incestuous. He did not reach the conclusion that these conflicts are universal in childhood, merely noting that the incest taboo is unique to humans. He also cited Ovid's observation that man is the only animal sexually deterred by the sight of the female genital. Other factors interfering with sexual performance noted by Montaigne are overwhelming excitement, too much respect for the partner, and attempts to have intercourse out of a sense of obligation. He described the nonlibidinal aspects of sexuality as well, such as the fact that sexual success bolsters self-esteem.

Although he stated that the most powerful appetites are the sexual ones, Montaigne, in agreement with Plutarch, at times deemed aggression to be an even more powerful impulse. Sadism is to be observed everywhere. He wrote that men are incapable of transcending either drive: they are beasts, not angels. Excessive ambition in the direction of overcoming the drives usually leads only to bad behavior.

He alluded to sexual jealousy as a disease of rage and hatred for which he knew of no remedy. On the subject of homosexuality, he stated that among the Greeks, the love of men had not been based on peer relationships but rather on physical appearance. Thus these relationships were beset with the same problems as the heterosexual ones of Montaigne's day, when even upper-class women failed to receive sufficient education to be equal to their men.

16. IDEALS AND VALUES

Montaigne stressed the importance of ideals which enable

man to face difficulty and danger. Ideals are generally acquired by example; according to Montaigne, the most valuable identifications are those with the actual skills of others. For learning of any kind to become useful, the learner must *espouse* the matter as his own. The most effective regulator of conduct is such an internalized standard and total commitment to living by it, i.e., being true to oneself. The resultant satisfaction is not to be confused with naïve self-love.

It is most difficult to value anything different from oneself; thus man creates gods in his own perfected image. We do tend to value whatever is more difficult to acquire, however. Those who, like Montaigne, use higher standards rate themselves lower than do others, but this lack of presumption, the refusal to disavow one's limitations, may in itself be the most significant sign of worth. Activities which bring a low premium of glory are more difficult than those which bring public acclaim. The greatest danger in this regard is the tendency to set unattainable standards for oneself.

The specific ideals which Montaigne espoused, in the face of the difficulty of giving credit to himself for possessing some of these qualities, are contentment with one's own nature, Platonic friendship, deliberation, consistency, the mastery of reason, the acceptance of transience, commitment to thinking, the adaptation of one's ambitions to one's actual abilities, moderation, self-knowledge in preference to glory or riches or erudition or rank.

Finally, he noted that, exceptionally, people are able to change themselves in response to certain external influences which they adopt as part of themselves.

17. THE SELF AND NARCISSISM

Montaigne's aim was to win the power to live alone and be at ease, i.e., to "have oneself." He quoted Quintilian: "It is rare for anyone to respect himself enough" (p. 178). Not only does self-knowledge permit one to choose a proper field of action for oneself; it also prevents disdain for life and for oneself. Socrates was the best examplar of gaining wisdom through self-knowledge, having traversed a stage of despising himself and having then achieved true humility. Montaigne quoted his opinion that insufficient self-knowledge is betrayed by our cocksureness.

Montaigne described how one can inflate oneself into perfection, as lovers do with the beloved; one can also deflate oneself in an analogous fashion. According to Aristotle, both of these distortions in self-esteem stem from arrogance. Actual wisdom presupposes awareness of and acceptance of one's real powers: *"Mentre si puo."* Fantasies of omnipotence imply a lack of true capacity; to test one's capacity means the overcoming of resistance about learning its limitations. Thus one should care about oneself, but without passion! Montaigne restated this in saying that we owe ourselves friendship.

As this summary shows, he was very sensitive to the difference between self-acceptance and self-love or vanity, manifested as man's wish for immortality, his inability to value anything or to see beyond his own self, his pretensions to omniscience, his ambitions for reputation or glory, his wish to be other than himself, his extension of his self-love to his children or to the products of his mind, his self-absorption, his unrealistically high standards, his clinging to illusions, and his arrogance (the most extreme form of which is the gesture of declining greatness). All this he summarized with an epigram by Erasmus: "Everyone likes the smell of his own dung" (p. 709).

Montaigne. noted injuries to narcissism, such as losses of functional integrity, as well as obstacles to its healthy development, such as affliction with bodily deformity. He also showed awareness of problems in the consolidation of a sense of self. In people with such difficulties, borrowings from others may crowd out the true self. Until one becomes sure within oneself, one must turn to others for ideals, an experience Montaigne had lived through with dramatic intensity in his famous friendship, almost amounting to a merger, with Etienne de la Boëtie. The need to imitate others leads to failures of consistency, of the "ruling pattern" which should be found in men. Self-esteem cannot be consolidated as long as one must turn to others for approval. In Montaigne's words, one must use borrowings if one doesn't know oneself well enough.

18. CREATIVITY AND ADAPTATION

In his own work, Montaigne noted that he was led to his best thoughts via obscure paths. He believed that it is man's freedom to make use of his fancies that distinguishes him from the animals. The products of the mind are more truly one's own than are one's children. Such achievements must be fueled by passion—e.g., the triumph of exultant nobility shown by Cato's suicide. Nonetheless, Montaigne concurred with Seneca that true freedom consists of the attainment of power over oneself.

Thus the passions should be ruled by reason, and happiness, as Cicero claims, should result from gaining mastery over trouble. Subjective contentment is never simply a response to external circumstances which, in fact, may well constitute a sham. The greatest challenge to man's adaptation is the task of accepting death and functional impairments. Conversely, a healthy soul promotes somatic health. Adaptation should include reinforcement from the conscience, from experience, and from self-knowledge. It implies moderation and reliance on judgment, variety and flexibility combined with consistency.

19. PSYCHOPATHOLOGY

Montaigne was aware of the potential for succumbing to "fancies and visions" whenever the vigilance of reason is relaxed or if one has been stunned by some misfortune. Such errors as well as dreams are tools of the soul for the purpose of regaining contentment and security. They may therefore be expressions of the person's private wishes. Loss of integrated control may affect not only the mental functions but also the voluntary and affectomotor activities, e.g., vision or sexual potency. Conscious volition is frequently defeated by hidden contrary impulses. Montaigne also described psychosomatic responses involving the visceral organs.

Behavior guided by reason is consistent and virtuous; unruliness, lack of moderation, and vice betoken passive submission to the appetites or to certain states of mind. Man's "mental agility" predisposes him to difficulties such as madness and hypochondriasis, largely because he is capable of avoiding confrontations with unpleasure—without ultimately diminishing it, to be sure. He may thus allow himself to be dominated by figments of his imagination, e.g., "witches" with their delusions. Reason may be affected by various emotions, and excessive intensities of pleasure may be overwhelming. Even in manageable doses, strong feelings will cause regressions to primitive modes of behavior. Sexual needs in particular are therefore implicated in pathogenesis. Frequently, excessive fear also interferes with foresight and judgment.

Because man's state of being is determined by his own subjective judgment, his psychic condition is not directly related to the actualities of his situation. Mental states may, for instance, be the consequence of an identification with some other person. Responses to new situations are determined by man's character; e.g., he may be unable to adapt properly because of rigidity. In contrast, others are able to make whatever they find useful into their own qualities. Hence it is character that determines man's fortune. One pathological character type avoids all emotion, another actually seeks pain, while a third disdains his own self and even life. Some men have a need to subject themselves to a master, even to a woman. Thus man is dangerously ingenious in maltreating himself; this potential has been reinforced by the cultural idealization of suffering. Montaigne noted the frequency of asceticism, hatred of sexuality, the seeking of cuckoldry, and the prolongation of suffering through covert compliance with it. As Seneca had put it, "Slavery holds but few; many hold fast to slavery" (p. 195). Montaigne attributed much of this to the action of conscience which makes man punish himself, both in dreams and in actuality. However, he also knew that maladaptive behavior is often not self-punitive but an avoidance of the more difficult path of moderation, i.e., it is the acting out of excessive ambitions. The internalization of hostility may be experienced as persecution by demons if there has been a failure of reason.

Montaigne stated that internal conflict may lead to the withdrawal of certain mental contents from consciousness and that such a shift then leads to further pathogenic consequences, a perpetual agitation by illusions. One mechanism for crowding out relevant content is hypermnesia for insignificant details. As for the consequences of unresolved conflicts, one of these is the type of failure of volition already mentioned, another is the alternation between behaviors satisfying either side of the conflict, e.g., the commission of offenses followed by expiatory acts or the resort to magical formulae.

Montaigne mentioned certain developmental issues related to psychopathology: the unfavorable effects of bodily deformity on subsequent mental life, the need for family affection to mitigate the results of the impotence of old age, and the general difficulties of growing old, which lead to pride, prickliness, envy, and malice.

He alluded to a number of other issues more in passing: the intractability of sexual jealousy with its hate and rage, the destructive effects of malice on the person who hates, the correlation between weakness and cruelty. On the other hand, Montaigne showed a lack of understanding of phobias and other "eccentricities," which he condemned as if they constituted mere self-indulgence.

20. PSYCHOTHERAPY

Montaigne realized that certain emotional states are time-limited, i.e., that they are gradually overcome as they are worked through; other painful states, however, require a change in attitude for their modification. Attitude change can come about when the soul is made more active through self-knowledge and when threats have been mastered by having been confronted. In addition to such rational therapeutic methods, Montaigne discussed the efficacy of magic in producing symptomatic relief; he reported his success in curing a case of acute sexual impotence by these means. He also emphasized that patients' response to treatment largely depends on faith in the therapist, and he spelled out their responsiveness to suggestive influence. On the other hand, he also stressed that people may genuinely learn from appropriate models; it is particularly valuable to acquire *skills* by identification, rather than mere content.

Montaigne stated that cures of the diseases of the soul are necessarily painful. He quoted Horace on the fatuity of reliance on environmental manipulations: "Reason and sense remove anxiety, not villas that look out upon the sea" (p. 175). His therapeutic prescription concerned only attempted self-cures, however; he recommended introspective self-study but never developed a method of helping to initiate this process in others. His own efforts had helped him to gain victories over "disordered appetites" and imperfections of character, i.e., to change his actual qualities. "My book has made me," he said (p. 504). The prerequisite for such changes is the acknowledgment of one's emotional illness and of its source within oneself. If one is obliged to reveal everything about oneself, one will refrain from committing unmentionable acts; hence the value of communicating the results of self-scrutiny. However, for Montaigne, the core principle of treatment remained embodied in the dictum, "Let us only listen; we tell ourselves all we most need" (p. 822).

Montaigne's "System" and Psychoanalysis

The foregoing account of Montaigne's views about psychology may suffice to show that he had a coherent theory about man's psychic life. He based this on the pleasure-unpleasure principle and the dynamic, genetic, economic, and adaptive points of view. This psychology had developed through the use of systematic introspective methods, essentially indistinguishable from free association. These methods were aimed at illuminating man's inner life and the subjective meanings of his behavior, rather than focusing on the outward behavior accessible to an observer. Careful distinctions between thoughts and words, between consciousness and mentation, and between volition and the sum total of motivations bring this psychological system into close proximity to the topographic and structural theories of psychoanalysis. Montaigne explicitly understood a number of the other key concepts to be formulated by Freud or his followers. To mention only the most significant of these, he discussed psychosomatic correlations, autonomous functions, traumatization and working through, defenses, the signal function of affects, intrapsychic conflicts, internalized morality and ideals, characterology, the meaningfulness of dreams, narcissism and the cohesiveness of the self, psychopathology as a consequence of regression to archaic modes of functioning, and therapeutic change by means of insight.

As a matter of fact, it may be easier to understand the comparison between Montaigne's "system" and that of psychoanalysis by listing their differences rather than their points of agreement. In this regard, the most significant finding of our study may well be the fact that nothing in Montaigne's *Essays* is in disagreement with psychoanalysis, with the single exception of his unempathic condemnation of neurotic irrationality in phobias.[3] The differences between the introspective psychology of the sixteenth century and that of our age are attributable entirely to the fact that Freud succeeded in penetrating *further* into the opaque depths than Montaigne, or anyone else before him, had done. Thus Freud added to the accumulated knowledge of the Renaissance the psychoanalytic understanding of transferences across a repression barrier, the compromise formations in dreams, parapraxes, and neurotic symptoms, the distinction between primary and secondary processes (in other words, the decipherment of the language of the unconscious), as well as the import of infantile sexuality for neurosogenesis.

These are omissions of enormous significance, and they probably condemned Montaigne's contribution to its ultimate fate, that of making its principal impact on the community of humanists—in the generation immediately succeeding his own, figures such as Cervantes and Shakespeare, in the later ages Goethe, Flaubert, and Nietzsche (see P. Jones, 1937; Bouillier, 1921; Frame, 1955). Montaigne's self-analytic efforts were apparently successful, to judge by the testimony of the *Essays*, but they were suitable for emulation only by men

---

[3] Even this statement dates from the earliest period of Montaigne's writing. Although he failed to delete it in his subsequent revisions of his work, it sticks out as an incongruous element within it. Although we cannot here discuss the steady progress in Montaigne's psychological sophistication during the course of his authorship, it is not difficult to demonstrate in view of the availability of reasonably certain dating for almost every sentence of the *Essays*. The reader may rapidly confirm our estimate by comparing, as one example, the essay "Of Conscience" (written primarily in 1573-1574) with "On Repentance" (1585-1588).

of rare intelligence and courage who could, moreover, afford to devote themselves totally to the life of the mind. Mankind has seldom produced more than one or two such figures per century. Montaigne's personal problems appear to have lain in the narcissistic sector of the personality, and he may have been relatively free of neurosis. At any rate, his psychology has relatively little to say about just those matters which proved to be central in enabling Freud to apply his psychological discoveries to the treatment of other people. Some persons— indeed, some of the most eminent personages of his age—did turn to Montaigne for psychological assistance, but the difficulties which he encountered clinically were generally the most intractable of psychiatric disturbances, and he was unable to develop any systematic therapeutic approach. The application of an introspective psychology to therapeutics was destined to await an opportunity which would make persons with manageable, delimited neurotic symptoms present themselves for assistance to a psychologist of Freud's genius. Such an opportunity was to be made possible in the 1890's by Charcot's delimitation of hysteria as a syndrome worthy of study and treatment (see Chapter 5).

Introspective Psychology after Montaigne

Although Montaigne's psychological "system" did not and could not develop into a clinical discipline, other factors must be taken into account to understand the relegation of introspective psychology to the private domain of the greatest European writers from the beginning of the seventeenth century to the end of the nineteenth. Indeed, as a body of knowledge—even as a relevant field of investigation—the patrimony of introspective psychology was excluded from Western science until the intellectual triumph of Freud's ideas within our own lifetime. As a successor of humanism in the vanguard of intellectual life, science was born in the generation following Montaigne; perhaps one acceptable signpost of its emergence is Francis Bacon's description of the inductive method in 1621 in *Novum Organum*.[4]

In one sense, intellectual history has tended to neglect whatever knowledge had been acquired in earlier ages. More important than this prejudice against older traditions, however, is the philosophical revolution which accompanied and underlay the flowering of seventeenth-century science. This revolution was primarily effected by the impact of René Descartes, whose *Discourse on Method* (1637) laid down the epistemology required by the physical sciences. The disastrous results of Descartes's ideas for psychology have been cogently discussed by Whyte (1960): "... Descartes was the first thinker to assert a sharp division of mind from matter as the basis of a systematic philosophy claiming scientific clarity and certainty" (p. 26). This Cartesian dualism led to the equation of mental processes with conscious awareness and directed psychological inquiry into imitation of the physical sciences, an approach that is still prevalent in much of experimental psychology and behaviorism. Moreover, Cartesian materialism denied the capacity of reason to arrive at universal and necessary truths; hence the epistemology based upon it became an empiricist one. In psychology, the heirs of Descartes and of the English empiricists who followed him are the advocates of the predominant influence of nurture, such as Pavlov (see Rapaport, 1947).

The rich fruits of the scientific revolution in mathematics, astronomy, chemistry, and physics ensured the dominance of the Cartesian epistemology through most of the next two centuries. There were dissenting voices, to be sure, but they did not gain much of a hearing within the *scientific* community. Pascal, the renegade mathematician, could echo the introspectiveness of Montaigne in his critique of Descartes: "The heart has its reasons, which reason knows not" (Whyte,

---

[4] Incidentally, Bacon's personal copy of the Florio translation of Montaigne is in the possession of the British Museum. It is also known that Bacon's brother visited Montaigne at the latter's château. Shakespeare apparently had read the Florio version before 1600. For a review of the philosophical developments of the early seventeenth century, see Wright (1941).

1960, p. 91); but Pascal was a religious mystic whose point of view was opposed to the progress of science; moreover, he was an opponent of Montaigne as well, because he regarded the latter's skepticism as a danger to religion.

A more systematic reaction to Descartes was that of the idealists, among whom the best known is probably Berkeley. Idealism resorts to an exclusive reliance on reason, at the expense of paying heed to sensory data, which are regarded as completely unreliable. This point of view has been called the "rationalist" epistemology. As Rapaport has shown (1951, pp. 232, 519), this idealist-rationalist philosophy is no more suitable for a scientific introspective psychology than Descartes's empiricism had been because it cannot avoid the danger, always quite real for an introspectionist, of slipping into solipsism.[5]

A more satisfactory philosophical basis for introspective psychology found its lone seventeenth-century advocate in Gottfried Leibniz. In his *History of Psychology,* Boring had already detected this intellectual connection (see Rapaport, 1952). Whyte (1960) credits Leibniz with being the first European thinker (he means after the Cartesian revolution) to have given clear expression to the idea of unconscious mental activity. More important still, Leibniz's rejection of dualism was to have great influence on later thinkers, who were to correct Descartes's epistemological one-sideness. Leibniz succeeded in avoiding the pitfalls of idealism and of materialism at the same time. "Leibnitz [sic] asked: How is it possible that reasoning arrives at conclusions which coincide with the outcome of processes occurring in reality? or in his own words: How can there be a correspondence between 'vérité de fait' and 'vérité de raison'?" (Rapaport, 1951, p. 317). Leibniz's work did not reach publication until 1765, however, so that his attempt to bridge the gap between the alternative epistemologies of the seventeenth century could not influence the

---

[5] As a matter of fact, Rapaport's life work can be seen as an effort to safeguard psychoanalysis from the tendency to drift into an idealist position by anchoring it within the theories of cognitive psychologists such as Piaget (see J. Gedo, 1973).

general course of science until the end of the eighteenth. In fact, by that time, the philosophical underpinnings for a future psychology were provided by the more influential work of Immanuel Kant, whose *Critique of Pure Reason* appeared in 1781.

The relevance of Kantian transcendentalism for psychology has been cogently summarized by Rapaport:

> Kant maintained that the validity of a priori synthetic propo-
> sitions (as for instance Euclid's postulates) cannot derive from
> experience. To explain the origin of their validity he asserted
> that the mind synthesizes all experiences in terms of a priori
> forms of sensibility, that is, space and time; and in terms of the
> categories of pure reason, which he classified as categories of
> quantity, quality, relation, and modification. The validity of
> synthetic (a priori) propositions derives from the fact that all
> impingements of the environment are synthesized by the pure
> mind in terms of these forms and categories, and this synthesis
> lends them validity [1951, p. 177].

On the basis of transcendentalism, the German philosophers from Kant through the Romantics and Schopenhauer to Nietzsche gradually changed the view of mental life acceptable to science and thus prepared the way for psychoanalysis, i.e., for the reintegration of the humanist introspective mode into the scientific study of man. The history of these nineteenth-century developments as they pertain to psychoanalysis has yet to be properly studied.

We must keep in mind, however, that the influence of these philosophical developments did not penetrate into the realms of official science until late in the nineteenth century. The school of Helmholtz, to which Freud's teachers adhered, was firmly committed to a materialist-positivist outlook. As late as 1895, Freud's "Project for a Scientific Psychology" was still cast in a Cartesian mold. The enthusiasms of his youth through which we may detect his kinship with the psychology of Montaigne (his admiration for Horace [see Chapter 3], for Shakespeare [see Chapter 13], and for Cervantes [see

Chapter 4])⁶ remained split off from his scientific self. It was perhaps at his fateful lecture of April, 1896, to the Viennese Society for Neurology and Psychiatry (see Chapter 9) that Freud first gave evidence of setting aside the Cartesian deluge that had swept away the introspective psychology of the humanists.

Appendix

Page references in Montaigne's *Essays*, translated by Donald Frame, Stanford University Press, 1965, relevant to each numbered section in the summary of *Montaigne's Psychological "System."*

1. METHOD
   9, 75, 224, 229, 234, 244, 272, 273, 274, 278, 297, 303, 499, 504, 611, 767, 822, 824. See also "To the Reader."
2. GENERALIZATIONS ABOUT HUMAN BEHAVIOR
   5, 56, 62, 221, 239, 243, 244, 311, 334, 350, 533, 534, 610, 807, 856.
3. THE PSYCHIC APPARATUS
   31, 39, 73, 176, 220, 240, 242, 249, 271, 279, 337, 372, 401, 402, 412, 479, 484, 550, 621, 686.
4. AUTONOMOUS MENTAL FUNCTIONS
   37, 39, 77, 274, 310, 311, 334, 336, 405, 443, 444, 450, 468, 494, 754, 772.
5. TRAUMA AND ABREACTION
   7, 8, 14, 23, 63, 193, 364, 511, 686, 768.
6. MOTIVATIONAL DYNAMICS AND CONFLICTS
   8, 9, 14, 31, 45, 70, 77, 172, 187, 231, 240, 242, 244, 250, 271, 305, 308, 313, 316, 425, 450, 493, 550, 551, 599, 613, 615, 617, 633, 634, 637, 686, 771, 772, 794.
7. CHARACTEROLOGY
   44, 77, 181, 196, 220, 298, 303, 308, 311, 499, 615, 621, 772, 824.
8. CONSCIENCE
   42, 46, 83, 84, 100, 231, 257, 264, 265, 266, 466, 606, 612, 617, 620, 638.
9. OBJECT RELATIONS
   14, 24, 68, 136, 139, 176, 180, 285, 286, 293, 337, 346, 629, 769.
10. GENETIC FACTORS AND EDUCATION
    24, 78, 79, 83, 84, 113, 117, 122, 183, 196, 267, 279, 280, 281, 282, 283, 290, 291, 293, 311, 540, 651, 780, 844.

⁶ Although it is difficult to evaluate from whom Freud received the most significant intellectual nourishment, one gains the over-all impression from study of his mature work that Shakespeare may have been the foremost. In his writings he quoted from Shakespeare more often than from any other author, and he began to read the English dramatist at the astonishing age of eight. Unfortunately, no evidence has come to light about his responses to Shakespeare before the age of 16. See Chapter 3 for his attitude to Shakespeare at that time. Here we should like to stress again that Shakespeare, particularly in his later work, was strongly influenced by Montaigne.

11. TOPOGRAPHY

6, 22, 37, 39, 57, 224, 286, 305, 364, 365, 522, 555, 606, 621, 642, 686, 709, 766, 767, 768, 769, 785, 795.

13. AFFECTS AND DANGERS

6, 7, 8, 23, 37, 40, 42, 43, 46, 52, 53, 56, 68, 119, 175, 191, 193, 251, 268, 364, 365, 427, 510, 615, 630, 631, 767, 778,

14. DREAMS AND FANTASIES

10, 21, 39, 68, 69, 220, 224, 265, 297, 355, 395, 414, 451, 504, 522, 651, 790, 843.

15. THE DRIVES

7, 11, 14, 42, 56, 70, 72, 137, 138, 293, 313, 316, 347, 357, 493, 522, 550, 555, 627, 646, 654, 658, 856.

16. IDEALS AND VALUES

5, 9, 34, 105, 111, 131, 138, 196, 224, 240, 252, 254, 265, 274, 358, 381, 464, 481, 547, 614, 622, 633, 634, 638, 758, 769, 774, 856.

17. THE SELF AND NARCISSISM

9, 10, 12, 14, 40, 63, 101, 116, 132, 139, 169, 174, 178, 181, 183, 187, 221, 254, 266, 274, 275, 291, 293, 358, 370, 378, 396, 414, 478, 499, 548, 612, 615, 622, 624, 627, 633, 699, 702, 709, 721, 758, 766, 769, 770, 774, 789, 794, 809.

18. CREATIVITY AND ADAPTATION

27, 31, 38, 39, 44, 55, 56, 57, 63, 119, 177, 191, 252, 266, 267, 291, 293, 309, 336, 362, 427, 484, 487, 555, 612, 621, 622, 767, 800.

19. PSYCHOPATHOLOGY

21, 22, 26, 29, 33, 39, 42, 44, 46, 52, 68, 70, 72, 73, 74, 80, 101, 123, 195, 220, 235, 240, 251, 254, 264, 265, 285, 290, 337, 362, 363, 365, 395, 425, 493, 511, 522, 523, 555, 606, 612, 614, 620, 637, 642, 654, 658, 670, 686, 702, 789, 790, 809, 832, 856.

20. PSYCHOTHERAPY

7, 33, 39, 60, 71, 73, 75, 105, 111, 148, 175, 224, 308, 468, 504, 522, 550, 584, 630, 631, 642, 774, 788, 822.

2

FREUD'S CULTURAL BACKGROUND

HARRY TROSMAN

[*The Viennese Matrix*. Trosman's chapter on Freud's cultural background can serve as documentation for the latter's adherence to the humanist tradition during his formative years. This study does not pretend to exhaust the subject of the intellectual influences which Freud absorbed in his Viennese milieu; it focuses, instead, on a limited number of cultural currents which Trosman believes had major significance in Freud's development.

The experience which clearly anchored Freud within the matrix of humanism was his secondary education at a classical Gymnasium. Trosman reviews the extensive immersion in Latin and Greek literature which left an indelible mark on every prospective member of the late nineteenth-century Middle European intelligentsia. He also suggests, in persuasive fashion, that such an education provided a ready avenue for the absorption of the children of the newly emancipated Jews of Austria-Hungary into the mainstream of European culture. Perhaps the ideals of classical antiquity constituted the only possible ground on which the age-old conflict between Church and Synagogue could be disregarded in the attempt to forge a modern, secular, intellectual elite. At any rate, this educational experience confirmed Freud in his lifelong passion for history, especially that of the classical past.

Although Trosman gives ample emphasis to Freud's Jewish

First published in *The Annual of Psychoanalysis*, 1:318-335. New York: Quadrangle, 1973.

origins, he effectively refutes the viewpoint of Bakan (1958), who sees the Jewish mystical tradition as one of the principal sources of Freud's way of thought. Trosman attributes the similarities between psychoanalysis and Jewish mysticism to the fact that the latter shared many characteristics with the broader cultural movements of the nineteenth century which have been designated as Romanticism and which exerted their influence on Freud in an unequivocal manner. It is difficult for those raised in the English or French tradition to grasp how much more powerful this current in intellectual life was in the German-speaking countries than it was west of the Rhine. One example of this profound impact was the prevalence of *Naturphilosophie* and the cult of Nature. Incidentally, this post-Kantian recurrence of idealism demonstrates the ever-present danger of relapses into untenable epistemologies.

Trosman also brings to our attention the specific way in which the philosophers most relevant for psychoanalysis, Schopenhauer and Nietzsche, probably came to Freud's notice during his early years at the University, namely, through his participation in a pan-Germanic student movement which drew its inspiration in large measure from these avant-garde thinkers. Rieff (1959) noted the influence of another German Romanticist philosopher, Feuerbach, on Freud's later attitude about religion; the unpublished correspondence reviewed by Stanescu (1965, 1971) also reveals that Freud was indeed reading Feuerbach's work at that time.

In his approach to Freud's cultural background, Trosman takes the position that the classicism and the romanticism which are both to be found as major forces shaping his intellectual outlook are "the two broad movements in the history of Western thought." Even if we assume that this statement is intended to apply only to the intellectual history of the nineteenth century (the only period for which the contrast between classic and romantic can be said to be characteristic), it probably requires some qualification. As we gain increasing distance from the age of Romanticism, the contrast between it and the neo-Classicism that had preceded it seems less and less significant. Winckelmann does not impress us as all that different from Byron; David's cele-

brations of republican virtue, as in the *Death of Socrates,* are
not essentially discontinuous with Delacroix's protest against
the suppression of freedom in the *Massacres of Chios.* Whatever their subtle differences, neo-Classicism and Romanticism
were but successive fashions within one broader movement
which characterized the birth of the modern age, a nostalgia
for the exotic that gave expression to disillusionment with the
excessive hopes of the rationalist Enlightenment. It may not be
valid to see Freud's simultaneous classical and romantic
inclinations as a paradox; perhaps they are merely alternative
channels for correcting the positivist and materialist bias of
the culture of science—*Eds.*]

In order to do full justice to the scientific and cultural
tradition to which Freud's thought is related it would be
necessary to cover a wide variety of topics. In this essay,
however, I confine myself to influences on Freud which are
usually regarded as literary, political, or broadly cultural
rather than scientific; thus I do not aim at comprehensiveness.
In addition, the areas of this investigation are presumed to
have affected Freud early in his life before he immersed
himself in the scientific work of Brücke's physiological laboratory during his early twenties. In the following sections I shall
deal with Freud's link with Romanticism, particularly as
reflected in his view of nature, the political and cultural
milieu of Vienna in the latter half of the nineteenth century,
the Jewish tradition, and Freud's secondary school education
with its classical emphasis on Greek and Latin texts.

NATURE AND POLITICS

Men of thought who find a universe emptied of God fill the
conceptual void. The mind requires a manner of accounting
for order and energy, a regulatory agency, preferably impersonal and inoffensive to empiricism. With the passing of a
theological point of view and the coming of Romanticism at
the beginning of the nineteenth century, Nature was credited
with the power previously attributed to a deity.

Although the adolescent Freud showed an early interest in the study of nature, this interest vied with another derivative of the Romantic Movement—the arena of revolutionary politics. The revolutions of 1848, the subsequent concessions to bourgeois demands, the tottering monarchies and stirring nationalist movements made a political career a promising choice for able young men in the early 1870's. Thus nature and politics—the first a field for learning something of the world, the second the means for changing it—these were twin enthusiasms of young Freud.

Before discussing the view of nature in Freud's thought I shall briefly consider the broad cultural movement we have come to designate as Romanticism or the Romantic Movement. Beres (1965) has depicted the relationship between the Romantic tradition and psychoanalysis and described the elements they have in common. "Psychoanalysis is one of the culminations of the Romanticist literature of the nineteenth century," wrote Trilling (1950, p. 44).

Romanticism as a current of thought is an over-all attitude which tends toward spontaneity and high regard for emotional expressiveness. As a movement in the history of style in literature and art it can be viewed as a revolt against the neo-Classical style of the end of the eighteenth century. A shift occurred in the arts toward increasing concern with ordinary people and everyday speech. Forms became more experimental, previously tabooed themes were taken up, nature and the individual were glorified, and a heightened emphasis was given to passion and sensibility, as exemplified by Goethe's *The Sorrows of Young Werther.* A positive value was attached to the irrational; psychological processes of an unconscious nature were regarded as routes to higher truths. Man was seen as complex, his nature as conflicted and ambivalent. An appreciation for the value of early childhood experience and the conception of an unconscious hidden human nature were accompanied by a high regard for imaginative over logical mental processes.

Historically, the movement is associated with the political upheavals of the end of the eighteenth century, the American War of Independence and the French Revolution; both produced Declarations of the Rights of Man. Literary figures took up the interest in nationalism and liberation. The exploration of private mental states ("feeling is all," said Goethe) encouraged an interest in introspection, the dream, the uncanny and the supernatural. In its more extreme forms Romanticism led to a suspicion and depreciation of reason, knowledge, and rationality.

The Romantic Movement was given a great impetus by German writers of the early nineteenth century, many of whom Freud knew well and quoted. The lyric poetry of Goethe and Heine, the writings of Jean Paul Richter and E. T. A. Hoffmann, Herder and other folklorists, spread their influence throughout Europe. Their view of Nature is not unlike the theme of Wordsworth's poem:

> One impulse from a vernal wood
> > May teach you more of man,
> Of moral evil and of good,
> > Than all the sages can.
> > > ("The Tables Turned")

Although it is not the intent here to highlight the romantic influence at the expense of the positivist and rationalist side of Freud's heritage, it can hardly be minimized. Freud was fully aware of the literary and philosophic tradition not only in writings of German origin but generally in the half dozen languages he read. Goethe had translated into German Diderot's novel, *Rameau's Nephew*, which contains an explicit and unambiguous statement of the Oedipus complex, and Freud quoted the passage several times: "If the little savage were left to himself, preserving all his foolishness and adding to the small sense of a child in the cradle the violent passions of a man of thirty, he would strangle his father and lie with his mother" (Freud, 1916-1917, p. 338).

The conception of a hidden element in human nature and the dangers in blunting the emotional life are prominent in the writings of Byron—with whom Freud was familiar (E. Jones, 1953, pp. 55-56; Reik, 1956, p. 648).

The romantic influence had even permeated into the psychiatric writings of the nineteenth century (Ellenberger, 1970, pp. 210-215). Indeed, it was in part as a counterromantic reaction against an excessive reliance upon poorly conceptualized and vaguely understood subjective states that psychiatry moved into a more organic and objectively descriptive phase in the second half of the century (Zilboorg and Henry, 1941).

In its excesses, Romanticism tended toward one-sided attitudes of repudiation of rationality and reason, a rejection of all artistic norms, a glorification of force, and a revival of pantheism. The latter became identified with *Naturphilosophie* and the German philosopher Schelling. But most significantly, the Romantic Movement produced an essential shift in the mentality of the nineteenth century through the emphasis on Nature.

What is Nature? Nature may be characterized as anything which exists, is apprehended by the senses but not created by man. In its simplest sense (and omitting capitalization) nature refers to landscape—mountains and valleys, the world of growing things, trees, grass, flowers, animals—flora and fauna. Nature (now occasionally capitalized, as in *The Standard Edition of the Complete Psychological Works of Sigmund Freud*) also denotes the creative and controlling force of the universe. Nature is distinct from culture and society, if not indeed opposed to both. Nature may be benign or indifferent to man, but also cruel and attacking. Occasionally man-made artifacts which have some initial charm or beauty (such as castles and cathedrals) and show the ravages of time and the effects of natural forces, are considered a part of nature. The ruins of Tintern Abbey as experienced by Wordsworth became transformed into a natural object.

To the Romantics the state of Nature was simultaneously primordial and the fullest expression of man's being; a growing person's subsequent involvements with the world were anticlimactic if not corruptive. Civilized man could only strive for the reattainment of the original unity with the natural forces. The Philosophy of Nature, promulgated by Schelling, supported a belief in the indissoluble unity of natural and spiritual forces. Nature, it was suggested, could not be understood in terms of mechanical or physical concepts. The organic and visible world arose from a common spiritual principle, a world soul, which produces matter, living nature, and the mind of man.

At the risk of casting too wide a net, it is possible to note links between the Romantic philosophers and the more abstract theorizing in psychoanalysis. The Philosophy of Nature put forth a law of polarities, a dynamic interplay between antagonistic forces which govern the existence of natural phenomena. This dualistic principle later found its echo in the bipartite instinct theory of psychoanalysis.[1]

A notion of a primordial state followed by a series of metamorphoses also evokes recollections of the genetic and developmental approaches. To the Romantic philosopher, the unconscious was considered a true bond linking man with nature and permitting an understanding of the universe through mystical ecstasy or dreams.

The Romantic interest in Nature is discovered early in Freud's development. His choice of a career as a natural scientist was decided at 17 after having heard Goethe's essay on Nature read at a public lecture.[2]

> Nature! [exclaimed Goethe.] We are surrounded by her, embraced by her — impossible to release ourselves from her and impossible to enter more deeply into her. Without our asking and without warning she drags us into the circle of her dance and carries us along until exhausted we drop from her arm. . . . She has a purpose and broods continuously. . . . She reserves to herself an all-embracing intention, which no one discovers. . . . She has set me within. She will also lead me without, I commit myself to her. She may command me. She will not hate her

---

[1] Bernfeld and Jones regard "the solemn oath" sworn by Dubois-Reymond and Brücke when they embarked on their scientific careers as prototypical for the mechanistic school in which the young Freud learned the rudiments of science. Even this program, however, pledges the scientists to investigate "matter, reducible to the force of attraction and repulsion," thus recalling the duality of the Philosophers of Nature (S. Bernfeld, 1944; Jones, 1953, pp. 40-41). Cranefield (1966) has called attention to the Romantic underpinnings of Brücke's teachings.

[2] Or at least it was assumed by many that Goethe had written the essay. In actuality, the ideas were Goethe's and were recorded by a Swiss theologian, Tobler, in a conversation with Goethe. Years later, Goethe incorporated Tobler's essay into his collected works, believing its was his since the ideas were so consistent with his own line of thought (Freud, 1925b, pp. 8-9 fn.). For further discussion of Freud's career choice, see Chapter 3.

work. I have not spoken of her. No, what is true and what is false, it is she who has spoken it. Hers is all the blame; hers is all the praise [1780].

The essay is a challenge to uncover the hidden secrets of Nature, to find knowledge through a pantheistic mysticism. Man is powerless and submissive. Nature is pictured as an omnipotent mother who is unfathomable, creating and destroying, changing and eternal. Although no one can comprehend her fully, love is the only means of understanding her (Goethe, 1780).

Although Freud's first enthusiasm for science soon suffered because of an inability to find an arena in which he felt he could make use of his natural gifts (1925b), he did not lose his enthusiasm for the Goethe essay. More than 25 years later he referred to it as "incomparably beautiful."[3] However, by this time, he was also prepared to acknowledge that the Nature of the essay had other meanings. He cited a patient whose mental illness was attributed to the reading of Goethe's essay. The young man who cried "Nature! Nature!" and later castrated himself was referring, stated Freud, to the sexual sense of the word.

Freud's references to nature are extensive. Echoing Goethe, he wrote of the secrecy of Nature. Discovering the sexual etiology of neuroses, he told Fliess, "I have the distinct feeling that I have touched one of the great secrets of Nature" (Freud, 1887-1902, p. 83). Elsewhere he stated that it is one of the "constraints of Nature to which mankind is subject" in that procreation is entangled with the satisfaction of the sexual need (Freud, 1898a, p. 277). In Leonardo da Vinci's case, his interest in nature was viewed as a sublimation for the kindly mother who nourished him (Freud, 1910b, pp. 122-123). In another context Nature was credited with keeping love fresh and guarding it against hate (1915, p. 299).

But Nature in Freud is also cruel and terrorizing. The task of civilization is to defend us against Nature, which brings earthquakes, floods, storms, diseases, and death. Man first

[3] The German is *"unvergleichlich schön"*; poorly translated as "striking" in *The Standard Edition* (1900, p. 440).

responds to the inexorable power of Nature by humanizing what he has little control over. When he finds, however, that the natural forces conform to independent and autonomous laws, the forces of nature lose their human traits. They are the Moira (Fates), above the gods (Freud, 1927a, pp. 15-19). Finally, Freud combined Nature with the power of Eros, the power to create and multiply life. Our bodily organism thus becomes a minute part of the superior power of Nature. "Oh inch of nature," he quoted without recalling the source, in reference to the state of the helpless infant at birth (Freud, 1930a, pp. 121, 86, 91; Reik, 1956, p. 648).

Perhaps one of the most revealing references to Nature occurs in a repeated misquotation. Commenting on the advisability of not deceiving patients about their terminal illnesses, he stated, "Shakespeare says 'Thou owest Nature a death,' " counseling submission to the inevitable (Freud, 1887-1902, p. 276). The quotation, a remark of Prince Hal's to Falstaff from *Henry IV, Part I,* actually reads, "Thou owest God a death." Freud made the same error on two subsequent occasions, once in association to a dream, later in referring to the belief that death is the necessary outcome of life (1900, p. 205; 1915, p. 289). He thus partially impersonalized and deanimated those forces to which a man must submit, deprived the powers of their masculine identity, and removed the conception from a religious framework.

Thoughts concerning nature accounted for the immutable in the human condition. Nature might be a source of endless fascination, a storehouse of wisdom and creativity; man could do little but submit to its inexorable laws or merely fend off its destructive effects. Politics, on the other hand, insofar as it dealt with the man-made, held out the promise, at least during Freud's adolescence, of bringing about incisive changes. He recalled that as a boy of six, when his mother rubbed her hands together to show him that we are made of earth and he saw the blackish scales of epidermis, he acquiesced in the belief of our inevitable return to Nature (Freud, 1900, p. 205). But as a boy of 11 or 12 he could share in the hope of social reform promised by the first bourgeois ministry formed after the ratification of the new Austrian Constitution in 1867.

Indeed, until a few months before entering the University in 1873 he could still aspire to a political career and even after matriculation he still maintained a political interest.

In the latter half of the nineteenth century Vienna was the capital of a quasi-feudal state administered for six centuries by its ruling family, the Hapsburgs. The Austro-Hungarian Empire was made up of a polyglot collection of Germans, Magyars, Rumanians, and a variety of Slavic peoples; few of the inhabitants thought of themselves as distinctively Austrian. The "German spirit" of high culture and social humanism was admired by the German-speaking intelligentsia, and the monarchy felt threatened by political movements which promoted closer ties with Germany.

It is interesting to consider Freud's choice of career as a reaction to the bankruptcy of the liberal political culture of nineteenth-century Vienna. For a time, the liberal middle class, devoted to the values of advanced German thought, but not to a German nationalist ideal, was dominant. Several of the liberal cabinet ministers in the government of 1867 were Jews who, by and large, adhered to the values of the progressive German-speaking bourgeoisie (Freud, 1900, p. 193). One of their number admired by Jakob Freud and the 11-year-old Sigmund, Berger, stated, "The Germans in Austria should strive not for political hegemony, but for cultural hegemony among the peoples of Austria." They should "carry culture to the East, transmit the propaganda of German intellection, German science, German humanism" (Schorske, 1967, p. 343).

Although the bourgeois ministry urged a program of liberal reform and attempted to mitigate the power of the upper classes, its net result was failure. It did not succeed in unifying the divergent national elements within the Austro-Hungarian Empire nor could it control the explosive lower classes. Instead, states Schorske, "the liberals unwittingly summoned from the social depths the forces of a general disintegration" (Schorske, 1967, p. 344). New antiliberal and antimonarchical mass movements consisting of Czech nationalism, pan-Germanism, Christian Socialism, Social Democracy, and later Zionism, were ready to replace an ineffectual and short-

lived spirit of moderate liberalism. Although morally committed to supporting the rights of minority groups within the
Empire, the German-speaking middle class realized that any
concessions to Bohemia and Moravia would weaken their own
power and create disorganization. The academic intellectuals
—both students and faculty—by the early and middle 1870's
were prepared to give up imperial stability and middle-class
oligarchy for the promise of a unifying German nationalism.
But under the influence and eventual leadership of Georg von
Schönerer, the Germanic nationalist movement became progressively illiberal and totalitarian. In 1878, Schönerer declared in the Austrian Reichsrat, "If only we already belonged
to the German Empire!" The next year he began to show his
anti-Semitic leanings and railed against "the semitic rulers of
money and the world." In 1882 Schönerer raged at the
"sucking vampire . . . that knocks . . . at the house of the
German farmer and craftsman"—the Jew (Schorske, 1967,
pp. 351-352).

Schönerer's anti-Semitic appeals had a strong attraction for
the Austrian lower classes who were inclined to blame their
economic ills on the Jewish capitalists, and their more prox-
imate representatives, the Jewish peddlers. The artisan who
had previously made and sold the product of his trade in
his own home was now replaced by the itinerant peddler who
went from house to house developing his own clientele.
Schönerer's anti-Semitism was largely motivated by internal
needs and became apparent as one manifestation of an intrapsychic disturbance which finally culminated in social ostra-
cism and a jail sentence when he physically attacked a political
opponent. But the advantages of using prejudice to organize
latent social discontent were not lost.

A few years later, Karl Lueger made use of the anti-Semitic
feelings of the lower classes for opportunistic political purposes. Unlike Schönerer, he was a man of some culture and
charm and was less swayed by intense psychopathology. Five
years after Schönerer's initiation of anti-Semitic sentiment
into the German nationalistic movement, Lueger began to use
it as a focus for the organization of the Christian Socialist
Party. Pan-Germanism became of less interest to Lueger when

he had collected a sufficient majority of Viennese artisans to lead him to a political victory as mayor of Vienna in 1895. Schorske states that the last stand of Austrian liberalism may well have been the Emperor's refusal to ratify Lueger as mayor on two occasions before being forced to do so in 1897. The Fliess correspondence informs us that Freud broke a temporary smoking fast to celebrate this autocratic action of the Emperor against Lueger on the first occasion in 1895 (Freud, 1887-1902, p. 133). Lueger's anti-Semitism lacked the rancor of Schönerer's and apparently was modulated by treating some Jews with favor. "Der schöne Karl," as Lueger was known, became famous for his statement of flexible anti-Semitism. "I will decide who is a Jew," he stated.

Returning to an earlier phase of Freud's life, from 1873 to 1877, during his early university days, he belonged to a German nationalist group, the *Leseverein der deutschen Studenten* which, after several years, was disbanded through governmental pressure because of its anti-Austrian leanings. The association attracted young Viennese such as Freud, interested in political changes, who were Germanic in sympathy. Germany was regarded not only as the seat of an advanced nationalism but also as a haven from an oppressive and outdated oligarchy (McGrath, 1967).

Freud, while still at the Gymnasium, seriously considered a political career, and until the spring of 1873 he planned on the study of law as a preparatory step (see Chapter 3). Much later, he wrote that Heinrich Braun, his inseparable friend of the time, had awakened in him a "host of revolutionary feelings" (see E. Freud, 1960, p. 379), and during his early adolescence these competed with his budding scientific interests.[4]

It is ironic that the political movement of German nationalism, which was originally associated with freedom from the

[4] Freud eventually lost touch with Braun; however, Braun is referred to in the associations to the "Count Thun" dream as one of his school fellows who "seemed to have taken Henry VIII of England as his model." Braun married four times and later had a distinguished political career. It is noteworthy that the dream association concerns a revolt against an unpopular schoolmaster. Although Braun was the moving spirit in planning it, the leadership in the assault was left to Freud (Freud, 1900, pp. 211-212).

Austrian yoke and attracted enthusiastic young intellectuals, shortly became repressive and baldly anti-Semitic. In the 1870's it represented the highest aspirations of students like Freud who saw in the movement toward pan-Germanism closer links with the culture of Goethe as well as a more genuine expression of their political identity. Indeed the adherents, many of whom were young Jews, saw alliance with Germany as a socialist goal. The students of Freud's generation, in contrast to their fathers for whom German nationalism was no positive objective, were radicalized through their pride in German culture. In the *Leseverein,* discussion frequently revolved around the manner in which the "stable bourgeois world of their liberal fathers could best be overturned" (McGrath, 1967, p. 185).

Bismarck's creation of a united German Empire in 1870 had given a sense of reality to the aspirations of the German-speaking students at the University of Vienna. Freud's *Leseverein* (reading society) took as ideational leaders Schopenhauer, Wagner, and Nietzsche. It was believed that a new and artistically vital culture, opposed to the excessive rationalism of the past, had to be created. Political activity was to appeal to the integrated man and not regard the rational as if it were more important than the emotional side. Freud's friend, Heinrich Braun, was elected to office in the *Leseverein* and participated actively over several years. In 1877 Braun was one of the joint signers of a letter to Nietzsche declaring devotion to his outlook and offering to follow in the wake of his criticism of liberal society. It is doubtful whether Freud's active interest continued much beyond his first years at the University. Even in an early debate with Victor Adler, the subsequent leader of the Austrian Socialist party—which probably occurred at a meeting of the *Leseverein*—he was already "full of materialistic theories" (Freud, 1900, p. 212). Soon he was to become totally immersed in scientific activity.[5]

Thus Freud from his early adolescent years was swayed by

[5] Of interest, however, is the fact that Freud's subsequent teacher, Theodor Meynert, whom he initially followed with "deep veneration," was an active participant in the *Leseverein* and frequently lectured to the membership on psychiatry (Freud, 1925b; McGrath, 1967).

the Romantic regard for nature and the world of practical politics. He retained a love for the Moravian woods of his childhood and the beautiful ruins close by the town of his birth (Freud, 1872-1874, p. 426; see also Chapter 3). His response to Goethe's essay, a latter-day expression of this interest, already heralded his transition to a scientific orientation. *Pari passu,* under the influence of Heinrich Braun, he developed an interest in revolutionary politics. By the time anti-Semitism had become an ingredient of German nationalism in the early 1880's, Freud had dissociated himself from political goals. His membership in the *Leseverein* ended in 1877 a few years before the society was prohibited by governmental edict. But it is likely that his interest had already waned the previous year when he entered Brücke's laboratory and for the first time felt that he had found his niche (Freud, 1925b, p. 9).

Interestingly enough, we hear of an appeal to the remnants of Freud's nationalistic interests several years later. In 1885, Freud had gone to Paris to study with Charcot at the Salpêtrière (see Chapter 5). One evening at a gathering at the home of Charcot, the French neurologist, Gilles de la Tourette, baited Freud by predicting a ferocious war between France and Germany. Freud promptly countered that he was a Jew, aligning himself with neither Germany nor Austria. That evening he wrote Martha that he found such conversations very embarrassing for he felt stirring within him something German. However, he immediately added, he had long ago decided to crush such stirrings (letter of February 2, 1886, in E. Freud, 1960, p. 203).[a]

In spite of the political ferment, several observers are united in the belief that the vitality of Vienna in the last half of the nineteenth century fostered a spirit of creativity (Zweig, 1943; Barea, 1966; Schick, 1968-1969; Sachs, 1944). Intellectual values were highly prized, learning was treasured, art and science were idealized. "There is hardly a city in Europe where the drive toward cultural ideals was as passionate as it was in Vienna," wrote Zweig (1943, p. 12). A community which for

[a] See Chapter 12 for a discussion of the stirring up of Freud's German nationalism with the outbreak of war in 1914.

centuries had been politically expansionist now found itself in competition with superior military powers and looked for supremacy on artistic levels.

A striving for excellence was not characteristic of the totality of the educated classes. The Austrian ruling class, the old aristocracy of the Emperor's court, settled for the *status quo*. They were content to practice their casual refinements and enjoy their intellectual sluggishness. In this regard, they resembled the French courtiers who had preceded them by a century.

The drive toward scientific and artistic supremacy was characteristic of the flourishing middle class and was encouraged by the wide receptiveness of the city to the assimilation of divergent peoples and cultures. Viennese Jews who had lived peacefully in the city for two hundred years—although without full civil rights until 1867—took on the sponsorship of art supported by the nobility in earlier generations. "Nine-tenths of what the world celebrated as Viennese culture in the nineteenth century was promoted, nourished or even created by Viennese Jewry" (Zweig, 1943, p. 22). Nor were the Viennese Jews artistically productive in any specifically Jewish way: Mahler and Schönberg in music, Hofmannsthal, Schnitzler, and Beer-Hofmann in literature, Max Reinhardt in the theatre—all saw themselves as European or Viennese rather than Jewish.

"What spirit engendered such a concentration of creative powers in Vienna?" asked Schick (1968-1969, p. 531). He inventoried the surrounding idyllic landscape, the well-planned educational system, the profundity of wit, the peculiar Viennese vacillation in prizing both reality and fantasy, and the simultaneous enjoyment and cynical disparagement of the creature comforts. But to catalogue such factors leaves one with a sense of dissatisfaction—particularly so, regarding the latter factor, when we consider how lacking in Freud's basic outlook is any suggestion of *fin-de-siècle* fashionable world-weariness. Antithetical to Freud's sense of the tragedy of the human condition is the well-known Viennese epigram, "The situation is hopeless but not serious."

Perhaps we do best if we consider creative activity such as

Freud's as operating in opposition to ongoing ideational currents. Freud had something like this in mind when he discussed the influence of his native city on his thought. Ridiculing the belief that psychoanalysis owed its character to the alleged sexual looseness of Vienna, he proposed that discoveries such as his were more likely to occur in the presence of exceptional restrictions on sexual satisfaction. Freud suggested that the crucial factor in respect to locality might well be the degree of openness with which observations are permitted. Here Freud was able to point with favor at his milieu. The Viennese, he believed, were less embarrassed and less prudish about sexual relationships than Northern or Western European city-dwellers (Freud, 1914c, p. 40). Cultural life was not characterized by hypocrisy or a need to practice dissembling for its own sake or in the interest of so-called higher cultural aims. Indeed Sachs, also no great lover of Vienna, made a similar observation, although remaining firm in the conviction that "the allegation that Vienna has put her stamp of origin on Freud's work is a hollow pretense" (1944, p. 19). However critical Vienna was of Freud, at least its character did not blur his vision.

THE JEWISH TRADITION

A more vital matter concerns Freud's link with the Jewish tradition and Jewish life and thought. Although he discarded any adherence to religious belief or ritual, he never repudiated his Jewish identity. Out of his early tendency to find Semitic military heroes for idealization, he freely and incorrectly attributed a Jewish identity to Napoleon's general, Masséna, and valued the link with the Carthaginian, Hannibal (Freud, 1900, pp. 196-198).[b] He believed it unworthy and senseless to deny one's Jewish identity at a time when baptism to Christianity was by no means uncommon (Bakan, 1958, p. 46). Being a Jew, he believed, prepared him to take a position of

[b] For the ambivalence behind the idealization of Hannibal, see Chapters 4 and 12.

solitary opposition against a compact majority (Freud, 1925d, p. 222), enabled him to be free of prejudices, repudiate arbitrary authority (Freud, 1926c, p. 274), and respect intellectual values (Bakan, 1958, pp. 48-49; Freud, 1939, p. 115). In later life he realized that his early familiarity with the Bible had had "an enduring effect" upon him (Freud, 1900, p. 97, p. 334; 1925b, p. 8).

The experiences of Freud's family of origin were typical of the lot of the Central European Jew. Toward the middle of the nineteenth century, with the new freedom permitted in traveling and in quest of economic opportunity, the Jews began to infiltrate the Central European cities from the Eastern countryside. The first known traces of the Freud family were in Lithuania; the family then moved to Galicia. Freud's father and mother were both born in Galicia and had moved to Příbor in Moravia by the time Sigmund was born. When he was three they moved to Leipzig for a year before settling in Vienna.[c]

In the towns of Central Europe the ancient laboring guilds were inadequate to cope with the needs of expanding populations. Hence Jews with commercial experience drifted from region to region as needs arose for the transmission of goods and services. "Many remained petty tradesmen looking for opportunity, always hopefully expecting something to turn up but rarely finding security," writes Handlin (1967, p. 165). Freud in later life described his father in similar terms.

In view of the uncertainty of the political and economic situation, and in response to emancipation, a secular education became an enthusiastically sought prize. Handlin points out that Jews who emigrated to America before 1900 showed no such eagerness for schooling. "In Austria and Germany, by contrast, the university became the object of young people's ambition.... In this society *Bildung*—the possession of defined cultural symbols—carried with it a status that could partially compensate for the disadvantages of affiliation with a minority discriminated against for centuries" (p. 165). Suddenly, the generation of Jews of which Freud was a member was precipitated into Western society and modern life. The

[c] For further details, consult Schur (1972) and Ellenberger (1970).

attempt to master the problems of their new secular lives led at times to great feats of creativity and innovation.

Commenting on the mode of thought transmitted through the Jewish tradition, Handlin says, "The insistent confidence that an orderly arrangement of the universe made all phenomena susceptible to rational comprehension was characteristic of a people whose culture, for centuries, had stressed the need for interpreting every particular action and event in the light of the Divine purpose of creation. The sense of divinity was no longer immediate for those whose outlook was increasingly secular; but the sense of purpose and meaningfulness remained even for those who had moved away from traditional modes of thought" (1967, p. 168).

In assessing the significance of his Jewish background Freud tended to designate a broad cultural attitude rather than systematic Judaic knowledge of specific content. Although Abraham pointed out the "Talmudic" nature of his thought to him, nowhere do we see any real familiarity with the Talmud, nor are there citations from it (E. Freud, 1960, p. 153; H. Abraham and E. Freud, 1966, p. 36). He was of course deeply interested in Moses. He particularly identified with the Jewish military leader. "I have often felt," he wrote Martha, "as though I had inherited all the defiance and all the passions with which our ancestors defended their Temple and could gladly sacrifice my life for one great moment in history" (E. Freud, 1960, Letter 94, February 2, 1886).[d] But specific Jewish sources for his thought are not striking.

Although Freud was provided with some religious instruction in his boyhood, his liberal teachers attached no great value to knowing the Hebrew language and literature (Freud, 1925a, p. 291). What he acquired in childhood he soon lost, describing himself as "ignorant of the language of holy writ" in his Preface to the Hebrew translation of *Totem and Taboo* (1912-1913, p. xv).

Bakan bases his supposition that Freud was influenced by the Jewish mystical tradition on similarities between psychoanalysis and the Kabbala, citing particularly the similarity in

---

[d] His identification with the Biblical Joseph, the interpreter of dreams, has been pointed out by Shengold (1971) and Eissler (1971b).

techniques of interpretation and the importance that both
attach to sexuality. He also points out Freud's interest in
numerological discussions and concern for discovering hidden
meanings in trivialities.[e] He suggests that Freud tried to conceal the mystical influence and took measures to cover his
tracks so that this would not be discovered. He proposes that
Freud's interest in law was related to his interest in becoming a
rabbi, and quotes from a Jewish scholar who claimed that he
had discovered the Zohar and other books on Kabbala in
Freud's library in Vienna.

Bakan's evidence is not impressive. He cannot discuss the
Jewish mystical tradition in terms of its unique attributes and
he acknowledges that there are many similarities between
Jewish mysticism and other cultural movements of the time,
for example, Romanticism. His interpretations are poorly
supported as, for example, when he suggests that the pseudonym *Dora* for one of Freud's patients is a cover for the word
Torah. We have far greater evidence that Freud was interested in the law as preparatory for a political career rather
than the rabbinate. The argument that Freud was interested
in hiding such mystical influence because he feared rejection
by the scientific community is contradicted by Freud's openness about his Jewish identity throughout his writings and the
pride he took in establishing links with his past. In my perusal
of the Freud libraries in London and New York, I found no
literature dealing with the Kabbala or any significant collection of Judaica.

Nevertheless, in attempting to evaluate factors in Freud's
cultural background, it is best not to dismiss readily a possible
source of influence. Freud himself came to believe that his
interest in the significance of numbers was related to an
unconscious incorporation of Jewish mysticism. In a letter to
Jung of 1909, he wrote:

> Some years ago I discovered that I had the conviction I would
> die between the ages of 61-62.... It all began in the year 1899,
> when two events occurred simultaneously; first I wrote *The
> Interpretation of Dreams,* and second, I was assigned a new tele-

[e] This issue has been clarified by Schur (1972) and extensively treated by Eissler
(1974).

phone number—14362. A connection between the two could easily be established; in the year 1899, when I wrote *The Interpretation of Dreams,* I was 43 years old. What more natural, then, that the other numbers should refer to the end of my life, namely, 61 or 62. Suddenly, there was method in the madness. The superstition that I would die between 61-2 showed itself to be the equivalent of a conviction that I had fulfilled my life's work with *The Interpretation of Dreams,* didn't have to produce anything further, and could die in peace. You will admit that with this knowledge the thing no longer sounds absurd.... You will find confirmation here, once again, of the specifically Jewish nature of my mysticism [Jung, 1961, pp. 361-363].

Reference has already been made to the affinity which existed between the Jews and the Germans in the nineteenth century. German culture in its universalist form, as exemplified by Goethe and Schiller, provided emancipated Jews with a ready source for involvement in the Western ideal. A Jewish writer of the 1880's wrote: "To no other people have the Jews grown so close as they have to the Germans. They are Germanized not only on German soil, but far beyond the German boundaries.... There must be correspondence in the basic disposition [of the two people] which made Germany and all things German particularly attractive for the Jews, and the Jews an especially useful complement to the German character" (Kahler, 1967, p. 24).

The special attraction of the Jews "for all things German," the love for the language, the literature, and the land, is illustrated by an anecdote years later. In the 1930's, after the German writer Erich Maria Remarque had emigrated, a Nazi official tried to woo him with the promise of much honor if he would return to Germany. When he refused, the Nazi said, "Are you not a bit homesick?" "Homesick?," Remarque said, "No. I am not Jewish" (Kahler, 1967, p. 33).

Freud responded to German culture, and as I have previously mentioned, while in Paris felt the Teutonic tug. However, he was not submerged by the attractions of national identity. He used his identity as a Jew to maintain a freedom from chauvinistic restrictions when nationalistic ideals were no longer useful to him. He experienced the attractions of nationalism, as well as the repudiation of such narrow allegiances. By his mid-twenties, anti-Semitism had clearly cast its shadows over nationalist aspirations and Freud was fully taken up with his scientific life.

FREUD'S CLASSICAL EDUCATION

By Classicism we denote certain values characteristically revealed in the literature and art of Greece and Rome. The essential elements have been filtered through the Renaissance and the neo-Classical revival of the eighteenth century and subsequently the emphasis was placed on restraint, order, serenity, and repose. Classicism has come to emphasize the ideal over the real, the abstract over the concrete, reason and intellect over the emotions. But, in actuality, the affective part of life was not neglected among the ancients.

Sterba (1969) has pointed out the intense humanistic bent in the Classicism of antiquity. Although order and integration were valued, there was no slighting of the instinctual life and the pleasure-seeking components to the personality. Freud wrote of the glorification of the instinct among the ancients in contrast to the modern idealization of the object (1905c, p. 149). He acknowledged the importance the Greeks attached to the dream and said that he was following in the footsteps of the dream interpreters of antiquity (1916-1917, pp. 86-87). Generally Freud, whose knowledge of classical writings and art was extensive, turned to antiquity more often to illustrate the power of irrational instinctual forces than qualities of order, control, and integration.

Freud's secondary education took place in the classical Gymnasium with its heavy emphasis on Greek and Latin. Under the influence of educators and humanists such as Alexander and Wilhelm von Humboldt, at the beginning of the nineteenth century German-speaking and European education rediscovered classical antiquity (Sterba, 1969). The humanistic tradition, developed during the Renaissance in Italy as a reaction against the authoritarian restrictions of the

Middle Ages, [f] found its visible form in the university preparatory schools of the nineteenth century. Universalism, order,
and harmony were to be arrived at through exposure to the
highest levels of Western thought as exemplified by the
classical ideal. The formal discipline acquired by the mind in
the mastery of the rudiments of the literature and language of
Greece and Rome would carry into other modes of thinking
and provide a basis for an educated outlook.

Along with the reverence for the classical ideal several side
effects resulted from the Gymnasium experience. The teachers
were usually ambitious men of learning and ability who saw
themselves entering careers of scholarship and advancement.
It was not unusual for universities to recruit their faculty from
the classical Gymnasium, and many scholarly papers, the
product of teacher and pupil collaboration in the secondary
school, were produced. The classical Gymnasium was the
school with prestige, and became identified with the attain-
ments of the "educated man." The author who wrote for
readers educated in the classical Gymnasium could leave his
Latin and Greek quotations untranslated. Robert Waelder described his culture shock following his arrival in the United
States when he discovered that educated men could not be
relied upon to understand Greek and Latin quotations (Sterba, 1969, p. 437).

The curriculum of the classical Gymnasium called for hard
work and skill with languages. After a two-year preparatory
period in Latin, which Freud began at nine, he was assigned
Livy's *History of Rome.* Freud read much of Ovid's *Metamorphoses,* with its poetic rendering of many of the Greek
myths. Sallust, the Roman historian, Cicero's *Orations,* Virgil's *Eclogues* and *The Aeneid,* Horace's poems, and Taci-
tus's *History* rounded out a rather full exposure to Latin. In
Greek, Xenophon's *Anabasis* and *Cyropaedia* familiarized
Freud with the Greek struggle with the Persians and with the
character and education of Cyrus. In Herodotus he read of the
death of Darius, Xerxes' invasion of Greece, and the Battle of

[f] For a further interpretation of the origin of humanism, see Kristeller (1961,
1965) and Chapter 1.

Thermopylae, Demosthenes' orations, Sophocles' *Ajax* and *Antigone,* Homer's *Iliad* and *Odyssey,* and Plato's *Apology* and *Crito* were read in the original over a period of almost six years.

Did the readings leave an impression?[g] Freud refers on several occasions to *The Aeneid.* Not only does he use a quotation from it as the motto for *The Interpretation of Dreams;* he recalled with ease Dido's curse on Aeneas when it was forgotten by a young man Freud described in *The Psychopathology of Everyday Life* (1901, pp. 8-11). In contrasting the classical reverence for instinct with the modern repudiation of instinctual life he doubtless falls back on Plato, Ovid, and perhaps Catullus. Freud first read of the favorite hero of his youth, Hannibal, in the pages of Livy. The assigned portion of the *History of Rome* covers the Second Punic War, the character of Hannibal, and the campaign against Rome. A line from a Horatian Ode read in 1873 is quoted as a memorial to Karl Abraham in 1926. The use of Greek names for crucial psychological concepts (Oedipus, Eros and Thanatos, Narcissus), the frequent references to classical myth, the shared values regarding morality and aesthetics, the fascination with Greek and Roman sculpture and archeology, all attest to the indelible impression of the classical Gymnasium.[h]

How did Freud react to his secondary-school curriculum? Darwin, similarly educated, stated that the classical curriculum had stultified his mind. The general negative reaction to the classical influence is highlighted in Butler's book, *The Tyranny of Greece over Germany* (1935). In Freud's case we hear of only one episode of rebellion directed toward his teachers. Once, when he was 15, he said, "We had hatched a conspiracy against an unpopular and ignorant master.... The leadership of the chief assault was allotted to me" (1900, pp. 211-212). We hear of no reprisal for this rebellious confrontation, nor did his conduct interfere with his making the honor roll that year as in every other year of his Gym-

[g] For a fuller discussion of Freud's response to this exposure to Latin literature, see Chapter 3.

[h] See Chapter 3 for a discussion of a poem written by Freud in 1875 in the form of a parody of an inferior Latin versifier imitating Homer. For a full translation of Freud's poem, see Rogawski (1970).

nasium career. He wrote of his teachers with affection when his secondary school asked its distinguished graduates to comment in a *Festschrift* celebrating the fiftieth anniversary of its foundation. It was his classical education which provided him with his "first glimpse of an extinct civilization which in my case was to bring me as much consolation as anything else in the struggles of life" (1914d, p. 241).

Freud's library, now in London, documents his fascination with the culture of Greece and Rome. His interest in the history, archeology, art, and literature of classical antiquity was lifelong. He had an extensive and distinguished collection of art and archeological objects, subscribed to archeological journals, and had more than an amateur's knowledge of the field. It is not surprising that the founder of psychoanalysis shoud be interested in glimpses of an extinct civilization. Archeology and psychoanalysis have obvious links with one another. Both value the understanding of the past through present-day remnants (S. C. Bernfeld, 1951). It is likely that an additional factor in Freud's love for the literature of antiquity was the opportunity it provided for authenticating the universal nature of psychoanalytic findings. He was sustained by the awareness that discoveries made in a specific clinical situation had a general applicability and had already been hinted at in cultures centuries old. Classical antiquity could provide a surety for findings clinical experience first revealed.

In summary, then, Freud in his prescientific days had already been exposed to a wide cultural and humanist tradition. Through an interest in German literature and particularly the writings of Goethe, he became conversant with the tradition of Romanticism and its regard for the irrational and unconscious. Although intrigued by the Romantic concern with the powers of nature, he responded not philosophically but with an interest in observation. Vienna provided an environment which did not interfere with an interest in observation and even encouraged an openness and acceptance of learning and innovation. His early political aspirations encouraged an attitude of independence and an unwillingness to bow to authority, and the Jewish tradition provided the strength to tolerate prejudice and opposition. His classical education provided a complex substratum against which universals concerning the human mind could be tested.

Although I started with a discussion of Romanticism, it is fitting that my ending highlights Freud's Classicism. In the sense in which psychoanalysis attempts to find order in chaos, synthesis among conflicting irrational forces, integration and self-knowledge in place of warded-off unconscious impulses, Freud blended the two broad movements in the history of Western thought. Both Romanticism and Classicism provided an impetus toward an empirical investigation of psychic reality.

3

THE "ICH." LETTERS

JOHN E. GEDO and ERNEST S. WOLF

A would-be master
will train precociously.
            Schiller, *Wilhelm Tell*

[*The Adolescent Freud.* The following chapter was originally prepared as a commentary to accompany the publication of the German text of the earliest known correspondence of Sigmund Freud. The Fluss letters were rediscovered among the papers of the late Ernest Jones to whom they had been made available in preparation for his biography of Freud. Although Jones (1953) did, in fact, use some of the information disclosed by this correspondence and noted the existence of these letters, he did not have the space fully to exploit their implications.

The correspondence deals, in large measure, with a most striking episode of Freud's adolescence, the fleeting love experience around Fluss's sister Gisela which was to constitute much of the subject matter of Freud's first autobiographical paper, "Screen Memories" (1899). On the basis of these letters, Gedo and Wolf disagree with Jones's conclusion that the disappointing outcome of the Gisela affair had led to a reinforcement of repression of Freud's erotic impulses and a corresponding increase of his scholarly and professional ambitions. Although the testimony of the Fluss correspondence should be treated with some reserve, as Freud was not

---

Translated from "Die Ichthyosaurusbriefe." *Psyche*, 24:785-797, 1970.

likely to be entirely frank about his feelings concerning Gisela
in writing to her brother, at least one of the letters after the
end of the affair (as well as parts of the Silberstein correspondence to be discussed in Chapter 4) demonstrates the
availability of much free libido—actually, quite amazing
intensity of libidinization in a boy as sexually inhibited as
Freud outwardly seems to have been. Gedo and Wolf propose
an alternative hypothesis to explain the significance of the
relationship to Gisela Fluss and Freud's subsequent reactions;
they base their formulation on the recent theories about
narcissism, specifically those about problems of idealization,
enunciated by Kohut (1971).

This paper has provoked disagreement on the part of Eissler
(1974). In a lengthy study dealing mainly with a beautiful
numerological fantasy elaborated by Freud in the Silberstein
correspondence, Eissler takes issue with Gedo and Wolf about
their interpretation of Freud's disillusionment with Gisela
Fluss as an expectable vicissitude of a normal adolescence.
Eissler does not accept Jones's view that Freud's adolescence
was a relatively tranquil one; he assumes that the disappointing affair with Gisela led to severe turmoil which, however,
Freud succeeded in keeping largely to himself. He does agree
with Jones's formulation that this frustration in the sphere of
love led Freud into a retreat from women in the form of single-
minded commitment to his career ambitions. Moreover,
Eissler believes that the change in Freud's career goals from
law and politics to natural science was a result of this pathological development and represented a regrettable, if necessary, postponement of the flowering of his genius, a kind of
self-burial in the physiological laboratory.

Whether one views them as expectable or as pathological,
there is no question that Freud was struggling with intense
conflicts during his adolescence; the fact that he could keep
them contained within himself, with no recorded trace of
outward activity derived from them, is both a measure of his
introspective genius and a differentiating quality which makes
his psychology seem quite distinct from that of other geniuses
like Leonardo and Goethe, as described by Eissler. If Freud
really did suffer from a relative lack of zest for life during this

period, as Eissler believes, this is more likely to have been caused by a splitting off of his unrealistic, grandiose ambitions than by romantic disappointments; such symptoms are characteristic of narcissistic conflicts and their presence would speak in favor of Gedo and Wolf's hypotheses.

In fact, it might be argued that it was precisely the shift into the field of natural science which permitted Freud to give free rein to the intensity of his ambitions and thus restored his full zest for life. Dreams of reforming Western society by way of a political career had become quite unrealistic for a Viennese Jew by 1872, as Trosman has shown in Chapter 2. Had he pursued the study of law with such a goal in mind, the best Freud could have achieved might have been prominence in the Austrian social democratic movement, like that of his admired acquaintance, Viktor Adler. Freud's actual course of action resulted, of course, in his having had a most profound revolutionary impact on our civilization; to achieve this, however, the detour by way of the discipline of the scientific laboratory was probably a crucial preparatory step. The "asceticism" of physiological research did not prove sterile for Freud; it saved him from scattering his talents in a life of political action where his literary gifts would very probably have found expression in pamphleteering and journalism.

The last consideration brings us back to the quality of these literary productions of the youthful Freud. In both form and content, they are in the tradition of the humanist letter, one of the principal areas of the humanists' professional activity. In consequence of the classical curriculum in which Freud was immersed at the time in his last year at the Gymnasium (see Chapter 2), his immediate model for his Epistles was not one of the Renaissance humanists but that of *their* preceptor, the Latin poet Horace. Here we may profitably recall that Horace had also been the favorite of Montaigne, the supreme introspective psychologist before Freud (see Chapter 1); Kristeller (1965) has designated Montaigne's *Essays* as humanist letters addressed by the author to himself. In this sense, Emil Fluss may be seen as Freud's provincial alter ego, an externalization of Freud's internal audience for the productions of a great German stylist — *Eds.*]

Psychoanalysts are destined ceaselessly to return to the life of Freud for inspiration and example to buttress their courage in the daunting quest for new depth-psychological insights. Although the main biographical outlines are now enshrined in Jones's (1953, 1955, 1957) indispensable *Life,* we have found ever more treasures in the successive volumes of letters (the correspondence with Fliess, with Abraham, with Pfister, with Arnold Zweig, and the selection edited by Ernst Freud). The complexity of a great man is brought more and more clearly into focus by each fresh approach to his sum of activities; the gain is particularly marked when we come into possession of primary data about the formative years. The recent rediscovery of a series of communications from Freud to a friend of his adolescence, Emil Fluss, now throws light on an earlier period of his youth than any of the previously published materials; their publication (Freud, 1872-1874) therefore has greater import than their relatively small number would otherwise suggest.

As we know from Jones, at the University Freud had a circle of friends, a *Bund,* which included Fluss. Our letters, however, come mostly from an earlier time, when Fluss was still living in their native town, Přibor in Moravia; only the last of the letters and the two postal cards, decidedly more cursory than the others, date from the period of student fellowship. Six letters (one of which was noted by Jones and published in Ernst Freud's [1960] selection) span the last academic year of Freud's studies at the Leopoldstäder Gymnasium. It was the time of his intimacy with the Eduard Silberstein who had accompanied him on the previous summer's vacation in Přibor; together they formed that Spanish Academy, the "Academia Castellana," which prefigured the Wednesday Evening Society and Committee of three and four decades later. An academy is a professional association for the pursuit of knowledge; Freud and Silberstein "learnt Spanish together and developed their own mythology and private words." They took the names of a pair of philosopher-hounds who engaged in a dialogue: it should be invaluable to examine these first creative efforts of the 16-year-old Freud.[1] While we await

[1] Silberstein preserved these letters, postal cards, and other memorabilia, and

their publication, we must delve into the Secrets of Cipion, *"pero en el Hospital de Sevilla,"* in terms of his reports to his provincial confidant, Fluss.

In his thoughtful and touching review of *The Letters of Sigmund Freud* (E. Freud, 1960), Eissler (1964) commented at length on the single communication to Fluss in that volume, a letter of 1873. Eissler noted the necessity of approaching it through the understanding of the psychology of late adolescence. In view of the fact that the letters to Přibor record the change in Freud's career goals from the law to natural science as well as the transformation of his given name from Sigismund, they might be seen as instruments in the resolution of the normative life crisis of adolescence. Like a serpent shedding its confining, outgrown integument, the young Freud emerged from his *Matura* in a state of consolidation, and feeling estranged from his past.

The impression one gains from reading about Freud's inner struggles confirms Jones's conclusion that he had a relatively tranquil adolescence. This is a finding of some significance, since other studies of the psychology of genius (e.g., Eissler, 1967) have revealed patterns of profound turmoil in this developmental phase. These letters also show, however, that Jones made decidedly unwarranted inferences about the dynamics of Freud's adolescent vicissitudes. He had assumed, on the basis of the allusion to the episode in "Screen Memories" (1899) and a letter to Martha Bernays in 1883, that the "calf love" for Fluss's sister Gisela had been an intense experience which was followed by strong repression of erotic impulses and reinforcement of scholarly-professional ambitions. (Incidentally, Eissler [1964] also stressed the predominance of narcissistic goals in Freud's youth. He believes that a better balance between narcissistic and object-libidinal aims was achieved in a restructuring of Freud's personality during the lengthy and abstemious courtship of Martha Bernays.)

With regard to Gisela Fluss, it seems more plausible to accept Freud's own report here that "there was more irony,

eventually settled in Romania. Of a total of over 70 items two complete letters, one poem by Freud, and a few excerpts of other letters have been published by Stanescu (1965, 1967, 1971). See Chapter 4 for an examination of the Academia Castellana.

yes, mockery, than seriousness in this whole flirtation" (28 Sept., 1872). A swain who can call his beloved "Ichthyosaura"[2] hardly appears to require further drastic defenses against his love of women. That Freud returned from Příbor in September, 1872, with his libido free and intact is sensuously reported in the "little adventure" which begins the Fluss correspondence.[a] It is therefore highly unlikely that Freud's swelling ambition was inversely related to his object-libidinal vicissitudes; this vignette is an excellent illustration of the validity of Kohut's view (1966, 1971) that narcissism and object love have independent lines of development. In the light of these considerations, Eissler's hypothesis about the effects of Freud's love for his fiancée on his ambitions may also have to be viewed with caution.

In general, this handful of letters provides an object lesson to the historian about the value of primary sources and the pitfalls of relying on even so excellent a guide as Jones. It is evident that even his spacious biography could not be intended as a repository for factual details; thus the following comments do not denigrate the value of Jones's work (within the bounds of his intentions). We merely wish to warn against its misuse as a historical record. These letters directly establish chronological sequences that Jones could only infer: the vacation in Příbor took place when Freud was 16; the trip to England, though planned for the summer after his *Matura,* had to be postponed (and must therefore have been taken at age 19). On other matters Jones is in outright error: Příbor is not in southeast Moravia but near the Silesian border, close to Ostrava; more significantly, the 1873 visit had not constituted Freud's only return to his native town—he specifically mentions an earlier stay (in 1870 or 1871) and alludes to the fact

[2] In Ernst Freud's introduction to the Freud-Fluss correspondence he erroneously designated the word "Ichthyosaura" as "jocularly coined by Freud." This would have been quite in keeping with Freud's ironic tone as well as with his characteristic tendency toward the original coinage of terms. However, *Ichthyosaurus communes* is, in fact, an extinct fish-lizard of the Jurassic period. Its use by Freud reflects his then current preference for metaphorical allusions derived from geology and paleontology.

[a] See Stanescu (1971) for a slightly later letter to Silberstein which brims over with eroticism just as clearly as this letter to Fluss, casting further doubt on the hypothesis of repressed erotic impulses as a reaction to the Gisela episode.

that his mother frequently went to a Moravian spa on her summer vacations. The evidence that she repeatedly took her beloved son with her suggests new lines of thought concerning the profound significance that traveling came to assume for Freud (see Chapter 12).

Perhaps the most exciting discovery in the Fluss letters is the precise recording of a turning point in Freud's life. "As for me, I can report what is perhaps the most important bit of news in my miserable life.... But the matter is as yet undecided" (17 Mar., 1873). Almost certainly Freud was here referring to the fateful lecture by Brühl at which he was so decisively impressed by hearing Goethe's poem on nature (see Chapter 2). Six weeks later, he was ready to lift the veil: he would become a scientist. "I shall gain insight into the age-old dossiers of Nature, perhaps even eavesdrop on her eternal processes" (1 May, 1873). It cannot be mere coincidence that this crystallization of manifold talents and goals into a lifelong identity took place in response to the stirring model of the outstanding post-Renaissance example of an artist-scientist: Goethe. (Freud's identification with Leonardo da Vinci, perspicaciously pointed out by Jones, must in part have been based on Leonardo's similar range of passionate interests.) These letters show ample evidence of Freud's awareness of his capacity for vivid, literary imagination; this is demonstrated with particular clarity by a more literal translation of his words than that of the version published in English. Thus the "little adventure" described in the letter of 18 Sept., 1872, is actually called a "small novel," and Freud's word is "narrative" in the passage rendered as "Any detailed description would have to be prefaced by Goethe's line: A fairy-tale . . . it was once upon a time' " (28 Sept., 1872). Similarly, the "little incident" in the letter of 7 Feb., 1873, is a free translation of "to relate an old tale." Freud did not succumb to the fear of inner excitement that so often leads adolescents to a sterile, defensive asceticism; instead, he channeled his imagination into the disciplined pathways of science, where he was to find unique scope for his towering psychological and literary gifts.

Eissler (1964) has said that "it was in Freud's report on his first scientific endeavor that his unusual capacities became for the first time manifest" at the age of 20. Now that we can study a fair sample of the 16- and 17-year-old Freud's efforts as an epistolary artist, the signs of future genius may fairly be said to be present in them. Like an infant Hercules, the youthful Freud can strangle twin forces; his powers are prodigious in the sphere of psychological observation and in that of German prose.

These letters abound in penetrating observations of human behavior, particularly in self-observation of unsparing introspectiveness. Excerpts from a single paragraph may suffice to suggest that we are face to face with the product of no common schoolboy:

> But once you are a melancholic, you will suck sorrow from anything that happens. This Exposition Universelle...does not suit me a bit. It adds to my laziness and provides me with a thousand excuses to exculpate myself before my tender conscience. I fear, through curiosity I'll fail the Matura, and through my sense of duty miss the World Exhibition. For the remaining two months...I am well stocked with the best of intentions, am so sensitive that I fairly dread your letter exultant with the kind of divine laziness from which an angel with a fiery sword has driven me long ago: all sorts of doubts and worries [1 May, 1873].

Awareness of inner conflict would be unusual enough in itself; the subtle grasp of issues of regressive longings, narcissistic investments, or rationalizations carries insight into the inner world to an extent available only to great artists; but the mark of genius consists in the cool irony with which Freud transcends his experiencing self. A more exact rendering of this text would read, "such doubts and sorrows." The capacity to view oneself whole, to acknowledge one's limitations without resort to illusions, is the sign of the transformation of narcissism into wisdom, humor, and creativity (see Kohut, 1966). Waelder (1965) has, in illustration of this point, quoted Auden:

> ... the power to enchant
> That comes from disillusion...

It might be said that to find extraordinary introspective and empathic capacities in adolescence in the greatest psychologist of Western civilization is so natural that it pales into insignificance in comparison with the musical talents of the infant Mozart or the draftsmanship of the child Picasso. Consequently it is much more striking to review these letters in terms of what they reveal about Freud as a litterateur. The German-speaking public has had the opportunity to study Schonau's detailed discussion (1968; see Niederland, 1971) of Freud's mature prose style; all the elements which he found to be characteristic of this unique and beautiful style can already be recognized in these youthful letters. We can but admire the discernment of Freud's German professor who openly acknowledged the merit of "a style at once correct and characteristic," so that the 17-year-old prodigy could tease Fluss about his lack of awareness of "exchanging letters with a German stylist" (16 June, 1873).

To start from the surface, there is the sheer quantity, the length of the letters, the obvious love of words and phrases, almost the *need* to write, coupled with an intense awareness of the importance of style in such expressions as "smooth-tongued platitudes" (18 Sept., 1872), "the word is a concession to your style" (7 Feb., 1873), "oracular tone" (17 Mar., 1873), or "to put it poetically" (7 Feb., 1873). Equally intense is the pleasure and the skill of the storyteller who narrates his travel experience as a little adventure and who, characteristically, expands one sentence taken from his friend's letter ("The other day I went ice-skating, and so did she" [7 Feb., 1873]) into an ironic and insightful little story. One is reminded of the mature Freud who was to take a sentence of a letter by Romain Rolland and expand it into the great essay, "Civilization and Its Discontents" (1930a).

No less important are the frequent literary citations and allusions, especially classical ones. In these seven letters we find Horace—"the unvarnished truth" (18 Sept., 1872) alludes to *"nuda veritas";* "similar circumstances always result in similar products" (18 Sept., 1872) alludes to *"fortes creantur fortibus";* "I have lost almost all recollection of past events, submit to everything as if dazed" (18 Sept., 1872) reminds one of "You ask me why a soft numbness diffuses all my innermost sense with deep oblivion."

We find the Bible: "the cup runneth over" [inadequately

translated into the metaphor of putting a lid on a pot]
(Psalms) (18 Sept., 1872); "the inscrutable workings of a
divine power" (7 Feb., 1873); "with fear and trembling" (Job)
(16 June, 1873); "an angel with a fiery sword" (Genesis) (1
May, 1873); "a Tower of Babel" (Genesis) (1 May, 1873);
"find ... favour in my eyes" (Genesis) (16 June, 1873).

We find Shakespeare: "suck sorrow from anything that
happens" (1 May, 1873) alludes to "I can suck melancholy out
of a song"; "more common ... than blackberries" (1 May,
1873) alludes to "If reasons were as plentiful as blackberries";[3]
"tender conscience" (1 May, 1873) alludes to "Conscience,
conscience! O, 'tis a tender place"; "to be content with cold
dishes" (16 June, 1873) simultaneously alludes to "The funeral
baked meats did coldly furnish forth the marriage tables" and
"He receives comfort like cold porridge."

We find the Mass for the Dead: "There comes the day, the
longest day, when..." (16 June, 1873).

Goethe is quoted twice and more often alluded to.

Heine's poem *"Heimkehr"* reappears in "fill a thousand
gaps from time immemorial" (16 June, 1873).

This necessarily brief list does not exhaust the rich literary
lode. Many other phrases call to mind a cultural heritage
without pointing quite so directly to a literary source. What
has been translated as "I have thrown myself heart and soul
into the future" (28 Sept., 1872) literally reads "I steer with
full sails," presaging Freud's love for the nautical metaphor:
he later used *"Fluctuat nec mergitur"* ("Swamped but not
sunk") from the insignia of the city of Paris as his motto for
"On the History of the Psycho-Analytic Movement" (1914c),
and in *The Interpretation of Dreams* (1900) we find *"Flavit et
dissipati sunt"*[4] which Freud in a letter to Fliess had already
considered for use as a motto. Among Freud's later favorites
were military metaphors which already make their apearance
in these letters: e.g., "to continue my reconnoitring," "to pass
in review" (18 Sept., 1872), and "reports from the theatre of
war" (1 May, 1873).

[3] Freud later (1914c) put the allusion to better use in the polemics with Jung and
Adler.

[4] "[God] blew and they were scattered" from a coin memorializing the defeat of
the Spanish Armada.

The hallmark of Freud's mastery of metaphor is his ability to use timeworn and flattened expressions in a novel and original context and thereby infuse them with new life and meaning. This raises some interesting questions about the role of the vivid literary imagination[b] as the spring from which flow the images that become metaphors on the way to being crystallized into scientific concepts and models. "It makes me feel like a scientist who is asked about the past of our planet. This whole period is as remote to me as can be, however much it once seemed part of me," says Freud (28 Sept., 1872). We recognize here the image of one of Freud's favorite and key metaphors, the metaphor of childhood as prehistory, a comparison that he first stated explicitly in 1898 (1898a) and that he used many times more in the ensuing years, even as late as 1938: "With neurotics it is as though we were in a prehistoric landscape" (p. 299). But we also discern in the 1872 image the idea of not quite involuntary forgetting—the concept of repression. One is left with the impression that for Freud metaphorical thinking served not only his aesthetic sensibility to communicate clearly and beautifully but was also a necessary step in the processes of insight and concept formation.

Much of the lucidity and persuasive power of Freud's mature style is the result of the reader becoming engaged in a fictive dialogue that leads him to think along with Freud, bringing forth objections and refutations. Freud writes with continuous courteous concern for the reader's affective experience. The letters examined here show the young Freud already using this device, even if not with the sure mastery of later years. We must therefore disagree with Schönau's (1968) suggestion that the fictive dialogue is ascribable to Freud's experience in the analytical consulting room. Rather, it seems that, analogously to Freud's use of metaphors, his fictive dialogue serves not only as a means of effective communication but also as the externalization of a necessary internal dialogue that disciplines the unfettered imagination into creative scientific ideas. "What conclusion would you draw from it?" (7 Feb., 1873) Freud asks Fluss in forcing him to

[b] Here is one concrete way in which Freud's specifically *humanist* qualifications, i.e., his natural use of the tools of poetry, had direct bearing on his psychoanalytic creativity.

think along with him. With courteous regard he says, "How well I can imagine your feelings" (16 June, 1873). Freud constantly keeps one eye on the reader, one eye on himself. "As you can see, I have not spared you my remark, my original intention notwithstanding" (18 Sept., 1872).

Finally, in these letters Freud shows his love for abbreviations, code words, new coinages. Most remarkable is the coinage of "Ichthyosaura" for Fluss's sister Gisela, which becomes abbreviated to the code word "Ich." This must have been the first time Freud used this designation which, characteristically, reappeared later in a new context and with a new meaning.

We have surveyed these youthful productions for those elements that Schönau has found to be "distinctly personal" in Freud's writing style; we believe that we have demonstrated their presence, some *in statu nascendi*, others sprung from their creator fully formed. Narrative skill and love of language, reverent and apposite use of the creations of great predecessors, creation and recreation of vivifying metaphors, invention of memorable codes, and the insertion of empathic contact with the reader into the explicit text in the form of internal dialogue constitute this cluster of characteristic stylistic elements.

Studies of the historical emergence of Freud's greatness as the peerless psychologist of the human depths have repeatedly stressed his unusual capacity to learn from contacts with suitable forerunners such as Breuer or Charcot (see Lowenfeld, 1956; also Chapters 5 and 8). It is of the greatest interest, although scarcely surprising, that in the development of his eminence as a writer he evidently made use of a similar mechanism of selective identification. This capacity is shown most obviously by the manner in which nuggets of the best in the heritage of European literature are incorporated into Freud's prose. There are a number of straightforward quotations, but in many more instances an image or a phrase is woven into the fabric of a sentence without showing a seam, and the process of internalization often goes a step further, giving the borrowed element an original twist which renders it barely recognizable. How many readers, even in the English-speaking world, will recognize in these pages Falstaff's black-berries or Jaques' melancholy?

Although more subtle and consequently more difficult to document, the Fluss letters contain another class of evidence pointing to the modes of Freud's absorption of literary influences. The curriculum of studies he was pursuing during the year of the letters is known (see Trosman's summary in Chapter 2). Of all of the authors the greatest immediate impact on Freud was made by Quintus Horatius Flaccus. "I read Horatian odes, you live them" (1 May, 1873).[5] We have made no effort to search out the doubtless numerous examples of borrowings from Horace that may have perfused these pages, for a single instance of a more cogent variety has suggested itself to us. A major portion of one of the letters is devoted to a description of the public procession on the occasion of the twenty-fifth jubilee of the accession of the Emperor Franz Josef (1 May, 1873). This is a clever parody, doubtless unconscious, of the noble civic poetry of Horace, most specifically of the *Carmen Saeculare*, that moving celebration of the zenith of Roman power, the Secular Games — another twenty-fifth jubilee, that of Augustus' defeat of the oligarchy at Philippi. Freud takes revenge for the suppression of Austrian democracy in 1848 through brilliant satire: that *"doctus chorus"* of praise, Horace's *"virgines lectas puerosque castos"* ("chosen youths and maidens"), are turned into street urchins who break into shouts at the sight of the Kaiser.

We can only conjecture why Freud was drawn to Horace in particular at this stage of his life. Surely the other classical

---

[5] In its formal aspects of structure and tone, the poem "Wedding Carmen" that Freud sent to Silberstein on October 2, 1875, resembles Latin poetry, specifically clumsy and slavish imitations of Homer. This effort has been translated by Rogawski (1970). In mock seriousness, a disdainful Freud celebrates the marriage of his first secret adolescent passion with jocular references to the "dull spirit" in a "small brain." Scathingly denouncing the groom as having studied the art of acquiring money, he dismisses the newlyweds as being "like worms and insects." Do we hear the disappointed Catullus fulminating against unfaithful Lesbia, or is Horace's satire on "How to Get Rich Quickly" reverberating in Freud's mind? Perhaps we can also discern the young Goethe's Anacreontic poetry. (For the emotional aspects of Freud's continued bitterness about Gisela Fluss, see Chapter 4.)

authors he was then reading exerted an equal influence on
him in the long run: in this regard we need merely mention
that of Sophocles, which turned out to be the strongest. The
most permanent quality of Horace retained in Freud's style is
the tone of detached irony aimed at a cultivated audience. It is
precisely the fact that the identification took place in terms of
a *formal* element rather than with regard to *content* that
makes the half-digested fragment of the *Carmen Saeculare* so
interesting as a clue to the process of internalization that was
probably taking place. We are left with a few lines of thought:
Horace was almost the first artist of the epistle and remains
unsurpassed in this form. He was also one of the first
introspective poets, and one who has been justly named "the
poet of Sanity" (Rose, 1936). Before his decision for natural
science (and in spite of the fantasy of studying the law),[6]
Freud must have been attracted to a model in an area for
which he already felt himself to be richly endowed. The boy
who was to write as yet uncounted thousands of masterful
letters might have begun this correspondence by enjoining his
friend to secrecy, but the fact that he was writing for posterity
also became part of the "unvarnished truth" (18 Sept., 1872)
he had promised: thus Fluss was told, "preserve them — bind
them together — guard them well — you never know" (16 June,
1873). In a more serious tone, Horace had written (Epistles
II — 2, 202-205):

> In this "human race"
> Where position and wealth and physical strength and good looks
> And talent and mental accomplishments all have their place,
> I come in last of the first and first of the last.

The 16-year-old Goethe, like Freud, had echoed these
Horatian ideals in August, 1765, when he wrote into the
album of his friend F. M. Moors upon the occasion of the
latter's departure to the University of Göttingen:

[6] Among the memorabilia preserved by Silberstein is a visiting card imprinted
"Sigismund Freud, Student of Jurisprudence," indicating Freud's interest, though
impermanent, was serious; he later sealed the finality of his choice of natural
science by changing his given name.

Almost like devalued money
That's how it looks, the best world.
(Can you hold back laughter, friends?)
            (Horace, *Art of Poetry*, Verse 5.)
The author has, when he writes,
Something certain, that drives him.
This drive also pulled Alexander
And all other heroes together.
Therefore I also write myself in here:
I would not like to be forgotten [our translation].

Freud's identification with both Horace and Goethe comes as no surprise. In Freud's Pantheon of heroes there is a poet's corner in which both occupy places of honor. Freud's intimate familiarity with Goethe's life and work is well-known and documented. Even the Academia Castellana faintly echoes Goethe's attempts to join the analogous "Arkadische Gesell-schaft zu Phylandria," a secret literary *Bund* of the town's noblest youth whose members pretended to names taken from Renaissance poetry. Indeed, Goethe is never far from us when we read these letters by the young Freud. Who is not reminded of the young Werther?

Perhaps we have come to the central thread in the discernible meaning of these letters. Freud's adolescence may have been outwardly tranquil, and his thought processes certainly showed the distinction of his future genius already, but he was still a half-formed boy with the emotional needs of his kind. It is therefore not unexpected that he was powerfully stimulated by a 12-year-old girl who could have been mistaken for a boy-angel. More significantly, he was an adolescent in search of greatness; he needed ideal imago figures for the consolidation of his self-esteem.[c] At this time, he could but joke about his greatness and read the works of a Horace, who was able to state flatly that he was first in talent and mental accomplishments. Freud had the capacity to find greatness in our common cultural legacy as well as in daily life: when a sage was "indeed a wise man," like a certain visitor from

[c] See Chapter 4 for some of the most significant ideal models Freud happened to find in adolescence. For a discussion of the implications of such choices for personality development in general, see Wolf, Gedo, and Terman (1972).

Czernowitz, Freud was able to pay homage and enjoy the association (16 June, 1873). Toward those who disillusioned him, he was still merciless, and he did not spare Fluss on occasion: "Oh Emil, why are you a prosaic Jew?" (16 June, 1873). After the cataclysmic events of the twentieth century, it is difficult to place such allusions into their original context. If Freud could write with rage about a "Madame Jewess and family" (18 Sept., 1872), it was because he still needed that those who were associated with him, no matter how remotely, should live up to ideal standards. Tolerance of frailty in others, especially those about whom he cared, was not to be gained without a lengthy struggle. Even in 1914, when Freud was no longer in any doubt about his own genius, he could wither Jung and Adler with Goethe's "Cut it short! On the Day of Judgment it is no more than a fart." By the time of Rank's defection, when Freud was about 70, mellowness had come.

The unification of Germany following the wars of Bismarck had brought with it the promise of civic greatness that enlisted Freud's enthusiasm. In the period of these letters he was politically committed to the cause of Germany, then seen as the most progressive force in Central Europe (see Chapter 2). We know, however, that he permanently abandoned narrow chauvinism, whether German or Jewish, when he no longer needed contemporary idealizations to free himself from the illusions of archaic imagos. Taking a Horatian distance he prepared to become a member of the "Society without a Father" of his ecumenical models, the classical authors. We see another example of idealization and disillusionment in these letters in the allusions to Professor Brühl whose lecture had led to Freud's decision about his vocation; a year later, "My opinion of him would be very different" (6 Mar., 1874). But Freud never had to revise his opinion of Cervantes and Horace, Sophocles and Shakespeare, Goethe and Schiller; Freud, in turn, never disappoints us, not even from his period of Moravian summers.

4

FREUD'S *NOVELAS EJEMPLARES*

*in which are related the picaresque
adventures of the ingenious hidalgo
Don Cipion Freud in the city of
Seville: with further comments on the
Academia Castellana and Miguel de
Cervantes Saavedra.*

JOHN E. GEDO and ERNEST S. WOLF

[*Juvenilia*. Gedo and Wolf continue their examination of
Freud's adolescence in this chapter by investigating the possible significance of his first known created product (aside from
his letters from the same period). This product was the
formation of a two-person secret society, the "Academia
Castellana," the existence of which was reported by Jones on
the basis of Freud's single reference to it in his letters to his
fiancée, Martha Bernays. Since the publication of Jones's *Life*
of Freud, it has come to light that Freud's letters to his fellow
in this society, Eduard Silberstein, have been preserved by the
latter's heirs. Dr. Heinz Stanescu, a Lecturer in the German
language and literature at the University of Bucharest, has
published several papers describing these memorabilia (1965,
1967, 1971), and their eventual publication by the Freud
estate appears to be assured.

Gedo and Wolf tackle the problem of the Academia
Castellana without reference to these unpublished letters;

First published in *The Annual of Psychoanalysis*, 1:299-317, 1973. New York:
Quadrangle.

their point of departure is Freud's statement, quoted by Jones, to the effect that the secret society, conducted in Spanish, had taken the form of a parody of a story in their Spanish language primer. This story, which consists of a dialogue between two dogs who live in a hospital (according to Freud, a hospital in Seville), was not identified by Jones. Gedo and Wolf have traced it to the great collection of short novels by Miguel de Cervantes, the *Novelas Ejemplares*. Alerted by this clue to the possibility that Cervantes may have been another significant literary precursor of psychoanalysis, the authors returned to Freud's published letters and found that he had undertaken to learn Spanish in order to be able to reread *Don Quixote* in the original. In the early stages of his courtship of Martha Bernays, Freud had once again immersed himself in Cervantes' masterpiece, and many aspects of his relationship to his fiancée seem to have acquired the flavor of a dramatization of certain aspects of the ingenious *hidalgo's* idealization of Dulcinea.

This study undertakes to investigate the connection between the emotional meanings inherent in the works of Cervantes and the psychological issues in Freud's life which may have made the great novelist's writings so personally significant for him. In other words, the tool of applied psychoanalysis is used in the service of illuminating the history of psychoanalysis itself. It is the only chapter in this collection which does this in a major way; however, in Chapter 6, Pollock relies on an interpretation of *Faust* to clarify one aspect of the career of Josef Breuer. Perhaps this departure from strict historical methodology will not arouse the rejection of the psychoanalyst reader; for those unfamiliar with the rationale or skeptical about the justification of the procedures of the psychoanalytic biographer, Kohut's extensive discussion of these matters in Chapter 16 may serve as an introduction. We can also recommend a recent Panel Report on this subject (J. Gedo, 1972d) as well as Kohut's earlier methodological essay (1959).

It will come as no surprise to the reader that Gedo and Wolf have concluded that Cervantes (like Shakespeare, an immediate devotee of Montaigne) served as one of the principal conduits through which the humanist tradition was acquired

by Freud. The Academia Castellana leads in a direct line from
Freud to Cervantes, from Cervantes to Erasmus, from Erasmus to Plutarch, and from Plutarch to Homer—*Eds.*]

"When I was a young student, the desire to read the
immortal *Don Quixote* in the original of Cervantes led me to
learn, untaught, the lovely Castilian tongue."[1] It was in these
proud words that in 1923 Freud recalled how, more than five
decades earlier, he had, "*sin maestros,*" embarked on his first
independent intellectual exploration. The self-proclaimed
conquistador of the terrae incognitae of the mind took his
maiden voyage in the wake of Miguel de Cervantes Saavedra;
like his admired predecessor, Columbus, he reached safe
harbor at Seville. In this essay, we shall attempt to trace the
route of this journey and to make an inventory of the treasures
he brought back from this New World.

The deep personal significance that *Don Quixote* had for
Freud did not escape the attention of Ernest Jones (1953, pp.
174-175). It could hardly be a coincidence that Freud returned to this book as soon as the departure of his fiancée's
family from Vienna separated him from his beloved Martha.
Moreover, he urged his prissily reluctant bride-to-be to share
his preoccupation: "But do finish *Don Quixote*," he exhorted
her on September 8, 1883 (E. Freud, 1960, Letter 20). He had
sent her a copy while he was once more immersing himself in
the adventures of the hero of his midadolescence: "While in
the midst of the book today I nearly split my sides; I haven't
laughed so much in ages. It is so beautifully done" (E. Freud,
1960, Letter 15). His response was by no means confined to
Cervantes' humor, of course; for Martha, he specified the
serious meaning behind it in this way: "Don't you find it very
touching to read how a great person, himself an idealist,
makes fun of his ideals?. . . [once] we were all noble knights
passing through the world caught in a dream, misinterpreting
the simplest things, magnifying commonplaces into something

[1] "Siendo yo un joven estudiante, el deseo de leer el immortal D. Quijote ed el
original cervantino, me llevo a apprender, sin maestros, la bella castellana"
(Freud, 1923d: original in Spanish, translated by Strachey.)

noble and rare, and thereby cutting a sad figure" (Jones, 1953, p. 175).

"A great person!" Can we doubt that here is another instance of Freud's unusual capacity readily to identify with great men, which has been demonstrated in a number of contexts?[2] It is essential to note that the identification is two-fold: not only with the wise and benign, yes, even loving smile of the author, but also with the ridiculous but noble hero. Freud felt like a fond father contemplating his offspring and seeing himself again: "...we men always read with respect about what we once were and in part still remain" (p. 175). In fantasy, he was quite capable of discarding the adult vantage point altogether; in a letter of November, 1884 (E. Freud, 1960, Letter 54), he reveals the source of the habitual address of Martha as his "Princess": "...do you remember the condition the hero makes to all knights he has conquered? They have to walk to Toboso and kiss the hand of the incomparable Dulcinea. Now my six students are kissing your hand." Thus even the Oedipal drama takes place on the *camino real* to Seville, rather than where three roads meet on the way to Thebes! And this is how dreams became the royal road to the unconscious, the dreams of noble knights passing through the world....

The struggles of his betrothal were not the first events which had made Freud enact one of Cervantes' dramas, and we shall have more to say about the circumstances which had impelled him to do so on a previous occasion. At this point, it may suffice to recall that we possess further evidence of the importance of Cervantes for Freud. He made several references to the novelist's insights into unconscious motivations, mostly put into the mouth of Sancho Panza, the "practical philosopher" (1901). He cited Sancho's awareness of the ambivalent significance of taboos (1912-1913) as well as his Solomonic wisdom in detecting a woman's unconscious collusion with her ravisher (1901). As late as 1920, he wrote Groddeck (E. Freud, 1960, Letter 188) that *Don Quixote* is "the immortal prototype of every humorous novel"; earlier, he

[2] See Jones (1953), Lowenfeld (1956), Schönau (1968), and Chapters 3, 5, and 8.

had written a superb summary of the heart of this chef-d'oeuvre:

> The ingenious knight Don Quixote de la Mancha is . . . a figure who possesses no humour himself but who with his seriousness offers us a pleasure which could be called humorous. . . Don Quixote is originally a purely comic figure, a big child; the phantasies from his books of chivalry have gone to his head. It is well known that to begin with the author intended nothing else of him and that his creation gradually grew far beyond its creator's first intentions. But after the author had equipped this ridiculous figure with the deepest wisdom and the noblest purposes and had made him into the symbolic representative of an idealism which believes in the realization of its aims and takes duties seriously and takes promises literally, this figure ceased to have a comic effect. Just as in other cases humorous pleasure arises from the prevention of an emotion, so it does here from the interference with comic pleasure [1905b, p. 232].

Perhaps all we need to add to this critique is the judgment of Spitzer (1969) that Cervantes' narrative is an exaltation of the independent mind of man — a historical miracle in the Spain of the Counter Reformation. Little wonder that the founder of psychoanalysis felt him to have been a kindred spirit!

Spitzer also reminds us of the curious cultural phenomenon that in Europe *Don Quixote* became a book read in childhood. Freud's letter of 1923 to his Spanish translator does not reveal how early he had first encountered the ingenious *hidalgo*, but it does show that the novel had sufficiently impressed him before he was 16 to move him to teach himself Spanish so that he might reread it in the original. Although extracurricular language studies may have been routine in nineteenth-century Central Europe, self-instruction in what was minimally a seventh language for a boy in the Gymnasium must have been rather unusual, to say the least. Perhaps the motive behind this strenuous effort is even more astonishing than its performance and underscores the vital significance that Cervantes had acquired for the young Freud. He needed to absorb the untranslatable qualities of Cervantes' style and language, to take in the formal elements in their original purity. This intense interest in the aesthetics of literature was

entirely characteristic of him; we can still sense his love for the
"*bella lengua castellana*" half a century later.[3] Clearly,
Freud's immersion into Cervantes had not been a child's
excited fascination for an adventurous tale but an expression
of the sensibilities which were to lead to the Goethe Prize for
Literature 58 years later.

That more was involved than the study of literary style was
revealed in a letter of February, 1884, to Martha Bernays (E.
Freud, 1960, Letter 37) which describes the relationship to
Freud's fellow student, Eduard Silberstein:

> We became friends at a time when one doesn't look upon
> friendship as a sport or an asset, but when one needs a friend
> with whom to share things. We used to be together literally every
> hour of the day that was not spent on the school bench. We
> learned Spanish together, had our own mythology and secret
> names, which we took from some dialogues of the great Cer-
> vantes. Once in our Spanish primer we found a humorous-
> philosophical conversation between two dogs which lie peace-
> fully at the door of a hospital, and appropriated their names; in
> writing as well as in conversation he was known as Berganza, I as
> Cipion. How often have I written: *Querido Berganza!* and signed
> myself *Tu fidel Cipio, pero en el Hospital de Sevilla!* Together
> we founded a strange scholarly society, the "Academia Cas-
> tellana" (AC), compiled a great mass of humorous work which
> must still exist somewhere.

Harbinger of Wilhelm Fliess and the International Psychoanalytic Association!

Mirabile dictu, some of the records of the Academia
Castellana, Sigmund Freud's earliest creative efforts, are still
in existence; Stanescu (1965) has summarized what has been
preserved. There are 70 letters, of which 13 are partially and
22 entirely in Spanish. Most of the letters are signed "Cipion,"
a number of others "D. Cipion"; in several the signature is
accompanied by a code which stands for "dog in the hospital

---

[3] We have discussed the importance of the literary heritage for the adolescent
Freud in Chapter 2. (See also Wolf, 1971.) We have stated that Freud's letters of
1872 already showed evidence of his genius, both as a psychologist and as a writer.
It may be appropriate to add that the insistence on reading Cervantes in the
original is an even earlier manifestation of that genius—one which cannot be
precisely dated as yet, by the way. Eissler (1971b) has also stated the belief that
Freud's unique capacities stemmed from his supreme sensitivity to language.

of Seville, member of the Castilian Academy" or some variant. (See also Stanescu [1967, 1971]. In 1968, one letter was published in its entirety in the second German edition of E. Freud [1960].)

The fragments of the Freud-Silberstein correspondence thus far made public permit the conclusion that the two families were well acquainted. Whatever the externals of these relations may have been, they fade into insignificance in comparison to the psychic reality revealed by the dramatization of Cervantes' *Novelas Ejemplares* by the adolescent Freud. We gain unprecedented insights into the roots of psychoanalysis through Freud's chance encounter with the celebrated *Colloquy of the Dogs* and his twinship with Silberstein. Freud could still describe the psychic reality of this relationship in 1928, three years after Silberstein's death: "Several years during my boyhood and youth were passed in intimate friendship, yes, even in brotherly fellowship with him. Together, *sin maestro*, we learned Spanish, read Cervantes—signed our letters to each other with the names of the two *perros en el Hospital de Sevilla:* Scipione and Berganza!" (Stanescu, 1965; our translation). "Beloved Berganza! . . . ." For over a decade Cipion Freud poured out a stream of friendly advice, biting aphorism, exhortation, and miraculous insight to his brother Berganza in the manner of the Cervantes of the dramatic moralities, the *Novelas Ejemplares.*

Perhaps the most fascinating aspect of Freud's captivation by Cervantes is the significance of this Academia Castellana. The light thrown on the transformation of the genius in adolescence by the example of Freud may have broad applicability for a psychoanalytic theory of the formation of psychic structure. These aspects cannot be taken up in this context, however. Here we shall focus on the particular psychological strivings for which Freud may have found an outlet through the formation of this secret society, i.e., the manner in which *Don Quixote* and some of the *Novelas Ejemplares* expressed and satisfied some of his individual emotional needs at that time.

We assume that Freud's passionate interest in *Don Quixote* and his immediate elaboration of an intricate parody of *The*

Colloquy of the Dogs into an independent work of art provide us with an unprecedented avenue of insight into the deepest concerns of his adolescence. The secrecy surrounding these fantasy activities, the fragmentary nature of the clues from which their meaning must be reconstructed, and the unavailability of the full text of the Silberstein correspondence would discourage interpretation were it not for one circumstance: namely, that the works of Cervantes have such overt autobiographical significance. It is widely recognized that all of his literary productions are reflections of his personal experience, especially in their evocation of the land and people, in their descriptions of everyday life, and in their faithful reproduction of contemporary manners and civilization. In his immortal characters, Cervantes is generally believed to have created graphic and deeply revealing projections of aspects of his own self (see Starkie, 1964).

With such autobiographical art, especially when actual correlations with events in the author's life are possible, applied analysis may legitimately arrive at interpretations of unconscious meanings. These aspects of Cervantes can serve as mirrors reflecting the conflicts of the young Freud who was so gripped by them, and, as we have seen, identified himself with them explicitly.[4] It might be said that the Academia Castellana was the only "symptomatic product" (see Eissler, 1971a) Freud ever created, so that it may reveal more about his central conflicts than his mature works are likely to do (see Chapter 12).

We may be able to discern the meaning of the Academia Castellana for Freud through the interpretation of the hidden psychological themes in the works of Cervantes. To facilitate this exposition, we must first refresh the reader's recollection of some salient aspects of the author's biography. Cervantes was born in 1547 into an impoverished branch of a distinguished family of Castilian warriors and aristocrats. He spent a lifetime of tenacious and honorable effort to lift himself from poverty, scandal, and degradation in spite of repeated failures and disappointments. Even the literary triumphs of

---

[4] A more extensive discussion of the methodological problems of this type of applied analytic interpretation can be found in J. Gedo (1972c).

his old age did not prevent him from dying in real poverty in 1616, his hopes for the patronage of some discriminating grandee unfulfilled.

Cervantes' father was a physician without diploma "whose adult life consisted of dreary wanderings from village to village in flight from his creditors" (Starkie, 1964). Scandalous stories involving his beautiful aunt were the forerunners of similarly disreputable alliances by his sister and ultimately his daughter, women "who made their living out of rich men" (Brenan, 1969). At the age of 16, Miguel, along with his younger brother, became a pupil at the Jesuit school in Seville; there is a touching testimonial to the "loving care and industry [of these] pious fathers" in *The Colloquy of the Dogs*. He first published some verses at the age of 21 but soon after went into exile to escape the consequences of a forbidden duel. After brief service in the household of a Cardinal in Italy, Cervantes enlisted as a private soldier for the great campaign of 1570 against the Turks. He fought with conspicuous heroism at the pivotal battle of Lepanto where he sustained multiple wounds which deprived him of the use of one arm. After his recovery, he participated in the capture of Tunis. In 1575, a galley on which he and his brother were returning to Spain was captured by the Turks, and he was held as a slave in Algiers for five years. He became the leader of the prisoners there; some of them came to regard him as "their mother and their father." He organized several attempts to escape of such tenacity and courage that the Viceroy made him his personal property for better surveillance. These distinctions made it much more costly to ransom him, so that his freedom was not secured until several years after that of his brother. The frantic efforts to raise money to free two sons completed the ruin of the Cervantes family. After his liberation, Miguel therefore had no choice but to continue in military service, although his disability made promotion hopeless. He served in the campaigns to secure the Portuguese crown for Philip II, but he also resumed his literary efforts. At the age of 36 he left the army, and in 1585 he was married and published his *Galatea*, a pastoral romance.

Unable to earn a living as a littérateur, Cervantes obtained

a government job, that of a tax collector in Andalusia. His
mediocre writings for the theater had been unable to compete
with the genius of Lope de Vega. His success as an itinerant
bureaucrat was no greater. He became liable for a large sum
of money embezzled by one of his subordinates, and this debt
hung over him for the rest of his life. He was briefly in prison
and lost his position, but around the turn of the century, in
Seville, he began the first of his *Novelas Ejemplares*, the
supreme example of the picaresque tale, *Rinconete y Cortadillo*. The first part of *Don Quixote* followed in 1605 and took
Europe by storm, but this did not bring financial relief, and
Cervantes had to support himself through menial work. The
full set of *Exemplary Novels* was published in 1613 and the
second part of *Don Quixote* only a few months before the
author's death in 1616. In the theater pieces of his seventh
decade, Cervantes showed that he could learn from the
example of his great rival, Lope, and he was thus able to
crown his *oeuvre* with some signal contributions to the Spanish
drama of the *siglo de oro*.

In order to place our discussion of the works of Cervantes
into the context of their significance for Freud, it may be most
cogent to point out that the very idea of a mock-serious
Academia is taken from them. The profusion of pretentious
successors to Plato's Academy during the Renaissance was one
of the favorite targets of Cervantes' satire; it may be recalled
that even Quixote's Manchegan hamlet had its Academia of
Argamasilla. As Freud had taken the characters of Cipion and
Berganza from Cervantes' *Colloquy*, it seems reasonable to
assume that the Academia Castellana was similarly inspired by
the Academy of Imitators mentioned in the *Novela*; the latter
actually existed in Madrid for the purpose of emulating the
writers of the Italian Renaissance, imitation being the sincer-
est expression of admiration. The fatuity of such enterprises is
brought into high relief in another of Cervantes' *Novelas*
through the contrasting example of the "infamous academy"
of Monipodio, a confraternity and "school," which prepared
those who were willing to learn for the actualities of life in the
city of Seville. This matter is of more than passing interest in
the light of Ellenberger's recent suggestion (1970) that the

unusual structure of organized psychoanalysis constitutes a covert revival of that of the philosophical schools of antiquity. It would seem that we have all become members of the Academia Castellana!

The Colloquy of the Dogs is in its entirety a gentle parody and an extension of Erasmus's *Familiarium Colloquiorum Opus,* "a rich and motley collection of dialogues, each a masterpiece of literary form, well-knit, spontaneous, convincing, unsurpassed in lightness, vivacity and fluent Latin; each one a finished one-act play" (Huizinga, 1924, p. 156). Although the great humanist's excursion into satire was reproduced in a stream of editions and translations that flowed almost uninterruptedly for two centuries after the first edition of 1519, Cervantes' return to this precedent was in itself an act of courage, as in Spain "Erasmista" was a term of opprobrium for departures from Catholic dogmatism. The *Colloquia* of Erasmus, in spite of their tone of jesting and mockery, constitute "a profoundly serious moral treatise" which puts forward a "passionately desired, purified Christian society of good morals, fervent faith, simplicity and moderation, kindliness, toleration and peace" (Huizinga, 1924, p. 157). The literary tradition Freud had chosen to follow in his adolescence thus has impeccable humanist antecedents. In a letter of 1511 to Thomas More, Erasmus had defended the "sportiveness" of his theme by referring to the fact "that the same was practiced by great writers in former times"; specifically, he mentioned Plutarch's dialogue of Gryllus and Ulysses[5] as one of his sources (Erasmus, 1487-1535).

Cervantes' *Colloquy* takes the form of a dialogue between Cipion and Berganza who have suddenly and miraculously acquired not only the gift of speech but also that of reason, "whereas the difference between brutes and men lies in the fact that man is a rational animal and the brute an irrational one." Subsequently we learn that we may actually be in the presence of twin brothers changed into beasts through witchcraft — but more of that later. At any rate, there is plentiful

---

[5] This was an extrapolation of the Circe episode of *The Odyssey.* Gryllus was one of the men the sorceress had transformed into a pig. In Plutarch's dialogue, Gryllus expresses his preference for the porcine over the human condition.

internal evidence that the life story of Berganza, which takes up most of the dialogue, recapitulates that of the author. On the other hand, it is plain that Cipion, the Spanish form of Scipio,[6] also represents Miguel de Cervantes. He is clearly asserting his identification with the great Roman commander, Scipio Africanus the Elder, conqueror of Carthage.[7] It is a subtle reproach to the fatherland by the forgotten hero of Lepanto and assailant of *Carthago rediviva*, Ottoman North Africa. It must be recalled that 12 years after his crushing victory over Hannibal[8] at Zama, Scipio and his brother were brought to trial before the Roman Senate for alleged misappropriation of funds. How Cervantes must have longed to be able to respond to *his* accusers about the stolen tax receipts of Andalusia as Scipio had done in the same situation 18 centuries before him: as his brother was about to produce the accounts which would clear them, Scipio wrested them from his hands and in a magnificent—nay, *quixotic*—gesture, he tore them to pieces and scattered them on the floor of the Senate. Yet Scipio was no impractical dreamer; Cervantes recalled with admiration his aplomb when he stumbled and fell upon landing in Africa—to turn this omen to advantage, he promptly grasped the soil with both hands, exclaiming that he would not permit Africa to escape him![9]

The story of Cipion, that of the life Cervantes would have wished to lead, is never told in the *Colloquy*. He had had to settle for the life of the sycophant Berganza; the last episode of

[6] See Freud's slip from Spanish into Italian—"Scipione"—in his letter of 1928 (p. 93 above) which demonstrates his knowledge of this derivation. Moreover, one of his letters to Silberstein is signed "Cipion, *non imperador romano*," indicating that the connection to Scipio was of personal significance to him.

[7] One of the indications that this was a conscious and deliberate choice occurs in Quixote's paean to Dulcinea, whose merits are asserted in the face of her handicap of not being descended from illustrious ancestors like the Scipios. It should also be noted that both Scipio Africanus and his father before him had conquered Spain during the Punic Wars. Scipio, moreover, was founder of Italica, the Roman predecessor of the city of Seville.

[8] Freud's choice of the secret pseudonym Cipion for himself betrays that his openly declared identification with Hannibal (see Chapter 2) was ambivalent at best and more probably stood as a thin screen hiding his partisanship for Rome. This may account for his curious slip about Hannibal's Italian campaign, discussed in Chapter 12.

[9] See Don Quixote, Part II, Chapter 58. Reference to this book will henceforth be made in the following manner: (II/58).

the *Novela* concerns four artists in the hospital who have been unable to find an "intelligent, generous, and magnanimous" patron. The dogs comment wryly, "most persons of this sort come to die in hospitals." The very name "Berganza" may be a reference to sycophancy; it is probably a corruption of Braganza, title of the Portuguese duke who had a claim to the vacant throne equal to that of Philip II, but allowed himself to be bought off with extravagant bribes. Compare this to the rewards for Cervantes' extraordinary efforts in Philip's service, for his intrepid insistence on fighting in the forefront at Lepanto in spite of a debilitating fever. Listen to Cervantes' self-disgust about what he had been driven to do by necessity:

> It is of [humility] I avail myself when I would enter any household, having first taken a good look to make sure that it is the kind of a house that can afford to keep and maintain a large dog. I then station myself at the door, and when I see some stranger coming in, I bark at him, but when the master comes I lower my head and run up to him, wagging my tail and licking his boots. If they beat me, I put up with it and, with the same meekness as before, fawn upon the one who has given me the blows.

We may infer that Cipion and Berganza represent complementary halves of an internal dialogue in the mind of Cervantes. Although on the surface the adventures of Berganza form just another picaresque tale, albeit the most refined example of that peculiar Hispanic genre (see Putnam, 1952), the responses of Cipion add a deeper layer to the *Novela* which transforms it into something unique and without precedent, the record of a journey of introspection: "For it will be better to spend the time this way than in seeking to learn about the lives of others."[a] It would seem that the youthful Freud read his Spanish primer with full understanding and retained its precepts permanently.[10]

[a] Compare this to Montaigne's statements (Chapter 1) about mankind's general resistance to introspection and propensity to project undesirable attributes onto others.

[10] An interlocutor in the *Colloquia* of Erasmus had already put forward the ideal of refraining from irreversible actions until one acquires self-knowledge (see Huizinga, 1924). The analytic principle of abstinence had thus been prefigured in the 1510's.

Berganza's earliest memories concern the slaughter house of Seville where he served the "bullies and ruffians...without soul or conscience" who lived by killing, stealing the meat, and quarreling over the spoils. Their concubines shared this life of greed and low cunning. At that time, the dog's name had been Gavilan, meaning a member of a gang of rogues, and he recalls himself as having had a "dirty butcher's mouth." Fearing his master's disfavor, he escaped to the countryside, where he found similar conditions among the shepherds. He comments bitterly on the differences between these realities and the picture of pastoral life in romances such as Cervantes' *Galatea*. Cipion concurs with anguish: "...it is impossible for people in this world to get along together unless there is mutual trust and confidence"; yet in actuality "the defenders are the offenders... The watchman robs, and the guardians kill." So much for childhood.

In the next episode, Berganza becomes a student at the Jesuit school of Seville as an attendant of the pampered sons of the mercantile bourgeoisie. This fleeting exposure to people of good will and honor is soon terminated by "a calamitous fate," as he is reduced to a menial job and put at the mercy of the household slaves. His indignation at human depravity boils over when he is required to act as silent witness to their amours, and he ragefully attacks the black wench who is in control of his food supply. Once more he runs away, but his next master is a corrupt policeman in league with a gang of racketeers, and this adventure also ends with his turning on the unworthy person upon whom he is dependent. He then joins a company of soldiers on their way to foreign wars and receives training in the performance of tricks which permit him to earn his living on the stage. As the story proceeds, he becomes more and more self-assured and competent to deal with the world as it is; the incidents of his adventures parallel the life of Cervantes, with a period of relatively tranquil residence among the Moors and eventual entry into artistic circles. He finally joins Cipion in the service of someone connected with the hospital at Valladolid where the colloquy is actually taking place.

The turning point of Berganza's life, the encounter that

changes him from a childlike innocent, ever hoping for impossible ideal conditions and filled with narcissistic rage (see Kohut, 1971) about the actualities of society, into what Freud was to call a "practical philosopher," is the discovery of his own origins and the acknowledgment of his true nature. An elderly sorceress recognizes him as the enchanted son of a fellow witch, i.e., a human being. This is why "wrongdoing and the speaking of evil are something we inherit from our forebears and drink in with our mother's milk." Dogs are not afflicted with these characteristics. When Berganza recounts learning about the mysterious delivery of a pair of puppy dogs by a witch, we are suddenly shown that Cipion is his twin by the latter's excited abandonment of the posture of the detached philosopher in order to speculate on "the remedy for our plight." Cipion quickly concludes that the story must be a hoax; the witch "was at once foolish, cunning, and malicious — if I may be pardoned for speaking that way of our mother, or rather of your mother, for I will not have her for mine."

At any rate, the sorceress gave Berganza the precepts by which he was to live: "Always be as good as you can, but if you have to be bad, do your best not to appear so." In view of the fact that the old sorceress ended her days as a hospital matron, we are left with an uncanny doubt about the purport of the dogs' residence at the hospital. Throughout the dialogue, Cipion and Berganza are concerned about their tendency to be malicious but never succeed in curbing their backbiting, even when they decide to punish it by biting their own tongues. When Berganza commits the next offense, he reneges on this pledge with "today a law is made and tomorrow it is broken, and perhaps that is the way it should be... Leave tongue-biting to the devil; I don't intend to bite mine... What I want to do now [is] to refrain from biting my tongue.[11]

The Colloquy of the Dogs thus deals with the problem of evil: man's innate aggressiveness, his identifications with parental malice and corruption, and his narcissistic rage

[11] Cervantes is gently reproaching Erasmus through this device for having allowed himself to ridicule his intellectual opponents in the *Colloquia* (see Huizinga, 1924, pp. 157-158).

about the manifold disillusionments of life, especially those
provoked by the deficiencies of caretaking persons. This
existential dilemma can only be transcended by a few be-
witched individuals who will be regarded as children of the
devil by society at large—they are the creative personalities.
The fate of those untouched by this magic wand of fortune is
shown in the *Novela* closest in theme to the *Colloquy, Rinconete y Cortadillo.*[12]

These ordinary adolescents have escaped from backgrounds
of poverty and shoddiness to make their way in the world by
petty thievery and fraud. They are typical "picaroons"—lov-
able rogues who provide for their own needs with the innocent
rapacity of animals. When they attempt to get by through
these means in the Andalusian metropolis, they are promptly
sucked into the center of a sophisticated mafia which regulates
their activities, confiscates their spoils, and grants them a
meager wage. Everyone is corrupt, cowardly, cruel, and
faithless. Rinconete and Cortadillo are incorporated by this
Leviathan in spite of their desperate awareness of the fact that
it will consume them in a short time. Such, then, is Man's
Fate: the fate that awaited Miguel and Rodrigo de Cervantes
in Seville, Sigmund Freud and Eduard Silberstein in Vienna—
unless they could utilize some inner resource to create a novel
solution for themselves.

The solution of Cervantes is presented in *Don Quixote*. The
first part of this greatest of cautionary tales satirizes not only
childish literary genres; on a deeper level, it is an ironic
signpost to the desires of childhood "to reform the world by
force of arms" (Brenan, 1969), a memento to a discarded part

[12] We have thus far been unable to ascertain whether Freud was familiar with
any of the *Novelas* beyond the *Colloquy*. However, a man who presents his fiancée
with the works of Calderón (see Jones, 1953) is not likely to have missed these "set-
tings for the jewel of truth" (Bell, 1947). Moreover, the Academia Castellana de-
parts from the *Colloquy* in one major detail: in Freud's version, the hospital in
which the dogs live is relocated from Valladolid to Seville. We cannot exclude the
possibility that this may have been an unmotivated error based on truncation of the
story in Freud's primer (the early episodes of Berganza's adventures take place in
Seville and therefore it may be natural to assume that he also ends up there); we
prefer to believe that it represents a condensation of the biography of Berganza
with those of Cortadillo and Rinconete who make their way to Seville on the
camino real through La Mancha and enroll in the Academy of Monipodio.

of the youthful Cervantes, i.e., to his grandiose self. As Bell
(1947) has concluded, "the main theme of *Don Quixote* was
clearly the presumption of Don Quixote, the presumption of
Sancho, the presumption of Cervantes, of Spain, of modern
man." Freud, with his penetrating psychological vision, saw it
(1905b) as a comedy at the expense of childish reactions to the
actualities of life. We can best illustrate this point by comparing Don Quixote's reaction to the primal scene with that of
Berganza. In contrast to the dog's rageful response when he
had been made to witness the blatant sexual peccadilloes of his
masters, Quixote (I/46) reacts with total refusal to perceive
reality. When Sancho reports that he has seen the supposed
Queen Micomicona "rubbing noses with one that is here every
instant and behind every door," his master indignantly accuses
him of slander. The girl has to rescue Sancho from Quixote's
narcissistic wrath by suggesting that the "good squire" may not
have borne false witness: he had really seen what he had
reported, but this vision had been brought about by "diaboli-
cal enchanters." Every threat to the perfection of the infantile
self or to that of the idealized parental image is warded off
through similar magical thinking. In this regard, the very
name of the beloved Dulcinea is "rare and significant" (I/1);
this magical private meaning is betrayed by its etymology—in
old French, "doulcinée" signified a precious and ridiculously
unnatural girl, *une précieuse ridicule*, but for Quixote she is
precious in all earnestness.

The personal development of the mature Cervantes may be
inferred from his treatment of the theme of his daughter's
promiscuity in one of his late plays and in one of the
Exemplary Novels, The Jealous Estramaduran. In this work, a
rich man of 70 marries a naïve 15-year-old whom he keeps in
complete seclusion lest she be seduced by someone who can
offer her a sexual life. An adventure in the spirit of the
Decameron culminates with the old man observing the girl in
bed with a young rake. He states his reaction in these words:

> My vengeance shall fall upon myself, as the person most
> culpable of all, for I ought to have considered how ill this girl's
> fifteen years could assort with my threescore and ten. . . . I do not

reproach you, misguided girl...but that all the world may see how strong and how true was the love I bore you, I shall give proof on my death-bed. . . . [In my will I shall recommend that] she marry that young man. Thus she will see that...I wish her to be happy when I am no more, and to be united to him whom she must love. . . .

Cervantes then shows the consequences of this renunciation: instead of pursuing a life of sexual freedom, the girl became a nun "in one of the most austere and rigid convents in all Seville." The internalization of morality is shown to depend on the transformation of parental narcissism into empathy (see Kohut, 1966).

In the second part of *Don Quixote*, Cervantes summed up the experiences of a heroic life. The Knight of the Rueful Countenance ultimately learned to tolerate actuality and thus came home at the end "victorious over himself, which is the highest kind of victory" (II/72). We know that he now stood for the author in the most explicit way, for he speaks in his own voice on the last page: "For me alone was Don Quixote born, and I for him; it was his to act, mine to write; we together make but one." As Bell (1947) has pointed out, in his *Journey to Parnassus* Cervantes addresses himself in words almost identical with those he puts into the mouth of Quixote: "Everyone builds his own fortune and I have built mine, but not with the necessary prudence, so that my presumption has come to nought." Quixote only regrets that the destruction of his illusions has come about so late that it leaves him no time to devote his life to some better purpose (II/74).

Cervantes was fully aware of his own genius, however, as repeated references within his writings indicate, and he certainly did not look upon ambition as undesirable or a pathological trait: "...men of low rank...raise themselves by their ambition or by their virtues...only those are seen to be great and illustrious that show themselves so by their virtue, wealth, and generosity.... There are two roads...by which men may reach wealth and honours; one is that of letters, the other that of arms" (II/6). He amplifies this list beyond the spheres of his own capacities through the mouth of Sancho Panza (II/8) who is able to prove that no secular accomplishment can match saintliness in the degree of the ambition motivating it.[13]

Victory over oneself therefore did not mean the abandonment of ambitions or the surrender of high ideals; Freud was correct in discerning that Cervantes had remained an idealist. It was his capacity to see his own ideals through a screen of wisdom and humor, i.e., his triumph over his archaic narcissism, that constituted his victory and his greatness. Quixote ceases being a ridiculous, childish figure when (II/17) he makes a distinction between human behavior viewed from the vantage point of an external observer and its meaning within the intrapsychic world:

> No doubt...you set me down in your mind as a fool and a mad man, and it would be no wonder if you did, for my deeds do not argue anything else, but for all that, I would have you take notice that I am neither so mad nor so foolish as I must have seemed to you... All knights have their own special parts to play; let the courtier devote himself to the ladies, let him add lustre to his sovereign's court...but let the knight-errant explore the corners of the earth and penetrate the most intricate labyrinths, at each step let him attempt impossibilities...for to seek these, to attack those, and to vanquish all, are in truth his main duties. I, then, as it has fallen to my lot to be a member of knight-errantry, cannot avoid attempting all that seems to me to come within the sphere of my duties.

In this key passage, Cervantes conveys his knowledge of the road to victory over oneself: the choice of an activity suited to one's talents and endowed with the perfection formerly re-

---

[13] The successful attainment of seemingly unrealistic ambitions recurs as a theme in a number of Cervantes' works (e.g., the *Novelas The Little Gypsy* and *The Illustrious Kitchen Maid* as well as the play *Pedro, the Artful Dodger*). In each case, it is expressed through the revelation that the family-romance fantasies of a beautiful young girl have been based on reality after all. Cervantes' assessment is most clearly stated in the play. The voice of "rationality" is "all amazed at the imperious claim this humble girl is making, for though she is of low state her claims are all ambitious, and I marvel to see with what mad gusto she aspires to soar aloft and even touch the sky." However, the voice of wisdom, that of Pedro, the author's alter ego, replies, "She is right and you should not ridicule her. It pleases me to see with what fierce pride she brings her tools and drills her upward way. I, too, who am dull-witted, have my fancies, and dream of being Emperor and King; why there are times when I rave and believe that I am master of the entire world." (See Kohut, 1971.)

served for the self and its pursuit without reservations or regard for external criticism. In achieving literary success close to the age of 60 with the first part of *Don Quixote*, Cervantes had proved that the quixotic pursuit of seeming impossibilities may sometimes bear fruit: for him alone was Don Quixote born—it was Quixote's to act, Cervantes' to write.

The second part of the novel therefore celebrates the triumph of intrepid perseverance in imposing an artist's vision on the public, as well as the internal victory over his own archaic grandiosity. Everywhere Don Quixote and Sancho are now received as famous and worthy personages; everyone they encounter is delighted to accept their eccentric vision of reality, i.e., the *aesthetic* illusion, as an improvement over the naturalistic viewpoint of ordinary people. The spokesman for this cultivated audience is the gentleman of Barcelona who reproves those attempting to interrupt Quixote's activities (II/65): "O señor. . .may God forgive you the wrong you have done the whole world in trying to bring the most amusing madman in it back to his senses. Do you not see, señor, that the gain by Don Quixote's sanity can never equal the enjoyment his crazes give?. . . May Don Quixote never be cured, for by his recovery we lose not only his own drolleries, but his squire Sancho Panza's too, any one of which is enough to turn melancholy itself into merriment."[14]

The sustaining ideal of a vision of perfection is essential to the artist to give him strength to withstand the lengthy mortification of being undervalued as a person before he has imposed himself on the audience as a hero. As Quixote puts it (II/32), "To deprive a knight-errant of his lady is to deprive him of the eyes he sees with, of the sun that gives him light, of the food whereby he lives. . . A knight-errant without a lady is

---

[14] This theme was more fully developed in *The Man of Glass,* another of the *Novelas Ejemplares,* which deals with the vulnerability of the artist who has not as yet created what his genius promises to make possible. The belief that the self contains within it treasures that should be exhibited to the public, as in a glass case or *vitriera,* is concretized as a delusion. Cervantes implies that his decision to seek more immediate glory on the battlefield had been necessitated by his incapacity to tolerate the tension between the estimate of his own worth and the response of the public which—perceptively—failed to appreciate his juvenilia.

like a tree without leaves, a building without foundation, or a shadow without the body that causes it." There can be no question that Cervantes is referring to a part of his own mental structure. Furnished with such internal structure, he could even withstand the unbearable verdict pronounced on one of his characters by the latter's wife: *"Come me ve pobre no me estima"*—"She despises me because I am poor." And where do these sustaining ideals originate? Once more, let us listen to the wisdom of Quixote: "God knows whether there be any Dulcinea or not in the world, or whether she is imaginary or not imaginary; these are things the proof of which must not be pushed to extreme lengths. I have not begotten nor given birth to my lady though I behold her as she needs must be, a lady who holds within her all the qualities to make her famous throughout the world" (II/32). Sustaining ideals are thus self-created, albeit never by parthenogenesis.

Perhaps we have said enough about Miguel de Cervantes to provide some tentative answers to our problem, that of the meaning of the Academia Castellana for Freud; in any case, we must curb our own presumption before we embark on enterprises beyond our means. It may be fitting to close our survey of the universe of Cervantes by echoing the lines he wrote about himself in a prefatory sonnet to the *Novelas Ejemplares*:

Bien, Cervantes insigne, conociste
La humana inclinación.[15]

Sigmund Freud spent the summer of 1872 in Příbor; some of the earliest surviving records of the Academia Castellana were dispatched to Berganza from there. This was the summer of the disappointing affair with Gisela Fluss described a quarter century later in "Screen Memories" (1899, p. 313): "It was my first calf-love and sufficiently intense, but I kept it completely secret. After a few days the girl went off to her school. . . and it was this separation after such a short acquaintance that brought my longings to a really high pitch. I passed many hours in solitary walks through the lovely woods . . . and spent my time building castles in the air." In the light

---

[15] "Noted Cervantes, you knew Man's inclinations well" (our translation).

of Freud's intense preoccupation with *Don Quixote* earlier in his adolescence, one is forcibly reminded of that chapter of the great novel (I/26) "in which are continued the refinements wherewith Don Quixote played the part of a lover in the Sierra Morena." It may be inferred that Martha Bernays was not the first girl whom Freud had cast in the role of Dulcinea. Jones (1953) may therefore have reached a false conclusion in asserting that Freud had failed to speak to Gisela out of shyness: a knight-errant does not wish to converse with his lady; he needs her to embody his ideals. Freud's contemporary claim in a letter to her brother, Emil Fluss (see Freud, 1872-1874), that "there was more irony, yes, mockery, than seriousness in this whole flirtation" cannot be dismissed as mere sour grapes or concealment (see Chapter 3).

Let us recollect Freud's own interpretation of the screen memory from Příbor (1899): the core of the conflict which gave rise to it concerned the temptation "to give up your unpractical ideals and take on a 'bread-and-butter' occupation" (p. 315). Implicit in this conflict is the tension between the platonic and a coarsely sensual love for women. In some manner not known to us, Gisela Fluss did not meet Freud's ideal standards; perhaps this disillusionment is echoed in Sigmund's depreciating reproach to her brother, "Oh Emil, why are you a prosaic Jew?" On the occasion of Gisela's marriage in 1875, Cipion sent Berganza a scathing parody of Latin poetry celebrating nuptials in a corrupt Homeric style in which the bride is mocked for her "dull spirit," her "small brain," and her striving for *petit bourgeois* goals (see Stanescu, 1967). At any rate, by the time he returned to Vienna in the late summer of 1872, Freud invariably referred to Gisela Fluss as "Ichthyosaura" (i.e., an extinct fish-lizard): the knight-errant had lost his lady through the machinations of wicked enchanters.

Although we have disagreed with Jones's conclusion that the outcome of this affair led to the repression of Freud's erotic impulses (see Chapter 3),[b] we must concur with his view that

---

[b] See also the excerpt from the Silberstein letters in Stanescu (1971). The passage he quotes is charged with a lively eroticism. It was written more than a year after the Fluss affair and is sufficient by itself to refute Jones's interpretation.

it prepared the way for a decade of strict celibacy filled with scholarly pursuits. It was not until April, 1882, that Freud found his Dulcinea in Martha Bernays; after meeting her while she was visiting his sisters, he observed her from a distance for several weeks before approaching her with the verdict that she was like "the fairy princess from whose lips fell roses and pearls" (Jones, 1953). We assume, therefore, that the traumatic disillusionment with Gisela Fluss had reawakened Freud's extraordinary sensitivity to the imperfections of his archaic objects. As Kohut has shown (1968, 1971), before the secure internalization of a workable set of guiding ideals, such failures on the part of idealized objects generally lead to regressions to relatively more primitive states of the grandiose self—the mental states satirized in the first part of *Don Quixote*.

It is not possible to specify at this time the historical factors in Freud's early life which may have predisposed him to this narcissistic vulnerability in adolescence. Jones (1953) has noted that his father's business reverses caused the boy to be "disillusioned in a specially painful manner." He implies that Jakob Freud temporarily lost his son's esteem when Sigmund was 12 upon telling the latter about his humble submissiveness in the face of a crude anti-Semitic attack.[16] The severity of the problem was even more impressive in relation to women, if we may judge from Freud's readiness to form intense friendships with men in contrast with his hesitancy with girls. In his letters to Fliess (Freud, 1887-1902) Freud stressed the life-saving significance of the availability of a nanny after the birth and death of his brother Julius during his infancy. He recovered memories in his self-analysis about this woman encouraging him to steal from his parents in her behalf and about her being dismissed from the Freuds' employ for her

---

[16] Jakob Freud was apparently in agreement with Berganza about the proper method for getting along in a hostile environment. Jones contends that Freud's admiration for Hannibal stemmed from the Semitic general's refusal to submit to the Romans. It should be recalled, however, that Scipio Africanus defeated Hannibal in the end, thus avenging his own father's disastrous humiliation by the Carthaginian at the battles of the Ticinus and the Trebia. It is all very well to admire good losers, but adolescents need to identify with the bigger battalions!

thefts (see Letter 70). We need not belabor the disillusionment caused by the disappearance of such a figure; what perhaps deserves more emphasis is that the attachment to a surrogate mother at such an early age also betokens some disturbance in the primary mother-child relationship.[c]

Whatever the genetic precursors may have been, it would seem that Sigmund Freud entered adolescence still searching for idealized parental imagos and that he found what he needed in the writings of Cervantes. Identification with the great novelist's humor and wisdom concerning his own grandiosity as well as the unworkable idealizations of his characters apparently permitted Freud to avoid the consequences of acting out in a quixotic manner — the episode with Gisela Fluss having been the single known exception. He followed the example of the *Colloquy* in borrowing strength from twinship with someone who was presumably struggling with the same problems.[17] Most important of all, in Cervantes himself he found a great man who had successfully overcome the consequences of a background of poverty and degradation, paternal weakness and female corruption. The solution lay in the internalization of an austere morality adhered to through self-knowledge and self-control. Berganza ceased being a picaroon after learning about his real nature from the sorceress.

Freud was to make "learning about his real nature" into his life's work; the Academia Castellana thus prefigured in its core the whole psychoanalytic enterprise. The role of Cipion,

[c] Schur's recent biography (1972) has brought to light previously unknown facts about the actual circumstances of the Freud family during the early years of Sigmund's life. He has stressed the exposure to the primal scene, to childbirth, and to death in the overcrowded and underprivileged household. He also implies that the family may have been living with an unmentionable secret, that of the fate of Jakob Freud's second wife, whose very existence has been overlooked until very recently.

[17] Another permanent acquisition from the *Colloquy* became a regular feature of Freud's writing style: this was the employment of a fictive dialogue to express varying perspectives about some matter. We have described in Chapter 3 how, at about this same time, Freud was incorporating certain stylistic attributes of the Latin poet Horace. Doubtless he made similar identifications with selected aspects of other great men; Goethe and Shakespeare (whom he started to read at the age of eight and probably soon confronted in English) may have been as crucial to him at other times as was Cervantes in adolescence.

that of listening to a life's story and making occasional comments to facilitate the flow of the material, has left its stamp on the professional activity of the psychoanalyst. Even more crucial in its impact was the explicit purpose of the *Novelas Ejemplares*: that of the moral improvement of man. If the Academia Castellana was but an unpublishable, juvenile "exemplary novel," the *Psychological Works* of Sigmund Freud constitute the greatest accomplishment in the genre in the history of the modern era (see J. Gedo, 1972a) and Rieff has justly designated Freud as the saving moralist of our civilization (1959).

When Freud visited the Athenian Acropolis in 1904, he experienced an episode of derealization which later (1936) he interpreted as the result of his disavowal of the feelings of triumph and superiority he then developed in relation to his father. Jakob Freud had declared, when the seven-year-old Sigmund had invaded the parental bedroom to urinate, that his son "would never amount to anything" (Jones, 1953). Cervantes would have known better: the small boy who boldly reverses the situation of the primal scene, a Scipio avenging the ravages of Hannibal in Italy, would have pleased him for the "mad gusto...to soar aloft and even touch the sky."

And that is why the *camino real* from Příbor to the Acropolis of Athens traverses La Mancha on its way to Seville....

PART II

PRECURSORS

5

SOME ASPECTS OF CHARCOT'S INFLUENCE ON FREUD

JULIAN A. MILLER, MELVIN SABSHIN,

JOHN E. GEDO, GEORGE H. POLLOCK,

LEO SADOW, and

NATHAN SCHLESSINGER

[*Toward a Medical Psychology.* This paper from the Workshop on the Scientific Methodology of Psychoanalysis of the Chicago Institute was actually the last of the series prepared by that group. Their earlier efforts constitute Chapters 7, 8, and 11 of this collection. The Workshop had decided to study the influence of Charcot upon Freud after having investigated the latter's scientific activities of the decade of the 1890's. They had been impressed by Freud's self-appointed role as the Vienna representative of the French school of neuropsychiatry in that period. Clearly, the months Freud had spent in Paris in the winter of 1885-1886 had established him as exceptional in Viennese medical circles. Freud did not gain his first exposure to psychiatric patients at the Salpêtrière, however; as Jones has reported, he had already served for five months on Meynert's psychiatric service at the *Allgemeine Krankenhaus* in 1883. The nature of this psychiatric preparation has recently been described in greater detail by Wolf (1973a).

If it had been a change in the focus of Freud's clinical

First published in *Journal of the American Psychoanalytic Association,* 17:608-623, 1969.

interests that had decided him to study with Charcot, i.e., if the turn from neuropathology to psychiatry had actually preceded the Paris journey, we have to seek a better explanation of what he had actually found there that had such a marked impact on him. In this paper, the authors suggest that he found a man worthy of being called his Master. They quote his description of Charcot's lectures as comparable to the cathedral of Notre Dame in their perfection and his testimony about the fact that his new teacher made a greater impression on him than anyone had made before. We can only conclude that Charcot's charisma, a dramatic quality Freud described as similar to an evening at the theater, provided the young physician with a relationship of a kind that even his most revered Viennese preceptors, Ernst Brücke and Josef Breuer, could not supply.

For the first time, Freud had come into contact with a man whom he could look upon as great. As Gedo and Wolf have tried to show in the preceding two chapters, Freud had already used idealized figures from history with whom he shared literary interests as models for selective identifications that he was able to maintain for the rest of his life. In Charcot, he found a living model whom he could follow into the endeavor of bringing man's psychological vicissitudes into the realm of scientific investigation. In this way, Freud's decade of scientific preparation could be wedded to his natural humanist bent in the service of establishing an entirely novel area of intellectual life, that of a *scientific* introspective psychology.

To be sure, another decade was to elapse before Freud actually turned toward introspective effort as his major research activity. In this regard, Charcot did not provide a useful example, having been singularly deficient in self-critical capacity. The Master was primarily an acute observer of others and an ingenious experimentalist. His antitheoretical bias may have served as a useful antidote to some of the more dogmatic aspects of Freud's education in the school of Helmholtz. In a more general sense, his credentials as a man of the world, open to the worth of a variety of men and cultures, helped Freud to shed his German provincialism forever. Of course, in this regard, one cannot discount entirely the general impact of the Paris of 1885 as the cultural capital of the world.

However, Freud's published letters and the Jones biography suggest that the young visitor from Vienna availed himself very little of the resources of contemporary Paris. He attended the theaters with some frequency, but his strong preference for the cultural interests that were to preoccupy him in later life was already in evidence. He seems hardly to have responded to being at the center of French civilization, with the possible exception of his strong aesthetic appreciation of the architecture of Notre Dame cathedral. Characteristically, he sought out the antiquities in the museums: he did not see the Leonardos in the Louvre until after having written his essay on the painter in 1909! His favorite was the Musée de Cluny, clearly because the building had originally been a Roman bath; at least, medieval artifacts (which the museum houses) seem never to have appealed to Freud. All in all, he treated Paris rather as if it had been an archeological site!

Freud was able to maintain his internalization of the activities and qualities he had admired in Charcot in spite of the fact that his idealization of the Master could not be sustained indefinitely without qualifications. The authors review the lengthy process of Freud's increasing independence of outlook with regard to many of Charcot's views and procedures. Perhaps it was the fact that the disillusionment was a very gradual one that permitted Freud to retain so much of value that Charcot had transmitted to him. At the same time, Freud was able to discard what he no longer found useful or admirable without losing his respect for Charcot. He remained forever grateful to the man whose autographed picture still hangs over Freud's analytic couch at Hampstead—Eds.]

In Chapters 7, 8, and 11, members of the Workshop on Scientific Methodology will consider the origins and modifications of some early concepts in psychoanalysis. We shall pursue our interest in the influences impinging on Freud during the early days of discovery and concept formation. In this context, Freud's trip to Paris to study with Charcot seems pivotal in his shift from neurological and physiological to psychopathological work. Although Jones (1953) traced the principles upon which Freud constructed his theories back to the influence of Brücke, he also says: "It was assuredly the experience with Charcot in Paris that aroused Freud's interest in hysteria, then in psychopathology in general, and so paved the way for resuscitating Breuer's observation and developing psychoanalysis" (p. 75).

We have examined Charcot's writings (1877-1889) as well as those of others who have commented upon his work (Ellenberger, 1965; Guillain, 1959; Havens, 1966; Janet, 1895; Veith, 1965) to understand Charcot's theoretical perspective, his clinical technique, his research methods, and aspects of his personality, and to assess the relative impact of each of these factors upon Freud.

CHARCOT THE THEORIST

Charcot recognized hysteria as a mental phenomenon and formulated a specific etiological theory for it (Veith, 1965). Although he was quite aware of certain emotional factors relevant to the development of the disease, he simultaneously leaned heavily on a concept of an inherited neuropathic tendency. This oscillation between a psychosocial and a biological theory characterized his ultimate formulation of hysteria (Havens, 1966).

Charcot accumulated a large mass of clinical data until he was able to discern an organized pattern, and he had less concern for theoretical explanations than for subdividing clinical entities and for recognizing groups of disparate symptoms as whole syndromes. On this score, Freud wrote, "the whole trend of his mind leads me to suppose that he can find no rest till he has correctly described and classified some phenomenon. . .but that he can sleep quite soundly without having arrived at the physiological explanation of that phenomenon" (1886, p. 13).

Indeed, Charcot was one of the most brilliant observers and classifiers in all of psychiatric and neurological history. Freud (1892-1894) quotes his response to an objection to a clinical demonstration which was contrary to the Young-Helmholtz theory. He replied: *"La théorie, c'est bon; mais ça n'empêche pas d'exister"* ("Theory is good; but it doesn't prevent things from existing") (p. 139).

Of course, such an attitude is in keeping with the demand that theory explain observed fact or be altered—an attitude which maximizes empirical induction and potentially minimizes deduction.

In keeping with his extraordinary capacity to build syndromes out of disparate symptoms, Charcot pieced together the various components of hysteria into a single syndrome that was all-inclusive. Freud (1886) says that Charcot "began by reducing the connection of the neurosis with the genital system to its correct proportions by demonstrating the unsuspected frequency of cases of male hysteria and especially of traumatic hysteria" (p. 11). A linkage between sexual function and the hysterical neurosis was clearly made, but the next step, to implicate sexual feeling or drive, was not made. Other material suggests that a preconscious perception of psychosexuality related to hysteria was present but underemphasized or disguised by Charcot as in the following statement: "For my own part I am far from believing that lubricity always is at work in hysteria; I am even convinced of the contrary. Nor am I either a strict partisan of the old doctrine which taught that the source of all hysteria resides in the genital organs; but. . .I believe it to be absolutely demonstrated that, in a special form of hysteria—the ovary does play an important part" (1877-1889, Vol. 1, p. 247).

Charcot's ideas about the origins of hysteria derive in large believe that "lubricity" is involved—a concept he makes use of in his clinical descriptions, but not in his theoretical formulations of hysteria. In 1888 Freud, as a disciple of Charcot, was still writing, "As regards what is often asserted to be the preponderant influence of abnormalities in the sexual sphere upon the development of hysteria, it must be said that its importance is as a rule over-estimated" (1888a, p. 50). Freud acknowledged the importance of sexual problems but was ambivalent and doubtful, like Charcot.

Charcot's ideas about the origins of hysteria derive in large part from the experimental induction of hysterical phenomena through hypnotism. With this technique he was able to produce symptoms which exactly replicated the naturally occurring phenomena. This, of course, is a quite legitimate experimental technique (cf. "Koch's postulate"). To be able to produce symptoms by such a process was a significant advance and it opened many new possibilities in the study of hysteria. It is an abuse of the technique, however, to assume that the naturally occurring symptoms must invariably be produced in an identical manner.

Although Charcot made a significant contribution to the understanding of the origins of hysteria, he tended to over-generalize from the "experimental" replication. Our conclusion can be illustrated by the following: Charcot described two male patients who sustained brachial monoplegias following accidents. He was able to create the identical condition in two women who were patients in the Salpêtrière. After demonstrating that by suggestion he could create paralysis in his subjects, he went on to show that he could induce the same state without verbal suggestion but with a blow to the selected area—thus replicating even the manner in which the symptom was produced in nature (1877-1889, Vol. 3, p. 307).

With regard to this impressive clinical demonstration it is well to keep in mind that serious questions have been raised about Charcot's research methodology. He repeatedly tended to discount the effects of learning, training, and compliance with the experimenter.

After having demonstrated that he could produce a paralysis by the hypnotic technique, Charcot argued for the existence of a naturally occurring state in which hysterical symptoms are likely to occur in the same manner: "A peculiar mental condition often develops...which is very intimately connected...with the hypnotic state. In both of these conditions, in fact, the mental spontaneity, the will, or the judgment, is more or less suppressed or obscured, and suggestions become easy...the slightest traumatic action...may become the occasion of a paralysis, or a contracture, or an arthralgia" (1877-1889, Vol. 3, p. 307).

In another discussion of those with a predilection for hysteria, Charcot anticipated Breuer's hypnoid hypothesis by commenting as follows: "It appears that the hypnotic condition which in the case of the normal person is an artificial state may be for those singular beings an ordinary one, their normal condition. These individuals sleep, if you will allow the term, while they appear perfectly awake. They comport themselves in ordinary life as in a dream, treating as parallel the objective reality in the dream imposed on them, at least they make hardly any difference between the two."

In addition to his own observations Charcot was also aware of the ideas (Ribot, 1881, pp. 111-112) about different kinds of consciousnesss or "split-off" memories (later to be understood as dissociation).

Thus, Charcot developed a formulation which is strikingly similar to Breuer's "hypnoid hypothesis" elaborated in the *Studies on Hysteria* (Breuer and Freud, 1893-1895). In considering the lasting influence of Charcot on Freud it is interesting to note that by 1895 Freud had some reservations about the "hypnoid" theory, which postulated an altered state of consciousness at the time of the induction of the symptom (see Chapters 7 and 11). It seems clear that Charcot, like Breuer, had confined his study of psychological phenomena to certain selected patients, while it was to be Freud's task to overcome this barrier and to develop a universal concept of conflict and defense (Chapters 7 and 8). Nonetheless, in 1893 Freud was able to say: "M. Charcot was the first to teach us that to explain the hysterical neurosis we must apply to psychology" (1893a, p. 171).

CHARCOT THE CLINICIAN

Although Charcot's explanations of hysterical phenomena probably had limited impact upon Freud's theoretical formulations of hysteria, there is another area which we feel to be impressive and relevant from the point of view of his influence on psychoanalysis: this is Charcot's behavior as a clinician and as a psychotherapist. He used hypnosis, suggestion, exhortation, and environmental and transference manipulations in ways which were apparently effective and which are quite similar to their current use.

We have already alluded to Charcot's awareness—at least preconsciously—of quite important psychological correlations to hysterical symptoms. Although he did not integrate these psychological processes into his theoretical constructs, he described them in his clinical reports, which Freud heard and which he could later recollect as his own ideas developed.

In presenting his case histories, Charcot frequently included events of psychological importance. The inclusion of these data suggests his preconscious awareness of their relevance to the disorders of the patients. Despite his preconception about the etiological significance of a hereditary "neuropathic" tendency in the family, such traumatic phenomena as the death of an important person, exposure to a frightening experience, and ill-treatment by a parent in childhood are all cited as occurrences which Charcot assumed in some way to be relevant and in some cases quite important to the illness. As an example of this, we cite a case of a hysterical woman who became ill at the age of 15. Charcot writes: "...the ill-treatment she had suffered from her father, who was addicted to alcoholic excesses, and her subsequent career as a prostitute, have doubtless exerted a certain etiological influence" (1877-1889, Vol. 1, p. 277). His comments assign not a simple correlation but an etiological role to the experiential events and also show a linkage to sexuality as a relevant phenomenon without assuming the prevalent moralistic posture about it.

About another case of hysteroepilepsy he writes: "... the probable causes of these nervous accidents...deserve mention. She had, as she said, a series of frights; one, at the age of 11, she was terrified by a mad dog; two, at the age of 16 she was struck with horror at the sight of the corpse of a murdered woman; three, at the same age, she was again terrified by robbers" (1877-1889, Vol. 1, p. 278).

Although Charcot had no systematic way of conceptualizing or explaining the effects of emotional trauma, it appears that he had a striking perception of its importance in hysteria, whatever his statements about the predisposing factors may have been. As early as 1877, he described recoveries from hysteria which could occur as a result of severe emotional disturbance, such as shocking events in the hospital setting and other dramatic occurrences, like the pilgrimage to Lourdes.

By 1885 he seemed convinced that hysteria requires a mental treatment: "We have here a psychical affection, it is therefore by a mental treatment that we must hope to modify it." As illustrated by the case cited, in which Charcot described ill-treatment in childhood as a relevant consideration, he was aware of the deleterious effects that parents may have on children. In another case, Charcot describes a boy with headaches and hysterical seizures who could not be cured until his father would consent to leave him in a sanitarium and effect a complete separation (1877-1889, Vol. 3, p. 83).

A similar description of a girl with anorexia nervosa in whom he achieved a remarkable recovery illustrates this as well as his general intuitive understanding of parental implication in the child's psychopathology. He describes a consultation request from the parents of this girl to whom he gave the following instructions: "Bring the girl to Paris, place her in one of our hydrotherapeutic establishments, leave her there . . . and I will do the rest" (1877-1889, Vol. 3, p. 212). Some weeks later the patient was brought to Paris. Charcot's poignant account follows:

> I went to the establishment indicated, and there I saw a lamentable sight. She was a tall girl, 14 years of age, who had reached the last stage of emaciation, in a dorsal decubitus, with weak voice, extremities cold and blue and the head drooping. . . . There was, indeed, every reason to be uneasy, very uneasy.
>
> I took the patient's parents aside, and after having addressed to them a blunt remonstrance, I told them that there remained, in my judgement, but one chance of success. It was that they should go away. . . as quickly as possible. . . . They could lay their departure to my door, a matter which was of little importance provided that the girl was persuaded that they were gone and that they went immediately.
>
> Their acquiescence was difficult to obtain in spite of all my remonstrances. Perhaps I was eloquent for the mother yielded first and the father followed, uttering maledictions. . . . Isolation was established; its results were rapid and marvelous. The child, left alone with the nun who acted as nurse, and the doctor of the house, wept a little at first, though an hour later she became very much less desolate than one would have expected. The very same evening, in spite of her repugnance she consented to take half a little biscuit, and wine. On the following day she took a

little milk, some wine, soup and then a little meat. Her nutrition
became improved, progressively but slowly.

At the end of 15 days she was relatively well. Energy returned
and a general improvement in nutrition, so far that at the end of
the month I saw the child seated on the sofa and capable of
lifting her head from the pillow. Then she was able to walk a
little. Then hydrotherapy was brought into play and two months
from the date of the commencement of the treatment she could
be considered as almost completely cured. Power, nourishment,
appetite, left very little more to be desired.

It was then that the girl, when questioned, made the following
confession to me: "As long as poppa and mamma had not
gone—in other words, as long as you had not triumphed (for I
saw that you wished to shut me up), I was afraid that my illness
was not serious, and as I had a horror of eating, I did not eat.
*But when I saw that you were determined to be master, I was
afraid.* And in spite of my repugnance, I tried to eat, and I was
able to, little by little." I thanked the child for her confidence,
which, as you will understand, is a lesson in itself [1877-1889,
Vol. 3, pp. 212-214].

Thus, in his clinical vignettes, Charcot demonstrates an
intuitive grasp of many psychological connections. In his
reports we find him using these connections although unable
to formulate them further into a coherent system of psychopathology or psychotherapy. Although not necessarily consciously aware of their significance, he makes references to the
importance of childhood events for later psychopathological
syndromes, to a relationship between sexual life and hysteria,
to "cures" of hysteria occurring through solely psychological
(emotional) means, to the traumatic effect of fearful and
frightening experiences, to the problems of secondary gain
reinforcing a pattern of illness, and to the harmful effects
which parents may have upon children, which therefore may
necessitate isolation of the child if treatment is to be successful.

CHARCOT THE MAN

We should now like to consider Charcot's personal characteristics, especially those which he displayed as a clinical
teacher. Most of the clinical demonstrations took place at

Charcot's weekly lectures, which were quite spectacular, attracting not only a scientific audience but also "society people, actors, writers, magistrates, and journalists" (Guillain, 1959) because of their theatricality and showmanship. In his work with hysteria, Charcot's interest in dramatic impact seems to have superseded his passion for scientific accuracy. The suggestibility of the hysterics, together with the great pressure on them to perform for "the Master," influenced the field which he observed in a way which may not have been equally significant for his neurological patients who were presented in the same amphitheatre. The failure to recognize this made Charcot vulnerable and oversensitive to criticism. Guillain, his biographer, describes a man of "violent feelings," nicknamed "Caesar," who staged "shows" rather than scientific experiments. It may be this same quality which served as a more personal motive for his interest in hysteria. Hysterical patients offered a dramatic opportunity (something impossible with most neurological patients) not only for vivid demonstration but also for the exercise of an almost omnipotent, magical power as healer.

Freud did not seem to note these tendencies at first, but reported a different impression of his new teacher upon arriving in Paris: "I saw no sign, however, that Charcot showed any preference for rare or strange material or that he tried to exploit it for mystical purposes" (1886, p. 13).

Freud's statements about the impact Charcot had upon him are found in his letters of the time (E. Freud, 1960). On November 24, 1885, he wrote to Martha Bernays:

> I am really very comfortably installed now and I think I am changing a great deal. I will tell you in detail what is affecting me. Charcot, who is one of the greatest of physicians and a man whose common sense borders on genius, is simply wrecking all my aims and opinions. I sometimes come out of his lectures as from out of Nôtre Dame, with an entirely new idea about perfection. But he exhausts me; when I come away from him I no longer have any desire to work at my own silly things; it is three whole days since I have done any work, and I have no feelings of guilt. My brain is sated as after an evening at the theater. Whether the seed will ever bear any fruit, I don't know; but what I do know is that no other human being has ever affected me in the same way.

In another letter (January 20, 1886) he indicates the regard he has for Charcot by way of a humorous reference to the great man's daughter. In describing her to his fiancee, he wrote:

Mlle. Charcot is...small, rather buxom, and of an almost ridiculous resemblance to her great father, as a result so interesting that one doesn't ask oneself whether she is pretty or not.... Now just suppose I were not in love already and were something of an adventurer; it would be a strong temptation to court her, for nothing is more dangerous than a young girl bearing the features of a man whom one admires.

Freud was drawn to study in France with Charcot largely because of the latter's interest in psychological phenomena, particularly hysteria.

The French school of neuropathology...seemed to me to promise something unfamiliar and characteristic in its mode of working, and moreover to have embarked on new fields...[The] findings of the French school—some of them (upon hypnotism) highly surprising and some of them (upon hysteria) of practical importance—had been met in our countries with more doubt than recognition and belief.... I gladly seized the opportunity ... of forming a judgement upon these facts based on my own experience [1886, pp. 5f.].

Charcot had accepted hysteria as a legitimate topic for study; although we know little of the circumstances, we infer that he had personal motivations for pursuing this interest. Guillain, quoting Pierre Marie, offers only a perfunctory explanation:

What happened at the Salpêtriere was that...the administration took advantage of the evacuation of [a dilapidated] building finally to separate the nonpsychotic epileptics and the hysterics from the insane, and inasmuch as both groups of these patients manifested episodic behavior, it was considered logical to group them together and establish a special quarter called "Quartier des epileptiques simples." Since Charcot was the senior of the two physicians at the Salpetriere, this new service automatically was assigned to him. Thus, quite involuntarily and by force of circumstances, Charcot found himself engulfed in the problem of hysteria [1959, p. 135].

Since Charcot's position was without peer he could obviously have changed clinical services within a reasonable time had he so wished In fact, this kind of rotation was customary in Paris at that time. His perseverance in this arrangement suggests that more personal motives led him toward his psychological investigations. However, the grouping together of hysterics and epileptics, which seemed so fortunate in stimulating Charcot, also served as a source of error, since it produced, by virtue of the suggestibility of the hysterics, many of the major seizures Charcot described. Although he differentiated between the two types of seizures, his uncritical acceptance of the manifest symptoms, as well as deficiencies in his experimental methods, ultimately opened the way to serious criticisms of his results and methodology, especially by Liébeault and Bernheim.

That Charcot had a great impact upon Freud is attested to not only by Jones (1953) and Freud's own letters of the time, but also by the fact that he named his eldest son Jean Martin, after Charcot, and that his own study shows striking similarities to that of Charcot. In a letter to Martha Bernays of January 20, 1886, he describes Charcot's study:

> I just want to add what his study looks like. It is as big as the whole of our future apartment, a room worthy of the magic castle in which he lives. . . . Along the side walls of the larger section stands his enormous library on two levels, each with steps to reach the one above. . . . The other section has a fireplace, a table, and cases containing Indian and Chinese antiques. The walls are covered with Gobelins and pictures; the walls themselves are painted terra cotta. The little I saw of the other rooms on Sunday contained the same wealth of pictures, Gobelins, carpets and curios — in short, a museum [E. Freud, 1960].

The photograph of Freud's studies in Vienna (Jones, 1955, p. 400) and London show similar collections. Eissler (1966a, pp. 392f.) has cited further data suggesting that Freud had identified with Charcot.

Other letters Freud wrote to Martha Bernays (E. Freud, 1960) during his period in Paris illustrate Charcot's influence on him in more detail. The letters also illustrate the capacity Freud had for vivid description at the age of 29:

> At ten o'clock M. Charcot arrived, a tall man of fifty-eight, wearing a top hat, with dark, strangely soft eyes (or rather, one is; the other is expressionless and has an inward cast), long wisps

of hair stuck behind his ears, clean shaven, very expressive features with full protruding lips—in short, like a worldly priest from whom one expects a ready wit and an appreciation of good living. He sat down and began examining the patients. I was very much impressed by his brilliant diagnosis and the lively interest he took in everything, so unlike what we are accustomed to from our great men with their veneer of distinguished superficiality [Oct. 21, 1885].

I would love to give you a description of his home; but this must wait for another day. What's more, he invited me...to come to his house tomorrow evening after dinner; "Il y aura du monde." You can probably imagine my apprehension mixed with curiosity and satisfaction. White tie and white gloves, even a fresh shirt, a careful brushing of my last remaining hair, and so on. A little cocaine to untie my tongue. It is quite all right of course for this news to be widely distributed in Hamburg and Vienna, even with exaggerations such as that he kissed me on the forehead (à la Liszt). As you see, I am not doing at all badly and I am far from laughing at you and your plans [Jan. 18, 1886].

The allusion to Liszt's acknowledgement of Chopin when the latter took Paris by storm suggests the fantasy of surpassing the Master, in view of Freud's identification with Chopin.

Later Freud wrote to Martha of Charcot singling him out to work with his assistant:

I am now the only foreigner at Charcot's. Today...I had the chance of making a certain impression on him. He was talking about a patient, and while the others were laughing, I just said: "Vous parlez de ce cas dans vos leçons," and quoted a few words of his. This seems to have pleased him, for an hour later he said to his assistant, "Vous allez prendre cette observation avec M. Freud," then turned to me and asked if I would like to "prendre une observation" with M. Babinski [the assistant]. Needless to say, I had no objection. It is a case that Charcot seems to find interesting; personally I don't think much of it, but I shall probably have to write a paper about it with the assistant. Anyway, the point of the incident is that Charcot singled me out at all, and since then the assistant's behavior toward me has changed.... And all this in response to one nod from the Master! [Jan. 27, 1886].

DISCUSSION

There is evidence that the trip to Paris had additional personal meaning for Freud, beyond his contact with Charcot (see Chapter 12). A letter to Minna Bernays suggests that at that period of his life Paris had a meaning similar to that which Rome held at a later time. He writes (E. Freud, 1960):

> I am under the full impact of Paris and, waxing very poetical, could compare it to a vast overdressed Sphinx who gobbles up every foreigner unable to solve her riddles.... Suffice it to say that the city and its inhabitants strike me as uncanny; the people seem to me of a different species from ourselves; I feel they are all possessed of a thousand demons... As you realize, my heart is German provincial and it hasn't accompanied me here; which raises the question whether I should not return to fetch it [Dec. 3, 1885].

The explicit identification with Oedipus who solved the riddle of the Sphinx and thus became ruler of Thebes has the same possible significance as the previous reference to Chopin and Liszt.

These clues about the importance of Freud's visit to Paris lead to the consideration of what specifically he found there in this time of transition from neurologist to psychiatrist. Certainly it seems true that Charcot's attitude about the legitimacy of studying hysteria was important. Jones states (1953, p. 219): "Charcot's attitude to hysteria afforded very much encouragement—what psychologists call 'sanction'—to Freud, and he remained grateful to him for it." Beyond this "sanction," however, there seem to be two basic areas to consider: first, the actual knowledge and method which Charcot could communicate and teach; second, Charcot personally as a real and/or transference figure for Freud at this crucial stage (see Freud, 1892-1894).

We have inferred that the personal experience with Charcot and the encounter with Paris seem to have had a profound impact on Freud, but the conceptual framework that Charcot could teach was of limited usefulness. The clinical demonstrations were important, but the theories about hysteria contained little that would survive. Freud may have used the clinical examples to provide data for synthesis into a form quite different from that of Charcot. Indeed, the seeds of his intellectual disengagement from Charcot were visible even before Freud left Paris. In this context it is particularly interesting to note that in 1889 Freud went to Nancy to visit the severest critics of Charcot in order to perfect his hypnotic technique (Freud, 1925b). He did not discuss other reasons for the trip to Nancy, but he was at that time already aware of possible deficiencies in Charcot's ideas and techniques. In his Preface to Bernheim's *Suggestion*, which he had just translated, Freud wrote (1888b): "If the supporters of the suggestion theory are right, all the observations made at the Salpêtrière are worthless; indeed, they become errors in observation" (pp. 77-78). Thus Freud was finally able to consider the possibility that Charcot had induced symptoms in his patients by suggestion "in a manner of which he himself was unconscious" (p. 78) (see Guillain, 1959, pp. 169f., 174ff.).

Jones (1953, p. 229) points out an error in Freud's recollection of this period in his "Autobiographical Study" (1925b). Freud states that as a consequence of this Nancy visit he was stimulated to translate two works of Bernheim. Jones points out that Freud had already published one of the works with an extensive preface in 1888. The slip on Freud's part suggests ambivalent feelings about his need to seek validation about what he had seen in Paris insofar as it conflicted with his own scientific reality testing; i.e., a critical review of what he had taken from Charcot was taking place in him, albeit in the face of some resistance. By 1892 this emancipation had gone so far that Freud presumed to annotate his translation of the Master's lectures — and without asking Charcot's permission to do so. Although he went out of his way to deny that he was thereby setting himself above his "honored teacher," Freud stated his differences with Charcot very openly (1892-1894).

In 1925, Freud reviewed these events in "An Autobiographical Study":

> What impressed me most of all while I was with Charcot were his latest investigations upon hysteria, some of which were carried out under my own eyes. He had proved, for instance, the genuineness of hysterical phenomena and their conformity to laws..., the frequent occurrence of hysteria in men, the production of hysterical paralyses and contractures by hypnotic suggestion and the fact that such artificial products showed, down to their smallest details, the same features as spontaneous attacks, which were often brought on traumatically [1925b, p. 13].

As we have already suggested, Charcot's attitude in his psychotherapeutic work was that of an omnipotent character, powerfully manipulating the transference situation. Freud tried to imitate this stance but could never feel at ease in it, nor could he be satisfied with the limited effectiveness and understanding that were part of it. In this connection, an anecdote described by Freud expresses his attitude quite clearly: "When a patient [of Bernheim in 1889] who showed himself unamenable [to hypnosis] was met with the shout: 'What are you doing? Vous vous contre-suggestionnez!', I said to myself that this was an evident injustice and an act of violence. For the man certainly had a right to counter-suggestions if people were trying to subdue him with suggestions" (1921a, p. 89).

Freud developed new techniques, more rationally based, as he was able to separate himself and his technique from that of his teachers.

CONCLUSION

In this chapter we have attempted to assess the impact of Charcot upon Freud. Our study suggests that a powerful capacity for identification existed in Freud, accompanied by a capacity to modify that identification, selecting special areas in which it was retained while changing others that did not prove fruitful. It seems plausible to assume that the capacity for this kind of identification and differentiation is an important factor in unusually creative persons such as Freud. Lowenfeld (1956) has written:

> Identification with great men of the past seems to be an aspect of the growth of greatness in men, one of the conditions which make it possible. Greatness is deeply related to conflict—the struggle between powerful forces within, out of which the strength arises to stand alone and fight outside forces. Great father images appear to be necessary in the waging of this battle. Daring ventures into the unknown require protection in the history of revolutionary ideas or actions. Quite possibly, sublimations of the highest order are not achievable without such identifications [p. 685].

Our view corroborates Lowenfeld's thesis that Charcot served as one of a series of living models for these identifications, sublimations, and ultimate resolution within Freud. Earlier Brücke and Breuer probably served the same needs for him (see Chapter 8), as Fliess was to do later (see Chapter 16). Charcot has been characterized as a great pictorial artist who "lectured to enormous effect, evoked clinical pictures with unsurpassed clarity" (Havens, 1966, p. 516). Freud identified with this powerful figure and utilized Charcot's strength and sanction to investigate unexplored psychological phenomena, but he soon needed to differentiate his own ideas from those of Charcot. Freud's "daring ventures into the unknown" went far beyond the concepts of Charcot, but the experience in Paris served as a decisive propulsive force into this new venture.

6

JOSEF BREUER

GEORGE H. POLLOCK

[*A Voice in the Wilderness.* Josef Breuer's influence on Freud was probably even more important than that of Charcot; this estimate is reflected by Ernest Jones's decision, in his biography of Freud (1953), to call his chapter dealing with both of these relationships "The Breuer Period." Freud called Breuer the founder of psychoanalysis because of the latter's personal influence on Freud's development as a scientist and as a man; at least, Jones has pointed out that the designation could not have been earned for the discovery of any of the essentials of psychoanalysis as a discipline. Jones believed that most of Breuer's conceptual contributions had been borrowed, either from the physiological principles learned in Brücke's laboratory or from the French psychiatric school. We do not fully agree that Breuer made no original contributions; the development of the cathartic method, the conceptualization of its presumed mode of action, and the elaboration of the hypnoid hypothesis add up to a substantial innovative role. However, these theoretical contributions form only one part of the field of influence Breuer exerted on Sigmund Freud; he also provided narcissistic support and the essential stimulus for the transition from medical neurology to psychological work.

In the following chapter, Pollock devotes himself to an examination of Breuer's difficulty in carrying through the treatment of his most important case, that of Frl. Bertha

First published in *Journal of the American Psychoanalytic Association,* 16: 711-738, 1968, under the title, "The Possible Significance of Childhood Object Loss in the Josef Breuer-Bertha Pappenheim (Anna O.)-Sigmund Freud Relationship."

Pappenheim, "Anna O.," in the face of transference developments involving a pseudocyesis, and his parallel ambivalence a
decade later about accepting Freud's hypotheses about the
role of childhood sexuality in neurosogenesis. Although the
paper puts special emphasis on Breuer's scientific inhibition in
this particular area of inquiry, one must also keep in mind
that, in spite of his internal conflicts, Breuer did communicate
his crucial clinical discoveries to his young colleague, Freud,
within half a year of the termination of Frl. Pappenheim's
treatment. Later, when Freud had also had clinical experience in treating emotional disturbances, Breuer participated
in the task of developing the first theoretical system attempting to understand these on a psychological basis, and he
agreed to the publication of their joint findings. Thus Breuer's
brilliant clinical encounter with a patient who had her own
original contribution to make to the invention of the "talking
cure" must have confirmed Freud in his interest in psychology,
if it did not arouse this interest in the first place. Ten years
later, the intellectual collaboration of the two men eventuated
in writing *Studies on Hysteria* (1893-1895) (see Chapters 7-8).

Breuer's anxieties about dealing with the "unseemliness" of
the psychological depths are, for the first time, put into a
proper perspective in Pollock's chapter. His findings should
help us to empathize with Breuer's dilemma and to correct any
impression that he may have been lacking in courage. On the
contrary, it would seem that Breuer's participation in Freud's
research was a heroic feat, precisely because the subject
matter touched upon his personal conflicts in an unbearable
manner.

Viewed from this perspective, the significance of Josef
Breuer for psychoanalysis does, indeed, come close to Freud's
high estimate. It is not particularly important that eventually
Breuer did not have the strength to continue. Freud's disappointment and anger about this were unavoidable reactions
which say more about how much he still needed a collaborator
in order to accomplish his creative task than they convey any
objective assessment of Breuer. To put it in another way,
Breuer has been condemned for not being willing to lend
himself to the satisfaction of Freud's requirements rather than

pursuing his private goals. But, after all, *il faut vivre sa vie!* Upon losing Breuer as an alter ego, Freud had to fill the gap by finding a new relationship charged with personal meaning, the "friendship" with Wilhelm Fliess. It may be pertinent to note here that it was Breuer who introduced Freud to Fliess so that the two relationships were, in one sense, directly continuous. In his contribution to this volume, Kohut throws new light on the personal meaning of such relationships (see Chapter 16).

Even Jones, whose admiration for Freud occasionally led him into failures of empathy for some of the subsidiary figures in his biography, attempted to redress the balance by capping his unsympathetic portrayal of Breuer with the following qualification:

> The scientific differences alone cannot account for the bitterness with which Freud wrote about Breuer in the unpublished Fliess correspondence of the nineties. When one recollects what Breuer had meant to him in the eighties, his generosity to Freud, his understanding sympathy, and the combination of cheerfulness and intellectual stimulation that radiated from him, the change later is indeed startling. Where previously no word of criticism for the perfect Breuer could be found, now one hears no more of his good qualities, only of the irritating effect his presence had on Freud. The change had not, of course, been a sudden one. . . . The main reversal in Freud's feelings came in the spring of 1896, a date which coincides with the onset of the more passionate phase of his relations with Fliess [1953, pp. 254-255].

It will be well to remember that Breuer had not asked to be regarded as perfect and could not be blamed for the pain that Freud experienced as a result of the inevitable disillusionment and anger which had to follow this unrealistic idealization—*Eds.*]

In a letter to his betrothed, Martha Bernays, dated April 28, 1885, Sigmund Freud wrote:

> I have just carried out one resolution which one group of people, as yet unborn and fated to misfortune, will feel acutely. Since you can't guess whom I mean I will tell you: they are my biographers. I have destroyed all my diaries of the past fourteen years, with letters, scientific notes and the manuscripts of my

publications. Only family letters were spared.... Let the bio-graphers chafe; we won't make it too easy for them. Let each one of them believe he is right in his 'Conception of the Development of the Hero'; even now I enjoy the thought of how they will go astray. [Jones comments:] While appreciating Freud's conclud-ing chuckle in this interesting phantasy we nevertheless dare to hope that the last words may prove to have been exaggerated [Jones, 1953, pp. xii-xiii].

The genetic approach, implemented by reconstructions of the past, is one of the fundamentals of psychoanalysis. The facts upon which such reconstructions are based are fre-quently hard to obtain, be it due to the forces of repression or to realistic unavailability of crucial information. In attempt-ing to study the germinal relationship between Josef Breuer, Bertha Pappenheim (Anna O.), and Sigmund Freud, the investigator meets with various obstacles. Some facts are known; others seem to be lost, buried, or concealed. In order to study this critical period in the history of psychoanalysis, I have made use of existing information, heretofore unavailable historical data, and inferences derived from current psycho-analytic hypotheses.

The continuous interplay between theory and application is the basis of scientific endeavor. Hypotheses derived from many sources, tested in various ways, add to our explanatory and predictive knowledge, and provide a new perspective for re-examination and new understanding of earlier phenomena and events. My particular research has been fed by three streams. The first is my study of the mourning process. This investigation views mourning as a normal adaptive process, having various stages and an evolutionary history (Pollock, 1961). The second tributary has been the research of Fleming and her collaborators (1958) who have investigated the effect of parent loss in childhood on subsequent adult functioning. These workers have been testing two hypotheses: the first is that in some persons, adaptation to the death of a parent in childhood is associated with a failure to complete the work of mourning; the second is that the death of a parent in childhood may result in a degree of arrest of development of certain ego functions and object relationships at the childhood level achieved when the loss occurred. These adult patients, in analysis, seem to deny the loss of the parent internally and seek to avoid a meaningful psychoanalytic relationship if it endangers the existing level of adjustment.[a] The mobilization of the mourning process is a necessary prerequisite to the facilitation of the analytic treatment of these persons (Fleming and Altschul, 1963). I have extended the childhood loss study to include adult patients who have lost a sibling during childhood (Pollock, 1962). The findings of Hilgard (1953, 1969; Hilgard and Newman, 1959) on the significance of anniversary reactions in patients who had sustained such childhood object losses or object absences have been replicated and confirmed. Some of the studies referred to above have already been reported, and others are still in progress.

The third significant contributory antecedent of the present study, which drew my attention to Josef Breuer, has been the investigation of the *Studies on Hysteria* by the Workshop on Methodology at the Chicago Institute for Psychoanalysis (Chapter 7). This group found the styles of its two authors divergent and complementary: "Breuer displayed great freedom in hypothesis building based on deductive reasoning, while Freud subjected his inspirational hunches to thorough inductive revision in the light of the clinical evidence available to him." Even while recognizing that the actual process by which scientists work may be different from what appears in the published scientific reports, nonetheless the comparison of Freud's scientific style with that of Breuer showed sufficient overt differences to warrant the assumption of more basic differences in structure. Schlessinger et al. discuss this topic in another paper from the Workshop on Methodology (Chapter 8). These authors call attention to Breuer's impressive ability to observe objectively. Despite the threatening nature of the relationship developing in his treatment of Anna O., Breuer continued to observe and treat his patient intensively over a

[a] More than a decade after these formulations of the Chicago Parent Loss Workshop, we would also view such shifts in terms of the pathology of narcissism. At the start of treatment, such patients have regressed to an archaic grandiose position of aloof self-sufficiency. The loss of the parent has arrested them in this state if it has been experienced as a narcissistic injury. The capacity to mourn presupposes that the object is no longer being used for narcissistic purposes, i.e., to supply psychic functions not yet available to the self.

two-year period—a procedure most uncommon in late nine-teenth-century Vienna. The clinical situation became com-plicated in its terminating phase by the emergence of a transference-countertransference confrontation of which Breuer had had no previous experience, let alone under-standing. He withdrew from his patient and also seemingly abandoned direct clinical investigation of psychological prob-lems altogether.

I. TERMINATION OF THE CASE OF ANNA O.

In 1907 Breuer repeated his earlier assertion that the case of Anna O. was carried to a successful completion without the discovery of a sexual basis for her illness in spite of the patient's avowal of her love for him (Cranefield, 1958). In 1895, Breuer had written:

> On the last day—by the help of re-arranging the room so as to resemble her father's sickroom—she reproduced the terrifying hallucination which I have described above and which con-stituted the root of her whole illness. During the original scene she had only been able to think and pray in English; but immediately after its reproduction she was able to speak Ger-man. She was moreover free from the innumerable disturbances which she had previously exhibited. After this she left Vienna and travelled for a while; but it was a considerable time before she regained her mental balance entirely. Since then she has enjoyed complete health.
> [In a footnote, the editor of the *Standard Edition* writes that] when the treatment had apparently reached a successful end, the patient suddenly made manifest to Breuer the presence of a strong unanalyzed positive transference of an unmistakably sexual nature. It was this occurrence, Freud believed, that caused Breuer to hold back the publication of the case history for so many years and that led ultimately to his abandonment of all further collaboration in Freud's researches [Breuer and Freud, 1893-1895, pp. 40-41].

Jones, writing of the same situation, states:

> Freud has related to me a fuller account than he described in his writings of the peculiar circumstances surrounding the end of this novel treatment. It would seem that Breuer had developed

what we should nowadays call a strong countertransference to his interesting patient. At all events he was so engrossed that his wife became bored at listening to no other topic, and before long jealous. She did not display this openly, but became unhappy and morose. It was a long time before Breuer, with his thoughts elsewhere, divined the meaning of her state of mind. It provoked a violent reaction in him, perhaps compounded of love and guilt, and he decided to bring the treatment to an end. He announced this to Anna O., who was by now much better, and bade her goodby. But that evening he was fetched back to find her in a greatly excited state, apparently as ill as ever. The patient, who according to him had appeared to be an asexual being and had never made any allusion to such a forbidden topic throughout the treatment, was now in the throes of an hysterical childbirth (pseudocyesis), the logical termination of a phantom pregnancy that had been invisibly developing in response to Breuer's ministrations. Though profoundly shocked, he managed to calm her down by hypnotizing her, and then fled the house in a cold sweat. The next day he and his wife left for Venice to spend a second honeymoon, which resulted in the conception of a daughter; the girl born in these curious circumstances was nearly sixty years later to commit suicide in New York. . . .[b]

The poor patient did not fare so well as one might gather from Breuer's published account. Relapses took place, and she was removed to an institution in Gross Enzersdorf.[1] A year after discontinuing treatment, Breuer confided to Freud that she was quite unhinged and that he wished she would die and so be released from her suffering. She improved, however, and gave up morphia. . . .

Frl. Bertha (Anna O.) was not only highly intelligent, but extremely attractive in physique and personality; when removed to the sanitorium, she inflamed the heart of the psychiatrist in charge. Her mother, who was somewhat of a dragon, had come from Frankfurt and took her daughter back there for good at the end of the eighties. . . .

Some ten years later, at a time when Breuer and Freud were studying cases together, Breuer called him into consultation over an hysterical patient. Before seeing her he described her symptoms, whereupon Freud pointed out that they were typical

---

[b] Jones's information about Breuer's daughter is not accurate. See below, pp. 143 and 146.

[1] Ellenberger (1966) has shown that there never was a sanitarium in Gross Enzersdorf. Ellenberger's more recent researches have traced the actual sanitarium to which the patient was taken. See Pollock (1973).

products of a phantasy of pregnancy. The recurrence of the old situation was too much for Breuer. Without saying a word he took up his hat and stick and hurriedly left the house [1953, pp. 224-226].

In 1932, Freud, writing to Stefan Zweig about an error in the latter's report of the Anna O. case, stated:

It declares that Breuer's patient under hypnosis made the confession of having experienced and suppressed certain *"sentimenti illecti"* (i.e., of a sexual nature) while sitting at her father's sickbed. In reality she said nothing of the kind; rather she indicated that she was trying to conceal from her father her agitated condition, above all her tender concern. If things had been as your text maintains, then everything else would have taken a different turn. I would not have been surprised by the discovery of sexual etiology, Breuer would have found it more difficult to refute this theory, and if hypnosis could obtain such candid confessions, I probably would never have abandoned it.

What really happened with Breuer's patient I was able to guess later on, long after the break in our relations, when I suddenly remembered something Breuer had once told me in another context before we had begun to collaborate and which he never repeated. On the evening of the day when all her symptoms had been disposed of, he was summoned to the patient again, found her confused and writhing in abdominal cramps. Asked what was wrong with her, she replied: "Now Dr. B's child is coming!"

At this moment he held in his hand the key that would have opened the "doors to the Mothers," but he let it drop. With all his great intellectual gifts there was nothing Faustian in his nature.[c] Seized by conventional horror he took flight and abandoned the patient to a colleague. For months afterwards she struggled to regain her health in a sanatorium.

I was so convinced of this reconstruction of mine that I published it somewhere. Breuer's youngest daughter (born shortly after the above-mentioned treatment, not without significance for the deeper connections!) read my account and asked her father about it (shortly before his death). He confirmed my version, and she informed me about it later [E. Freud, 1960, pp. 412-413].

[c] Freud is here alluding to the specific wording of Breuer's reference to the meaning of exploring man's psychological depths by way of a quotation from the second part of *Faust*. This statement of Breuer's will be discussed in detail below (see p. 150).

To attribute Breuer's anxiety about sexuality and hysterical pregnancy to unconventionality is insufficient. There seems to have been more to the story.

II. THE GENETIC DETERMINANTS OF BREUER'S AMBIVALENCE

Jones (1953) points out that Breuer's reluctant cooperation with Freud resulted from Breuer's unwillingness to follow Freud in his investigation of his patient's sexual life and the far-reaching conclusions Freud was drawing from it. "That disturbances in the sexual life were the *essential* factor in the etiology of both neuroses and psychoneuroses was a doctrine Breuer could not easily stomach" (p. 253). He wavered from one side to the other. Yet for a long time Breuer seems to have been quite convinced of the sexual etiology of neurotic disorders; in fact, he appears in some of his writings almost casual and matter-of-fact about it. Thus, in his theoretical chapter in *Studies on Hysteria*, he writes:

> The sexual instinct is undoubtedly the most powerful source of persisting increases of excitation (and consequently of neuroses) [p. 200].
> It is a matter of everyday experience that a conflict...between irreconcilable ideas has a pathogenic effect. What are mostly in question are ideas about processes connected with sexual life [p. 210].
> [With this conclusion about the disposition to hysteria] we are already recognizing sexuality as one of the major components of hysteria. We shall see that the part it plays in it is very much greater still and that it contributes in the most various ways to the constitution of the illness [p. 244].
> [Finally:] The most numerous and important of the ideas that are fended off and converted have a sexual content [p. 245].

It was Breuer who remarked to Freud that some neurotic behaviors are always connected with secrets of the marriage bed (Jones, 1953, p. 248; see also Breuer and Freud, 1893-1895, p. 246).

How then to explain Breuer's oscillations about the role of sexuality in neuroses and his need to withdraw and avoid the obvious diagnosis of hysterical pregnancy symptoms?

A clue is offered in the 1923 Curriculum Vitae that Breuer prepared for the *Akademie der Wissenschaften*. This was published in Vienna in 1925, and later edited and translated into English by C. P. Oberndorf (1953). In this report, Breuer writes extensively of his father, Leopold Breuer, "this man to whom I am indebted for everything." Leopold Breuer "grew up in the most stringent circumstances after the early death of his own father who had been the village surgeon." Leopold himself was a teacher of religion appointed by the official Jewish Community in Vienna.

> ...in 1840, he married a pretty young girl, my mother, whom I do not remember, as she died at the birth of her second boy, my brother, "in the blossom of her youth and beauty," as the inscription on her tombstone reads. After a little while her mother, a very wise and witty woman, came to live with us and assumed the command of the household and the role of mother to the motherless boys [p. 65].

Josef Breuer was born in Vienna on January 15, 1842. After his wife's death, Leopold Breuer never remarried and devoted himself to his children. For example, Josef Breuer did not attend public school, but was taught at home by his father. He writes: "I was able to read perfectly by the age of four." Nowhere in his essay does Breuer mention his age when his mother, Bertha Semler Breuer, died. Upon first reading this autobiographical item, I made the "prediction" that Josef Breuer's mother died at the height of his Oedipal period, and offered the formulation that Breuer's vulnerability to the hysterical pregnancies of his patients related to his own Oedipal fixation resulting from his mother's death in childbirth and at the peak of his Oedipal phase. Furthermore, I postulated that he assumed a benevolent, helping identification with his father, manifested in his relationships with "younger brother" figures such as Freud and later Fliess, and also with his patients. A reinvestigation of the case history of Anna O. revealed that, although no anamnestic data were given, there was an overabundance of careful observations of the ontological processes related to Anna O.'s mourning reactions to the loss of her father. Anna O. seemed to be identified with her dead father, and in her treatment heavy emphasis on death was manifest. It was postulated that Breuer's involvement with Anna O. included a mother transference to her, a "helping Father" identification and role, and an apparent fascination with her mourning and grief reactions. The need for evidence to test these hypotheses remained.

Such unpublished evidence was obtained from members of the Breuer family and from the *Israelitische Kultusgemeinde* of Vienna. They revealed:

1. Josef Breuer was between three and four when his mother, Bertha, died at the birth of the second child, a son. Breuer's father died in 1872, when Josef was 30 years old.

2. The father did not remarry.

3. His brother, Adolf, was ailing and died in his twentieth year of tuberculosis.

4. Josef Breuer had five children:

    a. Leopold Robert: born July 1, 1869, died in 1930. An internist with a large practice. Named after Josef Breuer's father.

    b. Bertha Hammerschlag: born May 19, 1870, died in 1962 in New York. Named after Josef Breuer's mother.

    c. Margarete Schiff: born December 4, 1872. She, her physician husband, and one of their children perished in a German concentration camp. One of her two surviving children committed suicide in the United States.

    d. Johannes: born October 8, 1878, died in 1926.

    e. Dora, the youngest daughter: born March 11, 1882. She did not want to leave Austria, hoping to be able to help her sister and her family, the Schiffs. She committed suicide when the Gestapo knocked at her door in 1944.

Breuer's wife, Mathilde Altmann (1846-1931), was a particularly beautiful and charming woman. Freud named his eldest daughter Mathilde after her (Jones, 1953, p. 167). Freud named his youngest daughter, Anna, after Anna Hammerschlag—a sister of Breuer's son-in-law and a favorite patient of Freud's (p. 223).

Breuer was spared additional mourning as he died before his wife, children, and grandchildren. Breuer ends his autobiography with the statement: "...I have been, and am, completely happy in my home; that my beloved wife has given me five sturdy, fine children; that I have lost none of them, and that none has ever caused me serious sorrow—then I may well consider myself a fortunate man—and one who even owns a shirt!" (p. 67).

III. BREUER'S CONTRIBUTIONS

Young Josef Breuer wrote that he grew up in favorable circumstances—neither in poverty nor in luxury, but in *"aurea mediocritas."* He received excellent primary instruction from his father, then went through the Academic Gymnasium and, after passing the final examinations, to the University of Vienna to study medicine. Following his father's advice, he spent the entire first year in the liberal arts. For example, he was very interested in economic history and philosophy. In 1859 he began the medical curriculum. The importance and lasting impact of his teacher, the physiologist Ernst Brücke, is well known. During the course of his clinical studies, Breuer came in contact with Johann Oppolzer, Professor of Internal Medicine at the University of Vienna, who soon recognized his great talent and scientific drive. As soon as Breuer passed his final examinations, in 1867, Oppolzer made him his assistant. Early in his assistantship Breuer made one of his most important scientific discoveries, the self regulating reflexive process in breathing. His mentor in this work, the physiologist E. Hering, presented Breuer's research to a meeting of the Section of Mathematics and Natural Sciences of the Imperial Academy of Sciences on April 30, 1868. Breuer's extensive report of his research appeared in the *Proceedings of the Academy* dated November 5, 1868.

Following Oppolzer's wishes, Breuer was appointed "Privat-dozent" for internal medicine, a position he kept until after Oppolzer's death in 1871. Breuer's own father died in 1872, the same year Breuer's third child was born. When Oppolzer's department was taken over by Bamberger, Breuer lost his position and its accompanying clinical facilities. He resigned his "Docentship" and thereafter devoted himself entirely to private practice and private research.

When Billroth, the great surgeon, then mentioned his intention to propose Breuer in the senate of the medical faculty for the rank of Extraordinary Professor, Breuer asked definitely that this plan be dropped, giving as reason the existing obstacles to teaching. Thus it came about that J. Breuer remained outside the Medical University guild, although its most outstanding representatives — to name only Professors — Brücke, Exner, Fleischl, Dumreicher, Billroth, Gersuny, Chrobak, Frisch, Kaposi, Schnabel — held him in the highest esteem and chose him as their constant medical consultant and confidant [Meyer, 1928].

Jones indicated that he was also physician of the famous Brentano's family.[2]

One senses that Hans Horst Meyer is at some loss to explain the — undoubtedly unusual — refusal to accept his nomination for the professorship and the equally unusual resignation from the "Docentship."

Eissler (1966a), quoting Wagner-Jauregg, wrote that Breuer resigned from his *Dozentur* "after he was, in his opinion, treated in an undignified way by the College [of Professors]." Eissler suggests "that Breuer took offense at not being appointed professor and successor to his chief Oppolzer." One is impelled to speculate that Breuer could not succeed his older teacher and advisor for internal as well as external reasons, particularly since his own father died at about the same time as did Oppolzer, and instead withdrew from the situation. Nevertheless Breuer's

...great scientific importance did receive public and most honorific recognition when in 1894 the Imperial Academy of Science in Vienna made him, the simple physician without academic position or title, its corresponding member; the honor was all the greater as it was done on the proposal of men like Ernst Mach, Ewald Hering, Sigmund Exner. To be sure, Breuer had already published two decades earlier his great and basically important study "On the Function of the Semicircular Canals of the Otolabyrinth and on the Static Sense," in the *Medizinische Jahrbücher* of 1874 and 1875 [Meyer, 1928].

Breuer was at that time only 32 years old, and relied exclusively upon himself and his own simple instruments for his

[2] H. K. Becker, Carl Koller's daughter, has written that "Dr. Breuer was my grandfather's family physician and was deeply admired by my father, who described him as almost Christlike in character and charity, wise, restrained, lofty in spirit, with that rare balance between the inquiring, intuitive mind and thorough, objective appraisal and research" (1963, pp. 326-327).

research work. Breuer's "penetrating clarity and sound judgment," his "extensive mastery of the literature," and the ingenuity of his experiments were described as noteworthy. Breuer dealt "with the remarks of his scientific opponents... which had been at times very brusque and even offensive... in a strictly objective fashion, sharply sifting them with finality but withal noble and considerate" (Meyer, 1928). When he was reproached for having confined himself to his pigeon experiments, instead of including mammals in his studies, Breuer answered:

> As for me, this omission is due to personal circumstances which I hope will exculpate me. I am a practicing physician, my working hours are the late evening and the night, hence my laboratory is my apartment. There I could work on pigeons but could not perform extensive surgical operations on mammals.
>
> [Meyer notes that] in spite of his very extensive medical practice, J. Breuer continued to work in this hidden, one would almost say secretive fashion, with tenacity and with undiminished joy and vigor for decades—up to about the age of seventy [1928].

In the latter half of 1880, Breuer began his work with Bertha Pappenheim (Anna O.). This treatment terminated in June, 1882. As mentioned earlier, Breuer's youngest child, Dora, was born on March 11, 1882. This fact is in contradiction to the account given by Jones; the child was *conceived* and *born before* the end of Bertha Pappenheim's therapy. Dora's conception and the fact of Mrs. Breuer's pregnancy while Breuer was treating Bertha Pappenheim may not have been kept a secret from his patient and may have played a significant role in her therapeutic relationship with Breuer.

In November, 1882, Breuer related the remarkable story of Bertha Pappenheim's treatment to Freud. It so impressed Freud that three years later, when he was studying in Paris under Charcot, he reported the case to him. Freud's active collaboration with Breuer, however, began in 1891-1892 and included the cases of Frau Emmy von N. and that of Frau Cäcilie M., as well as the discussion of the treatment of Bertha Pappenheim.

Breuer evaluated his work with Bertha Pappenheim as well as his own differences with Freud in a letter to Auguste Forel written November 21, 1907:

> The case which I described in the *Studies* as No. 1, Anna O., passed through my hands, and my merit lay essentially in my having recognized what an uncommonly instructive and scientifically important case chance had brought me for investigation, in my having persevered in observing it attentively and accurately, and my not having allowed any preconceived opinions to interfere with the simple observation of the important data. Thus at that time I learned a very great deal: much that was of scientific value, but something of practical importance as well—namely, that it was impossible for a 'general practitioner' to treat a case of that kind without bringing his activities and mode of life completely to an end. I vowed at the time that I would *not* go through such an ordeal again. . . .
>
> We were no less filled with doubt and surprise when the analysis of severe cases of hysteria (e.g., of 'Caecilie M' in the book) led us further back into childhood. This too, of course, was entirely a discovery of Freud's. . . .
>
> The case of Anna O., which was the germ-cell of the whole of psychoanalysis, proves that a fairly severe case of hysteria can develop, flourish, and be resolved without having a sexual basis. I confess that the plunging into sexuality in theory and practice is not to my taste. But what have my taste and my feeling about what is seemly and what is unseemly to do with the question of what is true? [Cranefield, 1958, pp. 319-320].

In 1925, Freud wrote in his obituary of Breuer:

> We psycho-analysts, who have long been familiar with the idea of devoting hundreds of sessions to one single patient, can form no conception of how novel such a procedure must have seemed forty-five years ago. It must have called for a large amount of personal interest and, if the phrase can be allowed, of medical libido, but also for a considerable degree of freedom in thought and certainty of judgement. . . . It seems that Breuer's researches were wholly original, and were directed only by the hints offered to him by the material of his case. . . . My merit lay chiefly in reviving in Breuer an interest which seemed to have become extinct, and in then urging him on to publication. A kind of reserve which was characteristic of him, an inner modesty, surprising in a man of such brilliant personality, had led him to keep his astonishing discovery secret for so long that not all of it

was any longer new. I found reason later to suppose that a purely emotional factor, too, had given him an aversion to further work on the elucidation of the neuroses. He had come up against something that is never absent—his patient's transference on to her physician, and he had not grasped the impersonal nature of this process [1925c, pp. 279-280].

It may be that Breuer was even more frightened of the personal countertransference reactions he perceived; his attempts at self-cure, especially when external reality too closely approximated his own repressed longings for his young attractive mother who died "in the blossom of her youth and beauty" at the height of his Oedipal conflict, caused Breuer to deny, withdraw, and attempt to isolate himself from what was too threatening. Yet there was a pull toward Freud's theories, which attracted him and in which he partially believed. Breuer's ambivalence toward Freud's ideas may have been necessitated by his own defensive needs.

IV. MANIFESTATIONS OF BREUER'S INTRAPSYCHIC CONFLICTS

Breuer, the careful observer and scientist, researcher and experimentalist, could report the behavior of his famous patient in great detail. He could not, however, discover hidden meanings, latent aims, or genetic roots. Instead, he focused on phenomenology. There is no anamnestic material in the reported Anna O. case. Breuer preferred his ontological hypnoid explanation to Freud's idea of defense neuroses, perhaps to avoid the threat to his own defensive structures. Although not opposed to the concept of the role of adult sexuality in hysteria, he could not accept the importance of infantile sexuality that Freud discovered and emphasized. It is suggested that, to serve his own defensive needs, Breuer sought physiological and phenomenological explanations and avoided genetic and dynamic concepts. In this way he could preserve his repression of aggressive and libidinal, maternal and paternal components of the Oedipal conflicts, greatly reinforced and fixated by his mother's death in his childhood. To discover more of psychoanalysis would have led to exposure and confrontation of his infantile neurosis, and this Breuer could not do. He withdrew from his patient, from other similar clinical situations, from Freud's theories which threatened him, and finally from Freud himself.[d] Breuer could observe and inquire of the outside, but he could not inquire of the "inside."

On one level Breuer's involvement and fascination with Anna O. seems to have reflected his own curiosity, his secret "study," and perhaps his Oedipal wishes toward her in a mother transference. In addition, there seems to have been an identification with her as the mourning Oedipal child. Anna O. was mourning not only for her dead father during her treatment with Breuer, but also for the Oedipal father who gave the baby to another. Her knowledge of Breuer's wife's pregnancy may have revived this earlier, never-resolved conflict from childhood.

Perhaps as a result of his identification with his teacher father, and in a brother transference to Sigmund Freud (later to Wilhelm Fliess, and still later to other younger physicians), Breuer could set the spark and allow the genius of Freud to discover and develop what he himself could not do. In his relationships with the older Oppolzer, Hering, Brücke, and others, Breuer may have replicated the son-father transference as it related to his giving, educating, and encouraging father. These multiple transferences, remaining from late childhood, were relatively nonconflictual and did not interfere with Breuer's work or development. However, the Anna O. relationship was threatening on several counts: the dangerous revival of repressed Oedipal conflicts, of repressed mourning for the dead mother, and of ambivalent feelings toward his brother. This may shed light on Breuer's withdrawal from Anna O. (who had the same name as his mother, Bertha, and who was young and attractive), on his reluctance to write about the case much later, and on his ambivalence about accepting Freud's ideas and subsequently Freud himself.

[d] Freud, conversely, was clearly disillusioned by Breuer's inability to persevere and responded with more than appropriate anger to the discovery of the clay feet of one of his idealized mentors. So Sancho Panza's wicked enchanters are able not only to transform a Dulcinea into a coarse peasant but also to reduce a great scientist into an obscurantist!

Confirmatory evidence is provided by Schlessinger (1965), who has elucidated the possible significance of Breuer's reference in *Studies on Hysteria* to Faust's mysterious researches as follows:

At the end of the first section of the theoretical chapter that Breuer contributed to *Studies on Hysteria*, he apologetically noted that before he could discuss the concept of abreaction, he must take the reader back to the basic problems of the nervous system. He wrote: "A feeling of oppression is bound to accompany any such descent to the 'Mothers' [i.e., exploration of the depths]. But any attempt at getting at the roots of a phenomenon inevitably leads in this way to basic problems which cannot be evaded. I hope therefore that the abstruseness of the following discussion may be viewed with indulgence" (Breuer and Freud, 1893-1895, p. 192).

The reference to the "Mothers" is an allusion to Faust's mysterious researches in Goethe's *Faust*, Part II, Act I. Viewed as a dramatic association to Breuer's state of mind, it offers striking testimony that he was grappling with the content of the Oedipus complex and was under the increased unconscious influence of it. He was forced to mobilize his ego defenses against the impact of the "activated" Oedipus complex; he did so by turning to a physiological discussion of intracerebral tonic excitations.

Goethe wrote Part II of *Faust* when he was an octogenarian, although the essential outlines of the work were clear to him some 30 years earlier. It is a grand allegory in which Faust typifies man as a symbolic figure engaged in a titanic struggle with his own passions against a backdrop of the political, social, and cultural developments of the ages. Faust grows weary of the artificial life of the court of the German Emperor, after achieving a place of power and influence by introducing a new financial system provided by Mephistopheles. When the Emperor demands that Helena and Paris be called from the Shades, Faust readily agrees to provide this entertainment for the court. In preparation for the accomplishment of this awesome feat, Mephistopheles sends him to the mysterious mothers (goddesses who dwell below, in an internal void, without space, place, or time) to be instructed in knowledge of the essence of beauty and the means of evoking models of beauty. On Faust's return, apparitions of Paris, a half-naked beautiful youth, and Helena, the seductive older woman, are raised in a special drama presented for the Emperor. The narrator, an astrologer, announces the name of the drama, "The Rape of Helena," as a youth, Paris, in response to her charms, clasps Helena passionately as though to carry her off. Faust is an enraged onlooker and determines that he must make Helena doubly his by rescuing her now that he has retrieved her from the dead. He attempts to seize the apparition, but the form grows dim as he turns against the youth, Paris. There is an explosion and Faust falls upon the earth. The Spirits dissolve in a vapor.

Faust is overcome with love and longing for Helena, the personfication of Beauty, and begins a pilgrimage toward her through a *Walpurgisnacht*. He determines to search for her in the nether world and is guided by Chiron to Manto, the daughter of Aesculapius, with the advice that she has healing powers for "an ecstacy that seems madness to the spirits." Faust will not hear of healing, but insists on pursuing his quest. He secures Manto's help and, finding Helena before the palace of Menelaus, joins her on the throne as a successful suitor, even though Menelaus, Helena's husband, is present and alive. In a fulfillment of their love, Helena bears him a child, Euphorion, who later vanishes in flame (like Icarus) when he attempts to fly. Only his garments and lyre are left behind. From the depths, Euphorion cries out to his mother, Helena, not to leave him alone in the gloomy void. Helena responds to his plea and takes her leave of Faust in a last embrace. Faust thus loses her once again, retaining only her garment and veil.

In his creative resolution, Goethe describes Faust, enlightened and elevated, his aim to bend Nature to the service of man. Faust conquers a great stretch of half-submerged land from the aimless force of unruly elements. Faust demonstrates his new-found wisdom and restraint, refusing to be implicated by Mephistopheles in the seizure of a little cottage on the

downs owned by an old couple. He takes pleasure in building
happy homes for coming generations of men. In Heaven,
Mephistopheles loses the struggle with the angels for the soul
of Faust.[3]

To the psychoanalyst, Goethe's magnificent poetry relates
to the Oedipal struggle and its resolution. As a variant of the
Oedipal theme, it is fascinating that Faust pursues a dead
mother. Symbolically, the dead mother may achieve universality as the mother of the past, but of course it has special
significance for the man who has lost his mother through
death and more particularly through death in the Oedipal
period of his life. The theme of irreconcilable longing for the
mother is poignantly reinforced by the poet in recounting the
episode of Helena's decision to heed her son's pleas and join
him in death, when Euphorion is the victim of his reckless
desire to fly (symbolically a representation of penile erection
and masculine endeavor).

[3] Gerhart Piers has called my attention to other phallic and maternal symbolism
in this section of *Faust*. He has translated two sections of Act I, Scene 5, to read:

Mephistopheles: Unwillingly do I reveal the higher
secrets. Goddesses are enthroned in
solemn solitude,
There is no space around them, time much
less,
To speak of them is but embarrassment.
It is—the Mothers!
Faust (startled): Mothers!
Mephistopheles: Are you—scared?
Faust: The Mothers! Mothers! It sounds so
eerily!
Mephistopheles: And that it is. . . .

Mephistopheles: Here, take this key.
Faust: That little thing!
Mephistopheles: First grasp it and do not rate it small.
Faust: It grows right in my hand! It glows, it shines!
Mephistopheles: You noticed soon what you possess in it!
The Key will scent the right spot soon:
Follow it down; it guides you to the Mothers.
Faust (shudders): The Mothers! It always hits me like a
stroke!
What is this word that I don't want to hear?

The essential content of Goethe's poetry suggests that Breuer's reference to it had a profound rather than a casual import, for it bears directly on Breuer's deepest motivations as a psychological researcher and a human being. It impinges on a central theme of his life, his ties to a beautiful young mother who died in childbirth when he was between the ages of three and four, confronting him with a disastrous loss at the height of the Oedipal period. After Breuer had left the field of psychological research, he developed a meaningful relationship with the poetess Maria von Ebner-Eschenbach, a woman 12 years his senior, with whom he engaged in a rich and tender correspondence for 25 years. Breuer seems to have succeeded in mastering a part of his traumatic past, without benefit of insight, in his relationship to Maria von Ebner-Eschenbach— an asexual platonic correspondence, a poetic transfiguration of the relationship to a newly found idealized mother figure (Meyer, 1928).

Meyer notes that his inspection of this lively correspondence revealed Breuer's continuing penetrating and manifold deliberations and also his emotionality. Thus Breuer wrote: "I don't know, usually I am really not such a passionate letter writer; but when you touch a point, the entire song goes off, as if I were a music box gone crazy." Breuer seemingly had an open system about all events which did not threaten his repressed infantile neurosis. Thus in a 1906 letter to Maria von Ebner-Eschenbach, he discussed the question of the relationship of character and talent:

> . . . he shows how they can coexist entirely independently of each other, quoting the incongruities in this regard in a great number of artists and philosophers from Filippino Lippi and the agnostic Pietro Perugino down to Schopenhauer, H. Heine and R. Wagner; how erroneous it is if one always wants to demonstrate the great human being in the great artist: granted the artist has to be able to empathize with noble feelings, just like the good actor; but his "will," that is, his moral character, can be quite differently oriented without influencing his artistic creativity. The creatively gifted and active man, however, has one obligation toward his work which—like the mother's obligation toward her child—is detached from all the other areas of obli-

gation: whether his work thrives depends not on the good or bad character of the creator but on whether he is able to go forth with his work [Meyer, 1928].

The implications of this for Breuer himself seem to indicate a dim awareness of an inner conflict which did not interfere with external work. Breuer's creative productivity was not inhibited, but was channeled into nonconflictual fields. His "medical passion," his wish to help younger men, and his efforts to "rescue" his patients also remained alive in him up to his death. "Following the outbreak of the war [World War I], in spite of his seventy-three years, he took over the treatment of sick soldiers in a far distant suburban hospital for wounded, and commuted there daily in the most cumbersome fashion on overcrowded trolleys, regardless of weather or cold or of his own fatigue—hardly reserving a couple of summer weeks for vacation" (Meyer, 1928).

What might have been traumatic to Breuer, had he not avoided it by withdrawing from the situation which threatened his defensive structure, in the hands of the genius Freud became a stimulus leading to further self-discoveries as well as to more general formulations and theories of the mind. We cannot hold it against Breuer that he was frightened of infantile sexuality and the Oedipal conflict; only a few great artists had discovered it before his time. The support which Breuer gave to Freud was very helpful in allowing Freud to go forward. Breuer communicated his knowledge and his wish to discover the new to Freud. Freud was capable of using this help and could move forward and beyond Breuer.

V. AMBIVALENCE AND TRANSFERENCE

The treatment of Bertha Pappenheim as it related to her own experience of childhood sibling losses, her mourning for her father, her ambivalent relationship with her mother, her Oedipal-phallic involvements as they may have been repeated with Breuer and his wife, as well as the very interesting subsequent course of her adult life have been discussed elsewhere (see Pollock, 1971, 1972, 1973).

At this point, however, I wish to refer to the Fliess correspondence (Freud, 1887-1902) which reveals further evidence for some of the ideas suggested above. E. Kris (1950b, p. 8) notes in the Introduction that it was Breuer who first advised Fliess to attend Freud's lectures on neurology in the fall of 1887. In 1892, Fliess married a Viennese girl, Ida Bondy, who belonged to the circle of Breuer's patients. Breuer's paternal attitude, seen earlier with Freud, seemed evident again with Fliess. (Fliess was two years younger than Freud.)[4] It was an attitude based on identification with his father and also on his need to take care of a younger brother, a situation which was repeated in his relationship with Freud.

Not only did Breuer refer patients, make loans, give gifts and advice to Freud, but he often took Freud with him on his rounds. As Jones writes: "These sometimes covered a considerable distance so that they would have to spend the night away from Vienna. On one such occasion in Baden, Breuer entered Freud's name in the *Gasthaus* book as his brother, so that Freud would not have to tip the waiter" (1953, p. 168). The manifest reason given for this seems thin.

Both Freud and Breuer were Brücke's pupils. They first met at the Institute of Physiology in the late 1870's. Sharing the same interests and outlook, they became friends. In some ways this tie with Brücke seemed to repeat a father-brother-brother situation that occurred later in the Breuer-Freud-Fliess relationship. Freud was Breuer's patient, and as late as 1894 consulted Breuer about his own ill health (Freud, 1887-1902, Letter 17).

Breuer's ambivalence toward Freud's theory of the importance of infantile sexuality in the etiology of the neuroses is also revealed in a series of Freud's letters to Fliess.

> I am delighted to be able to tell you that our theory of hysteria (recollection, abreaction, etc.) is going to appear in the *Neurologisches Zentralblatt* for January 1st, 1893, in the form of a

---

[4]This may have been significant for Freud, who had lost his next younger sibling, Julius, when he, Freud, was 19 months old. Freud wrote in a letter to Fliess (dated March 10, 1897): ". . . I welcomed my one-year younger brother (who died within a few months) with ill wishes and real infantile jealousy, and . . . his death left the germ of guilt in me" (Freud, 1887-1902, p. 219). Freud's relationship with Fliess may be important in this connection. Furthermore Fliess's (dead) sister was named Pauline, as was Freud's niece, who was one year younger and the sister of his older nephew John.

detailed preliminary communication. It has meant a long battle with my collaborator [Letter 11, Dec. 18, 1892].

Breuer...is a new man. One cannot help liking him again without any reservations....Not only does he spread your reputation abroad in Vienna, but he has become fully converted to my theory of sexuality. He has become quite a different fellow from the one we have been used to [Letter 24, May 25, 1895].

Not long ago Breuer made a big speech to the physicians' society about me, putting himself forward as a convert to belief in sexual aetiology. When I thanked him privately for this he spoiled my pleasure by saying: "But all the same I *don't* believe it." Can you make head or tail of that? I cannot [Letter 35, Nov. 8, 1895].

In 1896, Freud wrote: "Breuer and I have in earlier communications maintained that the psychical traumas (in hysteria) are concerned with the sexual life" (Jones, 1953, p. 254). Jones guesses that "Breuer's acceptance referred rather to the later ages, and what he balked at was Freud's views concerning the incestuous seduction of children" (p. 254).

After the summer of 1894, Breuer and Freud never collaborated again. In a communication dated June 22, 1894, Freud was complaining of the loneliness he felt "since the scientific intercourse with Breuer had ceased" (p. 296). The main reversal in Freud's feeling came in the spring of 1896, a date which coincides with the onset of the more passionate phase of his relations with Fliess (p. 254).

In a letter dated March 1, 1896, Freud wrote: "I believe he has never forgiven me for having lured him into writing the *Studien* with me and so committed him to something definite" (p. 312). But then a seeming reversal occurs again.

...An evening patient has left me. It was my most difficult case, and the most certain in regard to aetiology; for four years I could not get near it, and it was the only case sent me by Breuer. He kept sending the girl back to me after I had sent her away in blank despair. Last year I at last managed to get on terms with her, and this year I at last succeeded in finding the key, i.e., convinced myself that keys found elsewhere fitted her and, so far as the short time (December until now) permitted, I have deeply and vitally altered her condition. She took leave of me today with the words: "You've done wonders for me." She told me that, when she told Breuer of her extraordinary improvement, he clapped his hands and exclaimed again and again: "So he is right after all!" [Letter 135, May 16, 1900].

I did not give the lectures announced last Monday in the *Neue Freie Presse*. It was...Breuer who had been badgered by the Philosophical Society, who pestered me to do it. I reluctantly agreed, and then, when I came to preparing it, I found I should have to bring in all sorts of intimate and sexual things which would be quite unsuitable for a mixed audience of people who were strangers to me. So I wrote a letter calling it off [Letter 142, Feb. 15, 1901].

In a later letter to Jung, dated November 21, 1909, Freud indicates his seeming insight into Breuer's ambivalence about the sexual etiology theory, when he writes about Anna O.'s term "chimney sweeping" for the cathartic procedure: "The reason why a chimney sweep is supposed to bring good luck is that sweeping a chimney is an unconscious symbol of coitus, which is something of which Breuer certainly never dreamed" (Jones, 1955, p. 445).

At an earlier time, however, there is an indication that this may not have been so. In a letter (Number 14) to Martha Bernays, dated July 13, 1883, Freud writes (E. Freud, 1960, pp. 40-41):

Today was the hottest, most excruciating day of the whole season, I was really almost crazy with exhaustion. Realizing that I was badly in need of refreshment, I went to see Breuer, from whom I have just returned, rather late. He had a headache, the poor man, and was taking salicyl. The first thing he did was to chase me into the bathtub, which I left rejuvenated. My first thought on accepting this wet hospitality was: If Marty were here, she would say: 'This is just what we must have, too." Of course, my girl, and no matter how many years it will take, we shall have it, but the only miracle I am counting on is that you will love me as long as that. Then we had supper upstairs in our shirtsleeves (at the moment I am writing in a somewhat more advanced negligé), and then came a lengthy medical conversation on moral insanity and nervous diseases and strange case histories—your friend Bertha Pappenheim also cropped up—and then we became rather personal and very intimate and he told me a number of things about his wife and children and asked me to repeat what he had said only "after you are married to Martha." And then I opened up and said: "This same Martha who at the moment has a sore throat in Düsternbrook, is in reality a sweet Cordelia, and we are already on terms of the closest intimacy and can say anything to each other." Whereupon he said he too always calls his wife by that name because she is incapable of displaying affection to others, even including her own father. And the ears of both Cordelias, the one of thirty-seven and the other of twenty-two, must have been ringing while we were thinking of them with serious tenderness.

The reference to Bertha Pappenheim is of interest; however, association of both Martha Bernays and Mathilde Breuer to Cordelia may be significant.

Literary references, as already demonstrated above, are important inner as well as outer communications, and one should attempt to understand what they may mean. It is impossible to know with certainty what Breuer or Freud had in mind with the comparison to Cordelia.

In "The Theme of The Three Caskets" (1913), Freud discussed King Lear and identified Cordelia as the Death-goddess, the "dumb" one who "loves and is silent," Death itself. He notes that "Lear is not only an old man: he is a dying man." In the final scene Lear carries Cordelia's dead body on to the stage. "Cordelia is Death. If we reverse the situation it becomes intelligible and familiar to us. She is the Death-goddess who, like the Valkyrie in German mythology, carries away the dead hero from the battlefield" (p. 301).

Freud concludes his essay by saying that

> ...what is represented here are the three inevitable relations that a man has with a woman—the woman who bears him, the woman who is his mate and the woman who destroys him; or that they are the three forms taken by the figure of the mother in the course of a man's life—the mother herself, the beloved one who is chosen after her pattern, and lastly the Mother Earth who receives him once more. But it is in vain that an old man yearns for the love of woman as he had it first from his mother; the third of the Fates alone, the silent Goddess of Death, will take him into her arms [p. 301].

We can see that his interpretation of the meaning of Cordelia to Lear parallels that of the earlier reference to "the Mothers"—the longing for yet fear of reunion with the mother.

The linking of this with the Oedipal conflict was spelled out by Freud in his letter to James S.H. Bransom in 1934. There he states that "the last small section of the book discloses the secret meaning of the tragedy, the repressed incestuous claims on the daughter's love. . . . Cordelia still clings to him, her love for him is her holy secret. When asked to reveal it publicly she has to refuse defiantly and remain dumb." Later in the letter Freud comments that it is curious that in the play there is no mention whatever of the mother, that there must have been one, but the play deals primarily with the father's relations to his three daughters (Jones, 1957, pp. 457-458). I might add parenthetically that Breuer had three daughters, and the last child was his daughter, Dora, who was born on March 11, 1882, while Breuer was actively treating Bertha Pappenheim. My inference is that Breuer was relating to Bertha Pappenheim as Lear did to Cordelia; the reference to Cordelia is in the July 13, 1883 letter.

In searching the literature on Lear, I have found no mention of Lear's wife or of the mother of his daughters. The absence of his mother played an important role in Breuer's personality development. In the play itself, Lear's wife is mentioned only once (Act II, Scene IV, lines 133-134), when he says to Regan,

I would divorce me from thy mother's tomb,
Sepulchring an adultress.

It is beyond the scope of this study to comment further on this passage except to note that the one time Lear does refer to his wife, it relates death and sexual infidelity—a theme of great importance to Josef Breuer.

Returning to the Bransom letter, Freud concludes by referring to his earlier interpretation of the Lear story in "The Theme of the Three Caskets." He states that in this essay he tried to establish "the mythological content of the material, to which the connection between father and daughter was originally alien. With the insertion of this feature the saga gains a psychological interest which puts the earlier one in the background; I hope to show that in Shakespeare's Lear the old meaning shimmers at times through the new one" (Jones, 1957, pp. 457-458). Freud did not do this; however, the connection is not difficult to demonstrate.

Ella Freeman Sharpe (1946) suggests that Cordelia, emerging as a tender, sincere, forgiving figure, is a maternal image. She cites the Fool who tells Lear, "Thou has made thy daughter thy mother" in support of her thesis. Pauncz (1952) believes Lear is erotically involved with Cordelia and compares the relationship to a reversed Oedipus complex. He calls attention to the absence of Lear's wife and the mother of Lear's children in the drama. Cordelia is a motherless child, left with a father who initially disowns her but is subsequently reunited with her in death. It is Cordelia who tells Lear in Act I:

> You have begot me, bred me, loved me: I
> Return those duties back as right fit,
> Obey you, love you, and most honour you.
> Why have my sisters' husbands, if they say
> They love you all? Haply, when I shall wed,
> That lord...shall carry
> Half my love with him.

In Act V, when Lear meets Cordelia, he says:

> ...Come, let's away to prison:
> We two alone will sing like birds: the cage.

One may speculate about what Freud and Breuer had in mind when they talked of "strange case histories—your friend Bertha Pappenheim," "rather personal and very intimate" matters about his wife and child which Breuer asked Freud not to repeat to Martha until "after you are married," and then the Cordelia references. It sounds like the opening phases of the recognition of the then yet unnamed and undiscovered Oedipus complex. In any event, it was the first written reference to the later famous Anna O.

Jones feels that the first sign of some change in Breuer's attitude toward Freud, a shift from his former encouragement to one of "damping any enthusiasm of Freud's, both in his personal life and in his later work in psychopathology," was revealed one evening at the Breuers when Freud spoke of his approaching marriage: "when Mathilde Breuer entered into the theme with interest, Breuer started up crying, 'For God's sake, don't egg him on to get married,' and he advised Freud not to think of it for another two years" (Jones, 1953, p. 145).

Jones believes that Breuer's "attitude had been most satis-factory so long as Freud was a young son [or, I might add, a young brother] in need of help, but he seemed to grudge his growing independence as many fathers do with their children."

Freud sensed Breuer's reluctance to write about Bertha Pappenheim and tried to mend it by drawing closer to Breuer; however, as he notes in his letter to Minna Bernays (July 13, 1891), he was not optimistic about a full reconciliation:

> The "Aphasia" has just come out, as you will see by the enclosed, and has already caused me deep disappointment. Breuer's reception of it was such a strange one; he hardly thanked me for it, was very embarrassed, made only derogatory comments on it, couldn't recollect any of its good points, and in the end tried to soften the blow by saying that it was very well written. I believe his thoughts are miles away. In the midst of all this he enquired whether Dr. P. had arrived, and when the latter did turn up and shrank back at sight of me, I, of course, left at once. The breach between us is widening all the time, and my efforts to patch things up with the dedication have probably had the opposite effect [E. Freud, 1960, p. 229].

Freud's paper on "A Case of Successful Treatment by Hypnotism" (1892-1893) suggests that he still sought to main-tain at least theoretical closeness to Breuer. In this report, Freud seeks to link Breuer's idea of the "hypnoid" state with his own ideas about hysteria. This essay was almost con-temporary with the "Preliminary Communication" he wrote with Breuer in 1893 (Breuer and Freud, 1893-1895).

As we have seen above in the Fliess letters, the breach was not yet one that was fully externally established. Internally, however, Breuer's barrier had to be maintained, even though it meant a rupture in the very meaningful relationship with Freud.

James Strachey (1955a), in his Introduction to *Studies on Hysteria*, comments that a study of Breuer's contributions to the *Studies* yields "the picture of a man half-afraid of his own remarkable discoveries. It was inevitable that he should be even more disconcerted by the premonition of still more unsettling discoveries yet to come; and it was inevitable that

Freud in turn should feel hampered and irritated by his yoke-fellow's uneasy hesitations" (p. xxvi).

CONCLUSIONS

Inhibition in the service of defense can interfere with creativity at various levels—observation, interpretation, abstraction to more general theory or hypothesis formation. In the case of Josef Breuer, an attempt has been made to explain his ambivalence toward the role of infantile sexuality in the etiology of the neuroses, and to the concept of defenses. Creativity at the level of theory formation requires neutralized energy and utilization of the conflict-free sphere of the ego. Although the precise determinants of the creative process are as yet unknown, encapsulated, repressed intrapsychic conflicts relating to crucial developmental periods and relationships can be defensively anticreative. The creativity of Josef Breuer, particularly that connected with his contributions to psychoanalytic clinical theory, has been studied as illustrative of this proposition. Freud, unlike Breuer, presented his propositions with supporting evidence in a logically orderly fashion using deduction and induction, introspection, and empathy. Breuer, on the other hand, though capable of such logical presentation and a proven observer, experimentalist, and theoretician in other fields, presented ideas that were original and potentially useful, but in a fashion which reflected his wish to distance himself from threatening psychological formulations. Instead, his models were more anchored to physiological explanations. Breuer's subsequent, albeit ambivalent, disavowal of psychoanalysis, and especially of the infantile sexual etiology of the neuroses, seems to indicate a more personal need for distancing. An investigation of Breuer's life suggests possible reasons for his need to withdraw from something which, in truth, he had discovered. These relate to the death of his mother at the height of his Oedipal period (ages three to four) when his only sibling, a brother, was born. Persisting transferences have been postulated and evidence presented to demonstrate their existence. When external involvements threatened the eruption of repressed conflicts and existing defenses, flight mechanisms, including avoidance and withdrawal, occurred. This interfered with any additional theoretical contributions Breuer could make to psychoanalysis.

PART III

THE CREATION OF PSYCHOANALYSIS

7

STUDIES ON HYSTERIA:
A Methodological Evaluation

JOHN E. GEDO, MELVIN SABSHIN,
LEO SADOW, and NATHAN SCHLESSINGER

[*Freud as Scientist.* The following Chapter was the initial study undertaken by the Workshop on the Scientific Methodology of Psychoanalysis of the Chicago Institute. In some ways, it was the outgrowth of a seminar on psychoanalytic research offered to advanced candidates at the Institute by the then Director of Research, George H. Pollock. The senior author of this paper participated in the seminar on a number of occasions both as a student and as a coteacher, while one of the topics of discussion was the progressive development of Freud's psychological studies during the early 1890's. The paper is an attempt to document the impression gained by repeated reading of Freud's early writings on psychology, including the collaborative work with Breuer, that psychoanalysis as a science evolved in an internally coherent manner.

In 1962, Robert Waelder published a schema for the classification of every proposition forming part of a clinical science in accord with the degree to which each such proposition had been raised beyond the level of concrete observation. Waelder's schema, although it is by no means the only conceivable or meaningful way of classifying psychoanalytic statements, provided the first serviceable method for reducing the mass of Freud's communications into a series of discrete

First published in *Journal of the American Psychoanalytic Association*, 12: 734-751, 1964.

statements, the logical relations among which could be tested. Because a historical review of the clinical evidence on which the basic concepts of psychoanalysis were founded must begin with the case reports in *Studies on Hysteria* (Breuer and Freud, 1893-1895) the authors of this chapter reduced the book by Breuer and Freud to a series of discrete propositions. All of these were then cross-correlated, yielding a complex chart which showed the logical connection among observations, interpretations, generalizations, and more abstract theoretical statements. This chart enabled the authors to differentiate those propositions which were derived from the clinical evidence presented in this book by inductive reasoning from those others whose origins could not be traced. Some of the latter may have been arrived at through induction, but from observational data which Breuer and Freud did not make public; the majority of these propositions were probably the result of deductive reasoning, based on the tenets of the biological science accepted at the time. These were the principles of the physiology generally referred to as those of the "school of Helmholtz," a designation called into question by Ellenberger (1970). Both Breuer and Freud absorbed these principles from their revered teacher, Ernst Brücke, in whose laboratory they had first encountered each other almost 20 years before the publication of their collaborative work.

The application of the foregoing method yielded surprising results. Instead of showing the kind of logical progression in the growth of psychoanalytic theory which had been anticipated, it illuminated a sharp divergence between the scientific styles of Breuer and Freud in their respective contributions to *Studies on Hysteria*, albeit this difference may have produced a useful complementarity between them. Breuer displayed great freedom in hypothesis building based on deductive reasoning; Freud, on the other hand, clearly subjected his inspirational hunches to thorough inductive revision in the light of the clinical evidence available to him. In other words, the internally consistent evolution of psychoanalysis was a process which took place exclusively within Freud's mind. However necessary Breuer may have been to him until 1895 as a supporter, an idealized model, and a source of confirmation for the worth of his ideas, by the time the *Studies on Hysteria* were being written, the presence of an alternative voice for the communication of the findings of psychoanalysis could act only as a source of confusion and delay. Hence we may infer that a cessation of the scientific collaboration with Breuer would have been inevitable even if the latter had not recoiled from some of the "unseemly" findings of the joint research and, if Schur (1972) is correct in his estimate of the nature of Freud's cardiac difficulties in the mid-1890's, even if Breuer's activities as his personal physician had proved to be more satisfactory than Freud found them to be.

It might be added that this conclusion of the Chicago study would probably have come as something of a surprise to Sigmund Freud. At least, it did so to his daughter Anna, who told the senior author that her father, to the end of his life, had continued to regard Josef Breuer as the model of scientific rigor, in contrast to his own propensity for theoretical daring.

The method used for this study has not been applied to further portions of the psychoanalytic edifice because of the escalating difficulty of cross-correlating the rapidly expanding number of analytic propositions after 1895. Such studies would be quite useful, and they will become feasible with the application of computer technology. This realization is in part responsible for the transformation of the Workshop on Methodology into the Chicago Psychoanalytic Indexing Research Group—*Eds.*]

I

Psychoanalysis as a science seems to be rediscovering its classical past. The publication of James Strachey's 24-volume English edition of Freud's *Psychological Works*, Ernest Jones's extensive Freud biography (1953, 1955, 1957) and his autobiographical fragment (1959), the Fliess letters (Freud, 1887-1902) and sundries of Freud's correspondence with others (E. Freud, 1960), two volumes of the *Minutes of the Vienna Psychoanalytic Society*, and doubtless many other source materials which will soon appear provide us with the archives through which in our own psychoanalytic development we can recapitulate that of our science.[a]

The training process has always involved some review of the historical development of psychoanalysis, and in his lifetime Freud wrote several expository essays on this theme (1910a, 1914c, 1923a, 1925b, 1925c, 1926b, 1935). In the past quarter century, however (and, if we except Freud's own historical works, during the entire course of the psychoanalytic movement), there has been a relative neglect of the study of our roots. Concepts from the early days of Freud's analytic activity have continued to be used without much attention being paid to their empirical origins, often leading to reification, the dangers of which Hartmann, Kris, and Loewenstein (1946) have discussed so cogently. Consequently, the time may be ripe for re-examination of the creation of our classical psychoanalytic concepts.[b]

Historical studies always run the danger of lapsing into a stultifying scholasticism, either extolling some dogma or engaging in sterile iconoclasm. They prove to be fruitful only if used to discover currently pertinent questions as well as answers; the re-emphasis of old insights will have value when it is the outcome of genuine intellectual working through from evidence to conclusions. The spirit of our times seems to invite this process. For instance, Rapaport (1959) made an attempt at an exposition of the current structure of psychoanalytic theory, in the course of which he alluded briefly to "the initial

[a] As of early 1974, this list can be amplified with the publication of the final volumes of the *Minutes* (Nunberg and Federn, 1962-1974), and of Freud's correspondence with L. Andreas-Salomé (Pfeiffer, 1966), O. Pfister (Meng and Freud, 1963), E. Weiss (1970), E. Fluss (Freud, 1872-1874, see Chapter 3), and most significantly, with Karl Abraham (H. Abraham and E. Freud, 1966). The appearance of the Freud-Jung correspondence has just taken place (McGuire, 1974). The Silberstein letters (see Chapter 4) may be published in the near future. Another document of importance is the "Freud Journal" of Lou Andreas-Salomé (Leavy, 1964).

[b] A decade after this was written, the field of psychoanalytic history is no longer as sparse as the authors then judged it to be. To mention only the most prominent studies published in the interval: Anderson (1962), Amacher (1965), Eissler (1971b), Ellenberger (1970), Schur (1972), and Stewart (1968). The individual papers on the history of psychoanalysis have been too numerous to mention here; the interested reader may consult the bibliography in Ellenberger (1970, see especially pp. 550-570) as well as the one in this volume.

evidential grounds for the assumptions of the system and their strategic character." He was referring, of course, to the clinical evidence from which Freud had induced his hypotheses. Rapaport's concise monograph could barely point toward the fruitful possibilities of studies of the relation of psychoanalytic theory to the case material upon which it was presumably based. There are, however, a number of other investigations with the same orientation, ranging from Holt's (1962) article on the evolution of the concepts of free and bound psychic energy in Freud's writings to the extensive collaborative concept research carried out at Hampstead and reported by Nagera (1969-1970). These lines of parallel inquiry are indicative of efforts to survey our origins.

It was in attempting to devise a coherent framework for an exposition of the development of psychoanalysis as a science that we began to grapple with the history of the process by which Freud arrived at his theoretical conclusions. Our focus of interest soon narrowed to his published works, and we chose to start with his case histories, partly (it would seem) to follow Freud's intellectual tracks—i.e., to follow in our work one cardinal attribute of psychoanalysis, its emphasis on a historical point of view. As we wrote critical summaries of the major case histories, our interest in the relation of empirical data to theoretical conclusions increased. We decided to undertake a systematic examination of the scientific methodology of Freud's opus. The initial step consisted in a thorough sifting of all of his published works to prepare a list of all of the clinical material in them. We have found references to over 200 cases, most of them Freud's own patients, some patients of colleagues, others studied only through biographical or autobiographical materials. The most important case history of them all remains unavailable except for fragments—unless, of course, one presumes to use Jones's *Life* and the Fliess correspondence as sources about Freud's self-analysis. Our task was to organize the mass of clinical evidence reported by Freud, to determine what his purpose was in publishing precisely these data, and to evaluate how much of the edifice of psychoanalytic theory is inductively based on this empirical foundation. Thus the logic of our search impelled us to outline all of psychoanalytic theory and to do so along the historical time axis. This necessity gave our research its ultimate design; in order to trace Freud's construction of psychoanalytic theory, we had to study his papers in the order of their compositon. This approach focused .on the relation of observations to theory building, the first psychological work of consequence having been *Studies on Hysteria* (1893-1895) which contains almost half of Freud's major case histories.

For this particular step in our study we used Waelder's conceptual classification of psychoanalytic propositions in his review, "Psychoanalysis, Scientific Method, and Philosophy" (1962). He ordered these propositions hierarchically in terms of the axis of increasing remoteness from concrete clinical data. We reduced the *Studies on Hysteria* to a series of statements, each of which was classified according to Waelder's schema, as follows:

1. *The data of observation*—facts of conscious life, derivatives from the unconscious, and their configurations.

2. *Clinical interpretations*—interconnections among the data of observation and their relationships with other behavior.

3. *Clinical generalizations*—statements about a particular type or category (e.g., sex, an age group, a symptom, a disease, etc.).

4. *Clinical theory*—concepts implicit in clinical interpretations or logically derived from them (e.g., repression, defense, etc.).

5. *Metapsychology*—more abstract concepts, such as cathexis, psychic energy, etc.

6. *The author's philosophy or Weltanschauung* (e.g., scientific humanism).

The data of observation we call "lower-level" statements; clinical interpretations and generalizations we place at the middle levels of abstraction, while clinical theories and metapsychological propositions are at the highest levels. Their definitions will be amplified as we illustrate each category below. It should be emphasized that all levels beyond that of the data of observation contain some propositions which are merely hypotheses and others which have been validated. The term "clinical theory" does not imply anything about the validity of any hypothesis—it refers only to the position of the concept within the taxonomy of intellectual processes.

A complex cross-correlation was attempted between each proposition and all propositions on all other levels to which it was relevant. In this manner, we were able to retrace all the inductive and deductive reasoning Breuer and Freud had demonstrated in their respective sections of the book.[1]

II

We should like to state at the outset our disavowal of any preference for one-particular path to scientific truth over any other. Induction from the data of observation has acquired a totally irrational aura as the only legitimate scientific tool for theory building, probably as a consequence of the abuse of deductive methods during the era of scholasticism. It should be evident, however, that it is not deductive reasoning which constitutes the antiscientific core of a dogma—it is the refusal to submit the conclusions to appropriate validation studies. In reporting our work, we could choose to emphasize our findings about the evidential grounds for various propositions in the book. These could be reported only in a highly condensed manner in a presentation of this scope, however, and we believe that the impression of arbitrariness which would result would defeat our primary purpose of evaluating the scientific framework of psychoanalytic theory at its roots. Consequently,

[1]In reference to this, it will be recalled that only the reprint of the 1893 "Preliminary Communication" was signed by both authors. Aside from this, Breuer was responsible for the case history called "Anna O.," and for the "Theoretical" chapter; the remaining case histories and the chapter on "The Psychotherapy of Hysteria" were written by Freud alone. Ernest Jones (1953) has described in some detail the scientific rupture between the two which occurred between composition of the book and its publication, and Strachey (1955a) in his Introduction devotes several pages to "The Divergences between the Two Authors." While, of course, it is clear that Breuer and Freud did not publish all of the evidence upon which they based their interpretations, generalizations, and theories, we believe that our work permits us to describe a relatively unexplored aspect of their estrangement (see Sullivan, 1959)—the radically different processes of scientific methodology and concept formation employed by the two men, as demonstrated in this book.

we must omit extensive communication of these results and concentrate at this time on a handful of illustrations through which we hope to demonstrate the applicability of our method, as well as its limitations. By using these contributions of Breuer and Freud as examples, we wish to show a way of studying the scientific style of psychoanalytic researchers, thereby contributing to the understanding of creativity in our field (see Chapter 8).

The initial step in our study was the reduction of a book of 305 printed octavo pages to an outline consisting of a manageable number of discrete statements. The outcome, a 25-page (double-spaced typewritten) document, contains 309 separate propositions. It is perhaps self-evident that each of these constitutes one unit only as a matter of convenience, that smaller (i.e., more homogeneous) units would yield a more precise map of the book, but that the magnitude of the task of cross-correlating the individual statements is increased in geometric proportion to the number of units. This is not a crucial issue with regard to the reliability of our work, since this question is separate from that of the size of the units; it must be tested whatever unit size is chosen—i.e., a map may be reliable whatever its scale. Having chosen our scale so as to yield a convenient number of propositions, each of our units consists of a cluster of interrelated statements—each component of the cluster must belong to the same level of Waelder's classification as all the other components within the cluster.

We attempted to check reliability by assigning each section of the book to be outlined by at least two of us. The outlines produced were by no means identical, but the degree of consensus was consistently high. Discrepancies resulted from the omission of material judged by one or the other investigator as insignificant. The final list of statements includes the items selected by both investigators, eliminating the repetitions. We cannot claim total reliability and have no doubt that a more thorough sifting of the book would produce additional material. (This apparent source of error leads to our results being, if anything, an underestimation of the adequacy of the clinical evidence cited by the authors.) The problem of what to include could be solved only by the exercise of psychoanalytic intelligence and knowledge. One had to be able to recognize that a casual report of Emmy von N.'s insistence on being allowed to finish her intended subject is, indeed, an important new discovery which will lead toward the free-association technique, whereas the details of her complex hysterical symptoms were not to prove to be of any particular consequence.

Completion of the list of propositions in the book was followed by their classification according to Waelder's six-point schema. In practice, only five classes were used, since *Studies on Hysteria* contained no explicit expression of the authors' philosophy. Waelder's definitions of his categories are crisp and precise, but their application to the propositions we culled from the book did not always prove to be an easy task. Even at the simplest level, that of the "data of observation," it may be difficult to decide what is an observable "fact," what constitutes an inference by the observer, and how far the inference must go beyond description of a group of phenomena before it constitutes an interpretation. This particular question we resolved by defining each category to fit a range of propositions; i.e., as a segment of the continuum from the single description of a fact to abstract speculative explanatory attempts. This progression can be illustrated via restatement of the observed fact that Anna O.'s drinking inhibition disappeared when she relived her disgust about her governess's dog using a glass. We have stated this among the data of observation as "When spontaneous reliving [of a forgotten incident] with affect occurred, a symptom disappeared."

This observation already appears as an assertion in the "Preliminary Communication," where no specific evidence is cited for it. It thus becomes an explanation of a range of phenomena, and was therefore classified as the Clinical Interpretation, "When the precipitating event is recollected and its accompanying affect aroused and verbalized, the [hysterical] symptom disappears."

The attribution of the precipitation of the symptom to the forgotten event as well as the claim that the proposition is universally applicable are the inferences which require this statement to be classified as an interpretation.

A clinical generalization carries the process of abstraction further; it attempts to formulate a hypothesis to explain the phenomenon studied. An interpretation no longer refers to a concrete instance, but its accuracy for each instance is testable by the simple trying on of Cinderella's slipper; a generalization is a much more complex proposition which has to explain the interconnections among a number of observations and the interpretations derived from them. Thus, the interpretation just quoted rests squarely on the observation of the disappearance of Anna O.'s drinking inhibition—the first symptom removed by exploratory psychotherapy. Whatever additional evidence for it occurs in the book proves to be an exact duplication of this event. The generalization most directly related is: "The operative force of [forgotten traumatic] memories is ended when treatment allows the strangulated affect to find a way out to normal associative correction or removal by suggestion." Although the story of Anna O.'s symptom fits well within this explanatory framework, it is clear that much more evidence is needed to validate this generalization, which involves not only the issue of symptom removal by abreaction but also such questions as the normal discharge of affects and the causal connection between the "strangulation" of affects and symptom formation. As a matter of fact, evidence to validate this generalization with regard to such issues was not provided in the book.

The boundaries between generalizations and clinical theories are particularly hard to define. There is no problem about theories concerning ubiquitous phenomena such as "Symptoms are psychologically determined," or "There is unconscious mental activity," but those relating to narrower entities come close to generalizations; for example, "Excitation is borne away through associative pathways, but if it is withdrawn from association conversion may occur." Even for this proposition, however, the points of reference are the boundaries of a whole clinical entity. Broad, fundamental, and abstract as these concepts are, they remain at least potentially verifiable.

Metapsychological propositions, on the other hand, are pure constructs; the relevant question about them is not that of "truth" but that of usefulness. As Waelder points out, such concepts are not testable empirically, and the only criterion for evaluating them is the elegance of their explanatory potential. It is a remarkable fact in itself that Breuer and Freud's entire book contains only three metapsychological propositions. The first two of these are still stated in the language of neurophysiology (which was to be abandoned after Freud's "Project for a Scientific Psychology" [1895c] written a few months after publication of the *Studies*). Since all three are relevant to the example we have used to illustrate our categories, we shall present them here:

1. The brain works with a varying but limited amount of energy; this intracerebral tonic excitation is not uniformly distributed.

2. There is a tendency to keep intracerebral excitation constant.

3. Psychic forces operate in dynamic interrelationships.

After the classification of our 309 statements into five categories, we set up a list of the 91 observations, 79 interpretations, 85 generalizations, 51 theories, and three metapsychological propositions, and correlated each higher-level statement with every statement on lower levels of abstraction which could in any way have been used as evidence from which the more general or abstract concept could have been derived by induction. In this manner, we brought together propositions from all levels of abstraction arranged in pyramidal fashion, each pyramid representing the inductive process through which a theory was arrived at. In Table 1 we present the sparsest but most convincing inductive pyramid as an example: the evidence for the clinical theory of overdetermination ("Symptoms may be multidetermined").

TABLE 1

A. Observations:
   1. When symptoms were systematically handled by Breuer's cathartic method, memories of numerous traumata were recovered.
   2. It was repeatedly observed that the most minute details of the patients' verbalization proved to be meaningful in their original context.
   3. The numerous memories which determine a given symptom emerge in reverse chronological order from the way they originated.

B. Interpretations:
   1. Often a number of partial traumata summate as a provoking cause.
   2. If the story which came out under hypnosis remained incomplete, there was no therapeutic gain, whether details of content were left out or the affect remained inaccessible.
   3. When the patient stopped talking but the symptom persisted, it was assumed that all had not been told.

C. Generalizations:
  1. Persistence of a symptom after accurate interpretation of its meaning shows that there are additional meanings.
  2. There is a convergence of factors in the production of symptoms.

The most direct evidence is furnished by a series of observations from the cases of Anna O. and Emmy von N. which in themselves suggest the concept of overdetermination as a hypothesis. The earliest of these was the fact that symptoms systematically handled by Breuer's cathartic method led to the recovery of memories of numerous traumata. Secondly, the most minute details of the patient's verbalization proved to be meaningful in their original context, i.e., revealed various significant roots for each symptom. Finally, the numerous memories which determined a given symptom emerged in reverse chronological order from the way they had originated, suggesting that they were associated with each other in some regular manner, like a chain, each link of which plays a part in the final outcome.

These three observations lead to the conclusion that two patients' hysterical symtoms were multidetermined, but this proposition would not yet constitute a clinical theory; we could classify it as a clinical interpretation if no further support had been furnished for it by middle-level propositions which demonstrated its general validity. For instance, the interpretation that often a number of partial traumata summate as a provoking cause for symptoms (a restatement of our dynamic proposition in economic terms) was confirmed not only in the cases of Anna and Emmy but in a whole series reported in the book. For example, Katharina's anxiety attacks were precipitated by witnessing a sexual act between her father and a servant girl. This event did not seem to be a sufficient causative agent for her illness, however. It proved to be the last in a series of traumatic episodes, spread over a number of years, in which she had been threatened with overt incestuous relations, the full significance of which she had not understood until she was exposed to the primal scene.

In the case of Elisabeth von R., symptoms had first appeared in mild form, when she had been in conflict about her interest in a man and her filial duty toward her father during his terminal illness. They became more marked during a family reunion which brought her longings for her brother-in-law to a peak.

The case of Fräulein Rosalia H. is specifically inserted to illustrate this point; she developed certain symptoms in the course of the analysis which proved to be related to a series of traumata, extending back into her childhood, which had been revived by an unjust accusation of seductiveness toward an uncle. The case of Frau Cäcilie M. also demonstrated a complex associative web behind the symptoms—her facial neuralgia symbolized numerous insults which had seemed to her like "slaps in the face," but it had first occurred when she had felt guilty while suffering from a toothache.

Later clinical experience, with the technique of hand pressure, showed that a recurrent association had been "insufficiently worked over," i.e., there was no therapeutic gain, if details of content were left out or the affect remained partially inaccessible. Specifically, when Elisabeth stopped talking but admitted persistence of her pain, it turned out that she had not disclosed everything relevant about the symptom; similarly, Freud was able to get Lucy R. to recall forgotten aspects of the "traumatic events" which had determined her symptoms.

These additional observations and the interpretations based upon them permit the extension of the concept of multi-determination to symptoms of many varieties in a series of varied cases. This permits the generalization that "there is a convergence of factors in the production of symptoms." This is illustrated in the theoretical chapter by a special case vignette about a girl who developed fear of cats after having one jump on her on the same dark staircase where sexual advances had been made to her. A second generalization based on the same set of observations is, "Persistence of a symptom after accurate interpretation of its meaning shows that there are additional meanings." This proposition also finds further support in a case cited by Breuer in which hysterical symptoms (of pseudo-peritonitis) persisted beyond the resolution of the overt precipitating circumstances.

It is only on the basis of these two well-founded generalizations that the overdetermination concept can be elevated into a clinical theory of universal applicability. As our discussion of this theory demonstrates, in order to evaluate the adequacy of the evidence upon which higher-level propositions are based, it is necessary to check whether the particular middle-level propositions which constitute part of its inductive pyramid are themselves solidly based on induction from clinical data. In the illustrations we have used, each interpretation is backed by further observations (e.g., those from the cases of Katharina and Elisabeth); similarly, each generalization has solid roots in additional observations (like the case vignettes in Breuer's chapter), as well as support from further interpretations based on still more data of observation. One might say that the theory of overdetermination is truly multi-determined!

In contrast to this theory, which has so much clinical evidence to back it, we found a considerable number of interpretations, for the most part occurring in Breuer's theoretical chapter, which were completely devoid of supporting clinical observations. Outside of this chapter, only two of a total of 53 interpretations were without such backing. In Breuer's theoretical chapter, only eight out of 26 interpretations were supported by observational evidence. We then deleted those interpretations which were not themselves arrived at by induction from the lists of propositions from which higher-level statements could have been induced. At the level of generalizations, this step clarified that those propositions which were not directly related to any data of observation were most frequently supported only by interpretations which were themselves without supporting evidence in the book. Seventeen out of 28 generalizations in the theoretical chapter and three out of the other 57 were found not to have been based on inductive reasoning. When the same check was made of the propositions related to the various clinical theories, analogous results were obtained. There were 31 theories in Breuer's chapter, and 15 of these were supported only by middle-level statements which had been found not to be based on induction from clinical data. On the other hand, only one out of the 20 theories in the other parts of the book was found not to be based on such induction.

On the basis of these figures, we believe that we have found internal evidence (i.e., data about the two authors' respective scientific styles) to confirm Strachey's conjecture that the "Preliminary Communication" was actually written by Freud alone. It bears the hallmark of his method.

III

The significance of these findings does not consist in a verdict of "proved" for statements which had been arrived at by induction or "not proved" for the propositions lacking evidential support. As a matter of fact, many of the latter were quite sound and have found subsequent acceptance. One important example is a generalization by Breuer that the capacity of ideas to be conscious is determined, among other things, by their quota of affect (here defined as a feeling of pleasure or unpleasure). This brilliant conception foreshadows Freud's later relegation of consciousness to the role of a sense organ and the topographic division of the mental apparatus into the systems Preconscious and Unconscious. It should be the task of future studies using the method we are now reporting to determine whether clinical evidence to substantiate such propositions was ever published. Another striking illustration is Breuer's assertion that awakening from sleep is caused by intracerebral stimulation. In 1895, this interpretation was probably a deduction, but observational data obtained half a century later by neurophysiological techniques have amply demonstrated its validity. We refer to Magoun's work on the reticular activating system (Moruzzi and Magoun, 1949). It would even be unwarranted to assume that all of these propositions were arrived at by deduction from higher-level statements, since many may have been based on evidence not cited by the authors but known to them from their own clinical experiences or the reports of others. Indeed, Breuer specifically states that he omits documentation for his argument in the theoretical chapter because the evidence is so well known. A historical study of the sources of these ideas should be of great interest; more generally, the contributions of Josef Breuer to psychoanalysis deserve greater emphasis than they have received.

In our view, our findings are significant because they illuminate the scientific methodologies used by Breuer and Freud. Breuer gave free rein to speculative thinking, reasoning by analogy (particularly from the biological theories of the school of Helmholtz), and apparently he did not differentiate deductive hypotheses from concepts derived inductively from observations. The result is a brilliant intellectual feat of startling originality, presented with a high degree of assurance. (It is fascinating to recall in this connection that Freud complained bitterly in his letters to Fliess about Breuer's vacillation and indecisiveness.[2])

Ernest Jones has called attention to the polarity between Freud's scientific rigor and his tendency to imaginative constructions. In this book, however, no such polarity is demonstrated; instead, there is a fusion of the creative imagination with the discipline of a high order of secondary-process logic.[c] The number of basic concepts at the levels of generalizations and clinical theories already evolved in this first report of psychological research attests to the richness and originality of Freud's ideas. Even a partial list is like a drum roll of our most essential psychoanalytic tools: the dynamic point of view, repression, psychic determinism, unconscious mental activity, overdetermination, defenses, the economic point of view, resistance, the sexual etiology of neuroses, psychic trauma, psychic conflict, conversion, transference, and working through are only the most prominent of many.

Our tracing of the logical network within the book has shown the impressive tightness of Freud's inductive thinking,

[2]We are indebted to the medical historian, Paul Cranefield (personal communication), for the suggestion that Breuer's relative remoteness from clinical psychotherapeutic experiences by 1895 permitted him greater freedom for hypothesis building at higher levels of abstraction, while Freud's continuing immersion in clinical practice anchored him more narrowly to observational data and the middle-level propositions which could be reached from them.

[c] In terms of the difference of opinion between Eissler (1974) and Gedo and Wolf about the value of Freud's self-immersion in laboratory work for most of the 1870's (see Introduction to Chapter 3), this evidence of careful, scientific self-discipline may underscore that Freud's choice was a useful one.

and his restraint in refusing to outdistance his evidence, as Breuer consistently did. Freud's use of deductive processes is always clearly labeled in this work: he uses them sparingly, to strengthen the evidential chain because clinical predictions based on deductions from earlier theories were immediately tested in the consulting room. Thus, Freud deduced from the theory of repression that Lucy R. must have tried to forget some determinant of the precipitating event. This permitted him to interpret accurately, and the patient responded by recalling her love for her employer, which she had been trying to forget. A similarly accurate prediction led to the clarification of the precipitating events in the case of Katharina, namely, her having observed sexual relations between her father and a servant. Observational data obtained on the basis of such use of deductive logic are, of course, particularly convincing keystones in the validation of the whole theoretical arch. However, this device can be vitiated through overuse — *una volta salta il leone* (the lion only springs once), to quote one of Freud's apt similes.

Since our approach relied so heavily on the spelling out of the implicit logic of the *Studies*, it does not lend itself as readily to the elucidation of the other components of the creative process, the freedom to explore the unknown, to try out spontaneous associative pathways, to regress in the service of the ego, as Kris (1932-1952) has formulated it in another connection. Among his many contributions to the study of creativity, Kris's paper "On Preconscious Mental Processes" (1950a) is particularly germane here. He discusses "primitivization of ego functions...during many types of creative processes" as part of "the integrative functions of the ego... voluntary and temporary withdrawal of cathexis from one area or another to regain improved control" (p. 312).[d] Kris differentiated an "inspirational" from an "elaborational" phase in creation; in the former, he postulated a readiness to receive id impulses or their closer derivatives; in the latter, cathexis is said to lie with reality testing, formulating, and communicating. Kris saw the capacity to oscillate between

[d] For a different view of endopsychic conditions characteristic of creative activities, see J. Gedo (1970).

these two ego states as a crucial attribute of the creative person; he had Freud specifically in mind, since he concluded his paper by quoting Freud's oracular remark, "If the theory of sexuality comes, I will listen to it."

Freud "listened" to many theories in 1895, but he did not communicate them all in *Studies on Hysteria*. His choices were clearly determined, for the most part, by an appropriate use of the secondary-process function Kris assigns to the "elaborational phase." Those theories which did not survive the test of support from currently available clinical evidence were, by and large, not communicated to the scientific community, but reserved for his confidant, Wilhelm Fliess, alone. (Study of these drafts and the "Project for a Scientific Psychology" [Freud, 1887-1902] would constitute the natural target for extension of this research.) On the testimony of this book, Breuer was Freud's equal in the "inspirational" aspect of the creative process, but Breuer's presentation is lacking in logical coherence, as measured by our study. Another consideration, indeed the more familiar one, was his emotional inability to tolerate some of his discoveries—the well-known flight to Venice from the long-covert erotic transference-countertransference situation with Anna O., the doubts about the sexual etiology of the neuroses, and the sad turning of his immense talent away from the field of psychological inquiry altogether (see Chapter 6). Freud's achievement was in part made possible by his avoidance of the twin dangers to scientific thinking: that of uncritically reporting unverified inspirational hunches, and that of defensively suppressing, isolating, or calling into doubt well-authenticated data.

Our emphasis on the fusion of inspiration with scientific self-discipline in Freud's section of the book should not be misconstrued as a naïve claim that the creator of psychoanalysis went through the same laborious and explicit effort of testing the logic of his inductive reasoning that we have attempted in following his scientific footsteps. The whole history of his subsequent work testifies to the improbability of such a supposition. On the contrary, we believe that the kind of research we are here reporting is valuable precisely because it attempts to make explicit whatever is left implicit of the

preconscious mental processes in the creation of psychoanalysis. (We are suggesting an analogy to the function of a timely
interpretation as described in another paper of Kris's [1956]
on "the good analytic hour.") We believe that the relative
neglect of *Studies on Hysteria* — as judged by the paucity and
triviality of subsequent references to it in the literature (see
Reichert, 1956) and the tone of condescension with which it is
mentioned at all, as though it were a slightly embarrassing
and ludicrous photograph of our nakedness in infancy — is
caused by the difficulty of culling the scientific logic from this
monumental volume supersaturated with new concepts.[3]

The manifest organization of the book is actually no more
important than the smoothness of narrative in a dream. It is
cast in the conventional mold of research reports — an introduction stating the problem and the main hypotheses, a
presentation of clinical data, a theoretical discussion, and a
conclusion. Closer examination reveals a much more dis-
jointed picture, however. For instance, Freud's terminal chapter ("The Psychotherapy of Hysteria") is based on clinical
experiences and theories derived from them far beyond the
shaky consensus with Breuer in the earlier sections; the only
major case history which comes close to illustrating all this is
that of Elisabeth von R. (There are, however, several brief
case vignettes in this chapter providing the novel data of
observation on which these departures were based.) Actually,
each of the five longer cases reported in the *Studies* represents
a major new development in the 15 years of investigation
reported on. Anna O. marked the spontaneous discovery of
the cathartic method; Emmy von N. insisted on being allowed
to talk about whatever occurred to her, and since she was not
at all suggestible, her conflicts had to be "analyzed"; Lucy R.
could not be hypnotized, so that the "pressure technique" had
to be developed for her and with her, leading to the discovery
of the purposefulness of repression; with Katharina hypnosis
was deliberately dispensed with; this experiment was repeated
with Elisabeth von R., whose therapy was the first reported
one carried to completion, and the findings of adequate deter-
mination for the symptoms by a technique based on the theory

[3]Exceptions to this assessment do exist — e.g., Karpe (1961) and Glauber (1958).

of defense neuroses constituted crucial confirmatory evidence for it.

This steady historical progression in therapeutic technique brought to light new data which gave rise to more propositions on higher levels of abstraction. These accretions of theory are, however, more than usually removed from the clinical material in this book because of the peculiarities of its authorship and the artificial concentration of theoretical discussion in the "Preliminary Communication" and in Breuer's chapter.

8

THE SCIENTIFIC STYLES OF BREUER AND FREUD AND THE ORIGINS OF PSYCHOANALYSIS

NATHAN SCHLESSINGER, JOHN E. GEDO,

JULIAN A. MILLER, GEORGE H. POLLOCK,

MELVIN SABSHIN, and LEO SADOW

[*On Scientific Style.* Having made the unexpected discovery of a difference in the styles of scientific communication in Breuer's and Freud's respective portions of *Studies on Hysteria* (see Chapter 7), the Chicago Workshop on the Scientific Methodology of Psychoanalysis decided to investigate the scientific career of Josef Breuer in greater depth. In particular, they decided to search out whether Breuer's contribution to this collaborative effort had been typical of his scientific work. Although the thinking process which a scientific author tries to represent in his written report may actually have been different from what finds its way to publication, usually it is only the published version that is available for subsequent study.

One aspect of this investigation of Breuer the scientist was the study of his personal biography reported by Pollock in Chapter 6, where he correlates the biographical findings with the conclusions reached by the Workshop concerning Breuer's *oeuvre*. These conclusions are presented in the following

First published in *Journal of the American Psychoanalytic Association*, 15: 404-422, 1967.

chapter; they show that Breuer's psychological contributions are markedly different from his papers in the field of physiology.

Examination of Breuer's physiological research, both that which preceded his collaboration with Freud and that which followed it, revealed that it was characterized by perseverance, technical ingenuity, skill in inductive and deductive reasoning, and precision in reporting the results. The description of the case of Anna O. in *Studies on Hysteria* was still in keeping with Breuer's customary scientific style. The "Theoretical" chapter he wrote for this book contains many inspired ideas, but it also demonstrates much unsupported speculation and reasoning by analogy. From subsequent accounts of Freud's view of Breuer as a sober scientist, it is evident that he had not been aware of the fact that the evidence offered by Breuer to back his hypotheses was extremely scanty, and that his contribution to *Studies on Hysteria* represents a unique departure from Breuer's usual procedures. Moreover, Breuer seems to vacillate between bold speculations and cautious disclaimers about some of his own ideas.

Schlessinger and his co-workers attribute much of this difficulty to Breuer's withdrawal from active psychological work with patients after the disruptions experienced by both himself and Bertha Pappenheim as a result of the misunderstood transference developments in the course of her treatment (see Chapter 6, and Pollock's papers on Bertha Pappenheim [1971, 1972, 1973]). They assume that this avoidance was necessitated by Breuer's personal conflicts, a view elaborated and explained through genetic reconstructions in Pollock's biographical study of Josef Breuer. In contrast to Breuer's reaction stands Freud's sequence of efforts, reviewed by Schlessinger et al., consistently to understand his observations of his patients and, ultimately, of himself. They stress the significance of the interplay between Freud's creative inspiration and his careful observations, designed to confirm or to refute his hypotheses. In this sense, the Baconian scientific method which Freud had absorbed in the course of his medical education can be seen as the application of reality testing to the created products of his mind and, thus, as an essential prerequisite of fruitful research.

In addition to its elucidation of an aspect of intellectual history about the birth of psychoanalysis, this paper for the first time suggests a definition of *scientific style*. As such, it may have opened a new path in the study of scientific creativity. In this regard, the authors followed in the footsteps of Ernst Kris (1932-1952) who corrected the worst flaw of previous work in applied psychoanalysis, that of an exclusive focus on the content of works of art and their unconscious significance, to the neglect of problems of form and of the role of the more advanced sectors of the personality in creativity. Schlessinger et al. also take up the methodological problems inherent in studying the entire creative process on the basis of the final product alone, when this is the only stage within the sequence of creation available for investigation. This aspect of the chapter draws on a seldom-quoted discussion of style from *The Psychopathology of Everyday Life* (Freud, 1901).

This chapter does not go into the issue of the psychological roots of the estrangement between Breuer and Freud; much of this ground has already been covered, of course, in the biographies by Jones (1953) and Schur (1972). To their cogent discussions only one addendum should be made here, that of Freud's inability to tolerate the disillusionment Breuer inflicted on him by showing himself to be severely limited in his scientific freedom by neurotic conflicts.

Initially, for the child, the parents occupy the position of idealized figures; as subsequent development occurs, however, various successors supersede the familial figures who tend to remain in a fixed position. The functions they once performed for the person gradually shift, and the specific idealizations made around them may be discarded, to be replaced by a different set. No adult is without ideals and idealized figures. Seen in a developmental perspective, the succession of idealized persons gives rise to the moral, aesthetic, political, or professional ideals. In later life, the adult comes to include his own children or students within the orbit of his ideals as the carriers of his future hopes. This generational shift goes beyond the developmental transformations of particular contents within the system of ideals.

In the case of Freud, the loss of significance of the idealized figures of childhood can be followed in the various chapters of this book. Freud's disillusionment with his father went deeper than the oft-quoted episode of yielding to the violence of an anti-Semite. Much earlier in his childhood, he had already turned to his older half brothers as admired figures (e.g., in his fantasy that one of them had fathered his younger sibling). Perhaps it was this turning away from the father that Freud repeated with his angry response to Breuer's ambivalence about their joint psychological work; as on the previous occasion, Freud turned to a sibling figure for idealization in the person of Wilhelm Fliess—*Eds.*]

I

In Chapter 7, investigating the methodology of the *Studies on Hysteria* (Breuer and Freud, 1893-1895), a striking difference between the scientific styles of Breuer and Freud as manifested in this particular monograph was noted as an unexpected finding. Freud presented clinical evidence and theoretical propositions at various levels of abstraction which could be derived from observational data by inductive reasoning. His hypothesis formation through deductive logic was clearly labeled and sparingly employed. He used deduction to validate his theories by making clinical predictions which could then be tested in the consulting room. Breuer, on the other hand, presented some data of observation but mostly theory (indeed, the "Theoretical" chapter was his sole responsibility). We could not demonstrate a clear and consistent connection between his theoretical constructs and the clinical evidence presented. Nor could we find a coherent and progressively developing theoretical framework into which further observations could be fitted. This appeared in sharp contrast to Freud's contributions in the work, which demonstrated systematic methods of scientific thinking.

Breuer seems to have given free rein to speculative thinking. Frequently he reasoned by analogy and deduced ideas from theories which were highly abstract, often borrowing from other sciences, notably physiology. The value and usefulness of his work are amply demonstrated by the fact that many of Breuer's conceptions of 1895 have subsequently proved to be sound and fruitful. What is striking is the absence of specific data upon which the abstract concepts were based. This difference in "scientific style" between the two authors of the *Studies on Hysteria* piqued our curiosity, stimulating our interest in a comparison of scientific styles and in their significance. We became particularly interested in bringing into clearer focus the relatively mysterious figure of Josef Breuer, so important in the prehistory of psychoanalysis. The fact that we were impressed with the astuteness, capacity, and depth of involvement demonstrated in his contributions made his subsequent withdrawal all the more puzzling to us. We wondered about what led him to initiate and then to abandon his explorations, leaving to Freud the completion of the voyage of discovery.

The rationale of evaluating a man's scientific style on the basis of his published results requires some comment. We have assumed that scientific work consists of a series of stages or part processes which culminate in the process of communicating the results to the scientific community. From inspiration to finished product a process of reality testing unfolds, formally designated as scientific method, whereby fantasies and hunches are given shape and form and precise verbal expression, so that word representations correspond to thing representations as closely as possible. Breuer gave an apologetic poetic expression to this process in the "Theoretical" chapter when, in reference to physiological expositions of complex psychical processes, he described the best efforts as but shadows, noting, however, that even the weakest tries "honestly and modestly...to hold on to the outlines of the shadows which the unknown real objects throw upon the wall...in spite of everything, the hope is always justified that there may be some degree of correspondence and similarity between the real processes and our idea of them" (p. 251).

In an analogous context, Kris (1932-1952) has stressed the complexity of interrelated factors in the psychological understanding of a work of art. Thematic content and organization, relationship to the life history of the artist, his established style, the function of creativity, and environmental influences, such as historical circumstances in the development of the art, may determine in one way or another the mode of expression and the stuff with which the artist struggles in creation. The evaluation of a creative scientific contribution is no less complex. Our method has been to review the available biographical materials about Breuer, including his intellectual milieu, and to study many of his published scientific papers for clues about his scientific style. The insights provided by a study of biographical data in conjunction with Breuer's psychological research have been communicated in a separate paper by Pollock (Chapter 6). We shall here attend to the question of scientific style, divorced for the moment from biography.

The published report need not reflect the history of the process of discovery—indeed, it usually focuses away from this and concentrates on the content. What, then, can we learn of scientific style from a published report? In the broadest sense, scientific style designates the characteristic modes used by the scientist in various phases of the scientific process: creative thinker, observer, investigator, theoretician, and author. While the evaluation of the scientific style of a man from his published work alone has its limitations, the scientific report does offer evidence about the stage of elaboration of the ideas in question which the author wishes his audience to assess. Such an appraisal is made on the basis of logical structure, method, and correspondence to reality. This is true whether the work in question presents new hypotheses or models, validation with clinical evidence, or both. Inferences of a lower order of validity may be made from the published report about stages in the scientific process before the communication of results. Particularly where a sharp difference in writing appears in a series of scientific publications and a style of reporting that has been relatively constant gives way to quite a different form, one would expect this difference to be meaningful and would search for determinants of the situation under study in any available data bearing on it.

Changes in the style of communication may well be correlated with or suggestive of structural or economic changes in
internal psychic processes. Kris has discussed the function of
style in the creative artist, involving the transition from
immediate discharge in a masturbatory fantasy, through the
solitary daydream, to attempts at interposing organizing
factors into the production. He emphasizes regressive stylistic
phenomena occuring in the inspirational phase as a variety of
experience in the service of the ego. The final product must,
however, achieve a solution satisfactory to the internal audience—measuring up to the standards of the ego ideal so that
self-approval is maintained and superego criticism withstood.
The mastery of the ego over the content of the work and its
accompanying tensions are the significant intrapsychic ac-
companiments of the production. With submission of the
work for appraisal by an external audience, the response may
have important consequences, particularly for the artist who is
insecure. A positive reaction heightens his self-approval. An
unfavorable reception threatens his solution and the balance
of forces within him.[a] That the process of communication is a
critical step is illustrated by the fact that many artists have
destroyed their work or have refused to permit its publication.

The parallels with creative scientific discoveries need not be
belabored. The product in preparation and communication
must similarly pass muster before an internal audience, a
passage that may be marked by permanent suppression,
repression or disavowal (constituting a complete failure of the
scientific process), or by changes in style, influenced by
internal conflict, demonstrable in the final product and
signifying far more than a matter of semantics or literary skill.
Freud commented on this fact in *The Psychopathology of
Everyday Life* (1901):

> Even in forming an appreciation of an author's style we are
> permitted and accustomed to apply the same elucidatory prin-
> ciple which we cannot dispense with in tracing the origins of

[a] In 1974, these issues could better be stated in terms of Kohut's (1971) views on
self-esteem regulation and the continuity of a cohesive sense of self. Artistic style
may be understood as a reflection of such continuity.

individual mistakes in speech. A clear and unambiguous manner of writing shows us that here the author is at one with himself; where we find a forced and involved expression which (to use an apt phrase) is aimed at more than one target, we may recognize the intervention of an insufficiently worked-out, complicating thought, or we may hear the stifled voice of the author's self-criticism [p. 101].

In the 1910 edition, Freud added the following quotation from Boileau (*Art Poétique*): "What is well thought out presents itself with clarity, and the words to express it come easily" (p. 101).

II

In pursuing our investigation of Breuer's scientific style, we first examined his published reports before, during, and after his psychological research. At the age of 26, he published his famous "Study of Respiratory Physiology" in collaboration with E. Hering (1868). His investigations of the sense organ of equilibrium (see Breuer, 1888-1889) were published at the age of 32. The discovery of the cathartic method of psychotherapy was made when he was 40. *Studies on Hysteria* (Breuer and Freud, 1893-1895) was published when he was 53, more than 12 years after the conclusion of the treatment of Anna O.

The work on respiration started from the clinical observations of Türck, the laryngologist. Breuer conceived the idea of a self-regulatory process — a hypothesis of feedback control mechanisms which proved to have wide, general applicability. This was tested experimentally under the guidance of Hering. Breuer devised novel techniques which permitted observation of the natural excitatory processes occurring in pulmonary tissue during expansion and contraction of the lungs. Previous investigators had either stimulated or severed the vagus nerve, precluding observation of the normal physiological state. Breuer obtained meaningful data about the natural phenomena by inventing intubation techniques which permitted the measurement of air pressure within the lungs in the intact animal. Extensive work with a number of species attests to his thoroughness and indefatigability. The experiments demonstrated the accuracy of predictions he had made from his hypothesis. The results were reported at some length, as was customary at the time, without statistical evidence but with close and precise reasoning. Speculation is at a minimum in this report, all the more important because the absence of speculation was a somewhat unusual feature for papers of his day. The Hering-Breuer reflex has stood as a fundamental contribution to physiology and its details need not be reviewed here.

In his research on equilibrium and position sense, Breuer took the hypothesis of Goltz, the physiologist, that the semicircular canals served as the sense organ for equilibrium. His extensive experiments were performed on pigeons in his own home, and he worked completely alone. According to de Kleijn, the otologist, who wrote one of the Breuer obituaries (1926), these experiments and observations refined the theory so satisfactorily and tested it so well that 50 years of subsequent work had resulted in only minor modifications.

Similar conclusions were reached almost simultaneously by Mach and Crum-Brown, each of whom pursued a different methodological tack. However, it was Breuer's work alone which was buttressed with ingenious experimental research that permitted a step-by-step demonstration of the physiological mechanisms with little left to speculation. The crucial departure from previous work in the field was Breuer's meticulous avoidance of damage in the course of experimental surgery to the delicate structures he wished to observe. Other investigators had injured the brain in dissecting the semicircular canals, thereby hopelessly contaminating the results.

In his studies, Breuer demonstrated superior deductive and predictive abilities and technical ingenuity. He showed extraordinary perseverance in pursuing intensive anatomical research on fish, reptiles, birds, and mammals to test the generalizability of his findings. Moreover, he was able to meet rejection of his thesis by influential scientists whose prejudices were mobilized by it with judicious and patient rebuttals, including further experimental proofs based on new techniques. After his work in psychoanalysis, even at the age of 65 he was able to reinterpret data presented to attack his theory, successfully demonstrating that the phenomena could be explained on the basis of his ideas (Breuer, 1907). This attitude stands in marked contrast to his diffidence and hesitancy with regard to his psychological findings.

It is clear, then, that in his physiological papers Breuer used with consistent and consummate skill the rigorous scientific method acquired from his distinguished teachers of the Helmholtz school. Having through induction arrived at a hypothesis based on his own observations or upon those of others, he was able to devise crucial experiments in which predictions derived from his hypothesis could be tested. Painstaking and ingenious technical procedures permitted validation studies yielding definitive results. Natural phenomena were observed with the minimum amount of intervention required for study. The improvisation of tools and techniques to facilitate observation was an established characteristic of his research. Finally, and perhaps most important from our point of view, Breuer showed superior capacities in communicating his discoveries in a clear, consistent, and logically organized manner.

We can conclude that the mental equipment which Breuer brought to his fateful encounter with Anna O. combined a rigorous scientific attitude, profound respect for natural processes and their inherent lawfulness, an intense desire to understand, the capacity to improvise and facilitate observation while avoiding injury, and the therapeutic passion of a great clinician. All the more striking, then, are the variations in his style of reporting psychological research. His speculation, reasoning by analogy, and the meagerness of evidence offered to back his hypotheses in the "Theoretical" chapter had never occurred before and never occurred again in his published scientific work. It is a striking fact that the differences thus established between the "Theoretical" chapter and other parts of Studies on Hysteria demonstrate a change of style for Breuer in the book itself, since his description of the case of Anna O. is very much in keeping with his physiological reports.

A summary of the findings in our methodological evaluation of the Studies on Hysteria may be useful in focusing on dramatic differences revealed by examination of the hierarchy of observed data, interpretations, generalizations, clinical theory, and metapsychology. In Breuer's "Theoretical" chapter, only eight of 26 interpretations were supported by observational evidence, whereas in the rest of the book, two of a total of 53 interpretations were without such backing. At the level of generalization, if one deleted as supporting evidence those interpretations which were not themselves arrived at by induction, 17 out of 28 generalizations in the "Theoretical" chapter, and three out of 57 elsewhere in the book, were found not to have been based on inductive reasoning. With regard to clinical theories, analogous results were obtained. There were 31 theories in Breuer's chapter and 15 of these were supported only by evidence not based on induction. On the other hand, only one of 20 theories in the other parts of the book was found not to be based on an inductive pyramid.

Turning to a closer examination of Breuer's psychological research, we know that he discovered the cathartic method of psychotherapy when he was 40 years old and for the next 12 years collaborated with Freud in the elaboration of hypotheses based upon the observations of the case of Anna O. and other patients treated by Freud. After the publication of the *Studies on Hysteria*, when Breuer was 53, he turned away from psychological research to return to physiology. He did not again achieve the originality of the discoveries of his youth but continued to publish reports until he was 70. His correspondence, cited illustratively in H.H. Meyer's (1928) biography but unavailable in its entirety, reveals a broad range of cultural and intellectual interests and a remarkable erudition. His thorough familiarity with questions of epistemology is demonstrated in Meyer's account of his correspondence with the philosopher Brentano, as well as in his running commentary on research problems in his contributions to *Studies on Hysteria*.

In Breuer's psychological work with Anna O., we were particularly impressed with his ability to observe phenomena even in circumstances which were quite alien to his ordinary experience. In his obituary of Breuer, Freud (1925c) noted what a novel procedure it had been in 1880 to continue observing and treating a single patient over a two-year period. This departure from convention was particularly remarkable in Vienna, steeped in the German psychiatric tradition and far removed from the French school with its relative therapeutic hopefulness.[b] In his own evaluation of his work with Anna O., Breuer, with characteristic modesty, wrote "my merit lay essentially in my having recognized what an uncommonly instructive and scientifically important case chance had brought me for investigation, in my not having allowed any preconceived opinions to interfere with the simple observation of the important data" (Cranefield, 1958, p. 319).

The case history prepared for publication in 1895, more than a dozen years after the event, attests to the carefulness of the observations and their recording. Breuer's intense clinical interest, his amazing flexibility in being willing to be guided by the expressed needs of the patient in devising the technique of therapy, the inductive hypotheses he formed about the genesis of hysterical symptoms and then tested systematically, represent the application of his talents at their best. Thus he observed that symptoms would disappear when the unconscious processes from which they had arisen were made conscious.

The clinical encounter was aborted by the emergence of a transference-countertransference embroilment for which Breuer had no known precedent, so that he mistook its manifestations for an unmanageable reality. Not only did he withdraw from the patient; he also abandoned the direct investigation of psychological problems altogether. Breuer later wrote: "Thus at that time I learned a very great deal: much that was of scientific value, but something of practical importance as well—namely, that it was impossible for a 'general practitioner' [in English] to treat a case of that kind without bringing his activities and mode of life completely to an end. I vowed at the time that I would *not* go through such an ordeal again" (Cranefield, 1958, p. 319).

It is significant that in 1907 Breuer repeated his assertion of 1895 that the treatment of Anna O. was carried to completion

[b] Ellenberger (1970) has collected an impressive array of exceptions to this generalization without, however, invalidating it.

without the finding of a sexual basis, in spite of the patient's avowal of her love for him and her pseudocyesis and hysterical childbirth. The refusal to consider these manifest sexual phenomena as etiologically relevant suggests the continued operation of defensive disavowal and isolation. However, Breuer's interest in psychological matters continued after he terminated the treatment of Anna O. He referred many patients requiring psychotherapy to Freud, so that his discussions of psychological observations were necessarily made from a detached position. This was a significant departure from his usual scientific style as an active investigator, and we postulate that this departure was probably dictated by unresolved internal conflict.

The "Theoretical" chapter documents further consequences of this conflict. Strachey (1955a, p. xxiv) has noted the paradox that Breuer, who had devised a psychological treatment for hysteria, wrote a physiological treatise for *Studies on Hysteria*. His work was full of references to intracerebral excitations and analogies between the nervous sytem and electrical conduction phenomena, while Freud, who was seeking physiological and chemical explanations, merely recorded psychological observations and conclusions in the book. Breuer's intent to describe psychological processes in the language of psychology was convincingly justified by his arguments for it, but he was unable to carry it through. Instead, he wrote a brilliant speculative essay in physiological terms. In painful ambivalence he alternated between caution and boldness. His discomfort is shown in his emphasis on the danger of being tricked into creating a mythology by figures of speech— yet he uses spatial metaphors to express functional relations, returns repeatedly (albeit apologetically) to the analogy with electrical phenomena, and acknowledges that his physiological explanations can never explain complex psychological events. He carefully labels his entire effort as a first step in a new region of knowledge, referring to it as a clumsy hypothesis that conceals rather than bridges gaping lacunae. Such a reliance on a level of physiological explanation may be readily understood as an early step in the creative process. However, Breuer's apparent fixation at this level in published form, when he has argued for a psychological exposition, suggests an internal conflict that goes beyond the conscious elements recognized and expressed by the author.

It is also striking that Breuer states in his introduction that he will not attempt to distinguish between his own ideas and those originating elsewhere, and he claims originality for very little of what he has written. He justifies this on the ground that so much about hysteria was passing into the public domain at the time that it was difficult to remember the origins of specific ideas. By contrast, Breuer's other scientific writings carefully refer to antecedent authors. Considering the unusual nature of the material and a potentially critical audience, one would expect greater attention to the customary style of presentation. The introduction seems to disclaim responsibility for the content of the book, as though it were a detour from Breuer's accustomed work. One might attempt to explain Breuer's writing style in the *Studies* as the professional assurance of an older, established scientist. Such an evaluation is contradicted by Breuer's reluctance to publish the book, as well as by the absence of a similar casualness in any of his subsequent works. The disclaimer of responsibility and the ambiguity are consistent with an arousal of defensiveness in Breuer upon recathecting the Anna O. experience.

Further evidence of conflict may be noted in Breuer's ambivalence toward the question of the significance of sexual factors. He dealt with this ambivalence by making bold assertions which exaggerated the assurance he felt about the issues with which he was wrestling. He described sexuality as "the most powerful source of persisting increases of excitation" in the genesis of hysteria and even of other neuroses (p. 200) (e.g., "the great majority of severe neuroses in women have their origin in the marriage bed" [p. 246]). Yet Breuer was never able to accept this conclusion emotionally. In a letter in late 1895, Freud recounted that Breuer had announced his *conversion* to a belief in the sexual etiology of neurosis at a public meeting, only to tell Freud privately afterward that he did not believe it (Freud, 1887-1902, p. 134). In a letter of 1900, Freud wrote to Fliess about a patient referred by Breuer in whose case sexual factors had proved to be crucial. When she reported her improvement to Breuer, the latter (according to the patient) clapped his hands and said again and again, "So he [i.e., Freud] is right after all!" (pp. 319f.). In 1907, Breuer himself wrote that the prominent place assumed by sexuality in the *Studies* "arose from no inclination towards the subject but from the findings—to a large extent most unexpected—of our medical experience....I confess that the plunging into sexuality in theory and practice is not to my taste. But what have my taste and my feeling about what is seemly and what is unseemly to do with the question of what is true?" (Cranefield, 1958, p. 320).

While Breuer could thus recognize that personal reactions had little to do with what was true, their influence, once aroused, profoundly affected his function as a scientist. This may be illustrated again *at the level of theory formation.*

In 1895, the main theoretical disagreement between Breuer and Freud concerned the alternative hypotheses they espoused about the mechanism of symptom formation: Breuer's hypnoid hypothesis versus Freud's concept of defense, primarily against sexuality.

In reference to the hypnoid hypothesis, Waelder (1956) has pointed out that it was a theory conceived and held by Breuer in utter remoteness from contact with actual patients. It was a hypothesis which adequately explained the patient's perceptual distortions on the basis of postulated alterations in the receptor apparatus. This was in the tradition of Breuer's physiological concepts (which also dealt with the reception of stimuli from the external world, leading to the activation of reflex systems) and of Meynert's psychophysiology as well, with its emphasis on the return of memories of percepts when hallucinations occur. Unencumbered by defensive emphasis on physiological explanations, Freud had no need to cling to a psychology founded on the model of (external) stimulus-response. He became aware quite early (with the case of Lucy R., in 1891) that the problem of perception in neuroses was that of perceiving internal processes (later to be conceptualized as drive derivatives)—from this, the concept of "defense" followed as a logical inference. In a very real sense, Breuer was the victim of his previous successes; clinging to the same ideas could operate as a defense at this point. Freud's subsequent clinical experiments confirmed the usefulness of the concept of defense and led to the recognition of a dynamic unconscious producing transference phenomena in everyone, including the investigator.

In 1895 Breuer's concept of "unconscious" was that of a portion of psychic content experienced and elaborated during a pathological state and therefore continuously operative without being capable of becoming conscious. Such an "unconscious" is an isolated, unusual, pathological phenomenon —a conception which permits the observer to maintain maximum distance from the observed. This short-circuits the recognition of an unacceptable impulse life influencing behavior by transference across a repression barrier. It places the locus of the problem in a particular altered state of perception at the time of the traumatic event, at the expense of seeing the dynamic processes of intrapsychic life occurring in everyone.

Our critique of Breuer's style indicates the possible effects of internal conflict on his scientific endeavors in psychological research. However, his application of physiological concepts to the realm of psychology was a significant first achievement. S. Bernfeld (1944) has carefully demonstrated the origin in Brücke's teaching of the theoretical propositions in Breuer's chapter. The deterministic philosophy, the emphasis on forces within the organism, were essential tenets of Brücke's physiology. Like respiration, the mind is seen as a self-regulating process, depending on the relative quanta of energy in brain cells, brain, body, and external world. In spite of the emphasis on physiological language, the bridge to the dynamic and economic points of view is clearly apparent.

Many of Breuer's hypotheses have continued to be important for psychoanalytic theory. Strachey (1955a), in his Introduction to the *Studies on Hysteria* (p. xxiii), singled out three major concepts which psychoanalysis specifically owes to Breuer: the distinction between bound and mobile energy; the idea that hallucination is a retrogression from imagery to perception; and the thesis that perception and memory cannot be performed by the same apparatus. Breuer noted that the latter idea is one that had been expressed by Meynert (p. 189).

The sophistication and intuitive ability evident in Breuer's essay can be illustrated by two examples of hypotheses that have only recently been shown to be fruitful and highly significant. One is a passing reference to the significance of imprinting and its possible role in the genesis of somatic symptoms through ideogenic modifications in the nervous system. The second recognizes the significance of an absence of stimuli in creating unpleasure and discusses the concept of an optimal energy level. Recent advances in ethology and in the psychology of perception have begun to exploit these profound ideas. On examining the wealth of ideas recorded in the "Theoretical" chapter it is readily apparent that Breuer served as a most stimulating collaborator for Freud in their discussions. Thus Breuer's contribution to psychoanalysis is an important one, and our study of differences in style and attempts to understand its meaning are significant precisely because of the magnitude of this contribution and his ability in the field.

Cranefield (1958) has already focused attention on the essential agreement between Breuer's and Freud's assessments of Breuer's contribution to psychoanalysis. Breuer discovered that symptoms arise from the unconscious and disappear when the processes which sustained them are made conscious. He presented these discoveries to Freud and explored the theoretical implications with him. Freud pursued the clinical work alone, integrated Breuer's findings with the discoveries of Charcot, and discovered the phenomena of defense and repression and the significance of early childhood and of sexuality in neurosogenesis.

III

The conclusion we reach is that the essential difference in scientific style between Freud and Breuer, observed in our evaluation of *Studies on Hysteria*, did not consist in a difference in method. Freud was able to persist where Breuer withdrew in the face of internal conflicts stirred up by his discoveries. The fact that inner turmoil was also raging within

Freud during the crucial period of the birth of psychoanalysis is well documented in his correspondence with Fliess. For personal defensive reasons, Freud had a high investment in a theory of childhood seduction as an etiological agent in neurosis at the time of the publication of *Studies on Hysteria*. His aggressive pursuit of evidence to substantiate these views may have heightened Breuer's dismay about "unseemliness" and thereby hastened the rupture in their collaboration. The process of modification of the seduction hypothesis and of two other early hypotheses, those of hypnoid states and of actual neuroses, will be discussed in Chapter 9.

Freud's great and extraordinary achievement was his capacity to extend the range of psychological observation to include not only his patients but also himself. His own analysis opened the gate to his increased understanding of the problem of transference. The magnitude of this step and the struggle required to take it are illustrated by such anguished statements in his letters to Fliess as this one of July, 1897: "Something from the deepest depths of my own neurosis has ranged itself against my taking a further step in understanding of the neuroses" (Freud, 1887-1902, p. 212). The contrast between the attitudes of the two men is glaring when we compare Breuer's struggle to accept the unseemliness of others with Freud's motto borrowed from Terence: "Nothing that is human is alien to me."

In historical perspective, we can assess the obstacles that had to be overcome in the discovery of psychoanalysis. Although Freud was evidently fascinated by Breuer's account of the Anna O. encounter, which was communicated to him in 1882, he did not begin to engage in psychotherapeutic work immediately. His famous attempt to relate the story of Breuer's work to Charcot in 1886 is sufficient evidence of his interest; it also shows that he did not then dare to launch into these deep waters without sanction from recognized authorities. Indeed, even when he had become the Viennese missionary for the radicalism of the French, who were taking hysteria seriously as a subject for scientific inquiry, his actual clinical efforts did not consist in an application of the cathartic procedure. His preface to the translation of Bernheim's

Suggestion (1888b) shows him to be a thoroughgoing disciple of the French school. A case report from this period of his therapeutic activity, "A Case of Successful Treatment by Hypnotism" (1892-1893), shows no trace of Breuer's cathartic method. It was not until disillusionment with the therapeutic efficacy of suggestion had set in that Freud, perhaps in desperation, turned to Breuer's seemingly dangerous and explosive technique. The story of this disillusionment is recorded by Jones (1953). When Freud went to Nancy in 1889 to learn hypnotic technique from Bernheim and Liébeault, he took a difficult patient with him. Bernheim could not hypnotize her deeply enough either, and "frankly admitted . . . that his great therapeutic successes by means of suggestion were only achieved in his hospital practice and not with his private patients" (p. 238).

It is true that Freud claimed that he always used hypnotism to try to trace the history of the symptoms, but the first evidence of this occurs in the case of Emmy von N., begun in May, 1889. Even then, he took the precaution of hospitalizing the patient, and the suggestive method was tried concurrently. In other words, Breuer was by no means alone in recoiling from the implications of the Anna O. experience. From the perspective of 1889, Breuer's misadventure might be viewed by someone else with sufficient detachment to warrant a new trial for his technique. No disaster developed from the Emmy von N. experiment. It was perhaps uniquely fortunate that Freud's first cathartic patient produced a negative, hostile transference rather than an erotic one. This may have helped Freud to grasp the essential *concept* of transference, which then provided him with the means to maintain therapeutic distance, whatever emotional reactions were produced in the clinical situation.

In this sense, then, Breuer had served as the essential pioneer. He was the first to experience the full impact in a therapeutic situation of what we now know as a transference neurosis. He had no precedent to help him put it in perspective. Freud, encountering the phenomena of transference, had the experience of Breuer to fall back on in addition to his own analysis. He could recognize that the intensity of the patient's feeling toward him had also occurred with a previous psychoanalyst. To recognize that knowing of Breuer's encounter with the phenomenon contributed to Freud's being able to see it as a repetition and as something appropriate to an analytic situation in no way diminishes Freud's achievement.

To recapitulate, it was Freud's ability to include himself and to see processes of transference occurring in himself that enabled him to continue his discoveries in psychoanalysis. Breuer had not been able to breach the wall that separated the doctor from the patient and to recognize disturbances of internal economy in himself, in order to see them in their ultimate perspective.

In comparing the contributions of Breuer and Freud, we have shown that Freud's theories evolved from the data of his clinical (and self-) observations, traversing the entire hierarchy of abstraction, from interpretations to generalizations to clinical theories to metapsychology. Breuer, removed by internal conflict from contact with patients, was unable to use the inductive method to arrive at his clinical interpretations, generalizations, and theories. It is no coincidence that nonclinicians who attempt to classify psychoanalytic propositions (e.g., Sullivan, 1959) similarly leave a conceptual gap between data of observation and high-level theories. Wolman (1964) has stated similar views as follows: "There is no reason to minimize the importance of clinical evidence proper. Psychoanalytic case studies are neither quantitative nor controlled, yet they bring a wealth of empirical findings and can be conclusive. As a rule, the case study method should be the first step in inquiry. Case studies play a crucial role in finding out relevant variables. The necessity for the first-hand acquaintance with empirical data must never be overlooked in psychological research" (pp. 723-724).

The gap in the inductive pathway to theory building forces the nonclinician to rely exclusively on deductive reasoning. Breuer's deductive work was precise, but, of necessity, unverified. As we have shown earlier, where intrapsychic conflict did not interfere with his creativity, Breuer was also capable of brilliant inductive leaps. The psychoanalyst-as-scientist needs both skills.

At this stage in the history of science, it becomes more and more pretense to say that laws and theories are based simply on observation of facts. In fact, they are arrived at by creative leaps which may occur in either direction, i.e., inductively from observational data or deductively from pre-existing hypotheses. Einstein has gone so far as to state that basic concepts are freely invented and not discovered by any logical method. Yet their elaboration and development must include the freedom to use induction and deduction appropriately in the framework of the scientific method; Hutten (1962) has called methodology "the intellectual counterpart of the mental attitude of reality testing."

In a sense, what we have demonstrated is the importance of a consistent application of scientific method in the origins of psychoanalysis. The broad significance of this issue in scientific pursuits today has recently been emphasized by Platt (1964) in the description of a method he calls "strong inference." Essentially, he ascribes the tremendous strides taken in biochemistry and nuclear physics to the elaboration of basic discoveries through a concentrated and systematic conscious reliance on scientific method as set forth by Bacon. Platt emphasized the use of alternative hypotheses so that the major research effort is expended on discarding or modifying hypotheses that are fallacious rather than on proving and defining hypotheses that are favored. The implementation of such a concerted approach in the evolution of analytic theory may have fruitful consequences.

9

SAXA LOQUUNTUR
Artistic Aspects of Freud's
"The Aetiology of Hysteria"

ERNEST S. WOLF

[*Freud's Conversion to an Introspective Psychology*. Albeit the author has outlined the aims of his chapter as threefold, we are less concerned with the first two of these (his study of the formal aspects of a created product and the delineation of a distinction between the influence of derivatives of the archaic self and those of the archaic object) than with the last, the description of the historical import of one of the turning points of Freud's career. Perhaps because he has learned a salutary lesson from Freud's difficulties with his 1896 audience, Wolf has contented himself with the task of discussing these issues without pushing the reader toward particular conclusions. We should like to focus on some conclusions suggested by his discerning selection of materials.

We can begin with Wolf's demonstration that, in the case of Freud's lecture on "The Aetiology of Hysteria" (1896b), the content, insofar as it refers to the author's representational world, is confined to the sphere of idealized objects, especially in terms of their admirable activities; by contrast, derivatives of the archaic self are excluded from the manifest content but find their way to expression through a decisive influence on the style of the lecture. Wolf has proposed a plausible psychological explanation for this occurrence in the circum-

First published in *The Psychoanalytic Study of the Child*, 26:535-554. New York: Quadrangle, 1971.

stances in which Freud found himself in April, 1896. Although other motivations may also have been at work, this possibility is not to the point of the principal theme of this chapter.

We should recall a decisive methodological statement by Kris in this connection:

> While in their clinical work psychiatrists are accustomed to assess carefully the requirements of a specific environmental situation, the "reality" in which the artist creates is often neglected. "Reality" is used here not so much in the restricted sense of immediate needs and material environment as in another and extended sense: The structure of the problem which exists while the artist is creating, the historical circumstances in the development of art itself which limit some of his work, determine in one way or another his modes of expression and thus constitute the stuff with which he struggles in creation [1932-1952, p. 15].

In the art of scientific writing, tradition did not permit the presentation of the archaic self in 1896; indeed Wolf's paper shows us that even its intrusion into the style of the presentation as an unconscious "return of the disavowed" led to its total rejection. Explanations of this reaction based on the alleged prudery of the Viennese bourgeoisie overlook the simultaneous acceptance of overtly incestuous themes on the stage, as for instance in Wagner's *Die Walküre*. Decker (1971) has shown that the rejection of Freud's findings was confined in large measure to the explicitly psychoanalytic portion of his work. i.e., it did not include his writings of the mid-1890's.

We may contrast the traditions of scientific writing with those of imaginative literature through the contemporaneous example of Friedrich Nietzsche. The latter had been able to state his ideal aspirations baldly and in the first person by using the simple device of repeating the introductory phrase, "Thus spake Zarathustra." Transparent though this concealment of the self may have been, the need to resort to it indicates the persistence of powerful taboos into the late nineteenth century against the appearance of the grandiose self in art and thought. As the more extensive discussion in Chapter 1 attempts to demonstrate, this taboo was the legacy of a millennium that had conceived of the arts as the handmaidens of theology in the celebration of the City of God. One can survey the artistic products of some nine centuries following the Confessions of St. Augustine without coming across a focus on Man. Perhaps the earliest sign of the renascence of humanism was the *Vita Nuova* of Dante Alighieri. In the visual arts, the proscription was even more absolute and led to actual loss of the capacity to produce portraiture in the West. Aside from Byzantine court art, the earliest portraits that have survived are fourteenth-century representations of royalty. When Renaissance artists initiated self-portraiture, they generally smuggled these self-representations into their works by means of giving their own features to some subsidiary figure in the composition.

It is therefore no coincidence that Pico della Mirandola's overt celebration of the Dignity of Man and Albrecht Dürer's precedent-shattering self-portraits were produced simultaneously, in the 1490's. Renaissance literary self-scrutiny came to its peak in the works of Montaigne, in the last quarter of the sixteenth century, to pass into the mainstream of Western literature through Cervantes, Shakespeare, Goethe, and Rousseau. Introspective painting was only established by Rembrandt; the psychological penetration of his self-scrutiny remains unparalleled. Incidentally, it may explain why his work constitutes the sole exception to Freud's lack of serious interest in painting (see Jones, 1957, p. 412, and 1955, p. 52). As Gedo and Wolf demonstrate in Chapter 1, the triumph of introspection in Western art and its penetration of philosophy with the work of Nietzsche and Schopenhauer were not paralleled in the realm of science. It was still unthinkable overtly to introduce narcissistic elements into a scientific work in 1896. This factor is sufficient by itself to explain Wolf's findings about Freud's lecture.

There is another aspect of "The Aetiology of Hysteria" which lends special importance to this investigation. The chronological listing of Freud's psychological works reveals a unique gap in his productivity between the publication of this lecture in May, 1896, and that of his next analytic paper. In the meantime he did produce a 300-page neurological monograph as well as a compendium of the abstracts of his scientific writings of the previous two decades (1897). Freud's own verdict on his next paper, "Sexuality in the Aetiology of the Neuroses" (1898a), which deliberately avoided mention of the discoveries he had made since 1896, was a dismissive one. Thus we may consider his next analytic creation to have been "The Psychical Mechanism of Forgetfulness" (1898b), which appeared around October, 1898. This work and its successor, the better known "Screen Memories" (1899), already utilize the revolutionary innovation that was to characterize *The Interpretation of Dreams* (1900), that of basing the science of psychoanalysis primarily on the results of self-scrutiny (see Chapters 1 and 12).

The two-and-one-half-year pause in Freud's psychological creativity was more apparent than real, as this period actually marked the initiation of his self-analysis. Henceforth he was to give greater weight to introspective data than to those obtained by observing others. With this conversion in working method, Freud accomplished for science the same great liberating step which Dante, Montaigne, Shakespeare, and Rembrandt had taken in literature and art: that of explicitly moving the self into the focus of attention. The magnitude of this step and the quality of courage required to take it may be impossible to appreciate in our post-Freudian age.

Wolf's presentation of the strength of the taboo in Viennese medical circles may help us to empathize with the resistance Freud had to overcome in himself in order to place Apollo's Delphic command *gnothi seauton,* to know oneself, at the center of his scientific work. These considerations may also help us to grasp the reason for the relative delay in the psychoanalytic clarification of the psychology of the self, in contrast to the rapid evolution of insight into problems of object love. Even now, the primacy of introspective-empathic pathways to psychological discovery is by no means universally accepted: we still boggle at the immodesty of devoting our lives to self-study—*Eds.*]

Revolutionary eras or even times of pseudorevolutionary unrest usually do not present the most propitious moments for historical retrospective, but perhaps it is precisely then, and therefore now, when renewing one's acquaintance with the wellsprings of the past is most refreshing. Psychoanalysts, of course, are not likely to have forgotten this because psychoanalysis is not only a method or process or a body of data, but is also a new kind of science whose meaning can be fully encompassed only by seeing it as a history. It is therefore neither a lack of concern for the present nor a sterile impotence in facing the future that leads psychoanalysts again and again to examine the plans of its first master architect who built the fundament upon which the structure is being erected.

Historically oriented studies in psychoanalysis generally fall into two groups. The first of these comprises the tracings of the development of psychoanalytic concepts through the vicissitudes of changing context and meaning, with the purpose of clarifying theory in a developing science. The second group, loosely labeled applied psychoanalysis, attempts to relate biographical and pathobiographical material — and social, cultural, and other historical material in the widest sense — to the growing scientific structure as relevant determinants.

Applied psychoanalysis most generally has addressed itself to the *content* of a work of art or of science and has concerned itself with uncovering latent psychological meanings hidden by the manifest content. Among the numerous examples one might mention Freud's analysis of C. F. Meyer's *Die Richterin,* his discerning dissertation (1907) on Jensen's *Gradiva,* and the many other psychoanalytic investigations of literature and drama by Freud's followers.[1] Other researchers have attempted to delineate possible relationships between the psychology of the artist and the product of his creativity. In short, what has been studied has been primarily the "what" and "why" of

---

[1] An essay on *Die Richterin* was the first application of psychoanalysis to a work of literature. Freud included it in a letter to Fliess of June 20, 1898 (Freud, 1887-1902, pp. 256f; see also Niederland, 1906b). The first published application of analysis to a work of literature was the essay on Jensen's *Gradiva,* while the first psychoanalytic study of the formal aspects of a work of art is contained in Freud's essay on Leonardo (1910b).

the creative act. Rarely has the focus of attention been on the *formal aspects,* on the "how."[2]

In contrast to the more traditional applied psychoanalytic investigations of *content,* this inquiry is concerned with studying the *form* of a created work from a psychoanalytic point of view. In this I have been guided by several aims. The first is to demonstrate a method of relating psychoanalysis to the investigation of the purely formal aspects of a work of science. The formal aspect studied here is the *style* in which a particular scientific work was written. A second aim is to present the findings resulting from this approach, namely, the formal aspects of the created work which was examined and related mainly to the transformation of narcissism, while the content appears to be mainly representative of the vicissitudes of object love. Finally, this paper also aims at making a contribution to the history of psychoanalysis.

I shall focus on Freud as a writer of scientific prose. The recent investigation of Freud's prose style by Schönau (1968), the philologist, has created a basis for further exploration and has provided psychoanalysts with the literary tools needed in this area of mutual interest.

The particular work to be examined here is the lecture Freud delivered to the Viennese Society for Psychiatry and Neurology and subsequently published as "The Aetiology of Hysteria" (1896b). According to Strachey, this lecture was given on April 21, 1896, though Jones believes the lecture was given 11 days later.[3] Apparently the paper was not well received, and Krafft-Ebing, who was at that time president of the society, commented, "It sounds like a scientific fairy tale" (Jones, 1953, p. 263).

"The Aetiology of Hysteria" is a lecture of about 30 printed pages. In later years Freud gave his lectures without the use of written notes, a practice he probably already followed in 1896. In a letter to Fliess dated May 30, six weeks after the lecture,

[2]The formal aspects of Freud's scientific creativity have been highlighted in a series of papers by the Workshop on Methodology of the Chicago Institute for Psychoanalysis (Chapters 5, 7, 8, and 11).

[3]Strachey's lucid introductory comments (pp. 189f.) go far in clarifying the historical significance of this lecture in the development of Freud's thinking.

Freud wrote: "In defiance of my colleagues I wrote out in full for Paschkis my lecture on the aetiology of hysteria" (Freud, 1887-1902, Letter 46).

In general, contemporary witnesses were impressed by Freud's talents as a speaker. Kardiner (1957) thought Freud was the greatest orator he had ever heard and in this respect favored him over Winston Churchill. Wittels (1924) found Freud fascinating and never tiring to his listeners. Jones (1959) was so enthralled that he felt oblivious of the passage of time. One may assume, therefore, that the icy reception that Freud reported in 1896 had little to do with any lack in oratorical talent.

The goal of a scientific lecturer is very similar to that of a writer of scientific prose: to convey his information so that it will be understood and accepted. Notwithstanding the fact that Freud failed to achieve this goal with most of the members of that Vienna society at that particular time, a close study of the published paper reveals it to have been eloquently powerful and worth examining for the style of his approach.

Freud began: "Gentlemen, — when we set out to form an opinion about the causation of a pathological state ..." With the word "we" Freud immediately attempted to engage the audience by identifying himself as one of them and as a physician. Then, by picturing a situation of anamnestic investigation, he started his audience off from familiar territory. It is characteristic of good writers and good speakers, and Freud apparently was no exception, to have in mind a clear picture of the audience they are addressing. Freud needed to have a clear image of the audience's expectations, interests, sympathies, level of education, and especially of their prejudices. From previous discouraging experiences with this particular audience, Freud knew that they prejudged him as unscientific. Perhaps in order to counteract this feeling in the audience, he tried to deflect it toward the unscientific patient whom he characterized "by his lack of scientific understanding of aetiological influences, by the fallacy of *post hoc, propter hoc,*[4] by his reluctance to think about or mention certain noxae and traumas."

[4]After this, therefore on account of this (an illogical argument).

It is interesting to note here Freud's use of a Latin citation, though of course physicians of Freud's time generally had a classical education, were familiar with Latin and Greek, and occasionally used such citations. Freud did this to a much larger extent and with much greater variety than most. In this particular paper there are one French and three Latin quotations.

In the rest of the paragraph, Freud underlined in some detail the audience's and his own scientific attitude and skepticism in the search for truth. The obstacle was identified to be the patient, whose ignorance prevented him from collaborating in the scientific endeavor. From this basic position, Freud attempted to catch the audience's interest by hinting that perhaps these obstacles could be overcome: "You will readily admit that it would be a good thing to have a second method of arriving at the aetiology of hysteria, one in which we should feel less dependent on the assertions of the patients themselves."

In simple language he crystallized the painful feelings of frustration of his fellow physicians and held out hope for relief. In so doing he also gave a first definition of the scientific task and took his listeners on the first step toward his goal. Since this gain needed to be consolidated immediately, he proceeded: "A dermatologist, for instance, is able to recognize a sore as luetic from the character of its margin, . . . and a forensic physician can arrive at the cause of an injury, even if he has to do without any information from the injured person. In hysteria, too, there exists a similar possibility. . . ."

In this way two vivid images with which his listeners were thoroughly familiar were used as analogies to clarify and achieve agreement on the goal of the investigation, which was to demonstrate a new investigatory technique that had the merit of being both scientific and able to overcome the difficulties presented by recalcitrant patients.

The use of the word "forensic" may not be accidental. In the first paragraph Freud had used words such as "investigation" and "critical examination" and, most important, *"agents provocateurs."* The flavor is one of a criminal investigation, of a detective story. This stylistic device reappears throughout the whole essay. Again and again, like Sherlock Holmes, Freud led his listeners on the trail after his elusive antagonist who vanished again and again behind sudden new obstacles, but each time leaving enough of a trace to raise new hopes and expectations in the audience. One can almost feel the excitement of the chase.

But before he could proceed further, Freud had to introduce the listener to his particular method of investigation. To do this he chose "an analogy taken from an advance that has in fact been made in another field of work."

> Imagine that an explorer arrives in a little-known region where his interest is aroused by an expanse of ruins, with remains of walls, fragments of columns, and tablets with half-erected and unreadable inscriptions. He may content himself with inspecting what lies exposed to view, with questioning the inhabitants — perhaps semi-barbaric people — who live in the vicinity, about what tradition tells them of the history and meaning of these archaeological remains, and with noting down what they tell him — and he may then proceed on his journey. But he may act differently. He may have brought picks, shovels and spades with him, and he may set the inhabitants to work with these implements. Together with them he may start upon the ruins, clear away the rubbish, and, beginning from the visible remains, uncover what is buried. If his work is crowned with success, the discoveries are self-explanatory: the ruined walls are part of the ramparts of a palace or a treasure-house; the fragments of columns can be filled out into a temple; the numerous inscriptions, which, by good luck, may be bilingual, reveal an alphabet and a language, and, when they have been deciphered and translated, yield undreamed-of information about the events of the remote past, to commemorate which the monuments were built. *Saxa loquuntur!*

With this beautiful metaphorical image Freud succeeded in synthesizing the images of the detective and the scientist. He heightened the interest of his audience who could well remember the skepticism and the excitement surrounding Schliemann's discovery of Troy.[a] He prepared them for the difficulty of the journey and the hard digging work ahead. He warned them of the worthless rubbish that needed to be cleared away. Perhaps he threw a contemptuous look at those

[a]See also footnote 9 below (p. 225) for earlier precedents.

who just proceeded on their usual journey without first having done some excavating. But what a reward of riches he promised those who stayed and dug! "Stones talk." What a pithy phrase for an imperative summary.

One of the hallmarks of distinguished literary prose is the frequent and subtle allusion to the literary tradition and heritage of which it is a part. With *saxa loquuntur*[5] Freud reached back to the Bible, to Habakkuk, "For the stone will cry out from the wall"; to Luke, "I tell you if they were silent the very stone would cry out"; to Shakespeare's Macbeth, "The very stones prate of my whereabout"; and to Schiller's poem, *An die Freunde* (*To My Friends*).

Freud's intimate familiarity with Schiller's works is well known and there are at least 47 references to Schiller in the *Standard Edition*. It is not surprising, therefore, to find that Freud's beautiful metaphor of the undaunted archaeologist contains allusions to a Schiller poem. I shall quote the first stanza in Bowring's translation (1910):

> Yes, my friend! — that happier times have been
> Than the present, none can contravene;
>   That a race once liv'd of nobler worth;
> And if ancient chronicles were dumb,
> Countless stones in witness forth would come
>   From the deepest entrails of the earth.
> But this highly-favor'd race has gone,
>   Gone forever to the realms of night.
> We, *we* live! The moments are our own,
>   And the living judge the right.

Schiller not only evokes the scene of ancient ruins and stones but also emanates the stubborn spirit of life asserting itself and making these moments his own. Nothing less can be said about Freud's little story almost a century later.

Yet, one might also speculate about what, beyond literary aesthetics and rhetorical eloquence, moved Freud to choose this particular Latin phrase with its allusions. Did he perhaps feel that in the anti-Semitic milieu of Vienna a reminder of

[5]Buchmann's *Geflugelte Worte* (a widely used compendium of citations, probably also used by Freud) traces *saxa loquuntur* from Habakkuk and Luke to the thirteenth-century *Legenda aurea* of Jacobus de Voragine and then to L. T. Kosegarten's legend *Das Amen der Steine* (Buchmann, 1964, p. 82).

the common roots he had with his audience in both the Old and the New Testament might soften their prejudices? Did he, like Macbeth, feel he had to hide some evil? After all, he had expressed some rather forceful derogatory opinions about his listeners to Fliess and, in an unpublished letter, had referred to them as "donkeys" (see Freud, 1896b, p. 189). Closer to Freud's spirit, however, is the spirit of Schiller's poem, the spirit of youthful defiance, renewal, and affirmation.

It has been suggested that Freud's literary heritage and literary imagination allowed him creatively to form concrete metaphorical images out of vaguely apprehended introspective experiences, and that these images were then harnessed by his scientifically trained ego into scientific concepts (Chapter 3). Thus the vivid imagery not only serves an aesthetic and rhetorical purpose but may be a necessary step in concept formation itself.[6] The same is suggested by the archaeological metaphor that has just been discussed. At a time when Freud had already begun to appreciate the importance of dreams but had not yet finally formulated his theories, he talked about a yield of "undreamed-of information about the remote past" that could perhaps be "deciphered and translated," that might be "bilingual [and] reveal an alphabet and a language." It was not until four years later that he specifically compared the interpretation of dreams to the deciphering of hieroglyphics.

For the purpose of this paper it is not necessary to continue the detailed examination of Freud's style beyond these first few paragraphs. A few more points will suffice. Leading his audience back from the symptom to the scene from which that symptom arose, Freud frequently had to encourage his listeners.

> But the path from the symptoms of hysteria to its aetiology is more laborious and leads through other connections than one would have imagined.
> [Two paragraphs later:] Here we meet with our first great disappointment.

[6]In a similar vein Eissler (1968, p. 151) speculates that "Freud may have discovered the oedipus complex from his study of Shakespeare's tragic hero, as much as from his observation of clinical cases."

[Anticipating the objections in the minds of his readers:] The allegedly traumatic experience, though it *does* have a relation to the symptom, proves to be an impression which is normally innocuous and incapable as a rule of producing any effect....
[Two paragraphs later:] You can understand how great the temptation is at this point to proceed no further with what is in any case a laborious piece of work.

Freud used examples from railway accidents, not because they were particularly illuminating, but because he knew his fellow physicians were vitally interested, since in their practices they had to wrestle with cases of suspected malingering and insurance claims. Having used lucid examples to illustrate his points, Freud confessed that he had been obliged to make them up because the real examples were too complicated. Throughout, he enlivened the flow of his presentation with vivid analogies, for instance, when he compared chains of associations to a string of pearls, or the interconnections to a genealogical tree. He frequently coined new words or expressions by taking ordinary words, such as *nodal point* or *hysterogenic point* or *neurosis of defense,* and elevating them to the status of quasi-scientific terminology. Recognizing his audience's depreciatory view of infancy and childhood mentality, he attempted to dignify the memories of the earliest experiences by comparing them to "the most ancient nobility." *Pari passu,* he thereby also struck a blow against the concepts of hereditary degeneracy.

Freud's prodigious literary talents, which appear so strikingly in his 1896 lecture, were already evident in his adolescent letters (Chapter 3; see also Wolf, 1971). They stamp his whole opus of writings, scientific as well as personal, with the signature of a littérateur of the first rank and earned him the Goethe Prize for Literature. Characteristic is his clarity, his vividness of expression, his use of telling aphorisms and beautiful imagery, interlaced with citations and allusions to the great classics, and punctuated by the coinage of memorable new terms. Awareness of his gift as a witty storyteller moved Freud to apologize that his case histories read like novels (Breuer and Freud, 1893-1895). Notable is his craft in drawing the reader into participation by fictive dialogue, and by empathically sensing the resistances Freud was able to refute objections before they obstructed the discussion.

This rhetorical quality of Freud's prose deserves further comment. On the basis of his philological studies Schönau (1968) has identified Lessing[b] as the most influential model for Freud's *style*.[7]

Lessing was not only a great dramatist and critic, but he is also regarded as the father of German scientific prose. His writings are characterized by many of the same qualities as Freud's, especially the use of fictive dialogue. One also wonders about the influence of Michael Bernays, an uncle of Freud's wife Martha, who as Professor of the History of Literature at the University of Munich had written in 1892 about the specific forms that were demanded by scientific writing and who had recommended Lessing as a standard (Bernays, 1892). Freud himself is reported to have told Wortis (1954) that Lessing was his conscious and deliberate model.

The eloquence Freud manifested in "The Aetiology of Hysteria" is so remarkable that Jones (1953, p. 263) called it a "literary *tour de force,*" and one may be reasonably justified in asking whether special circumstances evoked this extraordinary effort.

The months preceding this lecture had indeed been a time of increasing isolation and tension for Freud: the first strains

[b] An earlier critic—Freud's German teacher at the Gymnasium—had pointed to Herder as the prototype. See page 227.

[7] A number of citations testify to Freud's intimate acquaintance with G. E. Lessing's (1729-1781) writings (Breuer and Freud, 1893-1895, p. 175; Freud, 1900, p. 176; 1905b, pp. 72, 92; 1905-1906, p. 309; 1925b, p. 62; letters to Martha Bernays [E. Freud, 1960, p. 17], Fliess [Freud, 1887-1902, pp. 109, 172], and Pfister [Meng and Freud, 1963, p. 129]). It was Lessing who had in the eighteenth century broken the bonds of chauvinistic patriotism and narrow theology and who paved the way for the great flowering of German literature in the writings of Goethe and Schiller. At a time when Europe was enthralled by belles-lettres Lessing boldly proclaimed the superiority of Shakespeare to Corneille, Racine, and Voltaire. His blank verse play, *Nathan der Weise*, is a dramatization of the idea of religious tolerance, a very meaningful play for Freud from which he paraphrased dialogue in a letter to Martha and whose motto, *Introite et hic dii sunt* (Enter, for Gods dwell here also), he had planned to use as "the proud words" with which to precede his "Psychology of Hysteria" (Freud, 1887-1902, p. 172).

in Freud's relationship with Fliess[c] appeared, and the hostility of the medical community to his ideas surfaced in the publication of a scathing review by Strümpell of the Breuer-Freud *Studies on Hysteria*. On February 6, 1896, Freud (1887-1902) complained to Fliess: "There has been an unconscionable break in our correspondence.... I am blowing my own trumpet for lack of anyone else to blow it for me.... Our book had a disgraceful notice by Strümpell in the *Deutsche Zeitschrift für Nervenheilkunde*." On February 13, he wrote again: "I am so isolated." With a kind of forced enthusiasm he encouraged Fliess: "Criticism will not affect you any more than Strümpell's criticism affected me. I really do not need to be consoled." But his real mood would not be denied: "My health does not deserve to be asked after.... I have grown grey very quickly."

In a letter of March 1, 1896, he advised Fliess on how best to arrange his forthcoming book: "But one should not provide the public with an opportunity of exercising its limited critical faculty, which it generally does to its own detriment, in the chapter devoted entirely to facts.... Otherwise I fear that readers might jump to the conculsion that ..." Surely, here is a writer who is consciously aware of the uses of rhetoric. Freud always knew well what Michael Bernays (1892) had written a few years earlier about scientific prose: formal artistic qualities are required to ensure that scientific work might endure; otherwise the scientific content is absorbed by science, while the author and his writings are forgotten.

Fliess seems to have been unhappy about Freud's comments. On March 16, 1896, Freud was very apologetic: "Do not think I am throwing doubt on your period theory.... I only want to stop you from giving the enemy, the public, something on which to exercise its mind—as I unfortunately always do— because it usually revenges itself for such a challenge." In a footnote to this letter Ernst Kris remarked that Fliess's reaction to Freud's previous letter paved the way to their eventual

[c]For a clear account of the gradual estrangement from Fliess, see Schur (1972).

estrangement. It seems clear that Freud felt menaced on two fronts, in his relationship with Fliess and with the public. But with characteristic humor he was undaunted in stating his secret ambition and conviction: "I am met with hostility and live in such isolation that one might suppose I had discovered the greatest truths."

On April 2, 1896, Freud was again self-depreciating with Fliess: "I am delighted to see you are able to substitute realities for my incomplete efforts." But Freud's drive to attain greatness was not shaken: "... we shall certainly leave behind something which will justify our existence.... I am convinced that ... I can definitely cure hysteria and obsessional neurosis."

These passages reveal that at the time Freud prepared his lecture, he oscillated between states of depressed self-esteem and heroic fantasies of eminence. Referring to Freud's relationship to Fliess, Kohut (1971 and Chapter 16) believes that at that time Freud needed an alter ego to mirror his archaic ambitions for greatness as well as for an idealized self-object as a magnet for his strivings for perfection. Fliess, whose own grandiosity never became transmuted into a secure self-confidence, must have felt deeply hurt by even the slightest critical remarks made by Freud and apparently reacted with the temporary withdrawal of his unconditional acceptance, thus greatly intensifying Freud's needs. Moreover, the concurrent publication of Strümpell's contemptuous review together with its associated reminders of the personally ill-fated collaboration with Breuer could only have increased the void that Freud felt. In this emotionally critical situation — many a lesser man's efforts would have collapsed at this point — Freud marshaled himself, defiantly, in the spirit of Schiller, into an achievement of superlative beauty and eloquence. No wonder Jones speaks of a *"tour de force."*

Perhaps I am being too speculative in drawing these far-reaching inferences from data which are limited in scope and incomplete. A recent paper by Schur (1966a), however, does offer some support. On the basis of unpublished letters to Fliess, Schur concludes "that while the actual final break in the relationship between Freud and Fliess did not occur until the last meeting, during the summer of 1900, the change in Freud's attitude was a gradual one, *with many ups and downs*"[d] (p. 69; my italics).[8] Fliess's mishandling of Emma's nosebleeds which, according to Schur, in 1895 became an important day residue for the pivotal Irma dream, may have been the great and decisive disappointment that started Freud's disillusionment with Fliess.

A brief summary may clarify our thinking before venturing into new territory. I started by taking a new look at a fragment of Freud's opus and noted its aesthetic beauty and power. I paid particular attention to some of the formal characteristics which transform prosaic writing into artistic prose; some evidence of the influence of great writers of the past and of the literary tradition was found. Then, from available historical material, I have reconstructed with reasonable plausibility Freud's psychological state at the time of writing his lecture. But what can one say about creating an admired work of eloquent beauty? Is more involved than merely the wish of an artistically gifted scientist to write in a clear and convincing manner like his admired models?

Let us return to considering Freud's presumable psychological state. Jones (1953, pp. 295, 297, 298) noted that he was "drained of the self-confidence he had transferred to his overpowering partner" (that is, to Fliess), whom "he had

[d] In his 1972 book, Schur surmises that Freud's first reservations about Fliess arose precisely in the spring of 1896, i.e., just before he delivered his lecture to the Society for Psychiatry and Neurology. A more precise disillusionment came about in December, 1897, when Freud found Fliess's theory of bilaterality to be unacceptable.

[8] Eissler (1963, p. 1382) comes to parallel conclusions: "In studying the lives of some geniuses, such as Dostoevski, one gets the impression that man does his best creating when he is caught in the pincers of grave dangers that threaten from within as well as without, whether the outward ones are real or only assumed ... one must conclude that suffering, so far from being an obstacle or impediment to creativity, is one of its prerequisites." Similarly, Jones (1953, p. 305) reports a self-observation by Freud: "I have come back with a lordly feeling of independence and feel too well; since returning I have been very lazy, because the *moderate misery necessary for intensive work* refuses to appear." This seems to document Freud's awareness of the creatively stimulating power of certain states of psychic tension.

endowed with all sorts of imaginary qualities" and to whom he had written on July 14, 1894, "Your praise is nectar and ambrosia to me."

Fliess's withdrawal, even if only temporary and vaguely sensed, is likely to have disturbed the "mirror transference" contained in Freud's relationship to Fliess. The gap left in psychological structure by the "absence" of the admired Fliess in whom Freud had been able to mirror himself needed to be filled with another self-object that would restore the former perfection of the self (Kohut, 1966, 1968, 1971). An artistically gifted person, like Freud, is able to fill the gap by creating a work of artistic beauty, which is psychologically experienced as part of the self; thus the lost beauty and perfection of the self is regained. This creative act is reflected in the *form* of Freud's writing, in its tone, its structure, its artistic beauty which evokes the aesthetic experience. Eissler's (1963) discussion of the vicissitudes of Goethe's relationship to his friends Lavater and Plessing while Goethe's genius was wrestling with writing Book III of *Wilhelm Meister* suggests that Goethe's needs to create artistically were similarly related to his narcissistic vicissitudes.

Returning now to Freud's lecture, one need not look very far to see elements of its *content* with which Freud obviously had identified himself. Perhaps the clearest example is the image of the great archaeological explorer who deciphers ancient alphabets. The allusion here is to J. F. Champollion, who had found the key to the decipherment of Egyptian hieroglyphics on the Rosetta stone. Freud's writings are full of identifications with the great heroes of history, as has been well documented by Jones (1953) and by Schönau (1968). Psychologically, however, such identifications often belong to the developmental line of the cathexes of the functions and actions of objects. In the instance demonstrated here, Freud's identification appears to be with the *activity* of the archaeological explorer but not with his *personship*, an inference that is also supported by Freud's ommission of Champollion's name. It is interesting to compare this with Freud's mentioning of Hannibal (1900, pp. 196f.): "Which of the two, it may be debated, walked up and down his study with the greater

impatience after he had formed his plan of going to Rome—
Winckelmann, the Vice-Principal, or Hannibal, the Com-
mander-in-Chief?" Freud added, "the wish to go to Rome had
become in my dream-life a cloak and a symbol for a number
of other passionate wishes. Their realization was to be pursued
with all the perseverance and single-mindedness of the Carthaginian." Clearly, among the various determinants Freud
seems predominantly to have identified with the tenacious
quality of Hannibal's and Winckelmann's actions of conquer-
ing new territory. Moreover, the mention of both names in the
same breath might be interpreted as de-emphasizing their
personality.[9] These findings seem to suggest that two separate
developmental lines find separate representation in the product of the artist-scientist's creativity: object relations that are
derived from identifications with the actions of others are
reflected in the content, while narcissistic transformations
shape the form of the created work.[10][e]

[9]In connection with the allusion to Champollion discussed above, it is doubly
interesting to note that J. J. Winckelmann (1717-1768) is generally regarded as the
father of classical archaeology and that, like Freud, he also had persevered in his
fascination with antiquity through an interlude of medical studies.

[10]Freud's analysis of tendentious jokes distinguishes two sources of pleasure: an
incentive bonus derived from its formal construction, especially its economy of
presentation, and a greater amount of pleasure derived from the content by the
lifting of repressions (1905b). Similarly, Freud said that writers bribe us by purely
formal aesthetic pleasures so as to make possible the release of greater pleasure
from deeper sources (1908). Might we discern in Freud's formulation indirect
support for the hypothesis being proposed here?

[e]In different historical circumstances, one should, of course, expect a different
distribution of the expression of narcissistic versus idealized-object representations.
One illustration of an identification with the activity of an admired predecessor
that led to formal developments, in addition to being incorporated into content, is
the reaction of the aged Picasso to the death of Matisse (see M. Gedo, in preparation). The latter had been the sole contemporary artist whom Picasso could still
idealize. When Matisse died, Picasso had a period of creative efflorescence in which
he consciously used both the subject matter and the style of the elder artist,
declaring that these had been bequeathed to him.

The possibility of various permutations of these factors in no way detracts from
the importance of Wolf's demonstration that an adequate psychoanalytic approach
to a work of art must consider it from the point of view of form and content; it
must, moreover, identify both derivatives of whole object relations and of
narcissism. It is merely premature to categorize the distribution of these separate
cathexes in any rigid fashion, even if the relationship of narcissistic factors to
formal characteristics and of identifications with objects to content should turn out
to be relatively frequent.

One further comment needs to be made about the public reaction to Freud's paper. Why was this superbly eloquent and beautiful lecture received so icily?[f] Were these sophisticated physicians really so shocked by sexuality even when presented in Freud's circumspect and delicate manner? Perhaps, but I would suggest another and more decisive reason. Freud failed to win acceptance not in spite of his beautifully eloquent presentation but precisely because of its aesthetic qualities. When Krafft-Ebing said, "It sounds like a scientific fairy tale," he was telling a half-truth: this work of science did have the beauty of a fairy tale and, to that audience, beauty in a work of science was suspect and unscientific. One can easily imagine that a more pedestrian and awkwardly embarrassed presentation might have been listened to with more respect. Could it be that Freud, a master of empathic understanding, did not know this? I would suggest that unconsciously the need to create a work of beauty took precedence over the need to persuade. An artistic work of science became a scientific work of art.

Indeed, not only do stones speak, sometimes they also shine.

Although it is useful in common parlance to make a distinction between creative artists and creative scientists, here I do not want to raise again the question whether Freud was more one or more the other. What I am discussing here are aspects of creativity that are shared by both. Freud, especially in his mature years, took vigorous exception to being thought of as an artist. In 1919 Havelock Ellis wrote an essay intended to show Freud as the creator of artistic production but not of scientific work. Freud (1920a, p. 263) replied that "we cannot but regard this view as a fresh turn taken by resistance and as a repudiation of analysis, even though it is disguised in a friendly, indeed in too flattering a manner. We are inclined to meet it with a most decided contradiction." In a letter to Lou Andreas-Salomé he stated it succinctly: "But, despite what

[f]Ellenberger (1970) disputes that the lecture was poorly received and attributes Freud's disappointment to his own unreasonable expectations. On balance, the evidence seems to support Freud's view of his reception. If Ellenberger's were correct, however, Wolf's conclusion would be still more valid: if Freud was angered by mere lack of enthusiasm, his lecture must have been permeated with his grandiose self and its exhibitionism.

some people say, I am not an artist" (Pfeiffer, 1966, p. 196).
Yet it is interesting to note that in earlier, less guarded
moments, Freud did allow himself to flirt with the idea of
becoming a great writer, at least in fantasy. As a 17-year-old
he reported ironically, though with pride, that his professor
compared Freud's style to that of Herder, "a style at once
correct and characteristic," and, jokingly, Freud challenged
his friend Fluss to preserve his letters—"you never know"
(1872-1874). Ten years later he teased his bride, asking her,
"Why didn't I become a gardener instead of a doctor or
writer?" (E. Freud, 1960, p. 40).

In fact, Freud's genius makes it difficult to separate the
artist from the scientist, and the attempt to set them apart
does violence to a deeper understanding of the creative stream
in Freud's personality. It is a false and destructive prejudice of
our time that seeks to isolate modern scientific man from that
part of himself which cannot be weighed or measured but
from which his creative energy flows.

Freud achieved an amalgamation of the artist with the
scientist into a harmoniously productive balance such as had
not been seen since Leonardo or Goethe. As early as 1896, in a
far-seeing review of *Studies on Hysteria,* Alfred von Berger
commented that "the attraction constantly exercised on me
springs from my artistic sensibility which in manifold ways is
stimulated and satisfied by the form and content of this book."
With remarkable foresight Berger also discerned "the idea
that it may one day become possible to approach the innermost secret of human personality." Freud finally must have
felt more secure about the eventual acceptance of his achievement as scientific for he did accept the Goethe Prize for
Literature "in equal measure to the scholar as to the writer"
(Paquet, 1930).

Lest there be any lingering reluctance to acknowledge, even
today, the artistic aspects of scientific creativity, it might be
well to take a brief look at some of the founders of modern
theoretical physics. The British physicist Paul Dirac, who
shared the 1933 Nobel Prize with Erwin Schrödinger for their
pioneering work in quantum mechanics, wrote as follows
about Schrödinger's discovery of the wave equation of the

electron: "Schrödinger got his equation by pure thought, looking for some beautiful generalization. . . . It seems that if one is working from the point of view of getting beauty in one's equation, and if one has really a sound insight, one is on a sure line of progress." Another prominent physicist, Max Born, is reported to have hailed the advent of relativity because, he confessed, it made the universe of science "more beautiful and grandeur." Poincaré wrote that what guided him toward new discoveries was "the feeling of mathematical beauty, of the harmony of numbers and forms, of geometric elegance. This is a true aesthetic feeling that all mathematicians know."[11]

Scientists often acknowledge a quasi-religious feeling of ecstasy in the contemplation of the beauty and order of nature. Einstein (1931) gave eloquent testimony to this "fundamental emotion which stands at the cradle of true art and true science. . . . A knowledge of the existence of something we cannot penetrate, our perception of the profoundest reasons and the most radiant beauty, which only in their most primitive forms are accessible to our minds" (p. 11).

As psychoanalysts we can discern here not only a defensive position derived from the danger situations that menace object-relational developments but also a striving for participation of the self in Nature's infinite beauty and goodness derived from archaic narcissistic disappointments.

For Freud, who was less assured of public acceptance as a scientist than are Nobel laureate physicists, it may have been good politics publicly to deny the poet inside himself. Perhaps, even more than by such external pragmatic considerations, he may have felt persuaded by inner voices to distance himself from the exhibitionism of his illustrious but ill-reputed predecessors such as Charcot and the hypnotists. But his opus is a monument to the undiminished power of the Muse, "for the words which we use in our everyday speech are nothing other than watered-down magic" (Freud, 1905a, p. 283).

---

[11]The quotations in this paragraph are from Koestler (1964, pp. 245, 147).

10

THE CRYPTOMNESIC
FRAGMENT IN THE
DISCOVERY OF
FREE ASSOCIATION

HARRY TROSMAN

[*The Evolution of Psychoanalytic Technique*. In order fully to appreciate the significance of Trosman's discussion of Freud's cryptomnesia about the source of the method of free association, it may be fruitful to review the development of the classical technique of psychoanalysis. Such a review would ideally include consideration of the setting of the psycho-analytic interview as well as the interrelated activities of the patient and the analyst. It is the logical progression in these parallel aspects of technique that makes the ultimate solution, Freud's return to a forgotten model he had first encountered as a young adolescent, so astonishing and revealing of his characteristic mode of creation.

We cannot undertake to cover this vast subject here, but we may briefly reconstruct the evolution of Freud's theory of technique from his description of his treatment procedures in the last chapter of *Studies on Hysteria* (Breuer and Freud, 1893-1895) and from his later expository works (1910a, 1914c, 1925b) on the history of psychoanalysis. After becoming disillusioned with the suggestive therapies he had learned from

First published in *Journal of the American Psychoanalytic Association*, 17:489-510, 1969.

A fuller version of the editors' introduction appeared in "The Question of Research in Psychoanalytic Technique" (Gedo and Pollock, 1967).

Charcot (see Chapter 5) and from Bernheim, Freud adopted Breuer's cathartic method. He gradually dispensed with hypnosis because of difficulties in hypnotizing certain patients and after coming to realize that hypnosis facilitates the development of transference love (see 1925b, p. 27). At this juncture, Freud devised the "pressure technique," illustrated in the *Studies* by the cases of Lucy R. and Elisabeth von R. This was based on his recollection that Bernheim's patients could, with insistence, be made to remember what had occurred in the course of their hypnosis.

This change in procedure produced an essential discovery: that of the phenomenon of resistance. This observation led to the conceptualization of neuroses of defense and to the corollary theory of technique, that of overcoming resistance against the recollection of pathogenic' traumata (i.e., of undoing repression), largely through transference, "the personal influence of the physician" (Breuer and Freud, 1893-1895, p. 283). The cathartic treatment thus gave way to psychoanalysis.

The change in the paradigm of technique described in the *Studies* is typical of later analytic advances in this area. Its cardinal features can be summarized as follows: an established technique, serving as a method of data collection, yields a body of observations that necessitates an evolutionary change in theory. The new theory compels a modification of the special theory of technique. New methods of clinical application are then devised to accomplish the goals called for by the new theory. These methods bring to light a new body of observational data, and the cycle can begin anew. In other terms, the theory of technique can progress only after a major conceptual advance in the psychoanalytic theory of behavior; each such advance necessitates applied research to fit a model technique into the newly formed model of mental functioning.

The shift in method devised by Freud after *Studies on Hysteria* is the subject matter of Trosman's contribution. The substitution of the free-association technique for that of hand pressure was accomplished more gradually than may appear from his discussion, however. In fact, it came to a definitive culmination only with the analysis of the Rat Man in 1907:

"The technique of analysis has changed to the extent that the psychoanalyst no longer seeks to elicit material in which he is interested, but permits the patient to follow his natural and spontaneous trains of thought" (Nunberg and Federn, 1962, p. 227). This was the manner in which Freud announced the initiation of the model technique at the Wednesday Evening Society on November 6, 1907.

Freud later (1925b) described this change so summarily that the laborious 15-year effort it represented may have become obscured. The treatment technique of 1895 had confronted Freud with his patients' dreams (e.g., Breuer and Freud, 1893-1895, pp. 62, 74), and he reported some of his early efforts to arrive at their understanding by attempting to analyze his own. As Trosman reports, it was the successful analysis of the Irma dream that marked the first application of the association technique to a specific set of data. It was barely two months after the publication of the *Studies* that, as Freud was to put it (E. Freud, 1960, Letter 137), "the Secret of Dreams was revealed" to him. We must assume that his own success in producing associations that invariably proved to be relevant to the understanding of his dreams led Freud to the application of the same method in his work with patients. Trosman's account does not emphasize that, at first, the process of associating was not entirely "free." As Jones (1953) has pointed out, "for a long time...[Freud] continued to use the symptoms as starting points, and this habit was reinforced when it became a question of analyzing dreams" (p. 244).

This transitional technique of what might be called "directed association" was used in the treatment of Dora (Freud, 1905d), carried out in the fall of 1900. By 1904, Freud no longer asked his patients to close their eyes while associating (1904, p. 250). Perhaps the unfortunate outcome of the excessive focus on analyzing Dora's dreams may have alerted Freud to the pitfalls of directing the flow of associations on the basis of the analyst's preconceptions. At any rate, the technical innovation he announced to his students in 1907 finally adjusted the technique of analysis to the theory of the mind Freud had propounded in Chapter Seven of *The Interpretation of Dreams*. Freud had sufficient confidence in this model of technique to plan a monograph on the subject; the concrete product of this project is the series of "Papers on Technique" (1911-1915).

These papers formulate the new discovery produced by the switch to a technique of true free association: the realization that elucidation of the resistance, i.e., insight into the nature of the transference, is the prime vehicle of bringing repressed content into consciousness. "In this way the transference is changed from the strongest weapon of the resistance into the best instrument of the analytic treatment" (Freud, 1925b, p. 43). This realization concurrently clarified that, with analyzable patients, the analyst's task consists of interpretation alone — *Eds.*]

Among the unintended contributions of Sigmund Freud to the understanding of the creative process was the revelation of a wide range of psychological processes within himself. We are informed of many of his life experiences, dreams and associations, fantasies, affects, cognitive processes, parapraxes, and conflicts. His autobiographical references are so free of reticence that he could justifiably challenge the unsatisfied reader to experiment with being franker (1900, p. 121). However, on three occasions his disclosures were so personal as to require the special kind of distancing characterized either by anonymous publication or by referring to himself in the third person. In 1899 he described an adolescent love affair in a disguised autobiographical illustration in the paper "Screen Memories" (see Chapter 3). In 1914 he published anonymously "The Moses of Michelangelo" (1914a), an expression of his reaction to the dissensions of Jung and Adler. And in 1920 he used the thin disguise of the signature "F" for "A Note on the Prehistory of the Technique of Analysis" (1920a) in order to reveal a source for the discovery of the fundamental rule of psychoanalysis.

In this note Freud referred to a short article by the German essayist, Ludwig Börne, entitled "The Art of Becoming an Original Writer in Three Days" (1823). Börne advised, "Take a few sheets of paper and for three days on end write down, without fabrication or hypocrisy, everything that comes into your head. Write down what you think of yourself, of your wife, of the Turkish War, of Goethe, of Fonk's trial, of the Last Judgment, of your superiors—and when three days have passed you will be quite out of your senses with astonishment at the new and unheard-of thoughts you have had. This is the art of becoming an original writer in three days!"[1]

Börne, was the first writer whom Freud read in depth. His works had been presented to Freud when he was 14, and 50 years later Freud still had Börne's book in his library as "the only one that had survived from his boyhood." Although he could not remember having read the essay, when he turned to it again, "He was particularly astonished to find expressed in the advice to the original writer some opinions which he himself had always cherished and vindicated." Other essays from the same volume "kept on recurring to his mind for no obvious reason over a long period of years." He concluded, "Thus it seems not impossible that [the rediscovery of the Börne essay] may have brought to light the fragment of cryptomnesia which in so many cases may be suspected to lie behind apparent originality" (1920a)

In writing the note, Freud wished to refute a suggestion that Havelock Ellis had made about the historical antecedents to the technique of free association (Ellis, 1919). Ellis had referred to J. J. Garth Wilkinson, a Swedenborgian mystic and poet, as a forerunner of the psychoanalytic technique, pointing out that Wilkinson used his method for religious and literary purposes rather than for scientific purposes and therefore "Freud's method is an artist's method." Freud denied this, stating that the method rested on an assumption of psychic determinism and could be confirmed by direct experience. However, he would not deny that there was also a "personal influence" in the discovery of the method and, with only the hesitation suggested by writing of himself in the third person, he was prepared to establish the connection between Börne and himself.

Thus Freud's note raises a number of intriguing issues which deserve further exploration. What is the significance of the essay among the factors instrumental in the discovery of free

[1]See Appendix.

association? Who was Ludwig Borne and in what manner could his influence be described as "personal"? By examining the specific link between cryptomnesia and apparent originality can we further our understanding of the effect of tradition on the creative process?

CRYPTOMNESIA

The phenomenon of cryptomnesia has evoked a mild but unsustained interest in the scientific literature.[2] Literally, the term means "hidden memory" and refers to the appearance in consciousness of memory traces which are not recognized as such but appear to be original creations. Organized ideas, thoughts, or images from the past which are not perceived as part of the past appear novel. The term originally appeared in the French scientific literature and was described by the Swiss psychologist, Flournoy, in 1900. In his prepsychoanalytic days, Jung described it twice, first in his doctoral dissertation (1902) and again three years later (1905). The mental content of cryptomnesia enters consciousness as a sudden idea or hunch, he observed, and often in association with the inspirational phase of creative work. Jung noted that Nietzsche incorporated into *Thus Spake Zarathustra* a passage from a book which he had read between the ages of 12 and 15. The similarities between specific verbal elements in both are immediately striking. Without giving good evidence, Jung suggested that Nietzsche's state of mind at the time of writing *Thus Spake Zarathustra* brought him close to the reality of the experiences of his early adolescence. Jung assumed that Nietzsche experienced an altered state of consciousness at the time of the original exposure. Jung also pointed out that cryptomnesia and plagiarism can be confused, particularly when the derived work is a verbatim account of something that preceded it. In the example of cryptomnesia he selected

[2]Recently Taylor (1965) has re-examined cryptomnesia and its link with plagiarism and suggested that the term has passed into disrepute because of its link with spiritualism. He offers little to explain the phenomenon, but does indicate a tie between cryptomnesia, unintended verbatim plagiarism, and excellent verbal rote memory.

from Nietzsche's writings, he believed plagiarism could be discarded as a factor in view of the minor significance of the passage in question. He attributed the cryptomnesic passage to the associational "law of similarity," and explained it in terms of "brain psychology." The brain harbors impressions, however slight, and under special conditions such as ecstasy or inspiration the re-emergence of old memory traces can occur. Jung in this context made no reference to Nietzsche's life experiences when he came across the original source, nor did he suggest that the period of early adolescence was particularly significant.

Another reference to cryptomnesia is made in a paper by Dukes (1915). The author states that one morning, while sitting in the coffee house, he read a newspaper article about the French general, Joffre, which pleased him. It began, "He has a good head for a house watchdog; calm, yet always ready to bite." He then returned to his study, found himself unable to concentrate on a book, began to browse about in his library, took down a volume, opened it, and found exactly the same sentence about Joffre in a book published the previous year. He believed that the automatically executed act of taking down the volume in his library was determined by his reaction to reading the sentence in the newspaper an hour before. He explained the phenomenon in terms of repression; insofar as he had no memory of having read the article earlier, repression had been strong enough to prevent the breakthrough of the memory into consciousness. Nevertheless, the repressed memory trace expressed itself in the form of an automatic act. The original quotation had made a strong impression which subsequently became absorbed in the repressive process. Dukes realized that he had repressed the content of the memory because he was reminded of a character trait of his own that he found unacceptable. Ferenczi added a confirmatory note to the paper from knowledge of the author's early life.

Bleuler referred to cryptomnesia in the following manner: "There are learned men who at first negatively reject every new idea and then digest it consciously or unconsciously and finally accept it, if it suits them, but then absolutely forget that these are no discoveries of their own, and even go so far as to present them as new to the very people who discovered them" (1916, p. 109).

Ferenczi (1920) offered an example of cryptomnesic rediscovery in a review of a book by the Viennese physicist and philosopher, Ernst Mach. Ferenczi pointed out that, although Mach had been familiar with established psychoanalytic ideas about memory functions, he incorporated them into a book, *Kultur und Mechanik*, as an original contribution. Here, also, Ferenczi suggested the mechanism of repression at work. Mach could not give credit to Freud because of his need to repudiate psychoanalytic ideas concerning sexuality. "Mach had to rediscover (cryptomnesically) the idea inspired in him by Breuer and Freud," he wrote (p. 396). Thus Ferenczi on two occasions made a rather clear link between repression and cryptomnesia.

Stekel (1922) offered several examples of cryptomnesic rediscoveries in music and poetry and suggested that "close preoccupation with an author often leaves unsuspected traces." He emphasized not a repressive force but the presence of an incorporative and identificatory process. "We feed on those who have gone before us" (p. 240).

During the course of the analysis of Else Frenkel-Brunswik, her analyst pointed out to her that she had established an identification with Cordelia, the youngest daughter of King Lear (Frenkel-Brunswik, 1940). She responded that, although she had read most of Shakespeare's plays, she had not read *King Lear* and, when the analyst elaborated the interpretation, she rejected it. Much later, in looking through some of her old papers, she discovered that at the age of 15 she had copied out the entire role of Cordelia. She remarked when describing the incident that, although she must have been very concerned with the fate of Cordelia with whom she had identified, she had repressed not only the identification but also all memory of the play. Like Freud and Nietzsche, Frenkel-Brunswik provides an example of a cryptomnesic experience concerning something read for which the memory trace had been laid down during the period of early adolescence. In her case, however, the derivative of the memory trace did not take the form of an original idea or a compulsion toward carrying out an automatic act but appeared as a specific character motif. In all likelihood, the identification with Cordelia was subsequently pulled into the area of the repressed because of its association with ramifications of the childhood neurosis. However, in this instance, as in other instances of cryptomnesic rediscovery, the powers of repression were not strong enough entirely to obliterate any actual expression of the repressed content.

Freud made several further comments about cryptomnesia and originally in his own work. In 1917, Georg Groddeck asked Freud officially to confirm that Groddeck was not a psychoanalyst so that he might conceive of himself as untrammeled by intellectual allegiances. Freud replied that he could not disaffiliate Groddeck because "The man who has recognized that transference and resistance are the hubs of treatment belongs irrevocably to the 'Wild Hunt.'" He expressed his concern that Groddeck had evidently

> ...succeeded so little in conquering that banal ambition which hankers after originality and priority. If you feel assured of the independence of your discoveries, why should you want to claim originality? And besides, can you be so sure on this point?... Is it not possible that you absorbed the leading ideas of psychoanalysis in a cryptomnesic manner? Similar to the manner in which I was able to explain my own originality? Anyhow, what is the good of struggling for priority against an older generation?...a man with unbridled ambition is bound at some time to break away and, to the loss of science and his own development, to become a crank [E. Freud, 1960, Letter 176].

Another example of Freud's effort to find antecedents for his apparently original ideas appeared in a short paper of 1923, "Josef Popper-Lynkeus and the Theory of Dreams" (see Chapter 14). In considering "the subjective side of originality," Freud pointed out that, although some sources of ideas are immediately apparent, other apparently novel ideas yield their hidden and long-forgotten sources only after careful investigation. "There is nothing to regret in this," stated Freud, "we had no right to expect that what was 'original' could be untraceable and undetermined. In my case, too, the originality of many of the new ideas employed by me...has evaporated in this way" (1923c, p. 261). In another comment regarding sources of his apparently original ideas Freud referred to a dual instinct theory in the writings of the philosopher Empedocles, and stated, "I am very ready to give up the prestige of originality for the sake of such a confirmation, especially as I can never be certain, in view of the wide extent of my reading in early years, whether what I took for a new creation might not be an effect of cryptomnesia" (1937, p. 245).

Since the early 1920's the concept of cryptomnesia has been neglected in the psychoanalytic literature, and a panel (Niederland, 1965) devoted to "Memory and Repression" makes no reference to cryptomnesia by name or an isolated phenomenon. To re-examine the phenomenon, a more detailed view of its appearance in the context of Freud's work is appropriate.

Intellectual Background and Clinical Setting in the Discovery of Free Association

Jones believed that one of the two great accomplishments of Freud's scientific life was his self-analysis. The other was the transition from the cathartic method to free association (1953, p. 241). Jones listed, as contributors to this discovery, Freud's patience and passivity, the acceptance of the principle of psychological causality and determinism, his understanding of the phenomenon of resistance which permitted him to account for the variability of the patient's thought processes, and, finally, the influence of Börne.

Freud's attitude toward the discovery of the fundamental rule was quite different from his attitude toward the theory of repression which, he stated, "certainly came to me independently of any other source; I know of no outside impression which might have suggested it to me." For a long time he believed that the theory of repression was entirely original. When Rank pointed out to him that Schopenhauer had referred to a similar conception, Freud remarked wryly,

"Once again I owe the chance of making a discovery to my not being well-read." Since others had read the passage and passed it by without discovering the theory of repression, "perhaps," he stated, "the same would have happened to me if in my young days I had had more taste for reading philosophical works." He added that he deliberately avoided reading Nietzsche in order not to be "hampered in working out the impression received in psycho-analysis by any sort of anticipatory ideas" (1914c, pp. 15f.).[a]

Freud's view of the discovery of free association and its "first fruits," the interpretation of dreams, was not accompanied by the same certainty of the absence of an outside influence. Indeed, 20 years after the discovery he stated that in deciding to replace hypnosis by free association he was "following a dim presentiment" (1914c, p. 19),[3] indicating that he felt himself directed in this course.

He knew of some historical antecedents and in *The Interpretation of Dreams* (1900) he quoted a passage from Schiller urging a young inhibited writer to give free rein to his imagination and release the constraint imposed by his reason: "Where there is a creative mind, Reason—so it seems to me—

[a]Freud's statements about not being well-read, particularly in philosophy, must be taken *cum grano salis*. Merlan (1945, 1949) has called attention to the influence of Brentano on the young Freud. We have already cited (Introduction to Chapter 1) the evidence from Freud's Silberstein correspondence, written while he attended Brentano's lectures, which reveals not only the keenest interest in the subject matter but also avid reading in it, extensive personal contact with Brentano, and a serious intention to add a doctorate in philosophy to the medical qualifications Freud was already seeking (see Stanescu, 1971). Freud's *deliberate* avoidance of Nietzsche must have taken place while he was making his early analytic discoveries; the philosopher's productive years had by then come to their end. Freud obviously knew enough about the congruence of Nietzsche's thought with his own findings to be able to decide on the need for his policy of avoidance. As Schur (1972) has reported, he resumed his study of Nietzsche in 1900. His later friendship with Nietzsche's friend, Lou Andreas-Salomé, must have been given added impetus by the fact that she represented a human bridge between the mature Freud and his intellectual forebear. Gedo and Wolf have noted (Chapter 1) that Andreas-Salomé also may have called Freud's attention to the *Essays* of Montaigne.

[3]Strachey's translation of *"Einer dunklen Ahnung Folgend"*: translated as "following an obscure intuition" by Jones (1953, p. 246), who believed the expressive quality of the phrase was lost in translation. When Freud wrote about the influence in this manner in 1914, he had not yet become aware of his early exposure to the Börne essay.

relaxes its watch upon the gates, and the ideas rush in pell-mell.... You critics, or whatever else you may call yourselves, are ashamed or frightened of the momentary and transient extravagances which are to be found in all truly creative minds" (1900, p. 103). Rieff (1959), indicating Freud's link with the Romantic Movement, noted the general interest among creative writers in promoting spontaneity by such means as inducing dream states, taking drugs, or whatever would reduce the watchfulness of the conscious mind and allow unconscious material to enter it (p. 99).

Bellak (1961) found antecedents to free association in Aristotle and the British associational psychological school of Hobbes, Locke, Hume, Berkeley, James Mill, and John Stuart Mill. Bakan (1958) emphasized the origins in Jewish mysticism, particularly in the works of the thirteenth-century Jewish philosopher, Abulafia, who offered a method of "jumping and skipping" for widening of consciousness in order to bring to light hidden processes of the mind (pp. 77f.). Zilboorg considered it likely that Freud was influenced by Francis Galton, who used the method of free association as a means for the recovery of memories. Galton wrote, "Ideas arise of their own accord.... These associated ideas, though they are for the most part exceedingly fleeting and obscure, and barely cross the threshold of our consciousness, may be seized, dragged into daylight and recorded" (Zilboorg, 1952, p. 493). Havelock Ellis (1919) added, as mentioned above, J. J. Garth Wilkinson to the list.

Although the list of those who anticipated the discovery is by no means complete, many authorities have been cited as having anticipated Freud. Indeed, the attempts to trace the influence have been so successful that Freud's contribution appears as a culmination of a historical continuum rather than as an innovation. As Zilboorg suggests, "a wealth of ideas and conceptions seems to lie around idly in full sunlight, ripening, maturing.... Then... a day comes when someone picks up that which seems a fruitful part of our scientific heritage. Such men we call creative geniuses. They are truly creative, yet they seem to have created nothing new" (1952, pp. 494f.).

The traditional sources for the discovery of free association were part of the intellectual heritage of the time and, although influential, hardly specific. Freud's practical concern, arising out of the medical setting, was the need to find a more adequate procedure for clinical investigation. A number of direct experiences with patients had played a role in directing Freud toward a method which would allow an unlimited range of reportable psychological material. From Breuer he had learned of Anna O.'s departure from the formalism of hypnosis toward the more liberating "chimney sweeping." As early as 1888 or 1889, Frau Emmy von N. had already revealed to him the possibility of making use of conversation as a supplement to hypnosis (Breuer and Freud, 1893-1895, p. 56). By 1892 he had devised a "concentration technique" and encouraged Fräulein Elisabeth von R. to lie down with eyes closed and concentrate on a symptom in order to recall the memories that were associated with its origin. Shortly thereafter he used a "pressure technique," urging patients to report faithfully whatever appeared before their inner eye when pressure was applied to the head. When associations were denied, his insistence took the form of repeating his injunction that ideas would occur if the patient would not disregard them as a result of "applying criticism" (p. 153f.). It is not clear whether he first used this technique with Miss Lucy R. or with Fräulein Elisabeth, both of whom he began treating toward the end of 1892, nor do we know precisely when he abandoned these various techniques, although we know that hypnosis was abandoned altogether by 1896. On one occasion, Fräulein Elisabeth reproved Freud for interrupting her with questions, and thus another step in the direction of free association was taken (Jones, 1953, pp. 243f.). Schur (1966a) surmises that "what Freud may have been attempting for the first time with the Irma dream was the systematic application of free association to every single element of the manifest dream." The date of this dream analysis—July 24, 1895—may thus serve as the precise date of the consolidation of the free-association technique (p. 48). By July 7, 1897, Freud had become quite clear which of the methods he preferred. "So far as technique is concerned I am beginning to prefer one particular way as the natural one," he wrote Fliess (Freud, 1887-1902, Letter 66, p. 212). By 1900, in *The Interpretation of Dreams*, he indicated that the success of psychoanalysis is dependent upon the patient "reporting whatever comes into [his] head" (p. 101). The recommendation of shutting the eyes continued as a remnant of the old hypnotic procedure. By 1904 that had also disappeared.

Although in retrospect the progression toward free association seems to fall "naturally" into place, there is no intrinsic reason why the progression could not have stopped at any of the substations along the way, as it apparently did for less intrepid investigators; hypnosis and suggestion were considered adequate by the French neurologists, and catharsis seemed more than adequate to Breuer. Apart from his dissatisfaction with manipulative techniques, and from his experience with helpful patients, Freud felt an unknown factor urging him forward and later considered that it may have been the residual of the Börne essay read in his early adolescence and subsequently forgotten.

BÖRNE AND FREUD

Karl Ludwig Börne, a German-Jewish essayist and political journalist, was born Löb Baruch on May 6, 1786, in Frankfort am Main, and died in Paris on February 13, 1837 (Freud, 1923c; *The Universal Jewish Encyclopedia*, 1939-1943).[4]

His father, Jacob, was a well-to-do banker and merchant who sent his son to Giessen at the age of 14 to prepare for a medical career. He soon gave up medicine and, when Frank-

---

[4] *The Encyclopaedia Britannica* (1963) states that Börne was born on May 6 or 24, 1786. Since the correct birthdate is of significance in accounting for Freud's interest in Börne, I am grateful to Professor H. Stefan Schultz of the Department of Germanic Languages and Literature at the University of Chicago for having cleared up the ambiguity. He points out that the following ten encyclopedic works give May 6, 1786, as Börne's birthdate: *Allgemeine deutsche Biographie* (1876): "Geb. 6 (nicht 18. oder 2.) Mai"; *Jewish Encyclopedia* (1902); *Meyers Grosses Konversationslexikon* (1906); *Der Grosse Brockhaus* (1929); *Encyclopedia Italiana* (1930); *Meyers Lexikon* (1937); Wilhelm Kosch, *Deutsches Literatur Lexikon* (1949); *Neue Deutsche Biographie* (1955); *Collier's Encyclopedia* (1964); *Encyclopedia Americana* (1966). Professor Schultz states that the *Encyclopaedia Britannica* date of May 24 is incorrect. Börne in his early writings always gave May 6 as his birthday and May 6 was the birthdate known to Freud.

fort became a free city and civil rights were conferred upon the Jews, he decided to seek a public career and became a government official. Following the collapse of Napoleon in 1815 and the dismissal of the Jews from public life in Frankfort, in 1818 Börne converted to Christianity and thus succeeded for a time in holding his appointment. He was a bitter foe of Metternich and was active in promoting political and social reform in his journalistic work. His vehement criticism of the reactionary political and social conditions in Germany and his championing of individual liberty subjected him to political censorship during which his journals were suspended and he was fined and imprisoned. During the last years of his life he settled in Paris and continued to promote German nationalist activity. With Heine, he was identified with the literary and political movement known as *Junges Deutschland*, which finally culminated in the revolutionary achievements of 1848. Börne was admired for possessing a unique German style and he was a master of wit and invective.

Börne was the first writer into whose works Freud penetrated deeply, and his political writings may well have appealed to a boy who at one time carried "a Cabinet Minister's portfolio" in his schoolboy satchel (1900, p. 193). In his early student days (1873-1878), Freud belonged to a German nationalist group, *Der Leseverein der deutschen Studenten,* which supported the annexation of Austrian territory to Germany (McGrath, 1967). Another aspect of his interest in Börne was probably based on their shared birthdays, since we know of Freud's propensity to find such items of correspondence with historical figures. An early hero had been Masséna, the Napoleonic general believed to have been Jewish, and of whom Freud said, "No doubt this preference was also partly to be explained by the fact that my birthday fell on the same day as his, exactly a hundred years later (1900, p. 198).[5]

Börne's book came to Freud's attention shortly after his dis-

[5]He was mistaken in the date of Masséna's birth, which was actually 1758, and probably in his belief about the general's Jewish origin. His later interest in Woodrow Wilson is attributed in part to the fact that they were born in the same year (Freud and Bullitt, 1967, p. vi).

illusionment with his father for his "unheroic conduct" when humiliated by an anti-Semite. The exposure to Börne was contemporaneous with his reactive idealization of Hannibal, "the Semitic General" (1900, pp. 196-198). Börne's essay, which suggests a way out from disillusionment with the older generation and traditional values, offered an appropriate substitute for disappointed longings toward idealization.[6]

The specific developmental tasks of the early adolescent are to resolve the biological instinctual upsurges of puberty and to separate from former object ties and effect interest in extra-familial love objects. As Blos (1962) has pointed out, the period of early adolescence appears, in reaction, an attempt to recover the "narcissistic omnipotence of childhood" (p. 77). "The heightened introspection or psychological closeness to internal processes in conjunction with a distance from outer objects allow the adolescent a freedom of experience and an access to his feelings which promote a state of delicate sensitivity and perceptiveness" (pp. 125f.). Jacobson (1964) has remarked on the narcissistic inflation of the period of early adolescence and its propensity for the consolidation of highly creative activity with a freeing of previous repression. Börne's injunction was particularly appropriate to a young adolescent whose sense of self was suffused by an intense sense of uniqueness. Börne wrote, "Whoever listens to the voice of his heart rises above the shouting of the market, and whoever has the courage to propagate what his heart has taught him will always be original."

It is possible that Freud took seriously Börne's injunction to write down his free associations and he may have collected this material for a period of time. At 28, he wrote that he had frustrated his biographers by destroying "all my notes of the past fourteen years" (E. Freud, 1960, Letter 61, p. 140). In his later adolescence he gave up his intrapsychic explorations, became immersed in a tradition of biological research, and turned his powers of observation toward external reality rather

[6]The fact that Freud received the Börne collection as a gift at about the same time as his Bar Mitzvah may also have served to authenticate his budding sense of independence and heightened the significance of the book for him.

than toward internal mental processes.[b] A harbinger of this turning away from the challenge of introspection and some of its upsetting consequences is seen in a remark at the age of 17, in a letter to his friend Fluss, "I don't mean to suggest that if you find yourself in a doubtful situation, you should mercilessly dissect your feelings...it is unfortunately not a firm basis for self-knowledge" (E. Freud, 1960, Letter 1, p. 5).

Freud's experience with the Börne essay warrants comparison with several other cryptomnesic incidents he reported. Shortly after his arrival in Paris, at the age of 28, before he was taken into Charcot's circle, he felt "lonely and full of longings," and greatly in need of help and protection. While walking the streets, he concocted a fantasy of a figure who boldly threw himself at the head of a runaway horse in order to bring it to a stop. A great personage stepped out of the carriage and said to the hero, "You are my savior. I owe my life to you. What can I do for you?" Freud subsequently realized that he had probably read an exactly similar rescue fantasy in a story by Franz Hoffmann between the ages of 11 and 13, and remarked that part of the difficulty in remembering the fantasy and its origin concerned his own difficulty in accepting protection and his resistance to being dependent on a protector's favor. A deeper meaning to the fantasy is suggested in his reference to Abraham's paper on "The Rescue and Murder of the Father in Neurotic Phantasy-Formation" (1901, p. 150, footnote added in 1924).

Another incident occurred in the summer of 1900. During a lively discussion with Fliess he remarked on the importance of assuming a bisexual constitution to personality. When Fliess

[b] This volume has made repeated reference to the difference of opinion between Gedo and Wolf, on the one hand, and K. R. Eissler, on the other, about the significance of Freud's self-immersion in the discipline of the physiological laboratory (see Chapter 3, especially the Introduction). This seems an appropriate place to repeat the view that had Freud allowed himself, at the age of 19, to plunge into his more passionate interest in moral and political philosophy, it is very unlikely that he could have developed those disciplines into the empirically based science he created in psychoanalysis. It may not be too speculative to suggest that his work would very likely have come to resemble that of his admired contemporary and *Doppelgänger*, Popper-Lynkeus (for details, see Chapter 14).

pointed out that he had made the same statement to Freud two and a half years previously, Freud could not recall it. During the next week, however, he remembered the entire incident, including the statement he had made on the occasion that he had not yet accepted the notion of bisexuality and was not inclined to go into the question (pp. 143f.). The cryptomnesic rediscovery had occurred at a period during which the friendship with Fliess was waning. Freud related his inability to remember Fliess's comment to the pain associated with having to surrender one's own originality.

Forgetting the conversation with Fliess is indeed remarkable in the light of several comments Freud had written to Fliess. On January 4, 1898, he wrote, "I seized eagerly on your notion of bisexuality, which I regard as the most significant for my subject since that of defense" (Freud, 1887-1902, Letter 81, p. 242). On August 1, 1899, he wrote, "Now for bisexuality! I am sure you are right about it. And I am accustoming myself to the idea of regarding every sexual act as a process in which four persons are involved" (Letter 113, p. 288). However, priority for the concept of bisexuality is not easy to establish. In a letter of December 6, 1896, a year before the Fliess statement, Freud had *already* stated, "In order to explain why the outcome is sometimes perversion and sometimes neurosis, I avail myself of the universal bisexuality of human beings" (Letter 52, p. 179). This confusion over priority may well be reflected in the subsequent cryptomnesia.

Although the several cryptomnesic episodes Freud recorded vary in their content, there is a unifying theme of liberation from tradition and the past. The earliest episode is a challenge to overthrow authority and seek the truth by setting aside the censorship to free expression (Börne); the next is a reminder of passive infantile longings for support and patronage, thinly veiling an attack on parental authority (Hoffmann); and the last, in the midst of rivalrous and hostile feelings, is a claim for priority that denies his previous collaborative need (Fliess).

The period of the early 1890's is in some ways parallel to the period of Freud's early adolescence. As he began to experiment with various offshoots of the cathartic method, he experienced his first disillusionment with Breuer as he had previously experienced a sense of disappointment in his father. More and more he tended to turn in the early 1890's to independent activity and innovations in procedure. He began to use introspection as a method of observation and subjective experience as data, just as Börne had advised. During this period he sought and received the support of Fliess, whom he described as "a person whose agreement I recalled with satisfaction whenever I felt isolated in my opinions" (1900, p. 117). This statement closely resembles his comment about Börne: "He [Freud] was particularly astonished to find expressed in the advice to the original writer some opinions which he himself had always cherished and vindicated" (1920a). Thus it is not unlikely that the encourager and supporter of Freud's creative work in the early 1890's was a *revenant* of Börne. The points of similarity between Freud and Börne — that is, their Jewish origin, the identical birthdate, their medical training, a shared interest in German nationalism and a political career, and a mutual impatience with authority — permitted Freud to find in Börne an ally modeled after aspects of his narcissistic self. Although he later turned to experimental and biological researches when he had no means for adequately integrating the fruits of Börne's advice to look inward, he continued to preserve Börne's book in his library as a token of the importance he attached to the injunction to trust his intrapsychic processes. Significantly, he visited Börne's grave in Paris as he was about to take a crucial step away from an interest in organic medicine toward psychological concerns (Jones, 1953, p. 246).

CRYPTOMNESIA AND ORIGINALITY

Although the interest in this study is in the relationship between hidden memory and apparent originality, there are other forms of cryptomnesic rediscovery that do not necessarily relate to creative work. A variety of functions may be related to the hidden memory. In the case of Dukes, reactivation of the memory served as an instigator to action; in the case of Else Frenkel-Brunswik, the repressed memory subsequently expressed itself in the character structure. In the clinical situation the content of an unconscious memory can be reconstructed and subsequently confirmed either because it is repeated in the transference, because information is sought about it through external sources, or, indeed, because the memory itself is eventually recovered.

In Freud's case, the specific experience of cryptomnesia[c] as described in the discovery of free association is not of the dramatic kind in which there has been a complete repetition of an identical mode of expression, as for example, in the case of Nietzsche. Freud did not evidence an exact duplication of Börne's thought. There are two specific elements of the Börne advice which are initially repeated by Freud in *The Interpretation of Dreams* (1900). Like Börne, who urged picking a topic, Freud advised associating to specific dream elements and, also following Börne, he followed the practice of writing out the associations.

The experience of reading the Börne article and the accompanying memory traces were probably repressed rather than, as is done in normal forgetting, initially subjected to a process of condensation or decathected. The emotional importance of the Börne article is suggested by the presumptive evidence of an identification with Börne, Freud's designation of Börne as "the first author into whose writings he had penetrated deeply," and the retention of the Börne book in his library for 50 years. Repression necessitated by the content evoked by the method as well as the antiauthoritarian and revolutionary attitude toward authority figures proclaimed by the article may well have played a part in the special form of preservation of content which customarily results from repression.

The specific function of repression as a factor in the creative process requires attention. Repression is not only operative in forgetting but performs a function in preserving mental content as well. The various aspects of the memory function can be broken down into the part functions of registration, storage, coding, retrieval, and reconstruction (Klein, 1966). The retrieval of a memory, as, for example, in the crypt-

[c]For another instance of cryptomnesia suffered by Freud, see Shengold (1972).

omnesic experience, need not be consciously experienced, but it does depend upon effective registration, storage, and coding. Unconscious retrieval may be contingent upon the revival of the same state in which the original registration of the memory occurred. This process is suggested in Freud's case by the similar emotional constellations at the time of the registration of the memory trace in early adolescence and at its re-emergence in the period of creative activity which led to the discovery.

Specifically, the cryptomnesic experience implies omission of a quality which accompanies memory traces when they are experienced as such, i.e., the experience of remembering. If the subjective sense of remembering is absent, the retrieved material is experienced as original. In this way, it is similar to the clinical symptom of *jamais vu*, the false sense of unfamiliarity in situations which have been previously experienced. Although the duplication of the memory in a new setting is an indication of a lack of erasure, its use for adaptive purposes suggests a transformation from a conflict-laden context to a context in which ego functions characteristic of secondary autonomy are operative. The availability of specific memory traces for adaptive purposes implies a decathexis of a drive organization of memory to an organization on a conceptual or secondary-process level. "A change of function" to a nonconflicted sphere has taken place (Hartmann, 1939). Freud's remark, that he would have been encumbered had he known of Schopenhauer's conceptions, suggests that he may have experienced his remarkable memory as a burden which interfered with his ability to use observation as an investigative technique. When the memory function became attached to a specific historical figure whom he admired, the reinstinctualization of the memory function may well have interfered with his ability to use his observational skill. The reinstinctualization was then experienced as a regressive intrusion into the adaptive functioning of the ego.

The period of later adolescence has been implicated as crucial in the life of the highly creative person (Eissler, 1961; Erikson, 1956). Although it is an oversimplification to attach undue importance to any one specific phase over another,

Freud's reference to the Börne article and the period of his exposure to it suggest a crucial influence during the period of early adolescence. Approximately the same phase of personality maturation is identified by Frenkel-Brunswik, Nietzsche, and Freud as the period in which the original perception for the later cryptomnesic experience occurred. In each of the three experiences there is an aspect of a narcissistic ideal represented in the hidden memory trace. Nietzsche described a Superman; Frenkel-Brunswik, an idealized self-characterization; and, in Freud's case, the percept referred to tapping internal truth-fulfilling potentialities. These instances suggest a heightened receptiveness to ideational influences in the period of early adolescence. These influences may determine subsequent channeling of creative activity. Particularly, this period may be crucial in the development of potentialities which lead to psychological insights.

Finally, the cryptomnesic experience suggests a protective and defensive operation the creator is likely to resort to when confronted by the emotional isolation which accompanies the view of a hitherto unrecognized sphere of inner or outer reality. In Freud's case, the uncovering of psychological processes in his patients and himself was likely to stimulate repetitive traumatic states before the ideational content became clear to him. As Kris (1939) and Kohut (Chapter 16) have suggested, the difficulties inherent in such explorations necessitated an alliance, a sense of association with a sustaining ally, real or fantasies, an "unseen collaborator."[7] Fliess fulfilled this function during the period of the great discoveries, Börne during early adolescence. In Freud's correspondence with Schnitzler, another Jewish, medically trained, introspective writer, he explained his avoidance of meeting the playwright as a reluctance of meeting his "double," a reincarnation of some essential aspect of himself (see Kupper and Rollman-Branch, 1959). Perhaps Freud also saw Börne as "a

[7] A. E. Housman (1940) has caught this need for a feeling of alliance in his poem:
    Others, I am not the first,
    Have willed more mischief than they durst:
    If in the breathless night I too
    Shiver now 'tis nothing new.
                    ("The Shropshire Lad")

double," a link with the past who insured him against excessive traumatization in his early adolescence and offered the promise of his still dormant potentialities. When his relationship to Börne was no longer available to consciousness, it nevertheless left its trace. Thus, when he came to describe the transition from the cathartic method to the discovery of free association, he saw it as a journey in which he felt himself to be following a path already prescribed, however dimly.

SUMMARY

Cryptomnesia occasionally accompanies an apparently original discovery in a highly creative person. A number of such cryptomnesic phenomena are described, and particular attention is paid to Ludwig Börne's influence on Freud's discovery of free association. The discovery is seen as the fulfillment of an adaptive task consistent with the scientific path Freud was pursuing. The cryptomnesic fragment, although related to conflict and thus an ideational remnant of a failure of repression, is also an indicator of the link between the creator and his intellectual and personal tradition in the form of a creative alliance. The period of early adolescence, when ideational content is patterned by narcissistically derived ideals, is suggested as critical to the potentially creative person in that bonds of attachment to the historical past permit acceptance of creative powers and give direction for potential investments. Figures for identification are likely to follow a design established by an assessment of specifically unique attributes. Börne was not only a minor source of the discovery of free association but also an early precursor of "the unseen collaborator" necessitated by the hazards of revolutionary creative achievement.

Appendix

The Art of Becoming an Original Writer in Three Days

Ludwig Börne

(Translated by Leslie Gable, M.D.)

There are people and writings which give instruction in learning the Latin, Greek, and French languages in three days, bookkeeping even in three hours. How to become a good original writer in three days has not yet been shown. And yet it is so easy! In doing so one has nothing to learn, but only a great deal to unlearn; nothing to experience, but many things to forget. In today's world, the heads of scholars, and their works as well, are like those old manuscripts from which the tedious wrangling of shabby church fathers, or the drivel of a monk, has to be scraped off in order to come upon a Roman classic. Each human soul has innate beautiful thoughts and, inasmuch as through each human the world is created anew, new ideas are instilled in him; but life and instruction write their useless things upon the soul and obscure the ideas. One gets a fairly clear picture of this situation if one perhaps considers the following. We recognize an animal, a fruit, and a flower for what they are; they are what they appear to be. But would the nature of a partridge, a raspberry bush, or a rose really be obvious if one were acquainted only with partridge pie, raspberry juice, or rose oil? This is the case with knowledge, with all things which we perceive with the mind and not through the senses; when they are placed before us dressed and transformed, we will not learn to know them in their raw and naked form. The mind is the kitchen in which all truths are slaughtered, plucked, minced, stewed, and flavored. We lack nothing more than books without intelligence, that is to say, books which contain things but not views. There are but few original writers, and the best differ from the inferior much less than one might conclude after a superficial comparison. Some crawl, some run, some hobble, some dance, some drive, some ride to their goal; but an objective and a manner they have in common. Great and new ideas occur only in solitude; but how does one achieve solitude? One could avoid people, then only to find oneself at the clamorous book-market; one could throw away the books, but how to rid oneself of all the traditional knowledge which instruction brought? As far as the art of making oneself unknowledgeable is concerned, the most needed and finest and practiced least and most unskillfully is the art of self-education. Just as there are among a million people only a thousand thinkers, there is among a thousand thinkers only one original thinker. At the present time, a people is like the rich ingredients of a soup which only a pot holds together; something as substantial and solid will be found only in the scraping of the lowest layer of the nation, and stock remains stock, and the golden spoon that scoops out a mouthful, although it has separated the parts, has not also broken up the whole.

The true learned endeavor is no Columbuslike voyage of discovery, rather a Ulyssean journey. Man is born among strangers; to live is to search for a native country, and to think is to live. But the fatherland of thoughts is the heart, and those who wish to drink a fresh draught should ladle at this source; the mind is only a stream — thousands lie around it, and make the water turbid by washing, bathing, steeping of flax, and other dirty handling of it. The spirit is the arm, the heart is the will; one can develop strength, one can increase this and improve; but of what use is all strength without the courage to use it? A disgraceful cowardliness in regard to thinking holds us all back. The censorship of governments is less oppressive than the censorship exercised by public opinion of our intellectual production. It is not lack of intellect but lack of character that prevents most writers from being better than they are. This weakness arises from vanity. The artist and the writer want to surpass and excel their colleagues; only if one measures oneself against another can one know whether one excels; only if one races against another can one know whether one surpasses. Therefore the good writer has so much in common with the bad one; the good one lies hidden by the bad, but the former is something more. The good one goes the same way as the bad, only he goes somewhat further. Whoever listens to the voice of his heart rises above the shouting of the market, and whoever has the courage to propagate what his heart has taught him will always be original. Sincerity is the source of all genius, and men would be cleverer if they were more moral. And here follows the practical application that was promised. Take a few sheets of paper and for three days on end write down, without fabrication or hypocrisy, everything that comes into your head. Write down what you think of yourself, of your wife, of the Turkish war, of Goethe, of the Fonk trial, of the Last Judgment, of your superiors — and when three days have passed you will be quite out of your senses with astonishment at the new and unheard-of thoughts you have had. This is the art of becoming an original writer in three days!

PART IV

FREUD'S MATURE WORKING METHODS

11

THE PROCESS OF
HYPOTHESIS CHANGE IN
THREE EARLY
PSYCHOANALYTIC
CONCEPTS

LEO SADOW, JOHN E. GEDO,

JULIAN A. MILLER, GEORGE H.

POLLOCK, MELVIN SABSHIN, and

NATHAN SCHLESSINGER

[*Progress in Psychoanalysis*. The chapters in Part III have described the genesis of psychoanalysis in terms of a fusion within Freud's mind of the two principal strands of his intellectual heritage. At the start of his activity as a medical psychologist, the traditions of empirical science with their reliance on external observation, inductive reasoning, and hypothesis testing through renewed observation were most characteristic of his work. Following the discovery of his method of dream interpretation in the summer of 1895 through the analysis of his own dreams, Freud began to return to the humanist introspective tradition which had characterized his early education and his adolescent activities. The development of the method of free association marked the successful amalgamation of the scientific method with the humanist goal of self-knowledge.

First published in *Journal of the American Psychoanalytic Association,* 16:245-273, 1968.

The chapters in Part IV focus on the working methods of Freud in his maturity, i.e., in that period of his productive career which was informed by the results of his self-scrutiny. The first of these chapters is a study from the Chicago Workshop on Scientific Methodology of the processes of change in the course of Freud's subsequent life in three early hypotheses of his psychological system: the hypnoid hypothesis concerning the genesis of hysterical symptoms, the seduction hypothesis about the childhood determinants of both hysterical and obsessional neuroses, and the concept of actual neuroses as psychoeconomic disturbances.

Detailed examination of the fates of these hypotheses revealed that, as new data became available to him, Freud attempted to change his theoretical system so as to maintain maximal generalizability for its propositions. The hypnoid hypothesis was dropped in favor of the much broader conflict and defense theory of neuroses. The seduction hypothesis gave way to that of the Oedipus complex as an etiological explanation; at the same time, the occurrence of childhood seduction became one of a whole nexus of observations and concepts involving infantile sexuality. The concept of actual neuroses was eventually subtly transformed into a metapsychologically subordinate aspect of Freud's second theory of anxiety. In other words, the original statement of some hypotheses was ultimately seen to be valid only as a special case in the framework of a new, more broadly based proposition.

Sadow and his co-workers tentatively conclude that a successful piece of self-analytic work may be a prerequisite for major theoretical innovation in psychoanalysis which involves real expansion of its explanatory power. This inference is most clearly demonstrated in their review of the development of the seduction hypothesis. This concept had been formulated, in large part, on the basis of a defensive projection of blame for infantile sexuality onto parental figures. When Freud succeeded in becoming aware of his own sexual wishes of childhood, including their contemporary derivatives, by means of his self-analysis, he was able to correct his theoretical error. In this way, he arrived at a universal hypothesis about neurosogenesis, that of the Oedipus complex—*Eds.*]

Psychoanalytic hypotheses, constantly being tested by clinical observations and undergoing continuous reformulation, reflect the dynamic state of our science. The aim of this report is the exploration of the process of hypothesis change in psychoanalysis. For this purpose, we studied three of the early hypotheses used or developed by Sigmund Freud.

In the investigation of concept change, one can focus on the continuity or discontinuity between successive stages. To see the first and last expressions of a given concept in their polar extremes emphasizes and contrasts changes and differences between them. Focus on continuity stresses the relationship between successive stages. In this presentation, we shall use both approaches.

A number of questions regarding the nature of the instituted modifications can be asked. How did the idea originate? When and under what circumstances did change occur? What was the advantage of the change and what evidence was there that the new formulation was better and of greater utility than the previous statement? What is the process of hypothesis revision? Are there any general principles that can be ascertained which relate to the broad question of hypothesis alteration?

The three early psychoanalytic hypotheses studied by us are: the hypnoid hypothesis; the seduction hypothesis; and the concept of the actual neurosis. These formulations have in common the fact that the original form of each was modified or abandoned, and derivatives are still retained in current psychoanalytic theory.

THE HYPNOID HYPOTHESIS

The concept of the hypnoid state was originally presented by Josef Breuer as an explanatory hypothesis for hysteria (Breuer and Freud, 1893-1895). Although it was accepted by

Freud, he began to move away from this concept even within the pages of *Studies on Hysteria,* as will be demonstrated below. Before we consider the details of the development of the concept, however, it is necessary to differentiate between two separate ideas which are both referred to as "hypnoid." These are the "hypnoid state" as a clinical description at the level of interpretation (see Waelder, 1962) and what we shall refer to as the "hypnoid hypothesis," the explanatory hypothesis at the level of theory with which we shall largely concern ourselves.

In the opening pages of *Studies on Hysteria* there is the following definition: "...we find, under hypnosis, among the causes of hysterical symptoms ideas which are not in themselves significant, but whose persistence is due to the fact that they originated during the prevalence of *severely paralysing affects, such as fright,* or during positively abnormal psychical states, such as the semihypnotic twilight state of daydreaming, auto-hypnoses, and so on. In such cases it is the nature of the states which makes a reaction to the event impossible" (p. 11; our italics). As a clinical description of a state of altered ability to perceive, related to a subliminal perception, this definition makes considerable sense.[1] As it is stated, the term "hypnoid state" is only descriptive of a particular, not unfamiliar, mental state and is devoid of more abstract theoretical implications. Note in contrast the following statement, also from the *Studies on Hysteria:* "...we have become convinced that *the splitting of consciousness ... is present to a rudimentary degree in every hysteria, and that a tendency to such a dissociation, and with it the emergence of abnormal states of consciousness (which we shall bring together under the term 'hypnoid') is the basic phenomenon of this neurosis"* (p. 12). The conception of "hypnoid" used here is much broader and is essentially a theory of neurosis. Further: "... the basis and *sine qua non* of hysteria is the existence of hypnoid states ... the ideas which emerge [in hypnoid states and in hypnosis] are very intense but are cut off from associative communication with the rest of the content of consciousness. Associations may

[1] See Holzman (1959) for correlation of the hypnoid state with ego psychology and the work on preconscious perception.

take place between these hypnoid states, and their ideational content can in this way reach a more or less high degree of psychical organization" (p. 12). In this comment the hypnoid hypothesis achieves a surprising degree of structuralization. In a sense, it can be understood as a primitive way of describing the organization of a consciousness other than the conscious in terms of associative linkages.

The direct clinical evidence on which the hypnoid hypothesis is based is meager. In the case of Anna O., Breuer details many separate instances of "absences" in which the patient appeared to exhibit an altered state of consciousness. In these she was relatively unresponsive and spoke of past events in a manner suggestive of a hypnotic state. Freud uses the concept to explain Katharina's forgetting what happened when she was first attacked sexually by her father: "The affect itself created a hypnoid state, whose products were then cut off from associative connection with the ego-consciousness" (p. 128).

As an explanatory hypothesis the hypnoid concept carried little conviction for Freud. It depended upon a postulated, but never observed, clinical state which had been present when the trauma occurred. In its more abstract aspects, as a clinical theory, the hypnoid hypothesis involved energy transformations and a special state of consciousness, different from ordinary consciousness but essentially parallel to it. The hypnoid consciousness was further assumed to be highly organized while at the same time not in communication with ordinary consciousness. The meager base of clinical evidence was insufficient to support such a far-reaching clinical theory (see Chapter 7).

From the very beginning, Breuer and Freud conceived of at least two varieties of hysteria which were referred to as *dispositional* and *psychically acquired* hysteria. The former was essentially hysteria based on a personality susceptible to the hypnoid state, while the latter resembled a defense neurosis. "Between the extremes of these two forms we must assume the existence of a series of cases within which the liability to dissociation in the subject and the affective magnitude of the trauma vary inversely" (p. 13). The concept of psychically acquired hysteria based on the reaction of a person to an external event became the primitive model for a defensive neurosis based on repression due to trauma. This was extended by adding the idea of a return of the moment of the original trauma, an idea which contains the seed of the return of the repressed as well as that of transference.

It is apparent from the foregoing that during the period of collaboration with Breuer, Freud utilized the hypnoid hypothesis while maintaining some degree of intellectual reservation about its explanatory power. Jones (1953, p. 274) notes that from the first Freud subscribed to Breuer's idea only half-heartedly. Not until the cases of Lucy and Elisabeth von R., however, is there a definitive statement of his early views of the defense concept. It will be recalled that in the history of Elisabeth there was a clear exposition of the development of conversion symptoms in a young woman whose love for her dead sister's husband was strongly opposed by her own moral repugnance. In this first full-length analysis, the abundant detailing of the emotional factors in the illness became possible because, as the patient could not easily be hypnotized, Freud was forced to modify his technique so as to obtain associations in response to hand pressure on the patient's head. These associations revealed with clarity the conflict between the sexual impulse and moral repugnance. This state of affairs could not be explained by the hypnoid hypothesis, since, as Freud said, "The incompatible idea [the love for the dead sister's husband], which . . . is later excluded and forms a separate psychical group, must originally have been in communication with the main stream of thought. Otherwise the conflict which led to . . . exclusion could not have taken place" (p. 167). Because the two sides of the conflict must exist within the same system of consciousness so to interact, Freud here arrived at an explanatory hypothesis of conflict and defense (and repression) which was far more generally applicable than the hypnoid hypothesis. At the same time he did away with the clinically implausible idea of separate non-communicating consciousness systems existing side by side, with one or another of them being in the ascendancy at any given time. The therapeutic advantages of the new concept were evident in the good result, and, in terms of theory, in the gain in explanatory power for discussing the case of Elisabeth.

Breuer accepted the idea of defense in his "Theoretical" chapter in *Studies on Hysteria* but felt that the concept of hypnoid state still explained most hysterias. The further history of Freud's relationship to the hypnoid hypothesis can be quickly summarized. In the "Psychotherapy" chapter of the *Studies,* Freud explicitly stated his suspicion that, since he had never seen a genuine case of hypnoid hysteria, although he accepted this thesis for the case of Anna O., the primary factor in hypnoid hysteria must also be defense. In 1896, Freud said that he often found no grounds for presupposing the presence of a hypnoid state and that the theory failed in that the traumatic scenes uncovered "lack suitability as determinants" (Freud, 1896a). Later, Freud (1905d) definitely dissociated himself from the hypnoid state and called it "superfluous and misleading." In 1909, there was a momentary return to at least the clinical part of the hypnoid concept, when "hypnoid state" was explained as the withdrawal of attention cathexis at the moment of satisfaction from the process of achieving it during coitus or, in hysterics, during erotized fantasies (Freud, 1909a). During orgasm, a normal withdrawal of attention cathexis produces a gap in consciousness. This gap becomes useful for the purpose of swallowing, as Freud put it, that which the repressing agency rejects from consciousness. By this construction, Freud explained the clinical aspects of the hypnoid hypothesis within the context of the theory of repression.[2]

If we compare the hypnoid hypothesis with other early psychoanalytic propositions in an effort to determine the ways in which such hypotheses were modified, a significant distinction is to be noted: of the three early hypotheses chosen for our study, only in the case of the hypnoid hypothesis did Freud seem to accept as correct a concept set forth by another scientist, Breuer. Thus it was an idea not original with Freud which he rejected altogether. In other words, in this case,

[2] Loewald (1955) has explored the "hypnoid state" from the point of view of an early ego state rather than an abnormal mental condition. He also sees the hypnoid state as a precursor of repression.

Freud had to separate the problem of the validity of the hypothesis from the problem of dealing with his transference to the originator of the hypothesis.[a] For the other two hypotheses, Freud had to separate the problem of validity from that of dealing with whatever narcissistic value he attached to his original ideas.

It will be demonstrated in our discussion of the seduction hypothesis that, while this original conceptualization moved from a general to a much narrower or more specific category, elements of the basic concept were nevertheless retained. The concept was delimited in terms of its explanatory power to certain types of cases, e.g., brother-sister incest, rather than remaining applicable to a broad range of psychopathology. By contrast, Freud dismissed the hypnoid hypothesis as superfluous and misleading as a whole. In spite of this disavowal, Freud, as we have discussed, later returned to the consideration of the clinical aspect of the hypnoid state as a special case of the theory of repression.

As the explanatory value of the hypnoid hypothesis proved to be limited, Freud began to construct a new hypothesis, a detailed description of which is beyond the scope of this paper. The record shows that except for the brief preliminary hints of the conflict-defense-repression concepts to come, the startlingly new material which came to light with the change in technique of treatment of Lucy and Elisabeth von R. set the stage for the first definitive statement of the conflict-defense concept. Further, this theoretical shift is the major one to come about before Freud's self-analysis which began in June, 1897; the increasing internal awareness which, as we shall demonstrate, was so instrumental in the seduction-hypothesis modification is not present here. The ultimate development of the ideas of conflict and defense into the dynamic and structural points of view are well known.

[a] The term "transference" is used in the loosest sense here. Freud was able to deidealize Breuer, the man whose special personal qualities he had so esteemed that he attributed Anna O.'s response to him to these realistic merits. As we have already noted (Introduction to Chapter 6), in the process of being disillusioned with Breuer, Freud developed an even less reality-based idealization of Wilhelm Fliess. For further discussion of these issues, see Kohut (Chapter 16).

Breuer's further elaboration of the energic aspects of the hypnoid hypothesis is interesting because of its possible relationship to some of Freud's later ideas. He conceived of a quantity of excitation in the nervous system which can be fully utilized in creative or other mental work. If, however, there is an inhibition in the flow of ideas, i.e., if discharge is reduced, then the excitation "is at the disposal of abnormal functioning, such as conversion." Affectively colored ideas may increase excitation. Inadequate discharge occurs in autohypnosis, fright, protracted anxiety. Such a combination of inadequate discharge with increased excitation is prerequisite for the hypnoid state. There would appear to be a relationship between this economic conception of mental functioning and the Freudian theory of the actual neuroses. In the latter, the inhibition of libidinal discharge is the basis of anxiety; this is Freud's earliest theory of anxiety. Thus, Freud incorporated at least this aspect of the hypnoid hypothesis into his later formulations.

As a clinical description of a state at the conceptual level of a clinical interpretation (in contrast to an explanatory hypothesis at the level of clinical theory), the designation of hypnoid state may have merit. The term might well be revived as a name for the state in which the special kind of perception called subliminal may take place (see Holzman, 1959), or for the state resulting when powerful affects overwhelm the vulnerable stimulus barrier, as in borderline characters.[3] From the frame of reference of the economic point of view, the concept of the hypnoid state may be related to such psychopathological entities as traumatic neurosis and actual neurosis.

The Seduction Theory

The seduction hypothesis, the concept that sexual trauma in the form of actual genital manipulation by a nurse or relative early in childhood is of primary etiological signifi-

---

[3] Dickes (1965) has recently written analogously about the hypnoid state, as in defense and resistance.

cance in hysteria and obsessional neurosis, was firmly grounded in numerous case reports from 1893 until 1897, when the
first serious doubts about its validity were raised by Freud.

The initial clinical evidence upon which the seduction
hypothesis was based was reported in 1895 in *Studies on
Hysteria* in the case of Katharina, who was stimulated by her
father's erect penis, and in the "Theoretical" chapter in the
case of a hysterical girl of 17 who had previously been seduced.
The pathogenic effect of the seduction was explained by a
formula described in the 1893 "Preliminary Communication."
This formula held that a foreign body (in the form of a
pathogenic memory) in the psyche (unconscious) would produce destructive effects until the resulting symptom was
connected with the memory in the conscious mind of the
patient.

Further clinical evidence to support the seduction hypothesis, although unpublished at the time, is to be found in the
"Project for a Scientific Psychology" (1895c, pp. 410-413).
There, in the case of Emma, who was under a compulsion not
to go into shops alone, the symptom was related to the
(unconscious) memory of sexual assaults by a shopkeeper when
she was aged eight. The next two published references to the
seduction hypothesis provided evidence for this thesis by
offering a large number of cases which were summarized with
much detail. Freud (1896a) refers to 13 cases of severe hysteria
in which he discovered the memory of a sexual trauma during
which the patient remained passive while there was an actual
irritation of the genitals. The incidents were remembered as
having occurred before the age of eight or 10 and after one
and a half; they had then been repressed. Specific clinical
data of observation are not given; only the clinical generalization, "In every case a number of pathological symptoms,
habits and phobias are only to be accounted for by going
back to these experiences in childhood, and the logical
structure of the neurotic manifestations makes it impossible to
reject these faithfully preserved memories which emerge from
childhood life" (p. 165). In hysteria, the sexual trauma was
passively experienced, explaining the greater prevalence of
this malady in females; in obsessional neurosis, after an early

passive sexual experience, sexual acts were carried out actively, leading to its greater incidence in males. Only one case of
obsessional neurosis is specifically referred to, the case of a boy
who was sexually abused by a servant girl earlier in childhood,
an apparent contradiction to Freud's hypothesis, according to
which this should have resulted in hysteria. Since Freud held
that behind each obsessional neurosis there is a nucleus of
hysteria, this reference may illustrate the first stage, that of
passive seduction, which formed the basis of the hysterical
nucleus. On the other hand, this may be the first clue to the
inadequacy of the hypothesis. The theoretical problem of the
deferred operation of the sexual trauma is explained away
here on the basis of purported arousal of the memory trace of
the experience by some postpuberty excitation.

Although the sex of the patient and his age at the time of
the sexual trauma are vaguely referred to, these variables are
not strictly dealt with. The result is a hypothesis of considerable generality, appropriate at the initial stage of theory
formation. It is to be noted, too, that the early theory makes
every seduction a trauma, a generalization contradicted by a
recent clinical investigation (Burton, 1965), as well as by a
more sophisticated consideration of trauma as an economic
phenomenon in terms of the emotional context in which a
given incident occurs and the developmental stage of the
patient.

The most decisive statement favoring the seduction etiology
of "severe neurotic illness" was presented in "The Aetiology of
Hysteria" (1896b). In 18 unselected cases, both male and
female, Freud found a sexually traumatic incident in puberty
and earlier unremembered severe sexual assaults directly upon
the patient's body. He divided the cases into three groups.

> In the first group it is a question of assaults—of single, or at any
> rate isolated, instances of abuse, mostly practised on female
> children, by adults who were strangers, and who, incidentally,
> knew how to avoid inflicting gross, mechanical injury.... The
> second group consisted of the much more numerous cases in
> which some adult looking after the child ... has initiated the
> child into sexual intercourse and has maintained a regular love
> relationship with it ... for years. The third group ... contains

> child-relationships proper—sexual relations between two chil-
> dren ... mostly a brother and sister [p. 208].

In two cases, confirmation was obtained from relatives.
Further evidence that such events were not uncommon was
presented by reference to pediatric publications which cited
cases of "regular sexual relations" by nurses, maids, or close
relatives with young patients.

Having offered such an impressive array of evidence for
seduction as the primary etiological agent in the psychoneuroses, Freud makes what is for him a rare departure from
strict clinical observation. In referring to the patients' extreme
reluctance to reproduce the picture of the seduction scenes
and their attempt to withhold belief in the reality of the
"memories" by stressing the fact that they had no feeling of
remembering them, Freud asserts that such withholding is
decisive in establishing the accuracy of the traumatic effect of
the seduction "memories." The passage reads:

> Before they come for analysis the patients know nothing about
> these scenes. They are indignant as a rule if we warn them that
> such scenes are going to emerge. Only the strongest compulsion
> of the treatment can induce them to embark on a reproduction
> of them. While they are recalling these infantile experiences to
> consciousness, they suffer under the most violent sensations, of
> which they are ashamed and which they try to conceal; and,
> even after they have gone through them once more in such a
> convincing manner, they still attempt to withhold belief from
> them, by emphasizing the fact that, unlike what happens in the
> case of other forgotten material, they have no feeling of remem-
> bering the scenes [1896b, p. 204].

Jones refers to this statement as displaying "less psychological insight than we are accustomed to from the skeptical
Freud" (1953, p. 264). Indeed, Freud, in reflecting on his own
statement 28 years later, pointed to this overvaluation of
reality and low valuation of fantasy in explaining his error; he
made no comment about the likelihood of observational error
resulting from the suggestive effect of his technique.

Since Freud was regularly using the technique of hand
pressure rather than direct suggestion at this time, his insistence that the patient remember the seduction scene represents reversion to a technique which had been characteristic of

his former practice. As we have previously reported (Chapter 8), such a regression may be indicative of a conflictual area in the scientific investigator. Even when the image he elicited was the memory of an actual event, Freud's prior suggestion made a differentiation between fantasy and actuality very difficult to establish

The seduction hypothesis was restated two years later (1898a), albeit in rather vague terms and without use of the term "seduction." One small advance was made beyond the original theory; namely, that it is the residuals of such experiences that become pathogenic, given the somatic and psychic development of maturity. This restatement was most curious, since in a letter to Fliess almost a year earlier (Freud, 1887-1902, Letter 69) Freud gave explicit reasons for abandoning the seduction hypothesis:

> The first group of factors were the continual disappointment of my attempts to bring my analyses to a real conclusion, the running away of people who for a time had seemed my most favourably inclined patients, the lack of the complete success on which I had counted, and the possibility of explaining my partial successes in other, familiar ways. Then there was the astonishing thing that in every case ... blame was laid on perverse acts by the father, and realization of the unexpected frequency of hysteria, in every case of which the same thing applied, though it was hardly credible that perverted acts against children were so general.... Thirdly, there was the definite realization that there is no "indication of reality" in the unconscious, so that it is impossible to distinguish between truth and emotionally-charged fiction. (This leaves open the possible explanation that sexual phantasy regularly makes use of the theme of the parents.) Fourthly, there was the consideration that even in the most deep-reaching psychoses the unconscious memory does not break through, so that the secret of infantile experiences is not revealed even in the most confused states of delirium. When one thus sees that the unconscious never overcomes the resistance of the conscious, one must abandon the expectation that in treatment the reverse process will take place to the extent that the conscious will fully dominate the unconscious[4] [pp. 215f.].

[4] In retrospect, a number of alternative hypotheses to explain why seduction memories appeared with such regularity can be advanced: (1) suggestion by Freud and compliance by the patient; (2) masochistic submission to the analyst; (3) seduction by Freud as the transference father.

On October 3, 1897, Freud reported to Fliess his self-analytic uncovering of libido directed toward his mother at two or two and a half. Finally, on October 15, there was the definitive statement: "I have found love of the mother and jealousy of the father in my own case too, and now believe it to be a general phenomenon of early childhood, even if it does not always occur so early as in children who have been made hysterics" (p. 223, Letter 71).

Just why Freud persisted in holding to the original statement of the seduction hypothesis in his published papers in the face of his discovery of the Oedipus complex in himself is not entirely clear. Perhaps the delay in publication was a manifestation of Freud's resistance to his discovery. But the data in the sequence of Letters 69, 70, and 71 to Fliess show that he was working through in his self-analysis the very conflicts he saw in his patients. At this point in his work, however, he still differentiated between neurosogenesis in general and in his own case. It is certain that the reasons he gave Fliess for the abandonment of his old position could never have been logically stated had it not been for his self-analysis, which enabled Freud to begin to grasp both the import of his own Oedipal fantasies and the inability of the mind to discriminate between memory of fact and memory of fantasy in the unconscious. Erikson (1955) has noted that Freud's wish to put the blame for seduction on the father was revealed to him in a dream and that resistance to insight into his own conflicts led Freud to hold on to the seduction hypothesis.

The first explicit published modification of the seduction hypothesis was made in the Dora case (1905d), which Freud wrote in 1901. Here Freud refers to the images of the neurotic as fantasies and not as memories of actual occurrences. Here, too, he makes the first clinical demonstration of hysterical symptoms based on repressed fellatio fantasies and homosexual urges. There is a coincidence in time between this definitive change in the seduction hypothesis and Freud's first visit to Rome in September, 1901, which can hardly be fortuitous. Jones (1955) strongly hints that this visit signaled the resolution of Freud's infantile neurosis. In the "Three Essays on the Theory of Sexuality" (1905c), Freud acknow-

ledges his earlier exaggeration of the frequency and importance of seduction, notes that a child's sexuality is aroused by
internal processes, and reverses the seduction hypothesis as an
explanation for polymorphous-perverse behavior. It is worth
noting, as Strachey (1953) pointed out in his introduction to
the "Three Essays" (p. 128), that it took Freud some years to
become reconciled to his own discoveries regarding infantile
sexuality.

Subsequent references to the seduction hypothesis in Freud's
writings reveal no further clinical evidence that can be
directed to disproving his earlier position. It is, however, true
that without exception the longer case histories are demonstrations, among other things, of the influence on development of repressed sexual fantasies as against memories of
actual occurrences. The seduction material remains part of
the clinical picture in all of the major case histories. But it now
refers largely to fantasies of seduction or to seductive behavior
upon which fantasies could be elaborated, such as exhibitionism in the case of Little Hans (1909b).[5] Here the idea of seduction has been broadened to include seduction of the parent by
the child. Where actual seductions took place, they were no
longer seen as central in the etiology of the neurosis (e.g.,
1909d). Later references to this hypothesis are acknowledgments of the earlier error, including the recognition by Freud
that he had been influenced by Charcot's traumatic view of
hysteria in giving so much weight to reports of seduction
(1914c), and indications of the theoretical advantages which
abandonment of the hypothesis gained for psychoanalysis.
Thus the insertion into the theoretical system of the patient's
fantasies based on and elaborated from repressed memories
enabled Freud to develop a consistent theoretical framework
of neurosogenesis (1905c). Another modification was the
elimination of that part of the early hypothesis which ascribed
a specific sexual trauma to a specific kind of neurotic resolu-

---

[5] The case of the Wolf Man (1918) is more complex. When R. M. Brunswick
reanalyzed him, she came to the conclusion that he had been actively seduced by
his psychotic older sister and she *does* attribute etiological significance to this event.
However, Brunswick may have seen the material from the frame of reference of the
earliest statement of the seduction hypothesis (see Brunswick, 1928, p. 86).

tion (hysteria being related to the early molestation of the patient by another person and obsessional neurosis to active reversal of the passively experienced sexual trauma): with this, the idea of accidental events influencing the subsequent development of the person in a primary way was minimized. This made possible the development of a sexual theory which encompassed both the normal and the neurotic.

In summary, the immediate evidence leading to the discarding of the universal-seduction hypothesis was essentially an observation based on Freud's self-analysis, and evidence from the major case histories solidly grounded a new hypothesis. But in Freud's last remarks on the subject, in the "Autobiographical Study" (1925b), there is little clinical evidence explicitly cited to contradict the original hypothesis, except for the case of Dora. It is, in fact, evident that Freud never entirely abandoned the seduction hypothesis. In a letter to Karl Abraham (July 5, 1907), Freud refers to "the mistake I made of believing the real aetiology of neurosis to be sexual traumas." He adds, "In my cases of recent years which have come from very good social circles sexual traumas before the age of five have been far rarer than autoerotism. From eight years onwards the opportunities of course proliferate in all social classes" (H. Abraham and E. Freud, 1966, p. 2). We would now refer to some of the early patients Freud was studying as "borderline characters" or "severe ego disturbances."[b] Thus it is likely that some of them accurately reported extremely disturbing early sexual experiences. For the purpose of explaining the psychopathology of these early patients, the seduction hypothesis was of value. When Freud came to deal with neurotics with less severe psychopathology—including himself—the fantasied basis of at least many of the stories he heard became evident and forced a revision of this theory.[6]

[b] In the decade since this was written, advances in the psychology of the self (Kohut, 1966, 1968, 1971, 1972) have led to a refinement of nosology; many of Freud's early patients would be classified as narcissistic personality disorders in the new schema.

[6] An explanation of the false findings of the seduction hypothesis based on Freud's use of the pressure technique has been offered by Schusdek (1966), who concludes that the use of such an energetic technique was sufficient to produce the data which led to the seduction theory as an artifact.

As a study in the progressive development of a hypothesis, that of seduction is almost a classic model. It began with a few clinical observations which were generalized into a theory of the etiology of the psychoneuroses in the papers through 1898. Once generalized, the hypothesis was essentially forced on fresh case materials although it did not fit at least some patients in the seduction-equals-actual-genital-manipulation form it then possessed. Freud raised a number of critical questions which were aired in Letter 69 to Fliess, although they were not made public for some years. Simultaneously, a revolutionary new source of data became available to Freud through his self-analysis. Oedipal fantasies were now seen to underlie the pathogenic effects. The study of the unconscious, of dreams, of the Oedipus complex, and of infantile sexuality became possible. It was not necessary entirely to abandon the seduction hypothesis since the new observations produced refinements rather than hard contradictions.

From our present position of psychoanalytic progress, Freud's earliest idea about seduction may in part be seen as an external representation of his own Oedipal fantasies. The scientific work he performed was to trace these back to their existence in his unconscious. In this sense, Freud progressively internalized the seduction idea. Then he applied the new, introspectively derived insights to his patients. Actual seduction became a specific clinical situation within a more universal hypothesis in which the effects of experience in reality and fantasy could be substituted for each other.

In current theoretical discussions of clinical material, seduction is infrequently talked about.[7] It almost seems as if the apologetic way in which Freud corrected himself in order to produce the more universal Oedipal hypothesis has been applied a bit too literally. As late as 1925, Freud said that "seduction during childhood retained a certain share, though

---

[7] For a notable exception, see Ferenczi (1933), where note is made of the frequency of reality seductions and the pathogenic consequences in identification with the guilt of the seducer. Barry and Johnson (1958) have also written on the significance of actual seduction. Also see Burton (1965). Adams and Neel (1966) have documented numerous intellectual and physiological defects in children which resulted from brother-sister and father-daughter incest.

a humbler one, in the aetiology of the neuroses. But the seducers turned out as a rule to have been older children" (1925b, pp. 34f.).[8]

In its original form and intent, i.e., as a theory with etiological significance, the seduction hypothesis is of little current use, having largely been superseded by the concepts of the Oedipus complex and of seduction by way of the construction of fantasies, which have much more general applicability. However, as a clinical phenomenon which helps to explain certain developmental distortions, it still has limited value.

THE ACTUAL NEUROSES

In marked contrast to the seduction hypothesis, the concept of the actual neuroses underwent few modifications for a long time. Freud then retrieved for psychoanalysis what had become an orphaned hypothesis. The process of gradual internalization of the previously projected Oedipal fantasies as a result of Freud's self-analysis, which was observed to alter the fate of the seduction hypothesis, finds a parallel in that of the actual neuroses, as we shall demonstrate. However, the original actual-neuroses hypothesis did not become a special case of a more generalized theory in quite the same sense. As a psychopathological construct, it retained its almost unmodified integrity until Freud fitted it into the metapsychological framework as a special pathological entity, the psychopathological core of psychoneurosis.

Since the actual-neuroses hypothesis and Freud's early ideas about anxiety were intimately linked from their very inception, some elements of the latter will enter our discussion. As in many similar situations, the hypothesis under consideration came into being as a result of Freud's dissatisfaction with the then-current descriptions of clinical states with which he was beginning to work in the late 1880's and early 1890's. Notable among these were neurasthenia and a number of related conditions. Freud noted that a prominent feature of many

---

[8] It may be noted that fantasies of seduction in the minds of the parents can be as traumatogenic as an actual seduction.

cases was anxiety, and he proposed (1895a) that a separate clinical entity be established which would separate from the main body of neurasthenic conditions those in which the anxiety was central. This he called anxiety neurosis. The etiology, as interpreted by Freud, was inferred from historical data on numerous cases (see 1887-1902, 1895a, 1895b, 1896b) and invariably involved increased physical sexual tension resulting from inadequate sexual discharge. The basis for the inadequate sexual discharge lay in such practices as coitus interruptus and the use of a condom, practices which, Freud believed, resulted in a physical inhibition of full orgasm. In normal circumstances, physical sexual tension results in psychical libido which leads to copulation or the discomfort of undischarged tension. Where physical sexual tension does not have its normal consequences but is dammed up instead, anxiety and reduced libido result (1895a). To state it differently, where sexual tension does not gain psychic representation as libido, the result is an increase in undischargeable excitation. In 1895, Freud referred to this excitation as anxiety and to the clinical state as anxiety neurosis, the first of the actual neuroses.

The hypothesis consists of two parts: a clinical description and a highly abstract economic explanation. In the section on the hypnoid hypothesis, we have attempted to show how closely related this idea is to the pre-existing hypothesis of Breuer on energy transformations in the hypnoid state.

The term "actual neurosis" was not used until 1898 (1898a), but even in 1895 (1895b) Freud bracketed anxiety neurosis with neurasthenia and, more tentatively, with hypochondriasis. These conditions, which were thought not to be of psychical origin, were therefore distinguished from hysteria and obsessional neurosis. Freud felt that, just as coitus interruptus was the specific etiological factor in anxiety neurosis, so was excessive masturbation the specific etiological factor in neurasthenia (1895a, 1906),[9] which was seen as a depletion

---

[9] Fenichel (1945) cites Balint and W. Reich to the effect that although masturbation per se does not cause neuroses, masturbation which is unsuccessful, in that it increases sexual tension without being capable of discharging it adequately, does result in actual neurotic symptoms (p. 188).

syndrome. True to the medical and physiological precepts of his day, Freud saw at least this significant segment of psychopathology in terms of a model in which an excessive external stimulus produced a quantitative energic derangement with a resulting liberation of a toxic agent (anxiety).

It is of interest to note that, in materials not intended for publication, Freud attempted to use the mechanism of tension accumulation to explain melancholia as well. Melancholia was seen as an accumulation of psychical sexual tension, as opposed to the physical sexual accumulation which produces anxiety. This idea, an attempt to generalize the mechanism he had postulated, apparently failed to pass the test of empirical evidence and was rejected without seeing the light of the printed page (see Freud, 1887-1902, Draft G).

A brief summary of Freud's views on the actual neuroses through the years follows. It is of some note that no clinical evidence was cited to support new developments or buttress old positions. A clear statement of the theoretical differences between the psychoneuroses, derivatives of sexual experiences in the remote past, and the "common" or "simple" neuroses with their contemporary origins is found in the 1906 paper on etiology of the neuroses. "Actual neurosis" refers to this issue of contemporaneity; i.e., the problem is an *actuality*. That the purely physiological etiology first advanced by Freud for the actual neuroses was no longer entirely satisfactory can be inferred from a subtle shift in 1906. The earlier explanation of anxiety resulting from an accumulation of physical sexual tension which failed to find release as libido gave way to the idea of insufficient libidinal discharge as the necessary etiological factor. Thus a rudimentary psychological theory was present at this early date, although Freud later (1916-1917) relegated the actual neuroses, as clinical entities, to medicine as a matter for physiological investigation before finally retrieving the concept for psychoanalysis in 1926.

In the paper on psychogenic disturbances or vision (1910d), "neurotic" visual disturbances, i.e., those due to increased erotogenicity of the eye, are differentiated from disturbances based on conflict and repression ("psychoneuroses"). The tie of the actual neuroses to toxic physiological changes is stressed. Freud's nonpsychological view at this time is evident from his prescription of treatment by "actual" therapy, which refers to specific environmental manipulation to alter the patient's somatic sexual activity (see 1910e). An interesting sidelight on his view of the relationship between this theory and practical clinical technique is afforded by some comments Freud made in a letter to Abraham (February 16, 1908):

> I myself still regard the old position as theoretically unassailable, but I see that pure cases of anxiety neurosis are great rarities and perhaps once again only abstractions, and that the not actually typical phobias permit and call for psycho-analytic resolution. I 'fancy' there is nearly always an element of hysteria in them. In practice what happens is that actual therapy is first attempted, and resort is then had to psycho-analytic therapy to deal with what turns out to be resistant. Forming one's own opinion experimentally is certainly justified in every case. True, when the actual therapy is omitted or cannot be undertaken, the emptied forms are again and again filled with new material, so that one never comes to an end of them [H. Abraham and E. Freud, 1965, p. 26].

Freud (1912) continued to maintain the distinction between "actual" and psychoneuroses, reaffirmed his belief that actual neuroses could not be analyzed, and added the thought that psychoanalytic treatment could have an indirect curative effect on actual neurotic symptoms essentially by what would now be called strengthening the ego. In "On Narcissism" (1914b), hypochondriasis was definitively added as the third actual neurosis in a move logically dictated by the conceptualization of ego libido which was thought to be dammed up in the affected organ in this condition.[c]

In the *Introductory Lectures on Psycho-Analysis* (1916-1917), the parallel between toxicity and the actual neuroses is concretized as an actual toxic substance resulting from improper sexual practices. Although Freud rejected this idea some 15 years later, at the time he was apparently convinced

[c] This conception of narcissistic overstimulation in terms of the cathexis of an organ with a type of libido has recently been supplanted by Kohut's (1971) hypothesis, according to which hypochondriasis is a regression from a cohesive self to the stage of autoerotism in which particular organs or mental functions come to occupy the focus of psychological interest.

that, because the actual neuroses were so physiologically grounded, their study should be given over to physiological research. Curiously, Freud here notes that he could make the same observations concerning the specific relation between particular forms of actual neuroses and specific sexual practices as he had previously made, if only he had at his disposal cases similar to those he had studied earlier. Just what had happened to the quality or type of his clinical material is not made clear.

The first substantive change in the concept also came in 1917 (1916-1917), when Freud saw the actual neuroses as the nucleus around which a psychoneurosis developed. There was still no basic change in the conception that actual neurotic anxiety originates in a transformation of libido in the monumental work "Inhibitions, Symptoms and Anxiety" (1926a). The concept of libido had in itself undergone a subtle change from a largely physiological one to a concept at the border between physiology and psychology. There was in this paper an important attempt to bring the actual neuroses back into psychoanalytic focus by moving toward a more unified theory of anxiety. The concept of the intensity of a trauma relative to the strength of the subject was explicitly introduced. It now became possible to define a traumatic situation as an experience of relative helplessness — relative to the strength of the ego. With so universal a definition of the traumatic situation, a broader synthesis became possible. Thus all dangers, originating internally or externally, whether instinctual or real, are dangers insofar as they impinge upon an ego which is helpless in relation to them. "Anxiety is the original reaction to helplessness in the trauma and is reproduced later on in the danger-situation as a signal for help" (pp. 166f.). The definition of anxiety now became consistent whether considered from the frame of reference of its longitudinal development within a person or from the point of view of the origin of the danger, i.e., from the environment or the id. Note here the creative use of the concept of actual neurosis in the *broader structural* framework. Two differing anxiety theories, i.e., the idea of anxiety arising either from transformed libido or from a threatened break through the repression barrier by an unacceptable impulse, were no longer compatible. A distinction was thus made between anxiety proper and the discharge of the surplus of unutilized libido, such discharge taking place via the generation of anxiety.

It was not until the *New Introductory Lectures* (1933a) that Freud finally rejected the idea that the origin of any anxiety was transformed libido. Anxiety was now seen as closely related to an automatic response to any trauma, the birth trauma being prototypical, i.e., not ontogenetic antecedent. Psychoneurotic anxiety was seen as a signal threatening a repetition of such a moment. By this theoretical explanation, the anxieties of the actual neuroses, of infantile phobias, and of the psychoneuroses were gathered into a single explanatory system. The concept of the actual neurosis as a clinical entity resulting from an accumulation of undischarged physical sexual tension was thus retained to the end, but anxiety was seen as arising out of the response of the ego to such tension accumulation, based on a primitive biological response to threat. By this means, a new coherence was achieved in the theoretical structure which now attained universality.

The concept of the actual neuroses began as a hypothesis to explain certain limited clinical phenomena. It lay dormant for many years until Freud again found it practicable, this time as a useful economic concept. Viewed retrospectively, the concept, as originally stated, can be described as the misapplication of a high level of psychoeconomic generalization to rather specific clinical details. The concept of a universal psychoeconomic phenomenon represented by the actual neuroses had to await a metapsychological framework of sufficient breadth to accommodate it.

Insight into the process of concept change, as differentiated from its content, cannot be achieved simply from a description of the formal evolution of a concept. Unfortunately, as far as we know, Freud did not leave biographical data in relation to late changes in his hypotheses concerning the actual neuroses equivalent to the 1897 series of letters to Fliess. The evidence we cite is therefore less anchored to objective data, and hence more speculative than we would prefer; but it points in the same direction as the material about the seduction hypothesis.

The year 1917 was a difficult one for Freud. Not only were there severe physical privations, but Freud was understandably concerned about his soldier sons (Jones, 1955). The first significant change in the hypothesis, as we have indicated above, occurred at that time. A considerable series of more or less catastrophic events and reactions beset Freud during the ensuing years. In 1920, Freud suffered the loss of his good friend, Anton von Freund, whose wealth was to have been a prime source of support for the penurious psychoanalytic movement. At about the same time, his daughter Sophie died very suddenly. In a letter to Ferenczi on February 4, 1920, Freud expressed his feeling: "Down deep I sense a bitter, irreparable narcissistic injury" (E. Freud, 1960, Letter 187). During the next year, Freud spoke of taking a step into real old age (Jones, 1957, p. 79). Then in 1922, Freud was "deeply shaken" by the death of his niece, Mathilde, the daughter of his favorite sister, Rose (p. 86). In 1923, Freud suffered two even more severe tragedies. Early that year the first evidence of his life-threatening malignancy appeared. In June, the death of his grandson shook Freud as did no other single event in his life. Jones indicates that Freud suffered his first depression at that time, and goes on to say:

> It was the only occasion in his life when Freud was known to shed tears. He told me afterward that this loss had affected him in a different way from any of the others he had suffered. They had brought about sheer pain, but this one had killed something in him for good. The loss must have struck something peculiarly deep in his heart, possibly reaching even so far back as the little Julius of his childhood.[10] A couple of years later he told Marie Bonaparte [in a letter, November 2, 1925] that he had never been able to get fond of anyone since that misfortune, merely retaining his old attachments; he had found the blow quite unbearable, much more so than his own cancer [1957, p. 92].

Finally, in 1924, Otto Rank, one of his most intimate associates, broke off relations with Freud (Jones, 1957). One may surmise Freud's perception of himself during this period by his reference to a portrait executed in honor of his seventieth birthday. "An etching which Schmutzer completed for the

[10] Freud's 11-months-younger brother, who died at the age of eight months.

birthday strikes me as excellent. Others find its expression too severe, almost angry. Inwardly, this is probably what I am" (E. Freud, 1960, Letter 221, to Marie Bonaparte, May 10, 1926).

It was within this context that the structural model developed and with it the imbrication of the actual neuroses into the broader theoretical framework. It will be recalled that "The Ego and the Id" was begun in July, 1922, after Sophie's death and after Freud's assertion about entering real old age (Jones, 1957). "Inhibitions, Symptoms and Anxiety" was written in 1925, after the other events noted above. It requires only a short leap to assume that Freud was increasingly beset with more or less undischargeable aggressive responses to events which were well beyond his personal capacity to influence. The ego's response to such helplessness is anxiety. Freud's way of coping with these relatively large aggressive tensions was associated with his conceptualization of the structural model and development of new insights regarding the specific place of the actual neurosis in the theory.

If the foregoing is correct, it would follow that the Freud of 1897 or earlier had been dealing with relatively greater libidinal drive "quantities," and the Freud of the 1920's with greater aggressive drive "quantities." These circumstances may have led in the first case to his discovery of the universal Oedipus complex, which was stated in largely libidinal terms, although including an aggressive component, and in the second to his formulation of the structural model and a creative reinsertion of the actual neurosis concept into the metapsychological framework. Our speculation points to the possibility of a special relationship between actual neurotic anxiety and the aggressive drive.[d]

The two underlying principles of concept change which were noted in the section on the seduction hypothesis are evident here as well. There was a progressive universalization of the concept from one which explained only a narrow range

[d] The issue can also be restated in such a way as to leave aside the question of drive psychology: both aggressive arousal and great anxiety about self-cohesion are generally present when severe narcissistic injuries have been sustained (see Kohut, 1972).

of clinical phenomena to one which constitutes a part of a very broadly conceived anxiety theory. Although there was no change in the economic concept which might correspond to the seduction-hypothesis modification, Freud developed a more creative use of the concept. If our historical speculations are correct, as Freud began to experience the frustrating problem of his cancer and the death of his grandson, he was able to arrive at the later modifications of his hypotheses about actual neuroses by means of introspection rather than the observation of others.

The value of the actual-neurosis hypothesis originally lay in its diagnostic power to separate certain clinical entities, anxiety neurosis and neurasthenia, from the mass of psychopathological phenomena. These entities made sense when considered as a unit, and some mastery over the problem of understanding and explaining the ubiquitous phenomenon of anxiety was achieved. However, the clinical aspect of the hypothesis is most useful in dealing with problems at a pre-structural developmental level — a conclusion we also reached about the hypnoid hypothesis. Thus it may have some current theoretical utility, not only as a psychoneurotic core phenomenon, but also as an investigative tool for a more intensive study of the borderline states.[11]

DISCUSSION

In order to study the process whereby hypotheses evolve, three early analytic concepts have been examined. We are aware of the interrelatedness of Freud's ideas and of the fact that our approach therefore does not constitute a comprehensive history of these ideas. However, to facilitate our study, each concept was approached in relative isolation. Furthermore, we know that theory formulation may occur in a manner different from what may appear in published papers;

[11] Even within the analysis of a psychoneurosis the need to control the concurrent core anxiety neurosis has been seen by at least one writer (Blau, 1952) as a significant technical problem. Kohut (1971) has stressed the ubiquity of this clinical issue in the treatment of the narcissistic personality disturbances.

however, the order of presentation is of significance, especially where linkages can be established. We also appreciate that while ideas may initially serve as coping devices for personal conflict, they may subsequently become autonomous.

A comparison of the fates of the three hypotheses we have studied demonstrates how Freud persistently pursued the goal of developing hypotheses of the most universal applicability. The seduction hypothesis evolved into the Oedipus complex and infantile sexuality; actual neuroses became a metapsychologically subordinate aspect of the second anxiety theory, and, in terms of clinical theory, a core around which a transference neurosis forms; and the hypnoid hypothesis was entirely dropped in favor of the much broader conflict-defense theory of neurosis. We would expect that an examination of almost any other early psychoanalytic proposition would similarly demonstrate that its vicissitudes took place within the context of Freud's continual striving toward universalization.

When we focus more sharply on the modifications of each of our three examples, another issue emerges. The seduction hypothesis fared very differently from the hypnoid hypothesis. Differences from the actual neurosis concept were less significant. The seduction hypothesis was the most thoroughly modified by the discovery of new evidence with the result that it was discredited as the major etiological factor in neurosogenesis. This insight led to many theoretical innovations. The point of difference between the seduction hypothesis on the one hand, and the hypotheses about actual neuroses and hypnoid states on the other, is most obvious when we consider the utterly new and original quality of the results of the changes in the seduction hypothesis. By comparison, the relatively modest shifts in the actual-neurosis concept proper and even the brilliant feat of bringing it into line with the developing theory of anxiety are less dramatic. At the other end of the continuum, the hypnoid hypothesis was dropped, as it was not sustained by clinical observations. On the other hand, the absence of clinical material also meant the concept could not be disproved in this fashion. Freud worked on the null-hypothesis model of scientific investigation. Although it remained vaguely tenable, the theoretical part of the hypnoid hypothesis ceased having any explanatory value. However, as we have observed, Freud did use the clinical part of the hypnoid hypothesis as part of his explanation of the more universal phenomena of repression.

There are a number of possible solutions to the problem of just how and why the seduction hypothesis fared differently from the others. It is certainly a much less abstract idea, having been based on a series of interpretations from concrete clinical observations. By contrast, the energy considerations of the actual neurosis and hypnoid hypotheses are very far removed from the data of observation. Yet the history of science abounds in examples where both abstract and concretely based ideas led to creative formulations. The hypnoid hypothesis originated with Breuer, and it may be difficult for any man completely to accept another's idea. The actualneurosis hypothesis, ultimately based on the constancy principle which was in one form or another already current in the Helmholtz school, might be another example of Freud's reduced ability to deal with another's creation at his creative best, although in this case Freud made a successful transposition of this complex physiological idea to psychology and there were creative developments in later years. Yet we know that Freud took over from Claude Bernard the defense theory, applied it to psychology, and proceeded to elaborate and modify the idea in a highly original manner, demonstrating superior capacities in the synthetic use of the ideas of others. Indeed, Freud himself commented on this important point in 1923:

> A scientific worker may sometimes ask himself what was the source of the ideas peculiar to himself which he has applied to his material. As regards some of them he will discover without much reflection the hints from which they were derived, the statements made by other people which he has picked out and modified and whose implications he has elaborated. But as regards others of his ideas he can make no such acknowledgements; he can only suppose that these thoughts and lines of approach were generated — he cannot tell how — in his own mental activity, and it is on them that he bases his claim to originality.
>
> Careful psychological investigation, however, diminishes this

claim still further. It reveals hidden and long-forgotten sources which gave the stimulus to the apparently original ideas, and it replaces the ostensible new creation by a revival of something forgotten applied to fresh material. There is nothing to regret in this; we had no right to expect that what was 'original' could be untraceable and undetermined.

In my case, too, the originality of many of the new ideas employed by me in the interpretation of dreams and in psycho-analysis has evaporated in this way [1923c, p. 261].

Another possible solution to the problem of the varying fates of the three hypotheses is the difference among them with respect to mode of origin. The seduction hypothesis was inductively arrived at, whereas our other examples were deductively devised from the precepts of the school of Helmholtz. It is clear, however, that whether a concept is inductively or deductively derived is not the critical factor, since the actual-neurosis hypothesis fared so differently from the hypnoid one.

There remains a fourth possible solution to this dilemma. Our findings demonstrate that the seduction hypothesis was most intimately tied into Freud's own psychic needs, followed in this regard by the actual-neurosis hypothesis. It was the internalization by way of his self-analysis of what must have been the previously projected seductive wishes Freud had experienced toward his own mother that led to the highly creative modification of the seduction hypothesis. The new source of data, the self-analysis, made new hypothetical constructs imperative. This movement from an extrapsychic to an intrapsychic explanation with the development of insight may be compared to therapeutic working through. We assume, though with scanty data from Freud's ongoing self-analysis, that a related development occurred in the 1920's, leading to the creative imbrication of the actual neuroses into the broad metapsychological framework of anxiety and structural theory.

The implication that fruitful hypotheses in psychoanalysis are frequently based on some successful piece of self-analytic work is the most important conclusion of our study, the validation of which awaits further work in the scientific methodology of our field.

12

FREUD'S SELF-ANALYSIS AND
HIS SCIENTIFIC IDEAS

JOHN E. GEDO

[*Freud's Psychoanalytic Creativity*. Heinz Kohut's clinical theories on narcissism have had a strong influence on the intellectual climate of psychoanalysis in Chicago for the past decade, and they have provided one significant direction for some of the papers on the history of analysis written during this period (see especially Chapters 3, 4, 9 and 14). Their specific application to the study of Freud's work began with Kohut's discussion of Schur's paper on the Irma Dream in 1966, some elements of which found their way into his book, *The Analysis of the Self* (1971). (For an expansion of these ideas, see Chapter 16.) The paper correlating the sequence of Freud's published analytic discoveries with the principal focus of his self-analysis which forms the next chapter was written shortly before Kohut had communicated these formulations. From a current vantage point, therefore, Gedo's paper does not take into account Kohut's attempt to differentiate Freud's "illness" and his creative use of its "analysis" from ordinary clinical situations.

This chapter should be read with maximal use of one's historical imagination: it describes what Freud may have concluded about his self-observations at the time he made them rather than what those data would mean to us today. At the risk of detracting from the reader's pleasure by giving away the denouement before he starts, it may be fitting to give

First published in *American Imago*, 25:99-118, 1968.

a brief account of the principal differences between these vantage points separated by more than half a century of analytic progress.

The first notable area of difference has to do with the phenomena discussed in the paper in terms of maternal transferences. Freud had clearly discerned their erotic significance, and his allusions give solid grounds for assuming that he also considered their pregenital meanings, albeit at the time he described these events this developmental concept had not as yet been proposed. Gedo's discussion is cast entirely in the mold of traditional libido theory. At this time, however, we should give greater weight to the idealizing aspects of Freud's relationships to such figures as Fliess or Jung, i.e., today we can regard these transferences as recreations of mergers with idealized parental imagos. In this light, the prime issue within these relationships is perfection: premature disturbance of the child's illusion of omnipotent control over his environment on the one hand, and traumatic disillusionment in the qualities of the idealized parent on the other. These were the most likely consequences of the family tragedy which overtook Sigmund Freud at 19 months of age. However, in the light of the new biographic data contained in Schur's (1972) book on Freud, we may also conjecture that part of the difficulty may have stemmed from the mysterious affair of Jacob Freud's second wife. Did his third wife, Amalia, turn to her first-born son Sigmund with special intensity in connection with some disappointment with her husband? Clearly we cannot answer these questions at the moment.

Another formulation which would be stated in different terms at this time is that of the residual conflicts which Freud did not manage to resolve by the time he broke off the relationship with Fliess. Although there can be no objection to calling them "separation" problems, as Gedo did in this paper, it might be more cogent to emphasize the continuing need for seeking out idealized objects. A corollary of this difficulty is a relative intolerance of circumstances which might stimulate fantasies of perfection. Freud's derealization experience on the Acropolis is probably best understood as a defense against overwhelming excitement produced by this triumphant adventure. Freud's youthful enthusiasm about the outbreak of the war in 1914 may be another example of a euphoric expansion of the self upon a psychic merger with an idealized entity, that of pan-Germanic nationalism.

The fact that, for the most part, Freud confined his idealization to a few causes and certain inanimate artifacts might be understood in the same context as an adaptive solution of these conflicts through the utilization of transitional objects and experiences. It should be kept in mind that the concentration on Freud's residual difficulties does not imply that these constituted the predominant modes of his personality organization. We are espousing a view of personality as a system of multiple modes of functioning (J. Gedo and Goldberg, 1973), and this conceptualization includes the premise that every individual has more or less adaptively resolved conflicts in a developmental sequence of crucial areas. Thus the focus on one or another of Freud's presumed conflicts is not an attempt to "diagnose" him as a total human being—Eds.]

In a study of the manner in which Freud altered some of his hypotheses (Chapter 11) Sadow and his collaborators suggest that a successful piece of self-analytic work had been the source of clinical evidence on which Freud had erected each portion of his scientific edifice. The fact that some of his momentous early discoveries had come about in the course of his self-analysis has been vividly illustrated in the Fliess correspondence (Freud, 1887-1902). Erikson has written (1955) that this correspondence reveals "that basic psychological insight cannot be approached without the involvement (and not gained without the analysis) of the observer's impulses and defences" (p. 6). Sachs (1944) also believed that Freud "had made his own mind his chief laboratory, his untiring self-analysis became the basis for all his analytic discoveries."

Freud's solution of the puzzle of understanding dreams through successful analysis of his own "Dream of Irma's Injection" (1900) and his discovery of the universal Oedipus complex by achieving insight into his infantile libidinal wishes toward his mother and aggression against his father (Kris,

1950b) are the most prominent examples of the process described by all these studies. Yet the examples of Freud's self-analytic discoveries have thus far covered only the period before 1900. The purpose of this essay is to show that Freud's later scientific ideas may have been the fruit of similar introspective efforts.

At the age of 80, Freud made a scientific contribution to the understanding of states of altered self-feelings, based on an autobiographical fragment, "A Disturbance of Memory on the Acropolis" (1936). A brilliant analysis demonstrates that the basis of an episode of derealization on ascending the Athenian Acropolis in 1904 had been a defensive disavowal of feelings of triumph and superiority in relation to his father. Freud reports that the incident had preoccupied him for some years (Strachey notes an allusion to it in 1927), and he concludes the paper with the suggestion that this memory had "troubled me so often since I myself have grown old and stand in need of forbearance and can travel no more" (p. 248).

The mention of the incident in "The Future of an Illusion" (1927a, p. 25) indicates that Freud had then already arrived at an explanation "of a wholly subjective nature," presumably the one he was to make public almost a decade later. Simultaneously, he produced a notable clinical contribution in his paper on "Fetishism" (1927b). Strachey (1961) has singled out the conclusion that the defense of disavowal "necessarily implies a split in the subject's ego" (p. 150) as the crux of this paper. It is reasonable to infer that Freud had become aware of splitting within his own self, an insight which he utilized in a number of his subsequent works (e.g., Freud, 1940b). His most explicit statement of this self-analysis is contained in his "Postscript" (1935) to "An Autobiographical Study": ". . . I myself find that a significant change has come about. Threads which in the course of my development had become intertangled have now begun to separate; interests which I had acquired in the later part of my life have receded while the older and original ones become prominent once more" (p. 71).

This cleavage in his personality consisted in the emergence of early identifications which could not be reconciled, as the historical data I have collected will demonstrate. I wish to re-emphasize that I am here giving one additional example of a process which has been well documented in other instances in order to stimulate further thinking about Freud's creativity.

SOME BIOGRAPHICAL DATA

Ernest Jones has pointed to Freud's traveling as an activity which must be understood in order to gain insight into certain aspects of his personality: ". . . Freud knew of few pleasures as satisfying as the enjoyment of beautiful scenery, and the sight of new parts of the world. . . . for pleasure, happiness and pure interest, the South was pre-eminent. Its softness and beauty, its warm sun and azure skies, above all its wealth of visible remains of man's early states of development . . . all this made an irresistible appeal" (1953, p. 331).

Freud's travels to Italy did not begin until 1895 when he visited Venice and its environs for a week. The following year, he went for two weeks, mostly to Florence, and in 1897 for another fortnight touring the rest of Tuscany and Umbria. In 1898, he took his wife to Dalmatia, but she was a reluctant traveler, and Freud went on by himself to explore Lombardy for some weeks. He did not go south in 1899 while he was writing *The Interpretation of Dreams,* but in 1900 he explored the Lake Region and the Italian Alps as well as Milan and Genoa. Jones gives a hint of the special significance of these trips in his statement that "the moodiness to which [Freud] was subject at other times seemed to disappear altogether at holiday time. Freud certainly displayed then high powers of enjoyment and an extraordinary gusto" (1953, p. 337). Jones's reconstructions of these tours are based on Freud's daily letters to his wife, whose inability to accompany him caused him much distress. Apparently he disliked traveling alone and usually made his trips with some companion— his brother Alexander, his sister-in-law Minna Bernays, later his favorite pupil, Ferenczi, and finally his daughter, Anna (1955, p. 16).

To resume a brief chronology of these travels, I quote from Jones: "In the late summer of 1901 there took place an event which had the highest emotional significance for Freud, one which he called 'the high-point of my life.' It was the visit to Rome, so long yearned for. It was something vastly important to him and consideration of it must therefore yield some secret to his inner life" (p. 16). Jones speaks of "the great happiness and even exaltation" which Freud experienced on this and every subsequent visit to Rome. The inhibition which Freud had to overcome in order to enter Rome has been widely discussed, and Jones has disposed of various fanciful interpretations of the underlying conflict which had been proposed. Freud himself had compared his hesitant advances toward Rome in 1897 to Hannibal's Italian campaign.

Jones states the opinion that:

> To Freud ... Rome meant two things ... There is ancient Rome in whose culture and history Freud was deeply steeped ... Then there is the Christian Rome that destroyed and supplanted the older one. This could only be an enemy to him, the source of all the persecutions Freud's people had endured through the ages. But an enemy always comes between one and a loved object and if possible has first to be overcome. Even after reaching his goal, Freud related how the sight of that Second Rome ... impaired his enjoyment of the first.... It is clear, therefore, that Rome contained two entities, one loved, the other feared and hated [1955, p. 18].

In other words, Jones implies that the inhibition about Rome was a reflection of Freud's positive Oedipus complex. He may not have been fully satisfied by this explanation, however, as he felt the need to write a separate, brief paper on "Freud's Early Travels" (1954) in which he contrasted Freud's attitudes about visiting Northern countries (England, Holland, and Germany) with his feelings about the classical South. The former represented work, energy, and duty; the latter stood for magic, beauty, fantasy, and happiness. The implication is strong that the North had masculine and the South feminine connotations for Freud. Jones does not comment on the position of France in this schema, although Freud's two Parisian journeys had preceded the Italian ones and had had great impact on him.

In 1902, Freud and his brother revisited Rome and went on to explore Campania. The following year, he did not venture

south, but in 1904 the two brothers undertook the brief
journey to Athens described in the 1936 reminiscence.
Strangely, in view of Freud's overriding passion for Greek
archeology, this was his only trip to Greece. Jones's account of
the trip differs in emphasis from that given in Freud's paper:

> The first impression was an unforgettable and undescribable
> one of the temple of Theseus.... The following morning they
> spent two hours on the Acropolis, for which visit Freud had
> prepared himself by putting on his best shirt.... He related that
> the experience there had surpassed anything he had ever seen or
> could imagine ... More than twenty years later he said that the
> amber-colored columns of the Acropolis were the most beautiful
> things he had ever seen in his life [1955, p. 24].

In 1905, Freud toured Lombardy and Liguria; in 1906 he
made a brief excursion into the mountains of the Trentino.
However, in 1907 he returned to Rome for a short stay. In
1908, he went to see his older brother Emmanuel in England
and had time for only the briefest visit to Lake Garda; the
following year, his trip to the United States prevented even
such a token visit to Italy. It was at this time that Ferenczi
became his traveling companion; in 1910, they went through
Florence, Rome, and Naples together and then spent almost
two weeks in Sicily. In the next three years, there were shorter
excursions to the Italian Alps, two stays in Rome, and the
introduction of Anna Freud to Italy on a quick Venetian tour.
During the war years, foreign holidays were impossible.

There is a curious mistranslation by Jones (1955, p. 179) of
a 1915 letter of Freud: "Greece will declare war on us in a few
days and then we shall not be able to visit the towns I have
most loved of any I have seen." It was, of course, Italy which
entered the war in 1915 (Greece did so in 1917). Freud had
actually written, "the classical country whose inhabitants will
declare war" (see H. Abraham and E. Freud, 1966). This
ambiguity points to Italy as having had the significance of a
substitute for an even more profoundly cathected attachment
to Greece. Sachs (1944) states categorically that in Freud's
"later years, Athens became a rival to Rome." Could it be that
the intensity of Freud's response to Athens had been so overwhelming that he was reluctant to repeat the acute episode of
derealization on the Acropolis? And could the earlier fear

about Rome have had the same basis? That all anxieties had not been mastered by the conquest of Rome in 1901 is demonstrated by the report that before the 1902 visit to Naples, Freud had a superstitious dread of dying, on the basis of the proverbial *Vedere Napoli e poi morire* (Jones, 1955, p. 21).

During the war, Freud seems to have arrived at a new equilibrium which did not require him to travel with the same intensity until the crisis of his surgery for carcinoma propelled him back to Rome once more. Inflation prevented him from going abroad in 1919, and in the following year he was able to go to Holland only because the Dutch analysts paid his expenses to attend the Hague Congress. He was shown some of the lesser-known parts of the country by his hosts and apparently experienced his usual pleasure in touring. In 1921, he met several members of the "Committee" in the Harz region which he explored with his characteristic energy. In 1922, he attended another analytic congress in Berlin. At this time, he still wrote to Ferenczi: "Strange secret yearnings rise in me— perhaps from my ancestral heritage—for the East and the Mediterranean and for a life of quite another kind: wishes from late childhood never to be fulfilled" (Jones, 1955, p. 84).

In 1923, he made his last journey to the South; he took his daughter Anna to Rome immediately after the discovery of his malignancy. His health did not permit him to travel as before—he had become old, in need of forbearance, as he put it later. In 1933, he wrote Edoardo Weiss, "One of the consequences of my failing health difficult to bear is that I can no longer come to Rome" (E. Freud, 1960, Letter 269). His travels were now replaced by a symptom—the recurrent preoccupation with the most moving and overwhelming experience on his journeys: the disturbance of memory on the Acropolis.

INTERPRETATION

In his assessment of Freud's personality, Jones has stressed the paradoxical contrast between his impermeability to other people's opinions on the one hand, and on the other, his gullibility. Jones interprets the resistiveness against influence as a defensive need because of Freud's basic credulousness—a quality which enabled him to believe "in the improbable and the unexpected," and sometimes in the ridiculous. In his early years, he made a great effort to check "the daemon of creative speculation" through scientific rationalism. Jones believes that Freud's self-analysis enabled him to reach an optimal balance in this regard, but that "in the last twenty years of his life [i.e., 1920-1939] he gave his speculative daemon a freer rein than ever before." Jones believes that Freud's insight into the personality of Leonardo is at the same time a self-description; i.e., that both great men were torn between the passion for scientific knowledge and that for artistic creation. This is, I think, another way of conceptualizing conflicting identifications. Jones has singled out Freud's excessive credulity in relation to a series of men and his subsequent disappointment with Breuer, Fliess, Jung, and others as one manifestation of these character traits. He is tempted to trace Freud's gullibility to the influence of his Catholic nanny, but dismisses the interpretation because the transference difficulties in adult life occurred in relation to men only.

However, Erikson (1955) has pointed out that the relationship to Fliess in the late 1890's included strong components of mother transference which were not understood by Freud at that time. Erikson focuses attention on Freud's anxiety about traveling (often labeled a "railway phobia") which Freud himself had attributed to the traumatic loss by migration of a "prehistoric childhood milieu" at the time of his family's removal from Moravia when he was three years old (see Freud, 1887-1902, Letter 77).[1] This move entailed the permanent loss of his nanny, whom Freud described as "that prehistoric old woman" and "the old woman who provided me at such an early age with the means of living and surviving" (Letter 70; see also Jones, 1953, p. 6). Erikson interprets Freud's "deep neurotic urge" to see Rome as a return of longing for his *Kinderfrau* and his *Reisefieber* as anxiety about oral supplies.

---

[1] Interestingly, one of the sources of infantile sexuality listed by Freud in his "Three Essays" (1905c) is mechanical excitation, especially that provided by traveling, and he explains railway phobias as symptoms in adults on the basis of repressed conflict around this issue.

Jones has stressed the phallic elements in the relationship of the child to his nanny, but certain statements in the Fliess letters (Freud, 1887-1902) tend to substantiate Erikson's view as equally sound. ". . . I was crying my heart out, because my mother was nowhere to be found . . . When I could not find my mother, I feared she must have vanished, like my nurse, not long before" (Letter 71). ". . . E. has . . . provided me with the solution of my own railway phobia . . . My phobia, if you please, was a poverty, or rather a hunger phobia, arising out of my infantile gluttony" (Letter 126). Although conclusive evidence about the reasons for the child's intense attachment to his nanny is lacking, the explanation may be found in some temporary disruption in Freud's unusually close relationship to his doting mother. (The intensity of Amalia Freud's preference for Sigmund is vividly described in Martin Freud's memoirs [1957].) The event most likely to have caused such a disruption during Freud's earliest years was the death of his brother Julius in infancy when Sigmund was 19 months old. (Jones's emphatic assertion that Freud had been "fed at the breast" seems to speak against the possibility that the nanny had actually been a wet nurse [1953, p. 5].)

The fact that the language used by the child with his nanny had been Czech, in contrast to the German spoken by his family, may have contributed to the profound differences between Freud's later reactions to travels in German-speaking countries and his response to "foreign" lands. (England, associated with his half-brothers Emmanuel and Philipp, had in this regard a special position of its own; unfortunately, very little is known of Freud's visit to Manchester at the age of 19.)[a]

The first journey to a non-German city about which we have records was Freud's 1885 sojourn in Paris to study with Charcot. His letters convey the deep emotional impact which the experience had for him, both in terms of the city itself and in relation to Charcot. I cite only a few excerpts to illustrate the similarity of Freud's reactions to Paris with those he later experienced in Rome and Athens.

[a] For that matter, it is not as yet known when Freud mastered the English language. He started reading Shakespeare at the age of eight, and his adolescent letters give clear evidence of being thoroughly familiar with the original in English (see Chapter 3).

Paris had been for many years the goal of my longings and the bliss with which I first set foot on its pavements I took as a guarantee that I should attain the fulfillment of other wishes also [Jones, 1953, p. 183].

My first impression on entering [Notre Dame] was a sensation I had never had before: "This is a church" . . . I have never seen anything so moving, serious and somber, quite unadorned and very narrow [E. Freud, 1960, Letter 85].

I sometimes come out of [Charcot's] lectures as from out of Notre Dame, with an entirely new idea about perfection . . . am I under the influence of this magically attractive and repulsive city? [Letter 86].

[I] could compare [Paris] to a vast overdressed Sphinx who gobbles up every foreigner unable to solve her riddles . . . the city and its inhabitants strike me as uncanny . . . As you realize, my heart is German provincial [Letter 87].

Another 10 days in Paris in 1889 preceded the start of Freud's Italian journeys. Incidentally, his railway phobia is said to have been at its peak from 1885 to 1897, although Sachs (1944) records that, in later years, he continued to arrive at railway stations more than an hour early when he had to catch a train.

Freud returned from Paris in 1886 divested of his German provincialism. His extensive identification with Charcot has been documented by J. Miller et al. (Chapter 5), who quote Lowenfeld's opinion that the capacity to identify with great predecessors is one of the conditions which makes possible the achievement of greatness. The paternal transferences Freud experienced in relation to Brücke, Breuer, Charcot, and Fliess have often been referred to. At this time, I would like to call attention to a different aspect of these relationships; needless to say, what I am about to suggest is only a supplement to previous interpretations.

The equation of Charcot with Notre Dame de Paris and of Paris itself with the Sphinx whom Oedipus defeated points to the existence of an underlying repetition of the maternal aspects of the Oedipus complex behind the more obvious paternal significance of Charcot. (In this context, Freud's odd sensation on entering Notre Dame—"This is a church"— seems like a precursor of the thought on the Acropolis—"So all this really does exist.") We should expect, at any rate, that every person who became a transference bearer for Freud would simultaneously have possessed both paternal and material significance for him. The complexity of these transferences was compounded by Freud's childhood situation of having, in effect, had two mothers. This constellation recurred in the proper setting during the Paris visit; Freud was related simultaneously to two persons who had maternal meaning for him—Breuer, a German-speaking Jew, and Charcot, a Gentile of alien speech—like his mother and his nanny.

After Charcot's death in 1893, and the gradual estrangement from Breuer during the authorship of *Studies on Hysteria* (1893-1895), Freud found a new relationship which took on a multitude of transference meanings—his friendship with Wilhelm Fliess. Erikson (1955) has cautioned that it was only when Freud submitted to nasal surgery at the hands of Fliess that the friendship assumed its transference qualities. Freud's letters reveal his need to experience Fliess as an equivalent to his longings for Rome which had emerged into the open by 1897. After a meeting with Fliess in Prague, he wrote: ". . . the Rome of my dreams was really Prague . . . Incidentally, my longing for Rome is deeply neurotic" (Letter 77). In October, 1898: "[I] study the topography of Rome, my longing for which becomes more and more acute" (Letter 99). In August, 1899: ". . . What would you think of ten days in Rome at Easter (the two of us, of course)" (Letter 116).

In his introduction to the Fliess correspondence, Kris (1950b) reviewed the progress of Freud's self-analysis in those years, and noted the immediate scientific utilization of the insights then achieved in Freud's published works. As Freud worked through the conflicts of his relations with his father in the transference, he was able gradually to emancipate himself from Fliess, whose magical ideation under the guise of science became increasingly unacceptable to him.[b] A parallel development was the overcoming of Freud's inhibition about going to Rome. In September, 1901, he wrote to Fliess from there: ". . . I ought to write to you about Rome but it is difficult. It

[b] For an alternative formulation, casting doubt on the causal connection between these events, see Kohut's remarks in Chapter 16.

was an overwhelming experience for me, and, as you know, the fulfillment of a long cherished wish. It was slightly disappointing as all such fulfillments are when one has waited for them too long, but it was a high spot in my life all the same" (Letter 146).

In a study correlating Freud's analyzed dreams (1900) with the Fliess letters, Buxbaum (1951) interprets the mastery of the inhibition about Rome as a consequence of working through the paternal-competitive aspects of the relationship to Fliess—the theme Freud had alluded to in his references to the Punic War. However, Buxbaum recognizes that the severance of the friendship with Fliess did not constitute a solution of other aspects of the transferred childhood conflicts. She focuses on the passive feminine side of the paternal transference as one of the unresolved residua. Buxbaum does concede that Freud's self-analysis led to his discovery of the importance of bisexuality for neurosis, as well as of pregenital issues, namely the anal phase. It seems likely, then, that the unresolved conflicts were of a different order.

Suzanne C. Bernfeld (1951) was the first to draw attention to Freud's interest in archeology as a sublimation acquired during latency, at a time when he was struggling to relinquish magical thinking and illusion. She relates that interest in archeology to Freud's "prehistoric childhood" in Moravia and quotes Freud's statement "I hate Vienna almost like a person" in support of the hypothesis that statues, vases, buildings, and towns were symbolic representations of loved and hated persons from Freud's childhood past. Bernfeld inferred that collecting (and I would add, "visiting") these objects could only become an actuality for Freud after his resolution of competitive conflicts with paternal figures. Freud's initial response to Paris points in the same direction.

It is my impression that, upon the decathexis of Freud's relationship to Fliess, the unresolved infantile longings for the two pregenital mothers found their expression almost exclusively in his travels to the South and in his archeological interests. I do not believe, however, that these activities can properly be termed sublimations, since they were carried out in a highly libidinized and aggressivized fashion. My own conceptualization of these experiences is that they constituted an acting out in the service of mastery, i.e., an attempt to turn a passively experienced, traumatic' event into an actively produced, manageable one. The travels to and from the South constituted a seeking, a finding, and a relinquishment of the object, very much like Freud's famous example in "Beyond the Pleasure Principle" (1920b) of his grandson's attempt to master the separation from his mother by making a toy disappear and reappear repetitively. That part of the self-analysis thus found its way into a scientific work around 1919, when Freud's need to travel had been alleviated.

For the purpose of finding both mothers simultaneously, Rome was an ideal transitional object: Catholic and non-German like his nanny, with an ancient prehistory which could symbolize the relationship to the nursing mother, disrupted by the birth and death of a sibling. Athens, on the other hand, is relatively free of Christian remains; the visit there may have had the significance of a return to the earliest self-experience and a single mother. In the ascent to the Acropolis, the experience exceeded Freud's capacity to bind excitation, and he never attempted to return to Greece, satis-fying his passion for Greek antiquities in the comparative safety of Italy.

In this connection I would mention Freud's explicit identi-fication with Oedipus, another man who had two mothers. It will be recalled that Oedipus came to die at Athens (at Colonus, about a mile from the Acropolis) and that his last wish was for reunion with his two lost daughters. On their restoration to him, Oedipus exclaims:

> ... I have what is dearest to me in this world
> To die, now, would not be so terrible,
> Since you are near me [Grene and Lattimore, 1959].

Oedipus then dies by mysteriously vanishing into the Attic earth, a symbolic representation of fusion with the mother. Spiegel (1959) has pointed out that the Acropolis must have formed "part of Freud's narcissistic identifications" to account for the occurrence of a derealization experience rather than that of a neurotic symptom when the conflict arose. (In a paper on this incident, Harrison [1966] focuses on the sym-bolic genital meaning of antiquities, which may be equally valid. Slochower [1970] also connects the incident to infantile scoptophilia.)[c]

In the light of these developments it must be concluded that Freud's self-analysis did continue beyond 1901 and remained interminable because of the impossibility of mastering separation conflicts in the absence of an interpretable transference neurosis. Freud was quite successful in his adaptation at the price of compulsive repetition of attempts to master the trauma. In spite of the popular witticism, therefore, it is not always a countertransference which stands in the way of self-analytic success.

SELF-ANALYSIS AND SCIENTIFIC PRODUCTION

Thus far, we possess very little historical evidence about the process of Freud's self-analysis for the period after 1901, when he ceased to communicate its results to Fliess. Whatever inferences we make about it have to be arrived at by reconstruction which attempts to weave together what is already known about Freud's life and personality with his available works. Conclusions must remain tentative because of the fragmentary nature of the data. As more and more of Freud's correspondence and unpublished manuscripts enter the public domain, many of our present impressions will have to be altered. Since my own study has been restricted to the materials thus far published in English, these reservations apply especially to the present essay.

Nonetheless, a review of even such a circumscribed portion of Freud's self-analysis yields an impressive array of themes which soon engaged his scientific interest. Certain preliminary correlations do seem possible, and I shall list some of these.

First, the equivalence of artifacts from antiquity with the earliest love objects from childhood was one of the most interesting themes implicit in Freud's (1907) study of Jensen's *Gradiva*, written in 1906, one of the years which did not

_____

[c] For the emotional matrix of Freud's experience on the Acropolis see also Schur (1966b) and his chapter on "The Revenants": "The Acropolis Episode" (pp. 225-242) in Schur (1972).

include a trip to the South. Did the vicarious journey in the wake of the archeologist Norbert Hanold suffice? As Strachey says (1959, pp. 4-5), Freud elaborated the analogy between the fate of Pompeii and "burial by repression and excavation by analysis." It has been overlooked, however, that the delusion of Norbert Hanold was based on a displacement of his love for a woman to a Greek bas-relief. Freud explains the hero's interest in archeology as a means of repressing his childhood love for the girl; it "left him with an interest only in women of marble and bronze" (p. 34). It should also be noted that this paper contains Freud's first substantial discussion of fetishism (p. 47).

Second, I wish to focus on a work produced in the next year which passed without a visit to Italy—1909. It was on his return from America that fall that Freud turned his long-standing interest in Leonardo into an effort to study the personality of his fellow genius in detail (Freud, 1910b). Freud attributed this crystallization of his interest to the fact that one of his patients seemed to echo elements of Leonardo's personality, but Jones's interpretation of Freud's identification hints at another piece of successful self-analysis (Jones, 1955, p. 432). Oedipus, Leonardo, and Moses—the three great figures with whom Freud showed his identification—each had two mothers, like Freud. The analysis of the "Madonna and Child with St. Anne" in particular betrays its source in Freud's own personality. Whatever the continuing controversies about the validity of Freud's hypotheses about Leonardo, this work deserves careful study for its psychoanalytic content and its probable derivation from Freud's self-analysis, particularly his insight into his identification with his mothers and into certain aspects of narcissism.

Next, I wish to examine Freud's response to the outbreak of the war in 1914 and to its concomitant restriction on his freedom to travel to Italy. Jones (1955, pp. 171ff.) comments on the fact that Freud's "youthful enthusiasm" about the war, "apparently a reawakening of the military ardors of his boyhood," was a surprising development. Freud wrote, "All my libido is given to Austro-Hungary" and that for the first time in 30 years he felt himself to be an Austrian. Allowing for some license to round off the number of years, this span of time must refer to the first trip to Paris in 1885 when Freud had shed his German provincialism. Presumably, then, his initial reaction to the loss of his travels echoed his childhood mastery of the loss of his early milieu by acceptance of his new, Viennese identity. This patriotism soon shifted to admiration of Germany, since the Austrian war effort was rather disillusioning. These "libidinal" shifts did not completely replace the need for the South since Freud spent much of his vacation at home, "minutely examining and describing his collection of antiquities." In spite of unrealistic hopes for a quick and victorious conclusion of the war, he wrote mournfully to Ferenczi about the probability "that after the war it would be long before one could visit England and perhaps also Italy." Moreover, by the end of 1914, his estimate of the chances of victory had dramatically diminished and a depressive mood made its definite appearance. Superstitiously, Freud believed he had only two more years to live.

It was in this context that Freud experienced one of his great spurts of creativity: ". . . in the spring and summer of 1915 he once more undertook a full length and systematic exposition of his psychological theories" (Strachey, 1957, p. 105). In many ways the most seminal and most original of this series of great papers is "Mourning and Melancholia" (1917a), the themes of which Freud presented to the Vienna Society in December, 1914.[2][d] Freud was at that time in mourning for his half brother, Emmanuel, in addition to having experienced the losses caused by the war. The concept of replacement of an object cathexis by an identification in melancholia seems to parallel the cathectic shifts within Freud himself at this time.

In July, 1915, he wrote Karl Abraham about his plans to spend the vacation in Bavaria (H. Abraham and E. Freud,

[2] Jones reports that Freud had discussed these ideas with him a year earlier. [d Anna Freud recalls (Jones, 1955, p. 99) that her father had appeared overtly depressed only once—in 1913, following the break of the personal relationship with Jung. The publication of the Freud-Jung letters (McGuire, 1974) enables us to confirm the hypothesis of this paper in terms of the function for Freud of this late edition of his pattern of special relatedness to certain men.] However, the stimulus for the elaboration of the germinal idea into its final form did not occur until Freud's depressive reaction to the war in late 1914 (Jones, 1955, p. 328).

1966, p. 225): "... I liked [Berchtesgaden] so tremendously, it far exceeded the memory of the five summers I spent there, that the only explanation I can offer is that my libido, having been set free by the loss of Italy, wanted to settle there."

However, this "love" for Germany was highly ambivalent— in the summer of 1916, Freud was to refuse to go to Bavaria to meet Abraham for reasons which he could not put into writing because of the censorship, and by the end of 1917, he expressed overt hostility toward Germany and equal condemnation of all belligerent nations. It seems reasonable, therefore, to explain Freud's feelings on the basis of an identification with Germany following the loss of his childhood objects. The motive of his ambivalence was expressed in a 1918 letter to Abraham: "My prevailing mood is powerless embitterment, or embitterment at my powerlessness" (p. 275).

We are not in a position to evaluate exactly how far self-analytic insights had carried Freud in the direction of his contributions to the understanding of depressions, but some clues about the depth of his self-scrutiny are available. Thus, he was quite explicit in stating "that his passion for smoking hindered him in the working out of certain psychological problems," and he was able to discern the connection between his mood and the availability of cigars (Jones, 1955, pp. 189, 192).

The creative outburst of 1915 was followed by relative quiescence during the remainder of the war years. As the attempted identification with Germany had failed, an entirely new equilibrium seems to have been attained: Jones thinks that "the increasingly dismal outlook at times even impaired his joy of living" (1955, pp. 193ff.). In some of his letters of 1917, Freud actually expressed a wish to die: "The superstition that my life is due to finish in February 1918 often seems to me quite a friendly idea." His main scientific work at this time was a joint exploration with Ferenczi of the correlations between psychoanalysis and Lamarckism. Although the scientific fruit of these discussions was a monograph by Ferenczi (1924) alone, Freud undoubtedly approved of this highly speculative effort so that we may conclude that, in 1917, he briefly relinquished the tight reins over his "speculative daemon."

After 1920, his published works gradually came to include a higher proportion of propositions without an evidential base (see Freud, 1920b, 1921b, the chapter on "Dreams and Occultism" in 1933a, 1939) alongside a continuing stream of carefully reasoned and validated hypotheses (e.g., Freud, 1927b, 1936, 1940b); thus the contrast between his identifications of the pregenital era with those of latency emerged in his writings.[e]

I have already alluded to the first overt emergence of the separation theme in Freud's published works in the example of his grandson's efforts to master this trauma in "Beyond the Pleasure Principle" (1920b). This crucial paper was written early in 1919. It marked the first extended and explicit discussion by Freud of "the problems of destructiveness," as Strachey puts it (1955b, p. 5). That this new insight was achieved via introspection appears to be likely in view of the fact that his dark moods of the previous years were succeeded by "cheerful resignation," although the reality situation had not improved in Vienna; in fact, the inflation was wiping out his life savings and he had to face the future at the age of 63 with no material resources. He wrote Jones, "We are living through a bad time, but science is a mighty power to stiffen one's neck" (Jones, 1957, pp. 6, 16).

When his daughter, Sophie, died in January, 1920, Freud responded with stoicism, "blunt necessity, mute submission," and with more self-scrutiny: "Quite deep down I can trace the feeling of a deep narcissistic hurt that is not to be healed" (Jones, 1957, p. 20).

Freud's ability to mourn for his daughter and his general well-being during this difficult period attest to the restoration of his optimal adaptive state. Sadow et al. (Chapter 11) have proposed that Freud's ultimate psychoanalytic achievement of outstanding significance, the conception of the structural theory of the mental apparatus, occurred in response to the mastery of the severe frustrations of his seventh decade of life, i.e., that this development was also a fruit of his self-analysis.

[e] In Kohut's (1971) terminology, such a discrepancy is called a "vertical split" in the self.

Conclusion

I have made an effort to reconstruct the manner in which one important unresolved conflict from Freud's earliest childhood may have influenced some of his relations with certain people, objects, and activities. My thesis is that an infantile depression, caused by some presumed interference with his original relationship to his mother, had been relieved by a close attachment to his nanny from whom he was separated at the age of three. This trauma was transcended through repression of pregenital issues. On the eve of marriage and professional independence, when Freud was 30, there may have been a recrudescence of this conflict with the development of a complex dual transference to Breuer and Charcot. The subsequent vicissitudes of the conflict and their emergence in Freud's self-analysis were examined (insofar as published sources provide clues for doing so).

Tentatively, I have concluded that this conflict was barely touched on during that portion of Freud's self-analysis which was reflected in his letters to Fliess, i.e., before his initial trip to Rome. Interpretation of the import of Freud's travels to Italy (and even more so to Greece) as a transitional phenomenon through which he attempted to master his separation anxiety led to the conclusion that Freud continued to struggle with these issues for the rest of his life. The attainment of certain insights in his self-analysis was followed by a related sequence of published psychoanalytic hypotheses in Freud's papers, including some from his ninth decade. Although, in the absence of an interpretable transference neurosis, his self-analysis was naturally interminable, Freud apparently penetrated deeply enough into his own psychic functioning to be able to discern—and to turn to prime scientific use—a number of fateful adaptive shifts in his equilibrium. The last of these was a chronic split in his personality which probably reflected the re-emergence of his earliest identifications with his superstitious and mystical mother and nanny. It was this development which permitted the partial release of Freud's "speculative daemon" in the last 20 years of his life in such nonscientific works as his papers on telepathy and Moses

(Freud, 1921b, 1922, the chapter on "Dreams and Occultism" in 1933a, 1939).[3]

However, the most significant implication of my reconstruction does not consist in its apologia for Freud's occasional departures from strict scientific rationalism. I believe it suggests that Freud's scientific work throughout his career followed closely the crucial methodological advance he had developed in 1895 when he was "able to breach the wall that separated the doctor from the patient and to recognize in himself . . . disturbances of internal economy, in order to see them in their ultimate perspective" (as Schlessinger et al. put it in Chapter 8).

[3] A related issue, which I do not feel prepared to discuss at present, is the meaning and function for Freud—and other psychoanalysts—of scientiic creativity and publication.

13

FREUD AND THE
CONTROVERSY OVER
SHAKESPEAREAN
AUTHORSHIP

HARRY TROSMAN

[*A Failure in Freud's Introspection.* Although Gedo's study
of Freud's self-analysis in the previous chapter touches on one
of the problems which was never definitively resolved in the
course of the latter's introspective efforts, his chapter is nonetheless focused on the fruits of Freud's successes in attempting
to understand his own conflicts. The contribution which we
present next may be a complement, demonstrating the essential limitlessness of the self-analytic task. With the exception
of Chapter 7, this paper by Trosman is the earliest in this
collection, and its explicit treatment of Freud's biography as a
source for new analytic conclusions marked the beginning of
such work in Chicago.

Trosman has chosen for examination a relatively obscure
lapse into irrationality on the part of the elderly Freud, that of
his lengthy flirtation with anti-Stratfordian positions in the
matter of the authorship of the plays of Shakespeare. As Jones
has pointed out in his *Life* of Freud, a number of departures
from strict scientific rationalism continued to punctuate
Freud's career after he was able to free himself from the need

---

First published in *Journal of the American Psychoanalytic Association*, 13:475-
498, 1965.

to give credence to Fliess's numerological theories. The most significant of these concessions to a "speculative daemon" may have been Freud's interest in the phenomena of extrasensory perception. Our understanding of this facet of Freud will be enhanced by study of the extensive correspondence between Freud and C. G. Jung (McGuire, 1974), another devotee of parapsychological research. Similarly, the unpublished correspondence with Ferenczi might throw light on Freud's collaboration with the latter during the years of the First World War on the biopsychological fantasies which were ultimately made public in Ferenczi's (1924) *Thalassa* (see Chapter 15).

Trosman perceptively picks out an inconspicuous thread running through a series of Freud's more controversial works, that of the explication of various matters by means of hypotheses based on a bias in favor of a fantasy of the family romance. This prejudice forms the common denominator in Freud's interpretations of Leonardo, Moses, and Shakespeare. Further, Trosman discerns what may well be a most cogent connection between this bias and certain aspects of Freud's cognitive style in other areas of his hypothesis building.

From another viewpoint, Trosman's contribution is probably the first effort to explore the enormous personal significance of Shakespeare for Freud. This issue has been alluded to in several of the chapters in Part I, all of which were written after this pioneering study. Trosman does not pretend to treat this problem exhaustively, but his conclusion that the dramatist filled a need for recreating the idealized parent of early childhood (to which we might add that thereby the narcissistic injury of disappointment in the perfection of the actual parents would be partially repaired) surely points the way in the right direction. The fact that Shakespeare, perhaps with Cervantes and Goethe, may have had the most to teach the would-be creator of psychoanalysis about the human condition surely cannot be coincidental in his choice of object for idealization.

Between the age of eight, when Freud is reported to have begun his reading of Shakespeare, and 16, from which time our earliest records of his correspondence now date, this prodigious schoolboy seems to have absorbed much of the Shakespearean corpus (for a demonstration of the extent of his mastery, see Chapter 3). The continued significance of the dramatist's insight into human psychology for Freud's own thinking is shown by the use of *Hamlet* for the demonstration of the Oedipus complex in *The Interpretation of Dreams* (1900). Indeed, Eissler (1971a) has suggested that the discovery of the complex may have occurred in terms of Shakespeare's drama first; i.e., that Freud applied his insights about Hamlet to his self-analysis, rather than vice-versa. As Trosman shows, Freud's interpretations of the play continued to depend on the correlation of its principle themes with events in the life of William Shakespeare, the actor from Stratford.

This paper does not attempt to explain what may have necessitated Freud's abandonment of his earlier views in this matter in favor of fantasies of exalted parentage for his great predecessor. This problem is taken up, however, in Trosman's collaborative study with Wolf on Freud's relationship with Popper-Lynkeus, which we have included as our next chapter. We shall return to this issue in our introductory comments there — *Eds.*]

In 1938, when Sigmund Freud arrived in England, following his flight from Vienna and the Nazi occupation, he received a cordial note of welcome from J. Thomas Looney, the author of *"Shakespeare" Identified* (1920) and the leading proponent of the Earl of Oxford as the author of Shakespeare's plays. In his response Freud referred to Looney's "remarkable book, to which I owe my conviction about Shakespeare's identity, as far as my judgment in this matter goes" (Feldman, 1953). Freud's remark was more than a superficial courtesy appropriate to the occasion. Nor was this the first such reference Freud had made to the question of Shakespearean authorship.

The present contribution is an attempt to describe Freud's fascination with the authorship controversy regarding Shakespeare and to indicate the general nature of the controversy by focusing on the Oxfordian position as put forth by Looney. This essay will offer some speculations concerning the motivation of those who support the anti-Stratfordian position, with particular reference to this interest in the life of Sigmund Freud.

Freud's knowledge of the Shakespearean canon was extensive. Quotations from Shakespeare came readily to his mind and their variety indicates a remarkable degree of familiarity with the plays. He began reading the plays when a boy of eight, and Shakespeare continued to be a popular topic of conversation when literary topics were discussed. Jones (1957, p. 425) says that Shakespeare was Freud's "favorite." He admired his psychological insight and used him as a standard against which the value of other great writers, such as Dostoevsky, could be assessed.

It is difficult to know when his doubts about authorship first took hold. He appears early to have been content with the orthodox view that William Shakespeare was the author.[1] Soon, however, he wondered whether the author might have been French, the name perhaps originally having been Jacques Pierre and subsequently made to conform to the English idiom. He thought the face "could not be that of an Anglo-Saxon" (Jones, 1953, p. 22). In view of his early predilection for a French author, it is of interest that his final choice for authorship was a man of Norman descent.

Jones mentions that he dallied with the Baconian claim for a while, but gave it up when he discovered it was supported by a Delia Bacon, and he suspected a vested interest. Freud also tended to reject Bacon on the grounds that "Bacon would then have been the most powerful brain the world has ever borne, and it seems to me that there is more need to share Shakespeare's achievement among several rivals than to burden

[1] He wrote to Martha Bernays on July 14, 1882 (E. Freud, 1960, Letter 5): "Remember the words of an Anglo-Saxon poet who invented many gay and sad plays and himself acted in them, one William Shakespeare:

'Journeys end in lovers meeting,
'Every wise man's song doth know.
    (*Twelfth Night*, Act II, Scene iii)

In each edition of *The Interpretation of Dreams* until the eighth in 1930 he stated his implicit belief in Shakespeare's identity by relating *Hamlet* to events in the life of the Stratford man (1900, p. 266).

another man with it" (Jones, 1953, p. 21). Multiple authorship appeared a possibility to him.

In spite of doubts he maintained about the identity of the author, Freud did not settle on any one claimant until 1923, when he was 67 years old. At that time he read J. Thomas Looney's book making the case for Edward de Vere, the seventeenth Earl of Oxford, as the true author of the plays, sonnets, and poems. He was immediately impressed, reread the book in 1927, and the next year tried to interest Jones in investigating the authorship problem psychoanalytically. When Jones was critical, Freud persisted and was disappointed in his refusal (Jones, 1957, p. 429). In 1930 he wrote Theodore Reik, "I no longer believe in the man from Stratford" (Holland, 1961, pp. 4-5) and in the same year for the first time declared his doubts publicly. Accepting the Goethe Prize, he defended the cause of the psychoanalytic biographers and said (1930b, p. 211): "It is undeniably painful to all of us that even now we do not know who was the author of the Comedies, Tragedies and Sonnets of Shakespeare; whether it was in fact the untutored son of the provincial citizen of Stratford, who attained a modest position as an actor in London, or whether it was, rather, the nobly-born and highly cultivated, passionately wayward, to some extent *déclassé* aristocrat, Edward de Vere, Seventeenth Earl of Oxford, hereditary Lord Great Chamberlain of England."

In the same year, for the eighth edition of *The Interpretation of Dreams,* following the section in which he expounds the repressed Oedipal strivings of Hamlet and suggests a temporal and psychological connection with the death of Shakespeare's father and son Hamnet, he added the following startling footnote: "Incidentally, I have in the meantime ceased to believe that the author of Shakespeare's works was the man from Stratford" (1900, p. 266). The passage is doubly interesting. It suggests that at the time of the original writing, 1899, Freud adhered to the Stratfordian position although he is tentative in his affirmation of a connection with the life events. We note, too, that although the footnote is a direct contradiction of the passage in the text, there was no attempt to remove the passage in the eighth edition. Two opposing views are presented and the reader is left with the barefaced inconsistency.

The dilemma moves toward a resolution in the next two years. In 1932, writing to a German translator of *The Sonnets,* Freud declared (Flatter, 1951):

> There are no doubts any longer about their serious nature and their value as self-confessions. The latter point is, I think, accounted for by the fact that they were published without the author's co-operation and handed on after his death to a public for whom they had not been meant.
>
> The contents have been made use of to ascertain the poet's identity which is still dubious. There lies in front of me a book, *Shakespeare's Sonnets and Edward de Vere,* by Gerald H. Rendall, London, John Murray, 1930. In it the thesis is put forward that those poems were addressed to the Earl of Southampton and were written by the Earl of Oxford. I am indeed almost convinced that none but this aristocrat was our Shakespeare. In the light of that conception *The Sonnets* become more understandable.

Two years later, in 1934, in another letter commenting on Lear, Freud again took the Oxfordian position. He related the three daughters of Lear to the three daughters of Oxford and described *King Lear* as a play deriving from Oxford's guilt as a wretched father (Jones, 1957, p. 458).

Freud's views on the Shakespearean authorship had not yet been communicated to English-speaking readers. In "An Autobiographical Study" (1925b, p. 63) he declared, "Shakespeare wrote *Hamlet* very soon after his father's death." In 1935, for a second edition, he added the following footnote: "This is a construction which I should like explicitly to withdraw. I no longer believe that William Shakespeare the actor from Stratford was the author of the works which have so long been attributed to him. Since the publication of J. T. Looney's volume *'Shakespeare' Identified,* I am almost convinced that in fact Edward de Vere, Earl of Oxford, is concealed behind this pseudonym." Strachey adds a footnote describing his reaction to this declaration (p. 64):

> When, in 1935, the English translator received the draft of this additional footnote, he was so much taken aback that he wrote Freud asking him to reconsider it — not on the ground of the

truth or otherwise of the theory, but of the effect the note was likely to have on the average English reader, particularly in view of the unfortunate name of the author of the book referred to. Freud's reply was most forbearing, as an excerpt from a translation of his letter will show. The letter is dated August 29, 1935. '. . . As regards the Shakespeare-Oxford note, your proposal puts me in the unusual situation of showing myself as an opportunist. I cannot understand the English attitude to this question: Edward de Vere was certainly as good an Englishman as Will Shakspere. But since the matter is so remote from analytic interest, and since you set so much store on my being reticent, I am ready to cut out the note, or merely to insert a sentence such as "For particular reasons I no longer wish to lay emphasis on this point." Decide on this yourself. On the other hand, I should be glad to have the whole note retained in the American edition. The same sort of narcissistic defence need not be feared over there. . . .' Accordingly in the English edition of 1935 the footnote reads: 'I have particular reasons for no longer wishing to lay any emphasis upon this point.'

Three years later, shortly after his arrival in England, Freud wrote the letter to Looney, already mentioned, and in his last book, *An Outline of Psychoanalysis,* he related Hamlet's Oedipus complex to the fact that the Earl of Oxford's father died when the presumed author was a boy and shortly thereafter his mother, whom he repudiated, remarried (1940a, p. 96).

Such, then, were Freud's written statements on the question of authorship. At first he appears to have accepted the Anglo-Saxon author as authentic. Although he came early under the influence of Meynert, who was a confirmed Baconian, Freud's letter to Martha in 1882 referring to the author of *Twelfth Night* as one who "acted" identifies the author as the man from Stratford. Eighteen years later he relates the psychological theme of Hamlet to events in the life of the Stratford man. From the time Jones knew Freud personally, after 1908, he found him fascinated with the enigma of the authorship issue. Freud could not take the position that authorship issues were trivial and that the important thing was the existence of the plays and poems themselves. Nor could Freud content himself with the statement that the actual facts about the author's life were too meager to permit speculation. He responded to the poor historical documentation as a challenge to his psychological skill. His attempts to flesh the bare bones with a definitive identity reveal something about the man and give us an additional insight into his cognitive processes.

The Looney Argument

The anti-Stratfordian position[2] goes back to 1785 when skepticism about the authorship of Shakespeare's plays was first expressed by the Reverend James Wilmot, who referred to a letter written by Sir Toby Matthew to Francis Bacon which stated, "The most prodigious wit that ever I knew ... is of your Lordship's name, though he be known by another." The first published statement was W. H. Smith's "Was Lord Bacon the Author of Shakespeare's Plays?" This paper appeared in 1856 and was soon followed by a vast literature supporting Francis Bacon as the author. Ignatius Donnelly in 1887 discovered many ciphered messages embedded throughout the plays "proving" Bacon's authorship, and for many years the Baconian position attracted a large group of followers. In 1920 appeared Looney's book making a claim for the Earl of Oxford. In 1952 Titherley published *Shakespeare's Identity*, stating the argument for William Stanley, the Earl of Derby, as the author. Calvin Hoffman, in 1955, proposed Christopher Marlowe as the real author, although Marlowe is reputed to have died in a drunken brawl in 1593, long before many of the plays were supposedly written. Hoffman argued that Marlowe's death was pretense. For a variety of reasons Marlowe left England for Italy where he presumably continued to turn out the manuscripts, sending them to his friend Sir Thomas Walsingham who then had them published under the Shakespearean name.

A variety of 57 claimants have been proposed and many prominent men, including Henry James, Bismarck, and Mark

[2]William A. Ringler, Jr., of the Department of English, University of Chicago, has pointed out to me that doubts concerning authorship have an ancient history. The plays of the slave Terence were believed to have been written by Laelius and Scipio Africanus. Cicero, Quintilian, Suetonius, and Montaigne believed that Terence did not write the plays. Of interest is the similarity to the Stratfordian controversy in view of the "lowly status" of the author.

Twain, have been anti-Stratfordian. I propose to concentrate on Looney's arguments since they were the ones that convinced Freud.

Looney's book is indeed an impressive piece of work. It is written with clarity of style, restraint, and freedom from abuse achieved by few of the Baconians.[3] In the preface to his book Looney states:

> The solution to the Shakespeare problem, which it is the purpose of the following pages to unfold, was worked out whilst the Great European War was in progress; and my wish was to give the matter full publicity immediately upon the cessation of hostilities. As this was found to be impractical, steps had to be taken both to ensure that the results achieved should not be lost, and also to safeguard what I believe to be my priority of discovery. With these objects, an announcement of the mere fact of discovery, omitting all details, was made in November, 1918, to Sir Frederick Kenyon, Librarian of the British Museum, and he very readily undertook to receive, unofficially, a sealed envelope containing a statement on the subject. As more than a year has passed since the deposition was made, and as no one else has come forward with the same solution, the question of priority is not likely now to arise and therefore, with the publication of the present work, the purpose of the deposited document naturally lapses.

He goes on to express his gratitude to Kenyon for freeing his mind while developing his arguments and preparing his manuscripts.

Looney was a Gateshead schoolmaster whose doubts were based on his minutely detailed familiarity with *The Merchant of Venice,* as a result of having taught the play repeatedly. Looney developed an image of the author quite different from what we know of William Shakspere.[4] In marshaling the historical evidence he gives an excellent introduction to the basis for controversy and points out the grounds on which doubts about the authorship were justifiable.

[3]"Sir Edwin Durning-Lawrence concludes each chapter in his book with the legend 'Bacon is Shakespeare' in block capitals" (Gibson, 1962, p. 24).

[4]In discussing the claimants and referring to the actor from Stratford, I shall follow the commonly accepted anti-Stratfordian position and spell his name as above, reserving "Shakespeare" for the true author, whoever he may be.

In summarizing the known facts of Shakspere's life, he describes the Warwickshire background as an "unwholesome intellectual atmosphere" characterized by dirt and ignorance, pointing to the well-documented fact that William's father was fined for keeping a dung heap on the street in front of his home, contrary to town ordinances, and suggesting the likelihood that neither of Shakspere's parents could read or write. There are no school registration records extant to indicate that William Shakspere ever went to school. As for a sense of community with rural Warwickshire, none of his writings display any identification with "the people." Unlike Robert Burns, his folk and peasant background does not appear as material for his artistic inspiration. There is no record that Shakspere ever owned any books. What specimens of his handwriting we have are "malformed specimens of penmanship," indicating that he "had but little opportunity for exercising his handwriting." There is no record that the supreme dramatist and poet of the English language stood out in any way from his fellow men, and any comments concerning his personality are unrelated to the magnitude of his creative genius.

We know the man from Stratford was married to a woman eight years his senior, and the marriage was probably forced since she gave birth to a child six months thereafter. When twins were born two years later, he left home for London and became an actor. There is no record that he appeared in a play by Shakespeare. Little is known of his life in London. The length of his stay is unknown. He had no fixed residence. There is no letter from his pen, in spite of many business transactions that had to be conducted between London and Stratford. There is no letter from any patron or literary person to him. The only surviving letter addressed to him concerns a request for a loan. The Stratfordians, says Looney, expect one to believe that after having written the best literature in the English language, the dramatist moved back to uncultured Stratford, confining himself to buying and selling real estate and showing no further interest in his previous ability and enthusiasm for literature.

Shakspere's will is a conventional legal document and makes no mention of his literary work; there is no record of any attempt to provide for the publication of his plays or to ensure any profit from them for his heirs. The will mentions nothing about a library. The three signatures to the will are "outrageous," resembling a child's handwriting. He died without any contemporary notice being taken of his death.

The public knew only that there was an author Shakespeare, but no connection between the author and the actor is mentioned during his lifetime. There was never a personal response commensurate with the literary value attached to the work currently. Although no one single point is irrefutable proof that "the actor from Stratford" was not the author, in summarizing his arguments, Looney became convinced, because of the accumulation of evidence, that one could not "marry the life record to the literature."

Therefore, persuaded that another man was the true author, Looney goes on to describe the characteristics of such a person. In the Shakespeare mystery, Looney reasoned, we are confronted by a deliberate attempt at self-concealment by one of the most remarkable of intellects. There was no deliberate attempt to reveal through cryptograms and secret messages in the plays, as the Baconians suggest. Any indication of a discovered identity would be the result of unconscious disclosures, not conscious intent. Looney's method of investigation was to start with the plays and poetry and to draw inferences regarding character and the circumstances of the author's life from them.

Among the general characteristics of the man, Looney concludes that he must have impressed his contemporaries as a genius who appeared, however, to lead a wasted life, doing nothing most of the time. He was an eccentric given to passionate action, set aside from his society by the powers of his mind and the intensity of his ambitions. However, his natural ability as a lyric poet may have proved too overwhelming for successful concealment and it is possible that he permitted the circulation of a lyric here and there under his own name. This was a man of superior classical education who habitually associated with educated people.

Among his special characteristics one can only assume he was an aristocrat, since his identification with royalty and aristocratic values is obvious. Only the kings and queens in his plays "live," the lower order is poorly depicted and used largely for background. The historical plays suggest a connection with Lancastrian supporters, an enthusiasm for matters Italianate, a sportsman with a particular interest in falconry, and a lover of music. His attitude toward money marks him as improvident and contemptuous toward commercial interests. Toward women he was simultaneously affectionate and mistrustful, and in religion he leaned toward Catholicism.

With such a sketch in mind, Looney turned to a lyric poet who stopped publishing under his own name in 1593 when *Venus and Adonis* appeared under the name of William Shakespeare and is described in the dedication as "the first heir of my invention." In comparing the meter and rhyme of the opening stanzas to other poems of the same period by Elizabethans, Looney found in an anthology of sixteenth-century poetry only one poem of striking similarity. The poem is the work of Edward de Vere, the seventeenth Earl of Oxford.

The criteria as listed above are all fulfilled when applied to the Earl. He was a lyric poet, of an eccentric and high-strung nature. He was born in 1550 and died in 1604, and thus had attained his maturity at the time of the publication of *Venus and Adonis*. He had strong literary tastes, an enthusiasm for the drama, a classical education, and a continuous association with educated men. He belonged to the foremost among the aristocracy, had feudal ancestry, a personal and direct knowledge of Italy, musical tastes, and was loose with his money. There is presumptive evidence of his interest in sports, his Lancastrian sympathies, his intense affection for but lack of faith in women, and his Catholic leanings.

Oxford had an established reputation as a writer of lyric poetry. Twenty-two of his poems are extant, all written before the time of Shakespeare's first published poem. There is a striking correspondence in the mentality and literary style of Oxford and Shakespeare: similar words and imagery are used, the subject of love is treated in a similar manner. The two streams of work give evidence of many parallelisms in expression and theme.

Looney addressed himself to the motives for concealment. Oxford had quarreled with many men in power, had fallen into disrepute, and wanted to be forgotten. Although he believed his work immortal, he wished it to be dissociated from the shame associated with his person. Although circulating poetry privately was acceptable, dramatic authorship was scarcely a respectable occupation for an aristocrat of de Vere's stature. For this reason he would not wish to bring shame upon his family by permitting others to know of his identity even after his death.

Biographical data on the life of Edward de Vere suggest a close attachment to a father who died when the Earl was 12. He subsequently became a royal ward. His mother remarried early in the young boy's life and he apparently had little to do with her thereafter, the estrangement offering parallels to *Hamlet*. Following Oxford's trip to Italy shortly after his marriage, he returned suspicious of his wife; these suspicions proved as baseless as Othello's. Evidence suggests that the Earl had a company of players who toured regularly in the provinces and possibly visited Stratford in 1584. Was this the year that Shakespeare left Stratford by joining this group of players and thus gave Oxford the opportunity to use the actor as his means of concealment? By 1590, the Earl at the age of 40 disappeared into seeming inactivity. He continued under a shadow because of his lack of sympathy with the "ultra-Protestant" tendencies of the Court and his leanings toward a universal Catholicism. Until his death in 1604 the record of his life is almost a total blank. A total of 12 years of apparent seclusion coincides with the outpouring of the Shakespearean masterpieces.

A difficulty remains in accounting for the publication of several of the outstanding plays following Oxford's death in 1604. Since writing and publication were by no means coincident, Looney argues that the plays were written before 1604. The death of Oxford, rather than retirement or lack of interest, is the best explanation for the unfinished quality of the plays and the inability of the author to arrange for their publication. No plays were published from 1603 to 1608; thus an arrest of publication occurred with the death of Oxford and began again on the instigation of friends.

Both *The Sonnets* and *Hamlet* are seen as self-revelations, close to the life of the original author. One finds love for and belief in the infidelity of women, a man who has lost his good name ("a motley to the view"), who practices concealment and "bore the canopy" of the great office of Lord Great Chamberlain. Hamlet is a prince with secret purpose, attached to his father, with intense affection for and distrust of women, whose mother remarries after his father's death—this could be none other than the Earl of Oxford.

Among anti-Stratfordians Looney displays an unusually benign attitude to what remains of the actor, Shakspere.

> In view of the glory he [William Shakspere] has enjoyed for so long, [his] role in life becomes now somewhat ignominious. Nevertheless, whatever inducements may have been held out to him he fulfilled his part loyally. His task was to assist a remarkable but unfortunate man in the performance of a work, the value of which he himself could probably not have estimated; and although it will be the duty of Englishmen to see that the master is ultimately put in possession of the honours that have for so long been enjoyed by the man, it will be impossible ever totally to dissociate from the work and personality of the great one, the figure and name of his helper [1920, pp. 361-362].

Looney died in 1944, having helped organize The Shakespeare Fellowship in 1922 in order to investigate the Oxfordian claim. The organization eventually broadened its claim to include a number of other coauthors as well. The Earl was credited with the leadership of a syndicate consisting of the Earl of Derby, Francis Bacon, Sir Walter Raleigh, the Earl of Rutland, the Countess of Pembroke, and Christopher Marlowe. The Shakespeare Fellowship even made room for William Shakspere, who was conceived of as "the honest broker who negotiated with the theatres and printers for the production and publication of the plays" (Gibson, 1962). Whether Looney himself came to support a multiple-authorship position is not known. It would certainly appear to weaken the emotional impact of his argument, since his investment was in uncovering the identity of a singularly great and neglected man:

> The picture of a great soul, misunderstood, almost an outcast from his own social sphere, with defects of nature, to all

appearance one of life's colossal failures, toiling on incessantly at his great task, yet willing to pass from life's stage leaving no name behind him but a discredited one: at last dying, as it would seem, almost with the pen between his fingers, immense things accomplished but not all he had set out to do: this, it seems, will have for the manhood of England that 'Shakespeare' most certainly loved, a power of inspiration far beyond anything contained in the conception we have displaced [1920, p. 368].

THE CASE FOR THE ORTHODOX POSITION

Among literary and historical scholars there is, of course, no question that the actor from Stratford was the author of the Shakespearean poems and plays (Bentley, 1961; Chambers, 1930; Chute, 1949; McManaway, 1962). Making allowances for the fact that genius is never fully understood and that a mystery always exists with regard to the creative process, the historical data are perfectly compatible with the Stratfordian position. Should anyone have any doubts concerning the authorship, an examination of the anti-Stratfordian literature would be enough to assuage them. Gibson remarks that he embarked on his examination of the claimants with an open mind about the authorship controversy. After thoroughly examining what passed for arguments, he became convinced that there was no basis for any position but the Stratfordian one (1962, p. 10).

The case for the Stratfordian may be briefly summarized. There are about 50 men who during Shakespeare's lifetime referred to him as the author of the plays. Concerning education, there is no reason to assume he did not receive a grammar school education, consisting of Latin with much Ovid and Virgil. The author of the plays was by no means a classical scholar, and what errors are present in his classical learning are those one would expect to result from the education of a middle-class Stratfordian. The plays show a familiarity with authors who were part of the grammar school curriculum.

There is no more lack of knowledge about Shakespeare's life than about that of any other dramatist of the time except Ben

Jonson. Jonson, unlike Shakespeare, was a scholar, and a rather quarrelsome man much concerned with his historical reputation who made efforts to ensure that he would be remembered.

To argue that the author must have had an aristocratic background does not give sufficient credit to the creative imagination of a genius. In point of fact, the author shows an ignorance of or disregard for aristocratic conventions. The plays disregard conventional social distinctions, and people of every ilk seem to have ready access to royalty, aristocracy, and nobility. This was far from true at the time, but aristocratic social conventions may not have been part of the knowledge of a dramatist whose exposure to the nobility was restricted to his performances for them (Byrne, 1960).

Dramatic works were not considered as serious literature at the time. Manuscripts had no value after a play was published. Authors wrote for playing companies and their plays then became the property of such companies. There is no manuscript extant for any play before the year 1640 and it was considered unnecessary to keep the original manuscript once the play had appeared in print. Indeed, at the end of the seventeenth century the Bodleian Library destroyed the First Folio edition of the Shakespearean plays when the Third Folio appeared.

The age was not one of casual letter writing or an interest in biography, and extensive personal references are lacking for all Elizabethan dramatists. However, Shakespeare is referred to as the author on the title page of many of the editions of the plays. Ben Jonson, who knew him well, refers to the author as "sweet swan of Avon"; Heminges and Condell, fellow actors who edited the First Folio seven years after his death, refer to him as an actor and poet. The latter two are mentioned in the will of the Stratfordian. He was fully accepted in his own day as the author and no question about authorship arose until 150 years after his death.

To Elizabethan historians and the present author, the anti-Stratfordian position appears too fantastic to be considered seriously. One is expected to believe that an actor in a company of players pretended to be the author of a series of plays which the company produced, but no word about this pretense was breathed to anyone or, if it was, the conspiracy was so successful that no reference to it was plainly made. One shudders to think what the life of the poor impostor must have been like. How did he manage to deal with revisions that were likely to come up when the play was to be produced? Were he ignorant or ungifted, everyone must have known how preposterous such an attribution of authorship was. If others were a party to the conspiracy, it is impossible that some reference to it would not have been made at the time, or after his death.

When Looney's position is examined more precisely, the entire argument disintegrates into a completely unrealistic projection of fantasy. The town of Stratford was not backward and ignorant. Shakespeare's father, far from having been an illiterate, was a prosperous businessman who attained the status of high bailiff, a position equivalent to mayor today. Although there is no record that Shakespeare owned any books, we have no record that many scholars of the time, including Ben Jonson whose learning was immense, had any either. There was not the sharp division between the London and Stratford life that Looney assumes and, for at least one occasion, there is documentation that Shakespeare returned from Stratford to London for business purposes. There is no reference to the plays in the will because the plays were no longer Shakespeare's property. They had become the property of his acting company when they were finished. Certainly in the First Folio there is sufficient indication that the author of the plays acted and was well known as both an actor and author.

To dispute the claim of the Earl of Oxford as the rightful author in the face of the absence of a problem regarding authorship is unnecessary. The argument from parallelisms is a constant source of delight to Stratfordians who, by using such argument, are able to show that many obscure Elizabethans have as rightful a claim to the authorship as anybody else. The meter and rhyme that Looney considered of such importance were common at the time and certainly not unique to the author of *Venus and Adonis* and the Earl of Oxford. The case for Oxford is thrown into further jeopardy by Looney's assumption that Shakespeare must have impressed his contemporaries in the same way he impresses us, as the master poet of English literature. Although it is likely that Shakespeare's literary skill and personal attributes were communicated to others, the Elizabethans did not attach an overpowering value to dramatic works; nor is it likely that Shakespeare must have been a man apart, who stood out in contrast to his society. Looney here seems influenced by the Romantic Movement which conceived of the poet in Byronic terms, and he draws his Shakespeare accordingly.

Looney's greatest problem with Oxford, of course, is his early death, several years before the publication of *Macbeth, Othello, King Lear,* and *Anthony and Cleopatra,* as well as the later comedies. A source for *The Tempest* refers to a shipwreck that occurred several years after the death of Oxford. Looney's solution is rather uncharitable: he decides that *The Tempest* is a completely un-Shakespearean work, and thus an inferior play and the product of an unknown hand.

In examining the Looney book one looks at the best side of the anti-Stratfordians. The wildest of the dissenters are probably the Baconians, who have managed to decipher secret messages Bacon left in the plays. Some of the Baconians have had the authorship problem resolved for them by communication with the author himself through seances. Some Baconians hold that their author was the illegitimate son of Queen Elizabeth and the Earl of Leicester, and assigned to him Burton's *Anatomy of Melancholy,* Spenser's *Faerie Queene,* all the works of Christopher Marlowe, the King James version of the Bible, and Montaigne's *Essays* in French. Others have claimed the plays for Queen Elizabeth, Mrs. Shakespeare, and an Irishman on the basis of Hamlet's "St. Patrick" oath. Surely it is facetious to suggest, in support of the Irishman, Hamlet's speech as he considers killing the king, "Now might I do it Pat" (Churchill, 1958, p. 55).

PSYCHOLOGICAL BASIS FOR THE CONTROVERSY

The entire anti-Stratfordian position calls for explanation as illusion, a projection of an internalized and shared fantasy.

When examined from this point of view, several interesting factors become prominent. It appears to be characteristic for the proponents of a particular man to denigrate the character of the Strafordian actor. He is accused of being illiterate, a poor actor, a drunkard given to the practice of usury and blackmail, and shabby in his treatment of women.[5] The depreciation is the reverse of the idealization of the hero. Through a process of splitting, the unacceptable characteristics are isolated and attached to one representation, while the more purified image is allowed to remain as the heroic author.

Along with the denigration of the actor from Stratford and the idealization of the "true" author, another common factor is the unqualified supremacy attached to the work. Looney's reference to the dramatic work as the best in the English language is typical of the anti-Stratfordian point of view. Here at least the claimants have the support of the Elizabethan scholars and the common reader. My purpose is not to cast any Shavian doubts but rather to suggest a relationship between the emotional investment in the authorship problem and the undoubted conviction that one is here dealing with the best work in English literature. The "best" literature seems to stimulate more opportunities for regressive identifications and projections. This combination of literary supremacy and the dearth of factual and documentary data enables the anti-Stratfordian to fill out the image with attributes of his own. This process can be seen in a historical context as the end result of a nineteenth-century purification and deification to which the author of the Shakespearean plays had been subjected. He became so highly regarded, so much the embodiment of all that was perfect, that the only attributes fit for him were mythical.

It is striking how frequently the attributes of the proposed candidate relate to the anti-Stratfordian in question. A common device is to pick a man already competent in an area un-

---

[5]Churchill gives several examples of anti-Stratfordian name-calling: "The drunken, illiterate clown of Stratford-on-Avon," "a miser," "a lying rascal," "the sordid money-lender of Stratford," "a drunken Warwickshire rustic," "the mean, drunken, ignorant and absolutely unlettered rustic of Stratford," "the miser Shakespeare, the lying rascal," "the Stratford butcher boy," "this unlettered rustic of Stratford, who cared neither for honesty nor morality," "the huckster Shagsper of Stratford" (1958, p. 51).

related to literature and then point out that he is capable of accomplishing the literary feat as well. The proponents of the various claimants are also men unrelated in any professional capacity to the field of literature: lawyers, physicians, retired army officers, civil servants, and so on. When they turn to a discussion of the authorship controversy, they appear to find their man in their own professional group. The Baconian Society is heavily patronized, for example, by men of law who are convinced the plays show extensive knowledge of the Elizabethan legal system.

Regarding Looney, he is referred to by an admirer as one who possessed "an intellectual range and a literary and philosophical culture far beyond the requirements of his professional avocation" (Wadsworth, 1958, p. 111). Looney's general demeanor was modest and unassuming, and he was "not by temperament anti-conformist." He surprised his acquaintances when his book appeared, so little did they suspect the nature of his work. "You would never know from his general conversation that he was producing a shattering contribution to the authorship question" (Demant, 1962). His partiality toward idealization is evidenced by his gift of Carlyle's *Heroes* to a young friend, with a special injunction to read it before the age of 20. Looney's identification with his concealed hero is also manifested by the manner in which he half expected that someone else would also make his discovery (see p. 315 above). Looney thus imagined in his own life a repetition of the situation he believed had taken place during Oxford's and Shakespeare's time. Through some untoward event Looney's identity as the discoverer might not be acknowledged and someone else would be credited with having solved the puzzle. By entrusting his deposition to the Librarian of the British Museum, Looney could well imagine that eventually *his* identity would be revealed as the original instigator of the Oxfordian position. In the same way that credit must be given "to the great Englishman" who actually authored the plays, credit would then be given to him who had made the Oxfordian discovery first.

Aspects of the family romance are evident throughout Looney's presentation of his thesis, most obviously in the conviction that the author must have been an aristocrat, of noble birth, a more exalted figure than the middle-class provincial actor. Freud (1909c) describes the family romance as a step in the liberation from the authority of the parents, a compensation for humiliation and a method for dealing with disappointments in the imperfections of the parents. In reaction, the child feels he is a stepchild or an adopted child, and the parents are replaced by others of better birth. The exalted father is in fact the original idealized one elaborated and transposed to a later era. The overidealization of the parent seen in the form of a change of paternal identity is thus duplicated in Looney's choice of Oxford. Frosch (1959) points out how the nature of the family-romance fantasy can find its locus in the treatment situation and thus determine the type of analytic transference. In a strikingly similar manner, the imputation of Shakespearean authorship to a historical figure is another example of the formation of a transference allowed to continue unresolved, continually buttressed by the discovery of "new historical evidence."

Another aspect of Looney's thinking concerns the obvious rescue fantasy. He speaks of a "long overdue act of justice and reparation to an unappreciated genius." He wishes to correct the reputation of a man previously seen as a wastrel and now to be recognized as the greatest genius in the field of English literature. Freud (1910c) described the rescue fantasy as a defiant wish on the part of the son to be quits with the father for the gift of life. "It is as though the boy's defiance were to make him say: 'I want nothing from my father. I will give him back all I have cost him' " (p. 172). Abraham (1922) and Frosch (1959) pointed out the aggressive component implied in a fantasy constructed so as to make rescue a necessity. One sees in the deliverance from obscurity another facet of the family romance which functions both to mask the hostile impulses and to preserve the lost omnipotent object.

FREUD AND THE CONTROVERSY

Freud's attitude toward the authorship issue was similar to that toward a hobby or favorite sport, engrossing for a time, a form of play rather than work, discardable when more serious issues were at stake.[6] And yet his approach reflects a cognitive style similar to modes he applied to more serious pursuits. One can detect in the manner with which he approached the controversy a style of thought similar to conceptualizations made in his scientific writings.

Looney's book must have made an immediate appeal to Freud because to a large extent Looney's method resembled his own. Looney paid close attention to the literary work and drew inferences from it about the personality and the true identity of the author. Freud had, on several occasions, used a similar method, most notably in his psychological study of Leonardo da Vinci (1910b). He concluded, from an examination of Leonardo's paintings, that Leonardo had in fact been raised by two mothers and this circumstance resulted in a split maternal image subsequently reflected in his work.

Freud had the type of mind that could never accept the obvious or the popular. His great achievement was to see mystery and concealment where others accepted the manifest unquestioningly. The style of his thinking is reflected in his greatest scientific work as well as in his willing acceptance of the anti-Stratfordian position. In *The Interpretation of Dreams* (1900) he describes transference in terms of preconscious contents which serve as a means of attachment for unconscious ideas. The preconscious contents serve as a cover or stalking horse for unacceptable impulses which, but for the protection of the preconscious idea, would have no medium of expression.[7] The analogy in his thinking to the issue of Shakespearean authorship is striking. He conceived of the Shakespearean actor as an indifferent decoy behind whom sat, hidden from public view, the powerful instigator of the Shakespearean work. The Stratford actor is equivalent to a precon-

---

[6]As with a hobby, however, his fascination with the controversy would on occasion intrude on his scientific studies (see above).

[7]"We learn...that an unconscious idea is as such quite incapable of entering the preconscious and that it can only exercise any effect there by establishing a connection with an idea which already belongs to the preconscious, by transferring its intensity on to it and by getting itself 'covered' by it. Here we have the fact of 'transference', which provides an explanation of so many striking phenomena in the mental life of neurotics. The preconscious idea, which thus acquires an

scious content, the Earl of Oxford to an unconscious idea. Could the tendency to conceptualize in terms of an overt and covert duality have played a role in his acceptance of the anti-Stratfordian position?

It is surprising to find Freud adopting a concept that relates genius either to high social status or to great learning. What he knew of the life of Leonardo was sufficient to point out the total lack of formal training in a mind of amazing originality. It is also surprising that Freud did not place sufficient weight on the richness of day-to-day experience as a stimulus of the poet's creativity. So much of what Shakespeare wrote appears more the product of his experience than learning in any academic sense. The achievement of Freud himself is sufficient indication that exalted social position is not a necessity for supremacy of work.

In spite of Freud's tendency to deal with unconscious motives and conflicts within the personality, at times he shifted his interest to the field of external reality. He tended to look for the kernel of external reality in a paranoid delusion, he accepted stories of childhood seductions as valid in the early days of his psychoanalytic work, he constructed the "scientific myth" of the primal horde to account for the Oedipus complex phylogenetically, and he imputed to Moses royal Egyptian parentage. Certainly, as Jones points out, Freud harbored tendencies toward a family-romance fantasy. Speculations concerning external origins often relate to such a fantasy, and Looney's "discovery" may well have reactivated a latent but cathected set of ideas.

The 25 years before the Looney book may also have predisposed Freud toward conviction because of experiences of his own. Having produced a body of work Shakespearean in its exploration of human motives, being disappointed in the

---

undeserved degree of intensity, may either be left unaltered by the transference, or it may have a modification forced upon it, derived from the content of the idea which effects the transference. I hope I may be forgiven for drawing analogies from everyday life, but I am tempted to say that the position of a repressed idea resembles that of an American dentist in this country: he is not allowed to set up in practice unless he can make use of a legally qualified medical practitioner to serve as a stalking-horse and to act as a 'cover' in the eyes of the law" (1900, pp. 562-563).

lack of response, misunderstood and discredited, he doubtless felt a partiality toward an *unrecognized* author who also worked in "splendid isolation." But what of the childhood situation to which the controversy had relevance?

Freud suggested the specific variant of the family romance to which the Shakespearean authorship controversy has reference. He pointed out that a shift in the fantasy occurs following the child's acquisition of knowledge of sexual relations. Doubts concerning attribution of parental identity become specifically related to an acknowledgment of the powers of procreation. More specifically, the question arises: Are the parents responsible for one's birth? Freud quoted the legal adage to the effect that the role of the mother is *"certissima"* although *"pater semper incertus est"* (the father is always uncertain) (1909c, p. 239). In the face of doubt a fantasy of exalted birth attains credibility. By this means, not only does the young boy deny his fear of retaliation for his positive Oedipal longings, he also removes his real father as a potential rival for the mother by denying paternal sexuality.

The issue of the Shakespearean authorship controversy appears to be a long-standing unresolved preoccupation with doubts concerning rightful paternity. The dramatist's "life-giving" power is a manifestation of the paternal generative power, deposed and unattributed until a suitable hidden and distant aspirant is found. The discovery of the creator is a rediscovery of the original idealized father of early, pre-Oedipal childhood now cast in a new light and projected into the arena of history.

Interestingly enough, there is evidence of doubt concerning his paternity in the mind of the young Sigmund Freud. In the complicated family ménage of his early childhood he was exposed to two half brothers from his father's earlier marriage — Emmanuel, 23 years older, and Philipp, 20 years older — a father he tended to think of as a grandfather, and a young mother of the same age as Philipp. The pairing of his mother and Philipp is revealed in an early memory following the birth of his sister, Anna. In the absence of his mother he screams for Philipp to open a cupboard. The cupboard is shown to be empty, and his mother walks into the room, slim and beautiful. Analysis revealed his fear of another sibling, denial of a new pregnancy, and his suspicion "that his half brother and his mother. .had cooperated in producing the usurping Anna" (Jones, 1953, p. 10). He speaks of the fantasy that "this brother. . . had in some way introduced the recently born baby into [my] mother's inside" (Freud, 1901, p. 51, fn. 2). In analyzing the slip in which he substitutes the name of Hannibal's brother for that of his father, he relates this to the fantasy of "how different things would have been if I had been born the son not of my father but of my brother" (pp. 219-220). Both half brothers, Emmanuel and Philipp, were to migrate to England where they established permanent residence.

Finally, in a letter to Fliess, of October 15, 1897, in which he first describes the early memory implicating Philipp as a partner to his mother's pregnancy, Freud states: "I have found love of the mother and jealousy of the father in my own case.... Similarly with the 'romanticization of origins' " (Freud, 1887-1902, p. 223). And of special interest for the subject of this essay, following the reference to the family-romance fantasy in himself, he devotes a paragraph to a discussion of his favorite play by his favorite author, *Hamlet* by William Shakespeare.

SUMMARY

Freud maintained a long-standing fascination with the Shakespearean authorship controversy. After reading J. Thomas Looney's book, *"Shakespeare" Identified*, in 1923, he became "almost convinced" that Edward de Vere, the seventeenth Earl of Oxford, was the rightful author of the Shakespearean plays and poems.

The Looney book is examined as representative of the anti-Stratfordian position. The arguments are compared with the position taken by the body of historical and literary scholars who support the "Stratfordian orthodoxy."

Lastly, an attempt is made to examine the controversy psychoanalytically. Some speculations concerning the motivation of those who support the anti-Stratfordian position are put forth. Freud's interest in the controversy is seen as the outgrowth of a specific cognitive style and a variant of a family-romance fantasy.

14

FREUD AND
POPPER-LYNKEUS

ERNEST S. WOLF and

HARRY TROSMAN

[*Idealization and the "Doppelgänger."* This collaborative study by Wolf and Trosman supplements the last two chapters to present a first approximation of a psychoanalytic approach to the subject of Freud's creativity. If the central ingredient of his method was identical to Montaigne's commitment to a life of introspection (see Chapter 1), his self-observations were generally organized through the use of tight inductive logic (see Chapter 7). Penetration into the depths of human personality never before plumbed by science (and involving many matters of unseemliness not to the taste of the times) isolated Freud from his colleagues and preceptors (see Chapter 8). As Kohut suggests (Chapter 16), the artist or scientist of creative originality exposes himself to certain dangers in the realm of narcissism in these circumstances.

Sigmund Freud's narcissistic vulnerabilities have been tentatively sketched by Gedo and Wolf in Chapter 4. In this chapter, Wolf and Trosman suggest that these conflicts may have been reawakened when Freud achieved his great scientific and artistic triumph, the creation of psychoanalysis. Wolf's previous report (Chapter 9) on the consequences of the exhibitionistic tensions awakened by Freud's initial major

First published in *Journal of the American Psychoanalytic Association.* 22:123-141, 1974. The chapter is based on materials in the Siegfried Bernfeld Collection of the Library of Congress.

discoveries in psychology may have pinpointed the early stages in this new phase in the definition of Freud's sense of self. Two symptomatic residua of these internal struggles which persisted throughout Freud's maturity are described in this chapter.

One of these problems is the increasing difficulty encountered by the man of genius in finding people in his environment who can serve as carriers for his needs for idealization as his own stature grows with his creative achievements. Freud's capacity to mitigate this dilemma by turning to historical precedessors was demonstrated during his adolescence; e.g., his use of Horace as a literary model (see Chapter 3) and of Cervantes as a source for personal values (see Chapter 4). Once he had created psychoanalysis as a *scientific* enterprise, however, he found himself in an area in which predecessors did not exist; once the break with Breuer had taken place (see Chapter 8), he paid the price for his singular originality of having to feel completely isolated in terms of the traditions in which he had been educated. In these circumstances, he first turned to Wilhelm Fliess with an idealization poorly based on the latter's actual qualities. After the disillusionment which inevitably followed, Freud was explicitly aware of his need to preserve certain illusions about the few men whom he grew to admire. As Wolf and Trosman report, he attempted to manage this in part by avoiding these men in person. As the possibility of idealizing actual contemporaries became more remote, Freud apparently experienced a need to remove any taint of imperfection from his image of his idealized predecessors, leading to the fantasy of noble parentage for Shakespeare (see Chapter 13).

The authors bring to our attention an even subtler dilemma faced by the mature Freud. Insofar as he succeeded in idealizing a few figures such as Schnitzler or Popper-Lynkeus, these persons assumed the functions of an alter ego for him; in them, Freud saw reflected the outlines of his own greatness. In avoiding his *Doppelgänger,* he was therefore shying away from being confronted with archaic grandiose ambitions with which he had apparently never come to terms. The one known incident which produced such a confrontation, Freud's ascent of the Athenian Acropolis in 1904, proved to be traumatic (see Chapter 12). In a discussion of this paper, Kohut expressed the surmise that Freud's consistent refusal to consider himself as a great man, in contrast to his proud and forthright claims for the greatness of his work, may have been based on his correct appreciation of his own incapacity to tolerate the role necessitated by achievements of genius. This may have led to his refusal to assume the leadership of organized psychoanalysis once he had gained adherents in significant numbers; it quite certainly showed itself in his refusal to attend all celebrations in his honor. Our estimates of the importance of these problems in shaping Freud's creative activities cannot be confirmed in any reliable manner, of course. They are in consonance, however, with the one analytic report about creative genius based on actual clinical experience (J. Gedo, 1972b) — *Eds.*]

Sigmund Freud's sweeping and enthusiastic praise for Joseph Popper-Lynkeus may strike English and American readers as puzzling (Freud, 1900, 1923c, 1932). Who was this man whom Freud called "one of the very greatest men of his time" (Doryon, 1940)? What was the nature of his achievement? Was Freud's tribute justified or did he have a personal reason for his high praise? The purpose of this contribution is to review the nature of Freud's comments about Popper-Lynkeus, to describe the thought and achievements of Popper-Lynkeus, and to examine Freud's interest in him in the light of current psychoanalytic thought about narcissism, idealization, and various aspects of the grandiose self. We are particularly interested in how these latter conceptualizations are pertinent to the psychology of the creative process.

FREUD'S REFERENCES TO POPPER-LYNKEUS

In 1909, for a second edition of *The Interpretation of Dreams,* Freud added a postscript to his extensive review of the literature on dreams in Chapter 1 (Freud, 1900). After dismissing the publications of the intervening nine years as having "produced nothing new or valuable either in factual material or in opinions" he cited with evident pleasure a view of dreams "in an unexpected quarter" which coincided with the core of his own theory, and hailed it "as the single discoverable instance in the literature of the subject of an independent thinker who is in agreement" with his theory (pp. 93-95). He referred to a story, "Dreaming like Waking" (1899b), which appeared in *Phantasien eines Realisten* (*Fantasies of a Realist*) and was published by Joseph Popper under the pseudonym "Lynkeus" (1899a), and he quoted several paragraphs from the story in the section on the dream work which described dream displacement. The quoted passage pointed out that dreams are never nonsense, that dream distortion is to be understood as a result of censorship, and that there is a continuity between waking life and dream life (Freud, 1900, pp. 308-309).[1]

A close reading of the passage in question, or of the entire story (1899b, English translation by A. A. Brill), suggests that Freud was more than generous in bestowing credit to Popper for his insight into dream psychology. Although Popper did understand that dreams are meaningful, and that seeming nonsense in the manifest content related to concealment, he had arrived at no conception of a censorship nor any understanding of the processes of the dream work. When Freud wrote that in Popper he had found "a view of dreams which coincided entirely with the core of my own theory" (1900, p. 94) he asserted a similarity of viewpoint hardly supported by the writings. In fact, Popper himself might well have been puzzled by Freud's belief in the uniformity of their views. Fritz

[1]Rosenzweig (1958), who also examined the link between Freud and Popper-Lynkeus, makes much out of the fact that Freud refers to the *second* edition of *Phantasien eines Realisten*, published in 1900. Rosenzweig believed that Freud was preoccupied with issues of scientific priority and was thus reluctant to credit Popper with publishing his ideas before the publication of *The Interpretation of Dreams* (1900). Such a view is untenable. Although the first edition of *Phantasien eines Realisten* appeared in 1899 within a few weeks of the appearance of *The Interpretation of Dreams*, it was quickly banned by governmental decree in Vienna, because of the radical and amoral views expressed in the stories. Subsequent editions were available because publication was permitted in Germany, and in all likelihood the second edition, which was not nearly as rare as the first, was the only one available to Freud.

Wittels, a psychoanalyst, a biographer of Freud, and a devoted follower of Popper-Lynkeus, pointed out that there was a crucial difference between an intuitional, fleeting flash of mind and Freud's systematic approach to dream psychology (1947). Indeed Popper-Lynkeus thought so little about his discussion of dream distortion that he did not even mention it in his autobiography. Late in Popper's life, when Wittels presented him with a copy of Freud's *Group Psychology and the Analysis of the Ego*, Popper returned it with the remark that he did not understand one word of it.

Freud's comment about the discovery of Popper's view "in an unexpected quarter" deserves an additional comment. Coming at the end of an extensive review of the scientific literature on dreaming, much of which was pedestrian and limited, it was "unexpected" to find a glimmer of understanding not in science but in the tradition of imaginative literature. Also, the "unexpected quarter" may refer to the proximity of the writer. After reviewing the writings of a large variety of contributors to dream psychology, separated from Freud in time and distance, it may have carried a special meaning that the closest view was shared by a man whose background was remarkably similar and who lived only a few streets away. The search for affinity was to characterize Freud's interest in Popper-Lynkeus in the years to come.

In "On the History of the Psychoanalytic Movement" (1914c) Freud again linked dream theory with Popper, pointing out that he had found "the essential characteristic and most important part of my dream theory" in Popper. Here he used language closer to Popper's when he stated that dream distortion is derived from "a kind of inner dishonesty," a less neutral term than "the censorship" (p. 20) and more in keeping with Popper's terminology.

In 1916 there was an exchange of correspondence between Freud and Popper. Popper had sent to Freud an early eighteenth-century book on dreams as a gift. In Freud's letter of thanks he recalled his surprise years before that Popper had been "the only one" to recognize that distortion in dreams was the result of censorship (E. Freud, 1960, Letter 174).

The first of the two published papers Freud wrote on Popper-Lynkeus appeared in 1923 shortly after Popper's death, in a periodical which was dedicated to promulgating Popper's proposals for social reform. Freud (1923c) pointed out that apparent originality is often a revival of an idea which has been forgotten and then applied to new material. With regard to dream theory, he was prepared to accept that many of his own ideas were previously proposed by others and thus influenced his thinking. However, he was unaware of the source of the idea that dream distortion resulted from the application of the censorship to hidden impulses which strove for expression. He then quoted again the passage from Popper's *Phantasien eines Realisten* which he had quoted in the second edition of *The Interpretation of Dreams*, asking the reader to compare the quotation with the short summary of his own views that he presented in this paper. He said that he had not yet read the passage when he published *The Interpretation of Dreams*, thus proposing that there appeared to be two separate paths to the discovery of a common truth. At the end of the essay he said, "I believe that what enabled me to discover the cause of dream distortion was my moral courage. In the case of Popper it was the purity, love of truth and moral...[lucidity]² of his nature" (1923c, p. 263). These were the attributes of the man in Popper's story who never dreamt nonsense, who dreamt as if awake, and thus whose dreams were interpretable because they were free of distortion.

Before the next publication, in 1932, there were two additional pieces of correspondence about Popper. In 1927, six years after Popper's death, Freud remarked in a letter to his niece that he had discovered a physical resemblance between Georg Brandes, the Danish literary historian and critic, Albert Einstein, and the bust of Popper-Lynkeus in the Rathauspark in Vienna, "three great Jewish personalities.... I am fond of looking for resemblances," he said (E. Freud, 1960, Letter 229, p. 376).

Three years later he was sent a biography of Popper-Lyn-

²The word is *Klarheit*. To translate it as "serenity" (rather than "lucidity" or "clarity"), as Strachey does, misses the subtle point for which Freud was striving here. He obviously wanted to emphasize the link between moral lucidity and transparency of interpretation. It was the unambiguous and clear nature of Popper's (and his protagonist's) moral position which made distortion unnecessary. Fearlessness and lucidity—both could be routes to discovery.

keus by the author, Heinrich Löwy, and he complimented the author on the dignity and truthfulness of the book (E. Freud, 1960, Letter 250, March 30, 1930, p. 396).

In 1932, on the occasion of the tenth anniversary of Popper's death, Freud wrote an account of his contact with him for a special number of the periodical founded under Popper's influence. He wrote of Popper in the highest terms as a man "wholly without evil and falseness" (1932a, p. 224). After being struck with Popper's insight into dream distortion, he read all his works and formed a picture of an unassuming, great man, a thinker and kindly humanitarian. Freud said that although he felt a special feeling of sympathy for Popper, both having experienced the bitterness of anti-Semitism and the hollowness of contemporary values, surprisingly, Freud never sought him out and actually met him. He had previously had feelings of disappointment when he had met men of whom he thought highly because of their lack of understanding of his work, and he was unwilling to expose himself to a rebuff from someone he so greatly admired. Nor was he willing to risk the possibility of a revision in his view that there was an agreement between the two on the problem of dream distortion.

In 1938 Freud wrote an Introduction to a book by Y. Doryon (1940) on Popper's social views entitled *Lynkeus' New State*, which was published in Jerusalem. He stated his belief in Popper as "one of the greatest men of his time" and expressed his regret that the bust of Popper in the Rathauspark had been removed and destroyed by the Germans. By that time Freud was already in London, having also "been removed" by the German occupation of Vienna.[3]

[3]In view of the fact that this Introduction by Freud (1940c) is so little known and has not been included in the *Standard Edition* of Freud's writings, we have translated it and herewith include it in its entirety.

"The Jew, Joseph Popper-Lynkeus, investigator, thinker, and friend of mankind, will surely be recognized and honored by the coming generations as one of the very greatest men of his time.

"A bust was dedicated to him in the Vienna Rathauspark by the Socialist municipal government during the short time of its rule in Vienna. When the Germans invaded Vienna this memorial was removed and probably destroyed.

"The book by Mr. Doryon is a first attempt to erect it again.
                    Sig. Freud   London, November 1938."

JOSEF POPPER-LYNKEUS, HIS LIFE AND THOUGHT

Josef Popper was born in Kolin, Bohemia, in 1838, and died in Vienna in 1921.[4] As a youth, he moved from Kolin to Prague, where he attended the Polytechnikum. Although he was soon judged an excellent and promising engineer, he could not obtain a teaching position at the University because of his Jewish background. For a while he held a menial position with the national railway in Hungary, and then moved to Vienna where he worked as a tutor and peddled articles to newspapers in order to eke out a bare subsistence. In Vienna he attended the lectures of the physicist Ernst Mach and they soon became lifelong friends.[5]

Popper's inventive and scientific ability soon became apparent. He invented a mechanical device which enhanced the working capacity and safety of engines by preventing the accumulation of carbonate deposits which formed on the interior of boilers. He also invented an air condenser which condensed the exhaust of steam machines, thus permitting condensed matter to be used as an engine fuel. He was one of the first to propound the possibilities of transmitting electric power and was highly innovative in his theories of gyroscopic motion and aeronautics. In 1888, he discussed the mechanical possibilities of flight by building lighter steam engines. It was not, however, until he was almost 60 that he was sufficiently secure financially to devote himself to social issues and literary pursuits.

Although, as Edwards says, today he is almost completely forgotten, at the beginning of this century "he became the center of what amounted almost to a cult" (1967, p. 401). Nor

[4] A full-length biography of Popper has not as yet appeared in English. This sketch is based on the accounts which appear in *The Universal Jewish Encyclopedia* (1939-1943), *The Encyclopedia of Philosophy* (Edwards, 1967), and *Encyclopedia Judaica* (1971). *The Encyclopaedia Britannica* carries no entry nor any reference to Popper. A succinct account in English appears in *The Encyclopedia of Philosophy* and is written by Paul Edwards (1967), the editor of the encyclopedia. The article gives a lucid summary of Popper's political and social views and includes a bibliography with available English translations of Popper's writings.

[5] Popper, Mach, Einstein, and Freud were all members of the Society for Positivist Philosophy (Ellenberger, 1970, p. 809).

do his writings sufficiently convey the particular impact of his personality. In addition to admirers such as Freud, Mach, and Wittels, he was highly regarded by Arthur Schnitzler, Stefan Zweig, and Albert Einstein. Einstein referred to him as a "saintly and prophetic person." "All who met Popper were impressed by his deep serenity, warmth and unusual genuine kindness" (Edwards, 1967, p. 401), and his writings are consistent with a profound and consistent humanitarianism.

In 1878 he published *Das Recht zu Leben und die Pflicht zu Sterben, sozialphilosophische Betrachungen, anknüpfend an die Bedeutung Voltaires für die neuere Zeit* (*The Right to Live and the Duty to Die, Social-Philosophical Reflections in Connection with Voltaire's Significance for Our Times*). This work was a defense of the value of the individual and expressed Popper's opposition to the nationalistic policies which submerged the individual to the state.[6]

In 1899, Popper published *Phantasien eines Realisten* (1899a) under the pseudonym of Lynkeus. Rosenzweig (1958) points out that the choice of the name is multiply determined. Lynkeus was the lookout man for the Argonauts, Jason and his companions, who sailed in search of the Golden Fleece. He was named for his keen sight, like the lynx. Lynkeus is also a character in Goethe's *Faust*, a man who is prophetic, a visionary. And Popper may even have had in mind a sardonic rebuff addressed to the most exalted aristocratic hereditary order of the Hapsburgs, also known as that of the Golden Fleece. The book itself consists of 80 sketches, short tales or dialogues, many of which deal with some controversial topic of the day. Popper in his autobiography said that at least one sixth of the stories were based on his own dreams and were recorded shortly after awakening. He collected these stories for 33 years without any conscious interest in publishing them, and when he did suddenly decide to publish he carried out his intent in secret.

In spite of being banned in Vienna, the printing of the book in German went into 21 editions. Three of the tales are of particular interest because of their link to Freud and psycho-

---

[6]It was, no doubt, this belief to which Freud (1932a) in part referred when he expressed his agreement with Popper about the hollowness of the ideals of present-day civilization.

analysis. "Dreaming like Waking," the story to which Freud referred in *The Interpretation of Dreams*, includes several dream specimens which have been examined by both Brill (see Popper-Lynkeus, 1899b) and Wittels (1947). Since the dreams are presented with no associational material, both attempts at interpretation are unsatisfactory. A second story, "The Fermenting Power of a Secret," describes an overt incestuous relationship between a mother and her son in a frank and nonjudgmental fashion. The manner of the presentation as well as the content may have played a role in the demand by some clerical members of the Austrian parliament that the author be subject to criminal prosecution. The third tale, "The Son of the King of Egypt," related that Pharaoh was warned by an oracle that he was endangered by the birth of a son. To lessen his fear, he ordered the death or abandonment of the first-born, in much the same way as Laius tried to respond to the birth of Oedipus. Although the story does not spell out that Moses was Pharaoh's son, the linkage was hinted at. In 1938, after the publication of *Moses and Monotheism*, Doryon wrote to Freud asking whether he had been influenced by Popper's story. Freud responded first that it was possible that Popper's hint might have influenced his thought about Moses' birth: although there was no doubt in his mind that he had read Popper's essay at an earlier time, he could not remember it, and this may have been another phenomenon of "cryptomnesia" which, he said, "happened often with me and has clarified the source of apparently original ideas." In another letter, a few weeks later, after he had had a chance to reread Popper's story, he could not deny a possible influence, but he pointed out that there was an essential difference between Popper and himself. For Freud it was crucial that Moses was not "half Egyptian," that is, an illegitimate son of Pharaoh, but "a whole one." "For me the negation is essential. Moses is as little the child of his Jewish parents as Cyrus is the grandchild of the King of Medes or Romulus that of the King of Alba Longa. In all such cases the first family is the myth, the fiction" (Doryon, 1946).

In 1912 Popper published *Die Allgemeine Nährpflicht*, which he regarded as his most important work. (The title means *The General Duty to Provide Nourishment*, a play on the word *Wehrpflicht*, which means compulsory military service.) It is the duty of society, he argued, to provide for the basic material needs of every individual. Among the necessities he included food, clothing, shelter, medical attention, and basic education. In order to provide a guaranteed minimum subsistence for all he proposed a term of labor service in a *Nährarmee* (Nourishment Army) of 12 years for men and seven years for women. Although the necessities would thus be regulated by the state, private enterprise would handle the production and distribution of luxuries. As Edwards points out, although currently leading economists of many persuasions support the idea of a guaranteed income, at the time it was first recommended this idea was considered extremely radical and opposed to natural law.

In view of Freud's opposition to Popper's ideas on the basis of their fundamental assumptions it may be of some interest to pursue Popper's theories in greater depth. Popper believed that no value is as great as the worth we attach to the unique individual. He believed in the sanctity of human life and his program of social reform is based on this fundamental precept.

> When any individual, of however little account, but one who does not deliberately imperil another's existence, disappears from the world without or even against his will, this is a far more important happening than any political or religious or national occurrence, or the sum total of the scientific and artistic and technical advances made throughout the ages by all the peoples of the world. Should anybody be inclined to regard this statement as an exaggeration, let him imagine the individual concerned to be himself or his best beloved. Then he will understand and accept it [quotation from Popper, in Edwards, 1967, p. 403].

A civilized person, in the presence of a fire in the Louvre, would save the human beings in preference to the paintings. A group, in conditions of starvation when some individual members have to be sacrificed, makes the choices by drawing lots. Shakespeare or Newton would not be rated higher than someone else. Thus any human life, aside from that of someone with the intent to kill another, possesses infinite value.

Popper found views such as those promulgated by the historian Treitschke particularly galling. When Treitschke wrote "One statue of Phidias more than makes up for all the misery of the millions of slaves in Antiquity," Popper proposed that Treitschke spend five years of service as a slave and then afterwards be asked how he felt about Phidias. Popper's views can be criticized on the basis of the *ad hominem* fallacy of the argument. However, he renders a service in pointing out that a position based on personal experience might be more profound than one based on logic and reason alone. If views which have universal application are considered in terms of the life of the individual, then important distinctions can be drawn between value judgments and statements of feeling or fantasy. What holds for the life of the slave in the age of Phidias must also be true for the historian, Treitschke, if *all* human life has infinite value.

In a letter to Wittels in 1925, Freud indicated that, in spite of his high regard for Popper as a man, he could not support his political philosophy (Wittels, 1947). Freud felt that Popper's ethical system was founded on narcissism and that the incomparable value that Popper attached to human life was not valid and could not be supported in nature. The demands of Eros are such that narcissism is at times sacrificed for the sake of others, for a cause, or even, one might add, for trans- formations of the cathexis of the self which have to do with the primary preservation of life. Freud expressed himself along similar lines in his 1932 paper on Popper when he said, "I reflected much over the rights of the individual which he advocated and to which I should gladly have added my support had I not been restrained by the thought that neither the processes of Nature nor the aims of human society quite justified such claims" (Freud, 1932a, p. 224). Unable to pick up the ideology of individualism, he could not subscribe to Popper's belief in the ultimate amelioration of the human condition through social reform. "My compassion lacks pa- thos," he wrote Wittels (Wittels, 1947).

FREUD'S IDEALIZATION OF POPPER-LYNKEUS

"One of the greatest [*ganz grössten*] men of his time" was Freud's final judgment on Josef Popper-Lynkeus. Freud expressed respect and admiration without stint for many

friends and contemporaries, but his praise was rarely excessive. His tributes to Popper-Lynkeus seem inordinate, however, even if we do not take into consideration the rapid
disappearance of Popper-Lynkeus's renown during the post-
war period. To be sure, Freud felt the warming presence of an
ally in spirit when he first read *Phantasien eines Realisten*
during the early bleak years of intellectual loneliness. Appropriately enough, he acknowledged Popper as "an independent
thinker" and gave him credit for his insight by adding a
postscript to *The Interpretation of Dreams* as well as append-
ing a footnote (1900, pp. 94-95, 308-309); again, in his
"History of the Psycho-Analytic Movement" (1914c) he referred to Popper-Lynkeus's achievement and lauded him as
"the famous engineer." But it was not until after Popper-
Lynkeus's death that Freud's encomia became lavish. In
writing of "the purity, love of truth and moral...[lucidity] of
his nature," Freud endowed the author of "Dreaming like
Waking" with the saintliness of the story's protagonist. The
epithets by which Freud described Popper had been applied
by Popper himself to the man in his story (Freud, 1923, p.
263). Indeed, Popper had made his leading character say:
"Order and harmony reign both in my thoughts and in my
feelings, nor do the two struggle with each other ... I am one
and undivided." Freud (1932a, p. 223) quoted these lines from
Popper when commemorating the tenth anniversary of his
death. Clearly, Popper had in mind an ideal of resolved
conflict and Freud identified the person of Popper with this
ideal: "And if Science informs us that such a man, wholly
without evil and falseness and devoid of all repressions, does
not exist and could not survive, yet we may guess that, so far as
an approximation to this ideal is possible, it had found its
realization in the person of Popper himself" (pp. 223-224).
Freud confessed that he was "overwhelmed by meeting with
such wisdom" and began to read all his works until "there was
built up clearly before my eyes a picture of this...[unassum-
ing][7] great man, who was a thinker and a critic and at the

[7]Strachey's translation of *schlicht* as "simple-minded" is totally out of keeping
with Freud's tone. "Unassuming" seems closest to Freud's intended meaning.

same time a kindly humanitarian and reformer" (p. 224). Freud, who had waged a heroic struggle in overcoming and lifting his repressions by dint of his "moral courage" (1923, p. 263), could but admire this "great man" who seemed to have achieved such serene, conflict-free sublimation through purity, love of truth, and moral lucidity.

Twenty-two years had passed since the publication of *Phantasien eines Realisten* when Popper died in 1921. During these years Freud and Popper shared the same city, many friends, and even wrote to each other. They never met. Staying away from Popper in the face of Freud's high estimation of him may take on an added significance. Arthur Schnitzler was similarly esteemed and similarly avoided by Freud. Recent extension of psychoanalytic theory encompassing the transformations of narcissism (Kohut, 1966, 1968, 1971) may aid in illuminating these complicated relationships.[a]

During the early years of his growth as a scientist Freud's creativity seems to have emerged out of the matrix of a collaborative relationship with a series of admired colleagues. The work with Breuer and the friendship with Fliess are the most prominent examples. The sense of isolation experienced by creative minds during the lonely exploration of the unknown is both exhilarating and frightening (see Chapter 16). A measure of relief is often sought by blending with a powerful person in the environment. This narcissistic relationship may either be a variety of mirror transference, a confirming reflection to aid the expansion of an active, creative self; or it may be an idealizing transference in response to the wish to obtain strength from an idealized object. "Fliess may well have been the embodiment of such a narcissistic transference for

---

[a] In a review of Eissler's *Talent and Genius* (1971b), Wolf (1973b) calls attention to the curious coincidence that both Freud and Popper-Lynkeus died at the age of 83. He notes that this apparent triviality may have some bearing on Eissler's suggestion that a genius like Freud might perceive some unconscious clues relevant to his actual span of life. Eissler mentioned this possibility in connection with Freud's lifelong numerological preoccupations about his eventual date of death. Wolf wonders whether Freud might have been afraid to face the cues about his alter ego which his unique perceptual capacities might have provided.

Freud during Freud's most creative spell; and Freud was able to dispense with the illusionary sense of Fliess's greatness. . . after he had accomplished his great creative task" (Kohut, 1971, pp. 316-317).[8]

Following his self-analysis and the termination of his relationship with Fliess, Freud's creativity became largely independent of narcissistic objects in his environment.[b] Nevertheless, the high regard for Popper, especially after the latter's death, unmistakably shows the signs of a narcissistic relationship to an idealized object. This impression is strengthened by the fact that although Freud somehow never found the occasion to meet Popper in the flesh he sought out his bust in the Rathauspark to pay his respects, and, after the bust was removed by the German occupiers, he was pleased that Doryon was erecting it again in the form of his memorial volume (Doryon, 1940).

Doubtless there were a number of motives that led Freud to avoid Popper while he lived. Among these the fear of disappointment by the idealized object is suggested in a number of communications. Popper had told Wittels (1947) that he could not understand one word of Freud's involved explanations. Certainly Freud was familiar with the incomprehension which his ideas aroused in otherwise well-meaning and intelligent people. Georg Brandes, the respected literary critic and historian, was highly esteemed by Freud. On March 4, 1927, Freud wrote his niece Margit (E. Freud, 1960, Letter 229): "I too had been very saddened by Brandes' death . . . After I had talked to Einstein in Berlin and seen the bust of Popper-Lynkeus in our Rathauspark, I discovered a more significant resemblance between these three great Jewish personalities." It is interesting to note that Brandes' death reminded Freud not

[8]Wolf has discussed some of the vicissitudes of the Freud-Fliess relationship with regard to effects on Freud's literary artistry (Chapter 9).

[b]This statement is largely correct in reference to actual persons: if "object" is taken in a broader context, it may be that Freud's creativity continued to be fed by his successful idealization of certain works of art and localities (see Chapter 12) as well as by his less adaptive resort to pseudo scientific fantasies exalting certain of his predecessors (see Chapter 13). The correspondence with Jung (McGuire, 1974) suggests that an attenuated repetition of the Fliess relationship did in fact take place between 1907 and 1913.

only of Popper but also of Freud's high hopes for recognition and their bitter disappointment. Recalling a visit to Brandes, Freud wrote Margit, "I didn't know anything about his hostility to psychoanalysis and approached him quite ingenuously, with unclouded respect.... His conversion was seemingly a matter of two minutes...prepared by your influence and disarmed by my guilelessness, he was ready to relinquish a prejudice where he was unable to form an opinion. He could not fail to realize how highly I respected him."

More disturbing even than the lack of recognition is the incapacity of the idealized object to grasp the new ideas: it shatters the illusion of the perfection of the idealized person and thus threatens his image as a source of strength that one may draw upon. Popper, like Brandes, was a potential cause of painful disappointment. Freud himself tells it simply (1932a, p. 224):

> A special feeling of sympathy drew me to him, since he too had clearly had painful experience of the bitterness of the life of a Jew and of the hollowness of the ideals of present-day civilization.... But I never sought him out. My innovations in psychology had estranged me from my contemporaries, and especially from the older among them: often enough when I approached some man whom I had honoured from a distance, I found myself repelled, as it were, by his lack of understanding for what had become my whole life to me. And after all Josef Popper had been a physicist: he had been a friend of Ernst Mach. I was anxious that the happy impression of our agreement upon the problem of dream-distortion should not be spoilt. So it came about that I put off calling upon him till it was too late and I could now only salute his bust in the gardens in front of our Rathaus.

Not until Popper had joined the company of immortals and could no longer disillusion Freud was the latter able to meet him in the Rathauspark.

POPPER-LYNKEUS AS FREUD'S "DOUBLE"

It may not have been fortuitous that Freud remembered Popper's association with Ernst Mach when explaining his avoidance of him. Mach was no friend of psychoanalysis, and when the second edition of Mach's psychological book *Die Analyse der Empfindungen* was published in 1900, Freud read what Mach said about dreams and said that he felt like the dwarf in the fairy story, delighted that "the princess doesn't know" (Freud, 1887-1902, Letter 137, p. 322). Freud dealt with his bitterness at the poor reception of *The Interpretation of Dreams* by finding a bit of satisfaction in the fact that Mach was far from understanding dream psychology. Freud mentions Mach in a footnote in his paper on "The Uncanny" (1919, p. 248) as having made two observations on the uncanny effect of meeting one's own image, unbidden and unexpected, the uncanny effect of a "double." Freud then reports a similar experience of his own. "Is it possible," Freud asks, "that our dislike of them was a vestigial trace of the archaic reaction which feels the 'double' to be something uncanny?" And, one might add, could it be that Freud's avoidance of Popper, linked as he was in Freud's mind with the uncomprehending Mach and the never-forgotten uncanny experiences, was also an avoidance of a feared "double"? It would not be a unique instance. In May, 1922, on the occasion of Arthur Schnitzler's sixtieth birthday Freud wrote to him: "I shall make you a confession. . . . I have been struggling with the question of why I have never, in all these years, made any effort to meet you. . . . I think I have avoided you out of a kind of fear of finding my own double" (Kupper and Rollman-Branch, 1959). Freud had seen in Schnitzler's work "presumptions, interests and conclusions" well known to him from his own thoughts and giving him a feeling of "uncanny familiarity." Is this not what Freud may have felt when confronted with Popper's work such as "Dreaming like Waking"?

Kupper and Rollman-Branch have given an excellent account of the many parallels in Freud's and Schnitzler's lives and works and it would not be difficult to find similar resemblances between Freud and Popper. However, biographical material cannot be decisive here; at best it may lead into areas that reveal presumptions and interests.

A closer study of Popper's other stories and dreams in *Phantasien eines Realisten* does indeed reveal a great similarity between his way of thinking and feeling about many subjects and Freud's. Doryon has commented on the resemblance of the ideas in Popper's "The Son of the King of Egypt" and Freud's *Moses and Monotheism*. Popper's narration "What Are They So Happy About?" (*"Worüber freuen sie sich eigentlich?"*) discusses the nature of the mystique of royalty which binds the subjects to their sovereign. At the base of this mysterious bond lies what Popper calls a "transcendence," which is the ability to perceive and to believe in things which one cannot see and for which there exists no basis. It is by exposing children to unending repetition of hymns and speeches about royalty, lies repeated over and over, accompanied by music, marches, singing together, and uniforms, that even the most rational, the professors and artists, come to believe in the mystique of royalty and can be roused by national anthems and glorious parades to fight foolish wars for the honor of the fatherland. Popper seems to have understood aspects of Freud's later ideas about the idealization of the leader in group formation and its infantile roots. Yet it is interesting to note that after reading Freud's *Group Psychology and the Analysis of the Ego* Popper said: "I have enjoyed what he quoted from the Frenchman [meaning Le Bon]. But when he came to his own more involved explanations, I must tell you, I did not understand one word" (Wittels, 1947). Probably he did not understand *The Interpretation of Dreams* any better. Though in the case of the Egyptian Moses Freud acknowledged to Doryon the possibility of a cryptomnesia, it seems unlikely that in either instance Freud really absorbed the idea from reading Popper.[c] Rather, these corresponding ideas grew out of comparable *Weltanschauungen*. Popper's (1899a) "Ein Tischgespräch bei Martin Luther" ("Conversation at Luther's Dinner Table") and "Des Erasmus von Rotterdam Besuch bei Sir Thomas Morus" ("Visit of Erasmus of Rotterdam with Sir Thomas More") show the same skeptical antireligious and anticlerical criticisms of church-fos-

---

[c]Shengold (1972) has demonstrated, however, Freud's cryptomnesia about a paper by Karl Abraham (1912) concerning Ikhnaton as the founder of monotheism. Perhaps Freud's too facile acknowledgment of Doryon's claim in behalf of Popper may be explained on the basis of some awareness on his part that he *had* suffered a cryptomnesia with regard to his Moses.

tered illusions that were present in Freud's thinking.[d] In the
latter story Popper's Erasmus also takes issue with the presumed innocence of children; his observations of thousands of
children have him convinced that they are man in a state of
nature "without experience of life, without understanding and
instruction in matters of morality, with thought directed only
towards profit and pleasures." This is not yet infantile sexuality but may have seemed quite familiar to Freud. In "Ein
Gottesurteil" ("A Judgment of God") Popper shows that even
in intelligent and civilized people there can be a sudden
eruption of sexuality in the form of lust and sadism.[9]

It therefore seems reasonable to infer that the "uncanny
familiarity" which Freud felt on reading Schnitzler also confronted him upon meeting the *Phantasien eines Realisten* and
similarly led to an avoidance of his presumed "double" in
Popper. Rosenzweig (1958), who also suggested that Freud
may have been inhibited by a *Doppelgänger* sensitivity, based
his inference on two further tales from the *Phantasien eines
Realisten*, "Gärende Kraft eines Geheimnisses" ("The Fermenting Power of a Secret") and "König Salomo als Maus"
("King Solomon as a Mouse"). Both of these stories reveal
facets of Popper's unconscious that impinge closely on some of
Freud's own preoccupations.

Names were often significant links in Freud's associations.
Jones (1953, p. 4) suggested that the name Josef always had
some special significance for Freud.[10] There was an uncle
Josef who had difficulties with the law and died of epilepsy, at
best an ambivalently cathected model. There were his friends

[d] Rieff (1959) has identified Feuerbach as the principal spokesman for these ideas
in the mid-nineteenth century. The Freud-Silberstein correspondence gives concrete evidence that Freud was reading Feuerbach with avidity in the early 1870's.

[9] Popper's "Die Troubadours im Grünen" ("The Troubadours in the Green
Countryside") deals with a gang of thieves modeled after Cervantes' *Exemplary
Novels* (*Rinconete and Cortadillo*). It could easily have reminded Freud of the
Academia Castellana, an adolescent parody of the *Exemplary Novels* he acted out
with Silberstein (see Chapter 4).

[10] Freud himself noted the importance of the name Josef. "It will be noticed that
the name Josef plays a great part in my dreams (cf. the dream about my uncle). My
own ego finds it very easy to hide itself behind people of that name, since Joseph
was the name of a man famous in the Bible as an interpreter of dreams" (1900, p.
484 fn.). See also Shengold (1971).

Josef Paneth and, later, Josef Breuer. For some years Freud lived on Kaiser Josef Strasse. Shadowy in the past is the Biblical Joseph who, like Freud, had been an interpreter of dreams, and who, like Freud, had a father named Jacob. A man with the name of Josef Popper might have evoked some of the same enigmatic associations. The name Popper also may have elicited links to the past. Freud's first love, the Dulcinea of his adolescence, had been Gisela Fluss (see Chapter 3). He worshipped her from afar and when she married—someone else, a man named Popper—he expressed his bitterness in writing an almost scatologically depreciating "Wedding Carmen" (Stanescu, 1967; see also Rogawski, 1970). Our Josef Popper, however, remained a single man who only married on his deathbed at the age of 83. Another nexus in this matrix of connections may have been the writer Börne (see Chapter 10). Freud had a special regard for Börne who had been a model for a method of writing which became the prototype of free associations. Ellenberger (1970, p. 466) points out that Popper was a disciple of Börne with regard to his style, and both men seem linked to each other and to Freud as prefiguring the psychoanalytic method.

NARCISSISM AND THE DOPPELGÄNGER

Dostoevsky, Poe, Stevenson, and E. T. A. Hoffmann, among the major writers, have dealt with the theme of the *Doppelgänger*. After Freud illuminated the phenomenon of the "double" psychoanalytically (1919, p. 248) it was taken up, among others, by Rank (1925, 1941), Bonaparte (1934, p. 90), and Kupper and Rollman-Branch (1959). Freud suggested that the dislike of the "double" was a vestigial trace of the archaic fear that the "double" is something uncanny. Freud distinguished two sources for the feeling of uncanniness: repressed infantile complexes and the archaic animistic beliefs of civilized people which have been, more or less, *surmounted* rather than repressed. It is the latter, the surmounted beliefs in the omnipotence of thought with secret injurious powers and in the possibility of the return of the dead, which can be reawakened by something that *actually happens* (Freud's italics). The old, discarded beliefs thus seem confirmed, a judgment that is experienced with the feeling of the uncanny. It is this judgment, "So after all it is *true*,"[e] that creates the uncanny effect on meeting one's "double."

Elkisch (1957) has noted the fascination with mirrors observed in certain psychotic patients as well as in children. This fascination, which often turns into panic, is shown by Elkisch to be derived from fear of loss of self. The mirror image, like the shadow, the echo, the portrait, and the twin is a variant of the "double."[11] One might say that just as the child's peek-aboo game serves to master his fear of losing his mother, so the mirror game serves to master the fear of losing the self by omnipotently creating another self. At a time when the cohesiveness of the child's self is not yet firmly established, mirroring provides a confirming reflection. The "mirror" of parental approval strengthens the child's feeling of being able to preserve his originally diffuse narcissism by concentrating perfection and power upon the grandiose self which, *pari passu*, is experienced in a grandiose fantasy. During the psychoanalysis of adults with narcissistic personality disorders a revival of this early developmental phase manifests itself in one of the varieties of mirror transference (Kohut, 1968, 1971). Under the benign aegis of such a therapeutically managed narcissistic transference relationship, repressed or disavowed aspects of the grandiose self may once again become conscious, albeit with intensely painful shame. The

[e]Compare this with Freud's idea on the Acropolis. "So after all, it is *real*" (1936). His explanation of the uncanny thus seems to support the assumption that the journey to Athens had the significance of confirming an archaic, disavowed, omnipotent fantasy system (see Chapter 12).

[11]It is interesting to note that the encounter with his "double" reported by Freud occurred when he was momentarily unaware of a mirror which was showing him his image. "I was sitting alone in my *wagon-lit* compartment when a more than usually violent jolt of the train swung back the door of the adjoining washing-cabinet, and an elderly gentleman in a dressing-gown and a traveling cap came in. I assumed that in leaving the washing-cabinet, which lay between the two compartments, he had taken the wrong direction and come into my compartment by mistake. Jumping up with the intention of putting him right, I at once realized to my dismay that the intruder was nothing but my own reflection in the looking-glass on the open door. I can still recollect that I thoroughly disliked his appearance. Instead, therefore, of being frightened by our 'doubles', both Mach and I simply failed to recognize them as such" (Freud, 1919, p. 248 fn.).

uncanny feeling accompanying the experience of the "double" is the apperception of the imminent reappearance and confirmation of the surmounted or disavowed belief in the omnipotent creation of another self, a grandiose fantasy which may *suddenly*[12] flood the self with shame and threaten its cohesion: a feared loss of self.[13] This may also explain why in folklore the *Doppelgänger* is a harbinger of death, and even stepping on a person's shadow is believed to cause him injury.

SUMMARY

Sigmund Freud's relationship with Josef Popper-Lynkeus, a man whom he highly esteemed but never met, is examined in the light of the link between narcissistic transformations and psychological creativity. Although Freud idealized Popper's psychological insights and the saintliness of his personality, Freud took no steps to have his convictions about Popper challenged by reality. Indeed he feared that in actually meeting Popper he would be disappointed, as he had been on numerous other occasions when confronted by the lack of comprehension of men whom he admired. In addition, Popper, like Arthur Schnitzler, was an alter ego or "double" for Freud, an archaic aspect of his own self which had to be kept at a judicious distance. Freud could acknowledge the greatness of Popper and their similarity from afar, but he avoided a confrontation which might have disturbed the idealization or brought about a feeling of the uncanny.

The nature of the Freud-Popper relationship suggests that narcissistic trends toward idealization and the formation of an alter ego may have wider applicability in the investigation of creative individuals. In Freud's case there are indications of an intense need to idealize and to establish a relationship with a man whom he saw as a double. The double counteracts the sense of isolation and estrangement which accompanies revolutionary discovery. On the other hand, the presence of the double threatens the creative person with a sudden regressive pull toward fragmentation and loss of the cohesive self.

[12]Freud (1919) describes this as "meeting one's own image *unbidden* and *unexpected*" (my italics).

[13]Kohut (1971, p. 64 fn.) links the shame response to the sudden deployment of disorganized exhibitionistic cathexes.

PART V

FREUD AND THE PSYCHOANALYTIC COMMUNITY

15

THE WISE BABY RECONSIDERED

JOHN E. GEDO

[*Freud's Paladin and Grand Vizier.* No portrayal of Freud's
creativity could pretend to touch on its essential aspects if it
failed to consider the effects of his personal influence on the
psychoanalytic activities of his immediate followers. Although
these accomplishments have been surveyed in *Psychoanalytic
Pioneers* (Alexander, Eisenstein, and Grotjahn, 1966), a book
which devotes a separate chapter to each one of Freud's early
disciples, and are alluded to in passing in Jones's biography of
Freud, the primary source materials upon which such assessments will have to be based are largely not yet accessible to the
public (for the exceptions see footnote a, Chapter 7).

At the moment, then, studies of Freud's influence on his
circle of close associates must, of necessity, concentrate on the
published work of each student, attempting to estimate the
extent of his borrowings from Freud as against his originality
and taking into account the effect on the work of direct communication between them. Gedo's paper approaches this
aspect of the intellectual history of psychoanalysis by examining in detail the life work of Freud's favorite student, Sándor
Ferenczi.

This paper stresses the unusual creativity of the men who
gathered around Freud at the beginning of this century: their
level of achievement seems to be out of proportion to their
small number. Gedo doubts that these men possessed a greater
degree of talent than did psychoanalysts of later vintage, and
he tries to explain their high level of creative success in terms
of the effects of the very partial personal analyses available to

Translated from *"Noch Einmal der Gelehrte Säugling."* *Psyche*, 22:301-319,
1968.

these pioneers. In the context of this volume, focused on the impact of Freud as a person, we have to emphasize the importance of another factor, namely, that of the facilitating force exerted by the presence of a creative genius on his collaborators.

In many of the preceding chapters (see especially Chapters 13 and 14), various authors have discussed the needs of the creative person for idealized objects in connection with Freud's relationship to Fliess, Shakespeare, Cervantes, and Popper-Lynkeus. We are suggesting that Freud's early followers benefited from the fact that Freud was a figure ideally fitted to fulfill such needs for them. The inspiring example of a truly great man has often created a milieu in which even mediocre followers have been able to produce major achievements. To cite only one example, the painter Raphael Sanzio organized a Roman studio which, under his personal leadership, produced a series of masterpieces in the Vatican; after his death, the quality of the work of his former assistants never again approached the level it had sustained with him. To assess the other side of this coin, in Chapter 16 Kohut discusses the difficulties created for his followers by the idealization of the man of genius.

Gedo reviews the psychoanalytic contributions of Sandor Ferenczi from the inception of his career in the form of digests of Freud's latest ideas, through a long period of developing original contributions in the context of ongoing discussion of each of his innovations with Freud before making them public, to the last phase, covering about a dozen years before Ferenczi's death, in which he worked independently but required Freud's approval for his work in order to maintain his self-esteem as well as his capacity for further creative achievement. If these conditions strike the reader as indicative of severe psychopathology (albeit not exactly of the type suggested by Jones in his account of these matters in his Freud biography), it must never be forgotten that Ferenczi consistently looked upon Freud as his *analyst*. Although this analysis took place within the framework of a complicated relationship which had numerous other aspects—disciple, adoptive son, paladin, and grand vizier—its partial failure must be attributed to the unavoidable historical circumstance that it was performed at a time when psychoanalytic knowledge had not yet reached the point that would have made possible the successful treatment of Ferenczi's type of pathology. Without mentioning Ferenczi's name, Freud described his case history and explained the unsatisfactory results of the analysis along these lines in "Analysis Terminable and Interminable" (1937)—*Eds.*]

It was Ferenczi who brought to the attention of psycho-analysts the inevitability of ambivalent attitudes toward great men (B. 273).[1] His own scientific reputation and the place currently accorded him in the history of psychoanalysis certainly constitute a painful confirmation of this insight. His greatness is uncontested; on his death, Freud wrote (1933b): "We cannot believe that the history of our science will ever forget him." Jones (1933) paid him the ultimate tribute of echoing Hamlet's "We shall not look upon his like again." Yet the present-day student of psychoanalysis may well complete his training without having read more than two or three of Ferenczi's papers, and the man whom Freud regarded as his "Paladin and Grand Vizier" is generally remembered for the inconclusive technical experiments through which he departed from the views of his teacher.

Although the unjustifiably hostile interpretation of Fer-

---

[1]Numbers in parentheses preceded by the letter B. are those assigned to Ferenczi's publications in the *Verzeichnis der Wissenschaftlichen Veröffentlichungen von Dr. Sándor Ferenczi* (Ferenczi, 1908-1933a, Vol. 4, pp. 295-327). This system has been adopted for the English edition of his psychological works (see Ferenczi, 1908-1933c, pp. 377-386). Of the works mentioned in this chapter, English translations of numbers B. 61, 66, 67, 75, 80, 85, 92, 100, 111, 114, 135, 136, and 146 appear in *Contributions to Psychoanalysis* (Ferenczi, 1908-1914); numbers B. 60, 65, 103, 109, 138, 139, 159, 160, 161, 187, 189, 190, 191, 193, 194, 195, 196, 197, 198, 210, 211, 215, 216, 217, 220, 232, 234, 243, 269, and 271 in *Further Contributions to the Theory and Technique of Psychoanalysis* (Ferenczi, 1908-1926); and numbers B. 63, 77, 86, 93, 235, 239, 244, 273, 278, 280, 281, 282, 283, 287, 291, 292, 294, 298, 299, 301, and 308 in *Final Contributions to the Problems and Methods of Psychoanalysis* (Ferenczi, 1908-1933c). Number B. 218 has been translated as *Psychoanalysis and the War Neuroses* (Ferenczi, Abraham, Simmel, and Jones, 1919), B. 264 as *The Development of Psychoanalysis* (Ferenczi and Rank, 1924), and B. 268 as *Thalassa: A Theory of Genitality* (Ferenczi, 1924). A translation of B. 277 appeared in *The International Journal of Psycho-Analysis* (Ferenczi, 1927). Numbers B. 92, 110, 124, 150, 151, 175, 184, 201, 204, 265, and 277 have not been translated.

enczi's late years put forth by Jones (1957) in his biography of Freud has been vigorously disputed by Balint (1958) and Lorand (1966), even incorrect allegations of psychosis are sufficient to "drag the sublime into the dust." Moreover, some of his passionate partisans have done him as much disservice as have his detractors by claiming him, posthumously, as a precursor of various departures from psychoanalysis unheard of in his lifetime (Thompson, 1944, 1950).

The recent reissue of *Bausteine zur Psychoanalyse* (1908-1933a), the German edition of Ferenczi's writings, has given me the opportunity and provided the stimulus to read Ferenczi's complete psychoanalytic *oeuvre* and to attempt, from the vantage point of 1966, an objective assessment of the lasting scientific contribution he has made to our field.

As I have immersed myself in this task, I have been compelled gradually to realize that the ideal of objectivity was unattainable. My own ambivalence was unavoidably stirred by the one man whom Freud came to address as his "Dear Son" (Jones, 1955, p. 166), the one disciple with whom he shared his most passionately cherished activity—the Italian journeys—and to whom he had written: ". . . I often wished that you would pull yourself out of the infantile role and place yourself beside me as a companion on an equal footing" (E. Freud, 1960, Letter 148). Perhaps the similarity of our backgrounds—born 50-odd years apart within 50-odd miles of each other—turns me into a biased historian of the premier psychoanalyst of Hungary. Certainly I cannot help asking myself whether my relatives in Miskolcz patronized the Ferenczi bookstore or whether my grandfather might have known him at the University of Vienna. When I read of his bachelor quarters at the Hotel Royal in Budapest, I am confronted with the memory of my childhood stay there; when the story of his Professorship of Psychoanalysis during the 1919 Revolution emerges, I recall my father's exciting stories of those confused and bloody months. In other words, thinking about Ferenczi suffices to undo a quarter century of American experiences and to make me into what I have always denied I am—an exile from Hungary. So much for objectivity. My assessment of Ferenczi's lasting contributions is offered, unabashedly, *con amore.*

I was prepared, when I began to review Ferenczi's contributions to psychoanalysis in the order of their publication, to be impressed once more by the brilliance of his better-known papers, and I expected to discover many delights in the lesser-known works which I had not read before. Nor was I disappointed in these expectations. The greatest interest in concentrated study of his lifelong effort, however, turned out to be the chance to grasp the pattern of development of a creative scientist. The *Bausteine* proved to be an immense quarry of psychoanalytic ideas, most of which are not specifically credited to their originator when they are used today. I do not intend to highlight clever insights mentioned *en passant*; the issues I wish to stress are the recurrent themes of Ferenczi's thought. Science, which is systematic activity directed toward more precise reality perception and its communication to others, should become permanently retained when it is structuralized into definite word representations, but all too often valid scientific concepts are forgotten because they encounter prejudices or transference reactions. Ferenczi's ideas seem to have suffered this fate, or, alternatively, they have been taken into the public domain and dissociated from their creator.

It is staggering to encounter Ferenczi's earliest psychoanalytic publications, which were printed within one year of his initial efforts with the analytic method in 1907. They consist of a series of masterful expository lectures to a medical audience, starting with the problems of adult sexual life and actual neuroses and proceeding through the exposition of intrapsychic conflicts to the rationale of psychoanalytic intervention and of supportive-repressive psychotherapies. His sophistication and up-to-date grasp of Freud's theory and technique are best illustrated by his description of the method of free association (see Chapter 10) which Freud had barely devised during his work with the "Rat Man" during the previous winter (B. 60, 61, 65, 66). This work is not yet original, but everything in it is documented with clinical material from Ferenczi's own practice or from his own dreams. The extent of his efforts of self-observation is further demonstrated in some fragments of this period (B. 299) which also reveal his direct observations of children, instantly correlated with his clinical work (B. 298). The distinction of the mind of this first-year student of psychoanalysis is exemplified by the statements in these notes that, since the Oedipus complex is nuclear in all neuroses, the essence of a syndrome (homosexuality is the one he was considering) must lie not in its content but in its structure.

Freud must have recognized the unusual talent of his new adherent very quickly, because he invited Ferenczi to accompany him on his American trip in 1909; they discussed the subject of each of the "Five Lectures" at Clark University (Freud, 1910a) on their morning promenades. Their intimacy grew during the next decade, although for several short periods it was changed into a formal psychoanalytic treatment. Jones (1955) has pointed out that the informal scientific collaboration between the two men was so extensive that it is impossible to be sure with whom any particular idea may have originated at this time.

Seemingly, Ferenczi's first independent psychoanalytic idea appeared in the paper he contributed to the *Jahrbuch* for 1909 (B. 67). It consisted of pointing out the similarity between hysterical identification and normal accretions of mental structure. He coined the term "introjection" to cover both phenomena as well as those of hypnotism, which he characterized as the return of an infantile mode of relating to an object. In 1910 he began his extensive activities as a reviewer, especially for the *Zentralblatt*; since his reviews, incisive and persuasive though they were, did not contain original work of his own, I shall confine myself to noting that Ferenczi was given the task of representing the psychoanalytic viewpoint in reaction to a number of major dissenting voices, such as those of Jung, Adler, Bleuler, and, much later, Rank (B. 124, 150, 151, 201, 277).

By 1911, Ferenczi had found his own voice as a psychoanalytic researcher, and until his call-up for military service in 1914, which meant the loss of his psychoanalytic practice, he had a period of extraordinary productivity, comprising clinical and theoretical papers of the highest caliber and in the forefront of the advances of psychoanalytic knowledge. This is the era of some of his best-known works, like "On Transitory Symptom-Constructions during the Analysis" (B. 85) and

"Stages in the Development of the Sense of Reality" (B. 111). Simultaneously, he began to produce a long series of papers of the utmost brevity—often describing typical clinical situations or illustrating psychoanalytic concepts and discoveries from literature, folklore, or pre-Freudian science and philosophy. The breadth of his interests compels admiration: in 1913 he published his last peacetime neurological contribution (B. 110) as well as a report of a case of child therapy (B. 114), the treatment of little Arpad's cock phobia, confirming Freud's finding with Little Hans.

Through this apparent diversity, however, one can discern a remarkable uniformity of approach and a major organizing principle—never explicitly stated by Ferenczi, and perhaps not even consciously perceived. The thrust of this work was an effort to map out human personality development through the collation of data from the analyses of neurotics and clinical observations of normal and emotionally disturbed children and adults. The model for Ferenczi's scheme of organization was Freud's "Three Essays" (1905c); however, it was Ferenczi who conceived of the idea of *lines of development* to designate the successive stages in the ontogeny of particular mental functions. He used the concept for the first time in a paper on obscene words (B. 75) in 1911; at the same time, he wrote to Freud about the line of development of the capacity to symbolize, and he was planning more ambitious studies to describe the developmental stages of the ego (Ferenczi, 1908-1933b). At the Münich Congress in 1912 he related the irrationality seen in transference relationships to regression, set in motion by the analytic process, along the line of development of the sense of reality (B. 109). The crowning achievement of this series of papers was the detailed description of this developmental line in 1913 (B. 111) in which Ferenczi discussed not only regressions but explicitly conceptualized *arrests* in development—an idea which is barely beginning to be elaborated in present-day psychoanalytic theory. Most important, he drew attention to the fact that, while the *nature* of symptoms depends on the level of libidinal fixation, the *mechanisms* used in symptom formation depend on the fixation points in ego development. Subsequently, he was to describe a special aspect of ego development in outlining the line of development of the sense of reality about erotism (B. 265); in 1914 he offered a sample from the development of symbolization in tracing the vicissitudes of anality (B. 146).

Such pervasive interest in developmental sequences led Ferenczi to the problem of character formation. At a time when this issue had been dealt with in libidinal terms alone, he was the first to conclude that character traits are universally determined by the *outcome* of the Oedipus complex (B. 92); further, he discovered that psychoanalytic treatment may produce character regressions, which therefore demonstrate the developmental line of character formation. These character changes he saw as equivalent to the new symptoms produced by the stirring up of conflict in the course of psychoanalysis (B. 85).

These considerations led to the conclusion that character formation might be influenced by pedagogy (B. 103), an issue Ferenczi had already discussed at the Salzburg Congress in 1908 (B. 63). He even arrived at the concept of critical periods for certain traumas (B. 196).

There were, of course, a number of contributions on other subjects, mainly of a clinical nature—e.g., on the phenomenon of giddiness on arising from the couch (B. 138), and on sleepiness as a resistance (B. 139). In this area, the most exciting work of the era was Freud's investigation of paranoia and its relation to homosexuality; Ferenczi, Jung, and Abraham all collaborated in this effort. Freud had had no clinical experience with paranoid patients since 1896 and relied heavily on the reports of his followers.[2] Ferenczi's first communication on the subject (B. 77) confirmed the narcissistic fixation, the regression, and the conflict about homosexuality which Freud had described in paranoia. Ferenczi stressed that the cause of the breakthrough of homosexual libido was unknown, however, so that the ubiquitous homosexual problem encountered in paranoid patients may not constitute an essential element of their psychopathology (B. 80). This crucial distinction is often overlooked to this day. In 1914,

[2]This lack of clinical material dictated the use of D. P. Schreber's *Memoirs* to illustrate Freud's conclusions (1911).

Ferenczi published a fine case history of paranoia in which insight into his homosexuality preceded the patient's fragmentation (B. 135). Hence Ferenczi concluded that a paranoid resolution may be essential to preserve some semblance of coherent personality, so that psychoanalytic treatment is contraindicated in these cases (see B. 159).

On the other hand, he was a pioneer in the effort to treat homosexuality through psychoanalysis. The most significant conclusions of this work (B. 136) were that a perversion can be used in the service of neurotic repression and that Don Juan behavior is an attempted defense against homosexuality.

The quality of Ferenczi's therapeutic work before the war may be gauged from a beautiful sample published in 1915 (B. 160), which shows his ingenuity in drawing inferences from the active dialogue he promoted with his patients. In view of his later, controversial views on technique, it is noteworthy that in 1912 he was already stressing that only affective reliving within the analysis can give the patient conviction about the findings of psychoanalysis; since this requirement applies equally to those who become practitioners of the discipline, Ferenczi drew the conclusion that a personal analysis was essential in the professional preparation of every psychoanalyst (B. 85). Moreover, he extended this principle to cover *scientific* work in psychoanalysis which, in his view, also requires the mastery of unconscious prejudices (B. 92). Adherence to any specific ethical system, for example, compels the exclusion of data which do not fit the system (see B. 93). During the controversies with Jung, Ferenczi was able to criticize the latter's procedures from the point of view that ethicoreligious indoctrination in therapy exploited the patient's regression and reinforced his submission to authority; only interpretation of conflicts about authority can lead to insight into irrational gullibility and skepticism (B. 109). He related the renunciation of omniscience by the scientist-analyst to the attainment of the highest stage in the development of the sense of reality (B. 111).

The outbreak of the war in 1914 and his induction into military service coincided with a deep personal crisis in the life of the 41-year-old Ferenczi. He sought analytic treatment with

Freud for some weeks, and continued the discussion of his problems by correspondence when he had to return to duty. I have no access to data about the issues which may have been involved and am therefore completely in the dark about the nature of this midlife crisis. In the spring of 1917, however, Ferenczi is reported to have suffered from thyrotoxicosis (H. Abraham and E. Freud, 1966, p. 250), and his marriage finally took place in 1919—scant data, but possible clues to the extent of his turmoil during the war years. These difficulties and the lack of opportunity to conduct analyses inevitably created a break in the continuity of his scientific work. He busied himself with the translation of Freud's "Three Essays" and provided an Introduction to the Hungarian edition showing much methodological sophistication and a subtle grasp of epistemology (B. 161). He continued to write reviews (see B. 175, 184, 201, 204) and some brief notes on clinical subjects (see B. 187, 190, 191, 193, 194, 197, 198), but he also produced popular articles for the press, and even a neurological essay on the treatment of brain injuries. Then the psychoanalytic study of war neuroses provided him with a novel subject for investigation worthy of his talents, and by 1916 he was able to publish a preliminary report (B. 189).

This encounter with unusual case material permitted Ferenczi to conceptualize "ego injuries," i.e., regressions which followed narcissistic blows. In the joint monograph on war neuroses with Abraham and Simmel (B. 218) he explained the regression as an attempted return to previously abandoned methods of *adaptation*, and he concluded from the extent of the regression that a narcissistic fixation must exist as a predisposing factor in such patients. This is work in the area of ego psychology, some seven years before the appearance of "The Ego and the Id" (1923b).[a]

An important extension of the research on war neuroses was the generalization of these findings to neuroses which arose as

[a]Nine years have passed since this passage was written; from a current vantage point, it is not the early awareness of the adaptive capacities of the ego that is most impressive in this work but the fact that Ferenczi was able to place the issue of narcissism into a developmental framework (see Kohut, 1966, 1971).

reactions to somatic illnesses of all kinds—conditions for which Ferenczi invented the designation *pathoneuroses* (B. 195). He postulated that the somatic pathology produced a narcissistic trauma by increasing ego libido, which focuses upon the affected organ. Reaction formations may be erected against these regressions, producing changes in character. Pathoneuroses occur only in excessively narcissistic persons and in cases in which either life itself or an organ with a high narcissistic cathexis (e.g., the genital) is threatened.

The war years also saw the beginning of Ferenczi's major work in the area of applied psychoanalysis, an attempt to wed the libido theory with Lamarck's biology. These speculations were extensively discussed with Freud, who spent his summer vacations in 1917 and 1918 in the Tatra Mountains with Ferenczi (see H. Abraham and E. Freud, 1966, pp. 261-262). Since they were not published for several years, however, this work will be considered later in this review.

At the Budapest Congress in 1918, Ferenczi was elected President of the International Psychoanalytic Association, and shortly thereafter he held his abortive Professorship under the Communist regime. One amusing aspect of this is the ironic coincidence that Ferenczi was the first to have pointed out the major flaw in the communist system: its disregard of human psychic life. At any rate, the end of the war, with its return to psychoanalytic practice, ushered in a new phase of creativity, with fertile contributions in a variety of areas.

What I find most striking in Ferenczi's work of this period is his constant attention to psychic structure. One finally gains the impression that, had Freud himself failed to arrive at the structural model of the mental apparatus in the early 1920's, this crucial advance in theory might very well have been accomplished by Ferenczi. To put it another way, Ferenczi was so close to such a formulation that his inability to synthesize the scattered elements of his theoretical thinking into one cohesive statement was all that prevented him from matching Freud's achievement in "The Ego and the Id." Whether this incapacity was inherent in Ferenczi's style of work or whether it came about as a result of his transference to

Freud is a question which cannot be decided without extensive biographical research.[b]

To illustrate Ferenczi's evolving conceptualizations, some of his papers from 1919 already contain a workable ego psychology. Thus he discusses the traumatization of the child's "inexperienced ego" by unexpected quantities of libido stimulated by adult exhibitionism, for instance (B. 217). The concept of a superego is implicit in his statement that "Sunday neuroses" are caused by a hypersensitive conscience spoiling the day of rest (B. 211). In some posthumously published notes of 1920 (B. 301) he was quite explicit about the need for psychoanalytic study of the ego which, he foresaw, would permit the understanding of various talents and their multiple determinants. This fragment prefigures Hartmann's work on the autonomous apparatuses 20 years later. In 1921, with his study on tics (B. 232), Ferenczi began to talk about *conflict inside the ego*—a concept which implies that the ego is a coherent system lasting through time, i.e., a structure. In the important 1922 monograph on general paresis (B. 239), he implied a principle of ego organization, with hierarchies, a tendency to unification, and the potential for dissolution into independent entities, which is accompanied by mega-anxiety.[c] These in turn consist of old identifications. Elsewhere (B. 244), he asserted that these identifications occur between the stages of narcissism and object love via the annexation of qualities of the object, i.e., introjection. He pointed out that ego psychology depends on data from novel sources, since the transference neuroses do not provide pertinent information about ego pathology. Another important concept in ego psychology which Ferenczi discussed (B. 243) is that of *relative autonomy* of split-off derivatives from the unconscious. Finally, he defined the primary task of the psyche as the *inhibiting function*, i.e., control of the paths to motility.

[b] Ferenczi's literary executor, the late Michael Balint, did not make use of extensive, historically important materials in his possession, including letters of Freud.

[c] Today, one would have to question whether the dissolution of the cohesion of the personality Ferenczi was describing is referable to the system ego or, rather, whether it may be more pertinent to conceptualize it as the reversal of a more primitive structuralization, that of the Self (see J. Gedo and Goldberg, 1973).

These theoretical preoccupations must be kept in mind in order to understand Ferenczi's controversial technical experiments of this period. These were all concerned with methods to deal with what today we call the defenses of the ego and were modeled on Freud's recommendation that in the analysis of a phobia it is ultimately essential that the patient give up his avoidances. Ferenczi extended the principle by demonstrating that certain behaviors within the analytic setting may have to be overcome in order to break through a therapeutic stalemate. The method he first used was the prohibition of the activity concerned (B. 210). He did insist, however, that such an exploitation of the transference must be interpreted before the analysis could be terminated (B. 215). Even such temporary departures from strict neutrality on the part of the analyst inevitably brought the problem of countertransference into sharper focus than it had had previously, and Ferenczi now started to emphasize that the observation and control of his countertransference was a necessary part of the analyst's task (B. 216). Evidently his technical advice had been seized upon in an indiscriminate manner, since at the Hague Congress of 1921 he felt obliged to reiterate that modifications of technique are justified only when an analysis is stagnant, and the "rule of abstinence" can be enforced via prohibitions only in the presence of a positive transference. In selected cases, however, he was now experimenting with setting patients certain unpleasant tasks so that resistance would be accentuated, i.e., to facilitate analysis of the ego (B. 234).

Parallel with these papers on technique, Ferenczi was making clinical studies of certain syndromes which involved ego fixations or regressions. His fame as a therapist now brought him many patients considered too difficult for others, so that the nature of his clinical experience apparently became somewhat atypical; at the same time, he had unusual opportunities for the study of various narcissistic neuroses. His own hypochondriasis had given him an early interest in such problems, and it had been he who had given Freud the idea that hypercathexis of a body part is experienced as pain, leading to the explanation of hypochondriasis as the actual neurotic core of the narcissistic neuroses (see Federn, 1933).

In 1919, Ferenczi published his study of the conversion mechanism (B. 220). He saw this as a "materialization phenomenon," i.e., a magical realization of a wish by means of the stuff available in the body. Such a primitive, autoplastic motor discharge implies regression to a "protopsyche," as yet incapable of ideation but using the soma for the purpose of adaptation by means of magic gestures. The 1921 papers on tics (B. 232, 235) point out that regression in tiqueurs is to a level more primitive than that found in obsessional neuroses. These patients are ruled by the pleasure principle; their motility is not under preconscious control. Many are psychotic and all are narcissistically fixated. Finally, the joint monograph with Hollós on general paresis (B. 239) explored the effect of injury to the brain, with its high narcissistic cathexis, and the psychotic defenses which usually ensue.

Ferenczi's fiftieth birthday in 1923 was celebrated by a *Festschrift* in his honor. This included a tribute from Freud (1923e), who noted Ferenczi's most significant papers and praised the mastery of his "powerful brother complex" which had permitted him to become "an irreproachable elder brother, a kindly teacher and promoter of young talent." This event seems to have marked the apogee of Ferenczi's reputation; there was now a brief pause in his productivity while he was preparing two monographs (B. 264, 268) which were to turn him into a controversial figure whose contributions could be slighted.

The Development of Psychoanalysis (B. 264) was written in collaboration with Otto Rank, whose imminent defection from psychoanalysis may have contributed through "guilt by association" to the image of Ferenczi as a "dissident" from Freud. That Ferenczi intended nothing of the sort is attested to by Jones's report (1957, p. 57) that Freud's partial disagreement with the book had "shattered" its author. This must certainly have been a transference reaction on the part of Ferenczi,[d] since the actual difference of opinion between them

---

[d] Kohut (1968, 1971) has given the name of "twinship" to transference reactions in which the patient is "shattered" by confrontation with any difference between himself and the object. They are frequently to be observed in the analyses of narcissistic personalities.

appears to have been minor; Freud laid more emphasis on the importance of genetic interpretations whereas Ferenczi stressed the crucial importance of affective reliving in the here and now of the analysis. Today it would seem that they were both right.

Each of the coauthors took major responsibility for one portion of the book; Ferenczi's section is closely reasoned and important. He had already grasped the revolutionary significance of the new model of the mind Freud had proposed in "The Ego and the Id" (1923b), and he understood that the next task consisted in the translation of this general theory into specific improvements in technique. He gave a beautiful exposition of the reciprocal influence of analytic theory and practice—the improvement of technique which follows advances in theory and simultaneously retests them. He was the first to spell out that analysis must be understood as a *process* to avoid confusion by its manifold details; thus, he pointed out, both symptom analysis and complex analysis had become outdated. An adequate analytic process must promote the reliving and working through of the infantile neurosis in a transference neurosis. This aim, Ferenczi explained, can be attained only by overcoming the resistance of the ego, certainly never by naïve attempts to fill the gaps in the patient's knowledge. Hence resistances, including the negative transference, must not be treated as undesirable or what is worse, sinful.

If this work is slightly disappointing in retrospect, the reason lies in what it fails to accomplish rather than in any real flaw in its contents. Ferenczi was never able to devise a theory of technique based on the new ego psychology, and in his papers on technique, which came to occupy an increasing share of his scientific production, gradually narrowed his focus to the special problems of the psychoanalysis of unusually difficult cases. Moreover, he was unable to clarify the difference between special modifications and an improved classical technique, a difficulty which was perhaps unavoidable in an era of rapid evolution in the standard technique of psychoanalysis, such as the work of W. Reich (1933) and somewhat later that of Anna Freud (1936). At such a time, even the subtlest of technical suggestions, such as Ferenczi's methods of encouraging the verbalizations of fantasies in patients whose fantasy life is impoverished (B. 265), is likely to be mistaken for a general formula.

Ferenczi made strenuous efforts to define indications and contraindications for his "active technique," and he gradually shifted his position about it in response to unfavorable results in his actual practice. He clarified that the "activity" must never be that of the analyst but always that of the patient, an effort to achieve better tension tolerance, particularly with respect to pregenital impulses (B. 269). By 1926 he came out against giving the patient any kind of command, including the setting of arbitrary time limits for termination, a measure strongly advocated by Rank with which Ferenczi had also experimented. At this time he saw "activity" as a mere preliminary to interpretation (B. 271). He never did explain, however, what criteria he used to decide that interpretative efforts alone would not suffice. Apparently he abandoned the active technique as a failed experiment, the sole conceptual result of which was his discovery of a precursor of the superego, the "sphincter morality" of the child in the anal phase. This aspect of his career was closed by his brilliant critique of Rank (B. 277), from whom he now completely dissociated himself.

Ferenczi went to New York for several months late in 1926 and some of his lectures there were subsequently published (B. 278, 280). However, these efforts were decidedly in a minor key, and a real slackening in his scientific creativity now became apparent. Evidently he was going through some personal crisis. According to Freud (1933b), on returning from America Ferenczi became absorbed in the need to heal, set himself goals beyond the limitations of the analytic therapy of the time, and held aloof from his colleagues until he would find a way to integrate his work into the mainstream of psychoanalysis. In a letter to Freud in January, 1928, Ferenczi was still expressing the need to show that his views did not depart from Freud's (Ferenczi, 1908-1933b), but by 1930 he was apparently reproaching the latter for having failed to analyze the negative transference when he treated Ferenczi during the war (see Freud, 1937). The radical technical experiments which Ferenczi introduced at this time are remembered by many as the overriding activity of the last years of his life. This judgment is correct but superficial. Although he was not successful in conveying the import of his work, Ferenczi, propelled by his own emotional crisis and his self-analytic attempts, was actually engaged in the pioneering study of borderline patients and their treatment by psychoanalysis.

The patients whom he was describing had been traumatized by parental failures in helping the child with the tasks of weaning, habit training, and giving up the status of childhood.[3] Excessive strictness or deficient external controls lead to the formation of a harsh superego. Generally, in children brought up in these ways, there is failure in differentiating fantasy from real action (B. 281). These patients cannot trust the analyst's dependability and will test him repeatedly, so that, before a positive transference can blossom, the negative transference must be analyzed. Consequently, the analyst must not be authoritarian, his formulations must be presented tentatively, and he must engage in constant self-scrutiny regarding his countertransference (B. 283). These traumatized persons develop characters which render them unable to observe the basic rule of free association and need unlimited time for working through. Therefore, termination in these analyses cannot be initiated by the analyst; it should occur because the mourning for the lost gratifications of childhood has been worked through (B. 282). Many of these patients are suicidal, with self-destructiveness so intense that it might exemplify the concept of a death instinct. Their Oedipal problems are unresolved, and they are preoccupied with what we have come to call existential concerns. Their early traumatization acts like a constitutional adaptive defect, as if a solid "life force" has failed to come into being because of the deficiency of "good care" (B. 287). The personality is fragmented by multiple splits which defend against the affective

[3]Ferenczi had previously stated that resolution of the Oedipus complex is the most important separation experience in normal development, i.e., is the crucial issue for leaving childishness behind (B. 277).

recognition of the infantile traumata, so that Ferenczi saw the pathology as quite similar to that of the psychoses (B. 291). The most sensitive issue for these patients is that of abandonment, against which they defend themselves through narcissistic withdrawal (B. 292).[e] Often, however, a precocious maturity is developed: some of these patients actually assume a protective role toward their parents during their childhood (B. 294). This masochistic surrender amounts to an identification with the opponent, with unconscious fantasies of devouring the aggressor. A failure of these pathological defenses leads to profound hopelessness and helplessness. The reality of the traumatic events is ultimately defended against by a pervasive doubt or depersonalization (B. 308).

The similarity of my synoptic account of Ferenczi's description of his patients to recent psychoanalytic views of the borderline states, such as those of Winnicott (1931-1956, 1957-1963) is apparent. The emphases on the failure of "good-enough mothering," on the development of a "false self," on narcissistic withdrawal and depersonalization, and on the difficulties of establishing a therapeutic alliance because of the patient's latent mistrust, were, once again, 25 years ahead of their time. The most astonishing achievement of this work may have been Ferenczi's explicit conceptualization of a *transitional object* (B. 281).

Because of the repressed helplessness behind these patients' accomplished facades, Ferenczi termed their syndrome that of "the wise baby." He was keenly aware that he had arrived at these prodigious insights through introspection, writing in his scientific diary (B. 308): "The idea of a wise baby could be discovered only by a wise baby."

This great scientific accomplishment has been overshadowed by the rejection of Ferenczi's therapeutic methods with these patients (not to speak of their uncritical acceptance in certain quarters as an appropriate model of the standard psychoanalytic procedure). Ferenczi started with the premise that these patients had to be analyzed in the same manner as

---

[e]Kohut (1971) believes that such schizoid defenses should forewarn the analyst that there are serious doubts concerning analyzability. Narcissistic personalities who *are* analyzable may retreat temporarily into aloofness and grandiosity whenever disappointed by their objects, but they are not chronically withdrawn.

children, i.e., as children were being analyzed by Anna Freud ca. 1927. He believed that little active effort could be demanded of them, and even that certain gratifications had to be given before the cautious introduction of analytic privations (B. 287). This method of indulgence had the aim of "creating an atmosphere of confidence and securing fuller freedom of affect," as in a normal nursery (B. 291). At times Ferenczi entered into the reliving of certain recollections in the manner of present-day psychodrama, subsequently working through the resultant material analytically (B. 292). He became aware that his patients needed tenderness, not erotic gratification, and he was also cognizant of the dangers of acting out on the part of the analyst when he used a technique of such flexibility (B. 294).

Because great trust in the analyst has to develop before these patients dare to experience their profound dependency, he must really show himself to be a sympathetic helper, strong enough to forestall the patient's destructiveness. Since frustrating these fragile people is eventually unavoidable, the realistic limits of the analyst's availability must be clarified. Each new trauma leads once more to splitting (i.e., primary repression), narcissistic regression, and "self-care." Nonetheless, real growth can occur only after the patients can permit themselves to re-experience their infantile helplessness and hopelessness, which entails real suicidal risks. At this time the analyst's "tenderness" gives the patient courage to make a *new beginning* from the pretraumatic state (B. 308).

None of this sounds in any sense radical or unusual today; on the contrary, it is becoming the orthodoxy of the day in the treatment of borderline patients. A generation ago, it may have seemed like a naïve attempt to cure through love, an impression compounded by Ferenczi's imprudent remarks to the effect that Freud's technique was excessively frustrating. People did not see this in the context of a transference neurosis as the "wise baby's" reproach to his analyst who had wanted him to be "a companion on an equal footing." Jones, for one, chose to believe that Ferenczi's attitude about psychoanalysis had "regressed" (1933). His failed experiments, like affectionate physical contact with some patients, were held against him, even when he reported their failure and abandoned their use. Unsubstantiated derogatory rumors about his conduct with patients have been reported as facts.

In the last year of his life, from June, 1932 on, Ferenczi's notes (B. 308) convey unmistakable preconscious awareness of a grave illness, the subacute combined degeneration complicating his pernicious anemia. For example, he chooses a patient unable to walk as a case illustration; he discusses hysteria in terms of lost cerebrospinal functions. In November, he notes that in degeneration of the brain, memory for details is lost before the capacity for abstraction. In December, he discusses the cure for hopelessness: ". . . to reflect on age, space, time and fitness."

With complete simultaneity, in September, 1932, a loss of scientific rationality makes its first appearance in Ferenczi's writings. He speaks of the possibility of an "ideal power" working magically, each telekinetic action subordinating externals to the will of the ego. The regression of the sense of reality to the stage of the omnipotence of thoughts must have been in the service of disavowing the dying man's helplessness. Moreover, it should be noted that this was merely an entry in a diary published posthumously, i.e., without the final revision every scientist must perform before he approves a product as a valid representation of his scientific reality testing. Ferenczi had never published anything prima facie irrational, in spite of Jones's assertion that he was a credulous and naive believer in occultism all along, in constant correspondence with Freud on the subject.[f] In Ferenczi's psychoanalytic works, the sole criteria on which his scientific contribution can be gauged, there are, however, few indications of magical thinking. In 1912 there had been a respectful reference to Fliess's nasal theory of neurosis (B. 100) and an indication of belief in phylogenetic memories (B. 86); in 1924 there was the publication of *Thalassa: A Theory of Genitality* (B. 268). This purely speculative essay in applied psychoanalysis had lain dormant since its wartime composition with Freud's quasi-collaboration. The decision to publish followed Freud's urging (see Freud, 1933b), and Ferenczi expressed his doubts in the

[f]The Freud-Jung correspondence (McGuire, 1974) tends to confirm this judgment from an independent source—one, moreover, biased in favor of the occult. Jung himself.

monograph by specific discussion of his nonscientific method-ology. Much of the argument leans on concepts which psycho-analysis and biology have since abandoned, although they were still respectable at the time: anxiety as transformed libido, the birth trauma, Lamarckian evolutionary theory, Haeckel's biogenetic law. This is, of course, a danger common to all efforts in applied analysis. However, the overt psycho-morphism and reasoning by analogy simply cannot be over-looked, and the occasional concepts of value (e.g., that of the unconscious fusion of coital partners via identification) do not redeem this embarrassing product of fantasy.

These lapses are, however, rather less spectacular than Freud's writings on telepathy or his speculative papers in applied analysis (see 1939) and therefore cannot account for the general reputation of Ferenczi as the wild man of psycho-analysis. In fact, many people have written very favorable reviews of *Thalassa*, including Federn (1933), Rado (1933), and of course Freud himself (1933b). In the aggregate, Ferenczi's psychoanalytic *oeuvre* is solid, broad, and deep; reading all of it has convinced me that his contribution to the field before 1930 is second only to Freud's. Of course, he has been dead for a generation, and the history of science is full of examples of work which has been half-forgotten and has had to be rediscovered afresh. However, this factor cannot explain the pejorative tone of much recent comment about Ferenczi. We are in an age of scientism and systematization which undervalues imaginativeness and the ability to create hypo-theses; yet we honor Freud for just these qualities, but not Ferenczi.

In my opinion, this state of affairs is probably best ex-plained by the interpretation that most of us share in ambiv-alence toward the great men of our field. After all, it was Jones (1910) who recognized the unconscious hostility of Hamlet toward his father, and it was again Jones who eulogized Ferenczi by echoing what Hamlet said about his father. Perhaps we solve the conflict of our ambivalence about Freud through splitting: Freud is idealized, and his closest collab-orator, Ferenczi, becomes the recipient of our hostility.

What is there, then, in the life work of Ferenczi that psycho-analysis has overlooked? In terms of content, I believe we have now caught up with the neglected portions of his product. Of course, my perspective is limited by the *Zeitgeist*, and in another generation a reviewer of the *Bausteine* may be struck by how much of what it contains I have been unable to appreciate. Nonetheless, I believe that Ferenczi's accomplishments have the most to teach us about the very process of creativity in psychoanalysis rather than about details of their subject matter. They are particularly valuable in this regard because studies of Freud's creativity may be questioned on the premise that a genius like Freud is unique and one cannot generalize from his case.[8] Ferenczi, on the other hand, was no genius, and we may confidently predict that many psychoanalysts today and in the future do and will possess talents, energies, and dedication comparable to his. Very few, however, have been able to approach him in their creativity.

One may be tempted to explain this on the grounds that the opportunities in a new, unexplored region of knowledge and the presence in the field of a creative genius of Freud's caliber produced a flowering of analytic productivity comparable to those of Periclean Athens or the Florence of Lorenzo de' Medici. Such an explanation would assume that creativity in psychoanalysis is essentially no different from that in other endeavors. If, however, the discovery of new insights about the human psyche should turn out to require very special conditions, e.g., to depend primarily on the capacity to make new discoveries about oneself — a statement which I believe to be largely correct about the contributions of both Freud and Ferenczi — then we may have to look for other reasons to understand the relative decrease of creative accomplishments in psychoanalysis since the days of the pioneers. It may be that the outcome of self-analytic efforts such as those of Ferenczi consisted in very little structural change but produced defensive realignments which facilitated the perception of hitherto unknown aspects of mental life, thereby avoiding the experience of affective repetition of the past.

The fascinating vistas opened by such speculations must await their exploration in the next psychoanalytic generation.

[8] This question is ably and extensively discussed by Eissler (1971b) in *Talent and Genius*, where he compares Freud's unique creativity with that of a productive analytic researcher with talents probably not quite equal to those of Ferenczi.

16

CREATIVENESS, CHARISMA, GROUP PSYCHOLOGY
Reflections on the Self-Analysis of Freud

HEINZ KOHUT

[*On the Study of Psychoanalytic History*. Heinz Kohut first presented the principal thoughts contained in this essay as a spontaneous discussion of Max Schur's "Some Additional 'Day Residues' of the 'Specimen Dream of Psychoanalysis'" (Schur, 1966a) at a meeting of the Chicago Psychoanalytic Society on September 27, 1966. As we have mentioned previously, his words had a profound impact and led some of the writers represented in this volume to reconsider aspects of their approach to the study of Freud's biography; many of the papers included in this book would have been written in a different way without the impetus provided by this event. Kohut himself did not follow up his original contribution, except for an abbreviated version of his thoughts in Chapter 12 of his book *The Analysis of the Self* (1971). It is therefore particularly fitting that the concluding chapter of this volume should be an expanded survey of the problems of the historian of psychoanalysis by this thoughtful critic of applied analysis (see Kohut, 1960).

Kohut examines the special difficulties the analyst has to face in studying Freud's biography by virtue of the fact that, in his training, every candidate is driven either into an idealization of the creator of psychoanalysis or into a defensive reaction formation against this attitude. Kohut believes that this state of affairs is likely to persist because it enhances group cohesion within the community of analysts by protecting individual members against narcissistic injuries in relation to current competitors; moreover, it builds up a needed sense of continuity in the group, albeit at the price of promoting excessive conformity in some and rebelliousness in others.

In his own attempt to interpret that unique event, Freud's self-analysis, Kohut questions the assumption that it was primarily a therapeutic procedure. He does not doubt that Freud derived personal benefits from the insights he gained, but he sees the entire process as a creative spell rather than as the necessary unfolding of a repetition of the past in relation to a contemporary transference figure. Although, by virtue of the geographical distance separating him from Freud, Wilhelm Fliess could serve well as a substitute for the analyst Freud could never have, the very fact of Freud's unparalleled creativeness during the most intense involvement in their relationship speaks against the interpretation that this should be thought of as a transference neurosis. (Incidentally, Eissler [1972] has also stressed the import of the distance separating the men for the specific value of Fliess for Freud.)

Kohut postulates that Freud needed a merger with an idealized, omnipotent other who, by lending himself to such an expansion of the self, could restore a depleted narcissistic balance in the throes of a supreme creative act. He assumes that the cathexis of the created product leaves the self of the great creator relatively empty and vulnerable, particularly when, as in the case of Freud, his actual isolation from a community of peers recreates childhood situations of emotional abandonment. An alternative to such a blending with an omnipotent self-object is the establishment of a twinship with a collaborator whose qualities mirror the grandeur of the self.

In the service of this examination of the psychological need filled by Wilhelm Fliess in the course of Freud's creation of psychoanalysis, Kohut delineates the characterological qualities possessed by persons who are able to fill the role of idealized self-object within a "transference of creativity." His description of messianic and charismatic personalities adds a promising new chapter to psychoanalytic characterology; at the same time, it illuminates the personalities of many great leaders who have performed similar idealizing functions for large groups on the stage of world history.

Kohut's essay and this book end with a program for a new beginning for the field of historical studies on the subject of psychoanalysis. It would be out of place to attempt to summarize his subtle and ambitious proposal here; it may suffice to note that, by insisting that the application of psychoanalysis to the phenomena of history in general had best begin with the examination of the history of the community of analysts, Kohut provides us with explicit justification for the efforts we have made in pulling together our past work in this area—Eds.]

1. THE PSYCHOANALYST AND HIS IMAGE OF FREUD

We are faced by uncertainties and difficulties when we investigate Freud's self-analysis: first, by those which, in all areas of applied analysis, arise from the fact that we are not participating in a living clinical situation; second, by those that arise from the fact that we might not be objective because Freud is for us a transference figure par excellence (specifically, we are prone to establish an idealizing transference toward him, or to defend ourselves against it by reaction formation); and third, by those that arise from the fact that Freud's self-analysis is a specific and, in some ways, unique event in the history of human thought.

This is not the place for an examination of the goals and methodological problems of applied analysis, but I will discuss two issues: the general difficulties that we confront when we undertake the study of Freud (aspects of his personality, his biography, his significance), and the additional, specific difficulties which we face when we attempt to interpret the meaning and to evaluate the significance of Freud's self-analysis. These specific difficulties arise from the fact that we are here dealing with a psychological situation which—as the first scientifically orderly introspective effort to scrutinize complex psychological states—is without recorded precedent in the history of human thought.[1]

It is always hard to achieve an objective evaluation of a great man, whether the evaluation be by the average biographer, by the historian, or by the depth psychologist (R. and E. Sterba's *Beethoven and His Nephew* [1960] contains an illuminating discussion of these problems; see in particular pp. 12-17). The great man is prone to become a transference figure for the beholder—usually, of course, a father figure—and the childhood ambivalences of the investigator may intrude to falsify results. Even more widespread is another pitfall, namely the biographer's apparently falling in love with his subject.[a] When examined more closely, I believe it turns out that not true object love is involved here but the establishment of a bond of identification. Frequently the choice of the subject is already determined by the investigator's identificatory predilections (dictated perhaps by needs emanating from structural defects or weaknesses of the biographer who is in search of identifications) and the long preoccupation with the life of the investigated is prone to reinforce the

[1]Here two points may need to be emphasized. (1) I am, on the one hand, not claiming priority for Freud's self-analysis (and, by extension, for the science of psychoanalysis) simply because Freud used the introspective approach to the complexities of inner life—this approach to the broad field of inner experience has been used from time immemorial by poets and mystical philosophers (see Chapter 1)—but because he did so in a scientifically orderly, systematic way and recorded and formulated the results of his observations in the terms of a more or less experience-distant theory. (2) I am, on the other hand, not claiming uniqueness for Freud's self-analysis (and, by extension, for the science of psychoanalysis) simply because he used the introspective approach in order to obtain scientifically valid psychological data—this claim could also be made for the self-observations of experimental psychology—but because his subject matter was the whole of psychic life in all its breadth and depth. It is the fact that Freud used the introspective approach in a systematic, scientific way without narrowing the scope of his subject matter (and that, by extension, psychoanalysis has continued to employ the introspective-empathic approach in the same fashion) which justifies the assertion that the introduction of the psychoanalytic method constituted a revolutionary step in the history of science. (For further remarks on this important topic see Kohut, 1959, especially pp. 459-465; Kohut, 1970a, especially fn. p. 466; and Kohut, 1973, especially pp. 14-15.)

[a]For another discussion of this issue, see the remarks of B. Meyer at the Panel on the Methodology of Psychoanalytic Biography (J. Gedo, 1972d).

identificatory bonds even further.[b] Still, one might expect that the pitfalls of such a scientific enterprise would prove to be least dangerous for the psychoanalyst. The analyst is, after all, specifically trained to observe and control his own reactions and he should be able either to set aside his childhood loves and hates and his narcissistic (e.g., identificatory) needs during his clinical and scientific work or at least to disqualify himself when he senses his inability to do so.

In general it would be justified to make such demands on the analyst and, on the whole, we may assume that there is at least a fair chance that he may be able to live up to these standards. As regards the figure of Freud, however, the task of the analyst is vastly increased and objectivity is hard for him to attain. In the following I will discuss the two major obstacles which stand in the analyst's way when he attempts to be objective about Freud.

The first obstacle which is in the analyst's way when he tries to assess the figure of Freud with scientific neutrality stems from the fact that analysts become acquainted with Freud during the crucial formative years in which their professional selves as analysts take shape. This fact alone is weighty enough. But there is, in addition, a peculiar circumstance that must not be underestimated. While he is a student at a psychoanalytic institute the future analyst does not primarily study Freud's life and his opinions—he is forced to identify with Freud from the inside, as it were, i.e., he is asked to think himself into the most intimate and detailed activities of Freud's mental processes. To be concrete: each student of psychoanalysis reads and rereads *The Interpretation of Dreams* (1900). As he undertakes the study of this fundamental volume he undergoes over and over again the peculiar experience of moving from the manifest content of one of Freud's dreams toward Freud's unconscious dream wishes and thus he participates in the intimate workings of the most intimate recesses of Freud's mind: Freud's preconscious and unconscious libidinal and aggressive strivings in the object-instinctual and narcissistic sectors of his personality over and

[b] See the remarks of M. Zeligs in J. Gedo (1972d) for an excellent illustration.

over again become the student's own, and so do Freud's resistances, conflicts, and anxieties. If the student of analysis does not want to deprive himself of the full, enriching experience of obtaining his basic knowledge from the genuine source of the report of the discoverer, given at the time when the discovery was still a recent, immediate, fresh experience, he is forced to identify with the deepest layers of Freud's personality. Such empathic closeness with total sectors of another person's mind, extending from conscious to unconscious levels, is not available to us in our day-to-day relationships, not even with regard to those we are closest to, i.e., the members of our family and our friends. True, once we are in the daily practice of clinical analysis, such contact with the inner life of others does indeed fill our working day; but this contact is diluted by the simple fact that we do not experience our empathic trial identifications with only *one* patient, but participate in the inner life of an increasing number of them. The convergence of the facts that Freud is the great father figure and teacher of our science, that we are studying him from the inside, as it were, and that this study constitutes our first, or at least a very early and basic, experience of identification with the unconscious of someone else—these facts combine to produce the effect that analysts tend to have a specific attitude toward Freud, i.e., an attitude of firmly established identification with an idealized figure (or, in reaction formation, of rebelliousness against this identification). The idealization of great teacher figures is undoubtedly encountered in other branches of science, too. However, in general these idealizations constitute simply a new psychological content which temporarily attaches itself to the permanent unconscious idealized images of the superego; they are by no means analogous to the deeply anchored, lasting identifications which develop in the analyst with regard to the figure of Freud.[2]

[2]Some psychoanalytic educators might draw the conclusion that a simple curricular remedy is alluded to here—namely the postponement of the study of Freud's *Interpretation of Dreams* until later in the career of the analyst and its replacement by the study of secondary writers and of more up-to-date approaches. Such a conclusion is unwarranted, however. The analyst must not attempt to sidestep psychological tasks by avoidance; on the contrary, the identificatory pull

Although the pull toward the establishment of a gross and uncontrolled identification with Freud, created by the early and protracted preoccupation with Freud's thought during psychoanalytic training, is strong, I believe that with the aid of increasing self-understanding (e.g., as acquired during the training analysis) the student should be able to resist it. And I believe that with the aid of insight even an already established identification with Freud would be dissolved—unless it is the symptomatic result of a persisting, unanalyzed, structural defect—if it were only for the causative factors that I have mentioned so far. However, there exists another factor whose influence weighs even more heavily in the balance.

The most important obstacle in the way of the analyst when he attempts to attain an attitude of objectivity toward Freud is the fact that the idealized figure of Freud plays a currently active role in the dynamics of the psychoanalytic community, i.e., that body of psychoanalytic practitioners, scholars, and researchers, which in the past was sometimes—unfortunately, and, I think, largely erroneously—referred to as "the psychoanalytic movement" (see Freud, 1914c). Specifically, I would like to suggest that the idealization of Freud by the individual members of the psychoanalytic community has played an important role—usually a positive one, but not always—both in the maintenance of the psychic equilibrium of the individual analyst and in the maintenance of group cohesion in the analytic community. It exerts its influence in particular by virtue of the fact that, on the level of the individual, it tends to forestall the development of certain exquisitely painful experiences of narcissistic imbalance in the analyst (such as the pangs of jealousy and envy) and, on the level of the group, it is a counterforce to the rash and indiscriminate formation of splinter groups, which tend to arise within it in response to the ill-controlled narcissistic demands of certain of its creative members (such as the tendency for new discoveries to stim-

---

should be faced openly through increased awareness of its existence, of the psychological defect which tends to submit to it, and of the psychological assets which can be mobilized against it. (In this context see the discussion of the crucial difference between gross and wholesale identifications on the one hand, and the result of the process of *transmuting internalization* on the other hand [Kohut, 1971, pp. 45-50, 165-167].)

ulate secessionist movements instead of becoming integrated into the previously accumulated body of knowledge). There is no need to expand on these formulations since they are fully in harmony with certain basic psychoanalytic tenets concerning group psychology. Ever since Freud's relevant pioneering contribution (1921a), we have taken for granted that group cohesion is mainly established and safeguarded with the aid of the imago of the leader who, as the ego ideal held in common by the members of the group, becomes that point to which all individuals look up, and to whose greatness they all submit in shared admiration and submission.

A detailed and comprehensive study of the advantages and disadvantages for the science of psychoanalysis which are related to the fact that psychoanalysts are held together by a shared ego ideal, the idealized imago of Freud, should someday be undertaken—it is, however, a task which is beyond the scope of the present essay. Here I will only point out one of the advantages which accrue to analysis from the fact that psychoanalysts are held together by powerful emotional bonds. The essential continuity of a group, its essential sameness along the time axis despite the changes brought about by growth and development, is a precondition for the healthy productivity of the group, just as is the analogous continuity of the self-experience, despite the analogous changes within the confines of a single life span, for the healthy productivity of the individual. To state it differently: a firm group self[3] supports the productivity of the group just as a firm individual self supports the productivity of the individual. Applying this maxim to psychoanalysis, and stating it in the negative, we can say: if—even on the basis of legitimate reforms in theory and practice—psychoanalysis should change so abruptly and to such an extent that the sense of the continuity of the science were lost, then the individual analyst would receive no further stimulation from his participation in the scientific community of analysts, would lose his sense of belonging to a living, developing body of scientific

[3] The concept of a "group self" will be discussed later in the present essay. See pp. 419ff.

knowledge to whose growth he can contribute, and his productivity would cease.[4]

Among the disadvantages which arise for psychoanalysis from the fact that analysts form strong bonds of idealization toward an internalized imago of Freud, I will briefly speak of two. The first — it seems to me to be the less deleterious one — is a tendency toward conformity. New thought, in other words, is in danger of being viewed with suspicion because it is experienced as potentially disruptive. Many analysts may thus tend to be overcautious with regard to new ideas, while some others, owing to the presence of a preconscious rebelliousness

[4]In harmony with my emphasis on the importance of a sense of historical continuity for the psychoanalyst, I continue to be an advocate of historically oriented presentations in the curricula of psychoanalytic educational institutions. Despite the fact that I realize that the systematic rather than the historical presentation of psychoanalytic theory and technique would have some advantages for the learner, I still believe that there ought to be a minimum of courses which acquaint the student from the beginning of his studies with the germinal thoughts of Freud and of his early pupils. The familiarity with *The Interpretation of Dreams* and with Freud's great case histories is of particular value in this respect. The study of these works is not only a splendid, and I believe still irreplaceable exercise in a difficult new mode of thinking (i.e., in the terms of the symbolic notations of metapsychology), it also sets up a historical baseline for the future analyst from which he can trace the development which led to the modern theories and clinical methods. The advantages of retaining a minimum of historically oriented teaching are immeasurable and, to my mind, outweigh the advantages of a totally nonhistorical systematic orientation. To follow the unbroken line of development from the original discoveries in their original form through the various changes of the early formulations to their present state, will allow the student to experience the development of psychoanalysis in the course of his psychoanalytic education and will provide the psychoanalyst with that firm sense of the cohesion and continuity of analysis which forms the secure basis of all future creative developments. The cognitive advantages of a historical orientation also must not be underestimated. Only by studying the origins and the way stations can the present theories be fully understood. And only by realizing how analysts have in the past struggled unceasingly to formulate newly discovered data with the aid of new concepts will psychoanalysis continue to fulfill its potential for further growth. I am convinced that the vitality of psychoanalysis as a growing science is far from exhausted. It has so far hardly scratched the surface of the human mind and it will deepen its investigations for a long time to come, if — and indeed here lies a grave danger — historical and political developments do not stifle its activities from the outside. The recognition of this danger — perhaps in the form of the ascendancy of an antipsychological, totalitarian, mass society — should, in addition to the detached desire to expand the frontiers of psychological knowledge, prompt the analyst to investigate the field of history with the hope of increasing man's mastery over his historical destiny.

against the encompassing presence of an unchanging ideal, will welcome new ideas not so much because they have convinced themselves of their validity but because they have experienced them as a liberation from a dimly felt internal bondage. The second unfavorable consequence of the fact that the imago of Freud has served as a stimulus for the mobilization of idealizing cathexes seems to me to be of even greater importance than the first. The channeling of the flow of a large part of the individual psychoanalyst's narcissistic energies toward the group ego ideal creates psychological conditions which are unfavorable to those creative activities which emanate from the grandiose self. To describe the situation in experiential terms: the ambitious strivings and the cognate self-expanding urge toward new discoveries—in the physical world, to move into new territories, i.e., a derivative of archaic flying fantasies—are not sufficiently engaged and will therefore not stimulate the growth and the refinement of correlated new sublimatory structures, i.e., of those ego functions (talents) which would perform in accordance with the pressures emanating from the grandiose self. The potentially creative narcissistic strivings of the individual psychoanalyst may, in other words, be committed in too large a proportion to idealized goals. No doubt all creative and productive work depends on the employment of both grandiose *and* idealizing narcissistic energies, but I think that truly original thought, i.e., creativity, is energized predominantly from the grandiose self, while the work of more tradition-bound scientific and artistic activities, i.e., productivity,[5] is performed with idealizing cathexes.

But we must leave these general and speculative considerations and return to the more narrowly circumscribed area of our present concern. We are dealing with the question of what constellation of psychological forces protects the analyst against a disturbance of his narcissistic equilibrium with the aid of a nonobjective, idealizing attitude toward Freud. The answer to this question will, of course, secondarily

[5] I first encountered the felicitious comparative juxtaposition of the terms "creativity" and "productivity" in a letter (February 5, 1968) to me from K. R. Eissler.

explain certain specific resistances against discarding the idealization of Freud, i.e., those resistances which are an outgrowth of the analyst's wish that his narcissistic equilibrium remain undisturbed.

I believe that the idealization of Freud protects each analyst in two ways against the experience of painful narcissistic tensions. (1) Genuine, i.e., nondefensive idealization in any form and with any content (it is most effective in the form of a strongly idealized superego, i.e., in the form of meaningful, high ideals) is always an important and valuable safeguard against the development of narcissistic tensions (e.g., shame propensity) because a substantial amount of a person's narcissistic energies will be absorbed by his ideals. (2) The idealization of a group model protects the individual member of the group against certain states of narcissistic disequilibrium which are experienced as envy, jealousy, and rage. If these narcissistic tensions remain undischarged, they are exquisitely painful; if, however, they are discharged (through actions, especially actions motivated by narcissistic rage), then they are socially dangerous. If, however, the present-day psychoanalyst can maintain that everything of importance in psychoanalysis was already said by Freud, if furthermore the imago of Freud has been securely included in the analyst's idealized superego and has thus become a part of the self, then he can disregard contemporary competitors, they are not a threat to his own narcissistic security, and he can avoid suffering the painful narcissistic injuries which the comparison with the actual rivals for the goals of his narcissistic strivings might inflict on him. Small wonder then that the deidealization of the Freud imago creates strong uneasiness in the analyst which mobilizes strong resistances against taking an objective, realistic attitude toward Freud, i.e., an attitude in which Freud is seen as a fellow human being with his assets and defects, his achievements and his limitations. True, as I stated before, the tearing down of the image of Freud is a not infrequent occurrence in the history of analysis. Such events, however, one may assume to be largely defensive: in many instances, at least, they testify to a persistent, unmitigated idealization of Freud in the detractor's unconscious.

Readers inimical to psychoanalysis may well gloat over the preceding statements and may feel justified in their criticism of psychoanalysis as an unscientific, semireligious enterprise. But I will leave aside the comparatively easy task of formulating an anticipatory rebuttal to such potential abuse of my considerations. Instead I will here propose that, in true psychoanalytic tradition, these insights, if indeed they are in essence valid, should be considered by us as a challenge to expand the domain of our awareness. Specifically, I would say that they are a challenge to deepen and broaden our training analyses in the narcissistic sector of our candidates' personalities. We must in particular be watchful concerning the detrimental possibility that the unconscious grandiose-exhibitionistic strivings of our candidates will escape from becoming sufficiently engaged in the psychoanalytic situation, and that, in consequence of this evasion, they will not become gradually sublimated and integrated into the reality ego of the future psychoanalyst. The incompleteness of the mobilization of the candidate's narcissism (and/or the incompleteness of the working-through process in the narcissistic sector) may be caused in a variety of ways involving the entire spectrum of resistances in the candidate and a motley array of blind spots, countertransferences, and theoretically buttressed attitudes in the training analyst. Here I would like to mention only one specific mode in which the narcissistic pressures in the candidate may be shunted aside and escape analysis: the implicit or explicit agreement between analysand and training analyst that the potentially disturbing narcissistic cathexes of the candidate are to be committed to an idealized imago of Freud. To end a training analysis on the high-minded note of a shared admiration for Freud is, because of its emphasis on fraternal and communal feelings, not only a socially acceptable step of great respectability, it can also be a moving experience for the candidate which soothes his pain at the parting and sweetens the inevitable bitterness of having to accept the reality of his frustrations in the object-instinctual and the narcissistic realms. It cannot be denied, nevertheless, that such a termination may in some instances tend to close off certain postanalytic potentialities for the future analyst. In particular, the commitment of his still uncommitted narcissistic cathexes to the imago of Freud may deprive him of the emotional pressure to search for individually valid solutions and may increase his structural conflicts (his guilt feelings) if he, in independent assertiveness, should try to express the pattern of his own self. The clinical issues concerning this whole problem area are too complex to be dealt with in the present context, and here I will add only one statement in order to give an appropriately balanced outlook: a (training) analysand's spontaneously arrived at, realistic, nondefensive capacity to admire Freud as one of the great minds of the Western world, and as a model of scientific rigor and moral courage, by no means indicates that the narcissistic sector has not been successfully dealt with in the analysis. On the contrary, it may at times even be considered to be a sign of analytic success, especially in personalities who were formerly unable to mobilize any enthusiasm for greatness, whether encountered in the form of admirable ideas or of admirable personalities.

2. FREUD'S SELF-ANALYSIS: THE TRANSFERENCE OF CREATIVITY

After the preceding (cautionary) discussion of some of the personal, social, and methodological problems which an examination of Freud (his personal life and his scientific activities) poses for the psychoanalytic investigator, I will now turn to the hub of the present inquiry: the evaluation of Freud's self-analysis during the years preceding the publication of his decisive scientific contribution and greatest work, *The Interpretation of Dreams* (1900).

The initial question to which I will address myself is whether Freud's self-analysis should predominantly be considered as analogous to all other analyses, i.e., to the therapeutic analyses conducted by Freud, by his immediate pupils, and by all the later generations of analysts, or whether the essential significance of Freud's self-analysis is to be sought elsewhere.

There is no doubt that the insights which Freud obtained were of benefit to his emotional health in the ordinary psychoanalytic sense of the word, i.e., his self-analysis lifted repressions, dissolved psychoneurotic symptoms and inhibitions, and thus secondarily put instinctual forces which had formerly been bound up in structural conflicts at the disposal of his ego. Seen from this, the traditional vantage point, we will say that the success of Freud's self-analysis was the precondition for his creativity. However, we may say not only that the inner freedom obtained by his self-analysis liberated the nameless creative forces which served as the instinctual fuel for his achievements, but also that he was, in addition, able, on the strength of the unique and specific endowment of his ego, to turn each personal insight into a suprapersonal scientifically valid psychological discovery[6] (see Chapter 12).

If we look at the relationship which Freud established to Wilhelm Fliess during the period of his self-analysis we will quite naturally assume that, lacking an analyst (who would, as we have since learned to demand as the basic minimum requirement of the analytic situation, become the focal point of the transference, i.e., the target of the object-directed and narcissistic, libidinal, and aggressive strivings from the unconscious), Freud would almost as a matter of course search for a suitable person in his environment who could play this role for him. Indeed, we will in this context admire the cleverness

[6]Here the objection might be raised that each analysis is simultaneously therapy and research. I would have no quarrel with such an opinion if the term research in this context is meant to refer broadly to a specific mental attitude (taken by analyst and analysand) of openness to the unexpected and the unknown. In this sense analysis may indeed be looked upon as a form of research—especially by comparison with the therapeutic processes of medicine in which known remedies are applied to cure known illnesses. True research, however, aims at the discovery of data and relationships which have not been seen before by anyone, while in the usual therapeutic analysis the open-minded attitude is directed toward the recognition—the *re*discovery—of already previously discovered configurations. True research requires in addition the intention—whether consciously acknowledged or not—of formulating the newly seen configurations in more or less experience-distant terms and of communicating the findings and theories to the broader scientific group. My claim that Freud's self-analysis was unique by being a combination of therapy and research therefore rests on the fact that here a therapeutic endeavor was not just combined with the rediscovery of what was already known but (1) with the creative discovery of configurations which had never been recognized before, and (2) with the courageous intention of communicating the findings to the appropriate representatives of society, the community of scientists and scholars.

of Freud's choice of Fliess, with whom he was not in direct contact most of the time, i.e., the behind-the-couch distance and thus invisibility of the ordinary analyst was here replaced by the distance between Vienna and Berlin which likewise kept the disturbing reality input at a minimum. It is in tune, it must be stressed, with Freud's psychological genius that he did not — as so many of our patients and training analysands are wont to do even though an analyst is in fact at their disposal — live out his transferences with his friends and family or, what must have been most tempting, with his patients through the formation of countertransferences. In summary, then, we will understand why Freud's analysis has been primarily taken to be a specific variant of an ordinary therapeutic one and why it was thought that no other hypothesis was needed in addition to the assumption that Fliess was called upon to fill the void of the empty chair behind the symbolic couch on which Freud struggled along his way toward insight and mastery.

Freud's self-analysis was not the first analysis ever conducted — Freud (and Breuer) had already approached the problems of many patients through the application of the psychoanalytic method. Yet, in certain respects — in particular if we consider the breadth of Freud's aim and the persistence of his investigative effort as he conducted his self-analysis — this analysis was indeed something new, even if we disregard the absence of an analyst. It was the first specimen of the type of analysis which the modern analyst is in essence still practicing, i.e., it was an analysis which aimed at the depth-psychological comprehension of the total personality, and was not narrowly focused on a pathological symptom or syndrome. It was — and indeed continued to be almost to the very end of Freud's life — the first specimen of "analysis interminable."

Even though Freud's self-analysis was the pioneering precursor of the broadly conceived analyses of today, not all of its features are equivalent to those with which we have become familiar in our usual therapeutic work. It is the specific historical position of Freud's self-analysis, not the fact that analysand and analyst were the same person, which accounted for those of its elements — in particular the meaning of the central transference — which set it apart. I will now turn to a discussion of these distinguishing features of Freud's analysis in order to offer an alternative—or to be more exact, a complement—to the traditional hypothesis about the significance of Freud's transference to Wilhelm Fliess.

At the height of the transference neurosis of the usual therapeutic analysis the analysand's extra-analytic activities and his capacity for full emotional responsiveness outside the analytic situation are commonly impoverished; creativeness, too, is generally curtailed and tends to appear only in the final stage of the analysis, after the insightful resolution of certain specific sectors of the transference has been achieved. During the time of his self-analysis, however, Freud was not only capable of responding to his environment with strong, deep, varied, and appropriate emotions, as can be ascertained by a perusal of his correspondence, but he was arriving at the most original insights, discoveries, and formulations of his life, as is attested by the great work which was the crowning result of the labors of this period.

If Freud's self-analysis had been primarily an act of self-healing through insight, one would have expected it to end, parallel to the termination of the analysis of the usual transference neurosis, with the discovery of the meaning of the transference and, simultaneously, its resolution. In Freud's case, however, there seems to have occurred a dissolution of the transference bondage without corresponding insight, i.e., Freud's understanding of the full meaning of transference came only gradually, much later, and was derived from his clinical work. Freud's transference to Fliess must therefore be viewed as a phenomenon accompanying creative work: Freud's self-analysis was a creative spell which was simultaneously worked through analytically.

This phenomenon is outside the realm of pathology;[7] however, it is distantly related to the clinically observable fact that a modicum of empathic contact with the analyst is necessary for the maintenance of a newly acquired capacity for artistic sublimation on the part of certain analytic patients.

---

[7] Ellenberger (1970), however, uses the term "creative illnèss" for such events.

Mr. E.,[8] for example, was suffering from a severe narcissistic personality disturbance with regressive swings that had the appearance of fleeting psychotic episodes. As a result of the systematic working through of his skillfully conducted analysis, however, he gradually acquired the ability to channel certain formerly pathologically employed narcissistic cathexes into emotionally absorbing and fulfilling artistic activities. Both the leading symptom of his psychopathology (a voyeuristic perversion) and his newly acquired artistic sublimation were offshoots of his lifelong intense concentration on the maintenance of visual contact with the world. Already in his earliest years he seems to have shifted the focus of his contact needs from his frustrated oral, tactile, and olfactory demands toward his vision, as could be reconstructed on the basis of transference fears that his intense gaze overburden and destroy the (mother-)analyst. (Throughout the patient's childhood the patient's mother had been ill with malignant hypertension—she was frequently very tired, never picked him up when he was a baby, and was unable to give to the child the self-confirming emotional sustenance which he needed. She died during the patient's late adolescence.) The significance of the patient's voyeuristic perversion—he was irresistibly driven by the dangerous urge to look at male genitals—can be gleaned from the details of the situation in which it made its first appearance. During the patient's early adolescence the boy and his mother were at a country fair. He had enjoyed himself alone on a high swing (undoubtedly in a preconscious elaboration of archaic flying fantasies) and, pleased with his skill and prowess, asked his mother to watch him perform. When the mother, who was tired and depressed, did not respond to his wish, however, he suddenly felt bereft of the buoyancy which he had just experienced, and felt drained and empty. It was at that moment that he turned away from his mother and walked to a public toilet, driven by the irresistible

[8]This patient was analyzed by a senior student at the Chicago Institute for Psychoanalysis under my supervision. This case is frequently referred to in Kohut (1971)—see pp. 10, 15, 117-118, 130-132, 136, 158-159, 173, 313-315. Especially relevant to the present discussion are the remarks on pp. 131-132, 173, and 314.

wish to gaze at a powerful penis (see Kohut, 1971, pp. 158-159).

In the present context there is no need to spell out the metapsychological substance of the patient's perversion beyond that minimum which is necessary for the understanding of the relationship between the patient's narcissistic transference bond which had established itself in his analysis and his ability to maintain a newly cathected artistic sublimation. The essence of the perversion could be gleaned from childhood memories (such as the episode at the country fair) and was confirmed over and over again as the transference was being worked through. The patient's developing self had been badly deprived of cohesion-maintaining narcissistic cathexes because of the dearth of appropriate responses (mirroring) to his narcissistic(-exhibitionistic) needs. His craving to fill an inner void, to obtain a sense of aliveness, therefore became intense; furthermore, there is little doubt that—because of innate endowment and accidental circumstances (e.g., the fact that he was deprived of tactile contact)—these needs became concentrated upon the visual sphere. Deprived as it was, and severe as his regression might be, his self would never permanently disintegrate, however—he never quite gave up the hope that he would ultimately obtain the needed confirming-approving-mirroring response from the narcissistic object. Thus he offered himself (visually) to his mother (e.g., in the country fair), and he did the same within the context of the analysis in the transference. (For an early, beautifully elaborated attempt by the patient to channel the analysis and its insights into the visual-artistic area, see the description of the method by which the patient attempted to cope with the trauma of a weekend separation from the analyst early in the course of the analysis [Kohut, 1971, pp. 130-132].) Whenever the hope for an empathic mirroring response was disappointed, however, a regression took place. Instead of persisting in his demands and renewing his attempts to obtain narcissistic gratification on the level of "mirroring," he turned toward the sexualized attempt to achieve his needed narcissistic sustenance through a visual merger with the symbol of powerful maleness with which he could thus identify.

It would be tempting to enter into a discussion of the meaning of the patient's perversion at this point, but—even in its briefest form—such an enterprise would lead us too far afield.[9] In our present context, however, we can say that in the transference the patient experienced over and over the following specific sequence of events: (1) he offered himself—or later his artistic product, i.e., the extension of his grandiose self—to the narcissistic object (the analyst in the mirror transference); (2) he was disappointed because of an empathic failure from the side of the analyst—or because of other narcissistic blows from him; (3) then followed a regression, leading to the intensification of the voyeuristic perversion; (4) the analyst responded with an empathic interpretation of this reaction; (5) the perverse urge now subsided and the patient renewed his attempt to obtain mirroring admiration. It was the working through of the repeated experience of this sequence which gradually increased the patient's mastery over the regressive trends and which buttressed his ability to persist in his creative efforts despite disappointments.

A specific episode which occurred when, after several years of analysis, the patient had already made considerable progress, is of particular significance within the context in which I am adducing the clinical material on Mr. E.—namely, in order to illuminate the role which the narcissistic object is called upon to play in support of the more or less precariously maintained ability to carry on creative activities. Mr. E.'s general condition had much improved by that time and his whole life was now more satisfying and on a higher level. His homosexual voyeurism had nearly disappeared and he not only derived considerable inner satisfaction from his art, but, since luckily he did indeed possess considerable talent, he also received sufficient external acclaim to satisfy some of his needs

[9]Those familiar with my studies of narcissism will have no problem recognizing that here again (as I first pointed out in my discussion of Patient A. [Kohut, 1971, see especially pp. 69ff.]) we can see that the perversion is not caused by the existing pregenital sexual fixations but that it is a manifestation of the need to fill a structural defect. The visual merger with the powerful penis (including the accompanying unconscious or preconscious fellatio fantasy) constitutes the attempt to obtain needed narcissistic sustenance (to fill a structural void) and to escape from a sense of emptiness and depression.

for approving, accepting, and (self-)confirming responses. The patient was now able to weather the usual weekend separations from the analyst without feeling endangered by the pull of his voyeurism—clearly an indication of the considerable progress which he had already made. On this occasion, however, he not only had to confront the tension created by the time gap between the last appointment of the present and the first appointment of the following week, he also had to confront the feeling of an increasing separation from the analyst in space. During this weekend it became necessary for him to undertake a trip to a city about two hundred miles from Chicago because of some artistic work which he had been commissioned to do there. As he left Chicago by train he was not only still in high spirits but his mind was creatively preoccupied with the work he was going to do upon his arrival. As mile after mile went by, however—specifically (as he reported in the Monday session), as mile after mile of distance interposed itself between him and the analyst whom, as he now began to realize, he had always fantasied as sitting in his analytic chair during the weekends, waiting for him to come back—the patient experienced again the old feeling which he had thought he had overcome: a sense of depression, a painful lowering of self-esteem, a sense of inner emptiness and a need to be filled up. As the train took him farther and farther away from Chicago, the sense of emptiness increased and, simultaneously, his interest in the artistic task, which had formerly been so stimulating to him, declined. Finally, about halfway between Chicago and his destination, he suddenly felt the urge to follow a sailor into the toilet. It was at this moment, however, that he was able to make use of the analytic insights he had acquired. He grasped the essence of what was going on in him, resisted the temptation, went through with his trip and his assignment (though not as zestfully and creatively as he had anticipated), and returned to Chicago. On the trip back he could observe in himself that his self-esteem began to rise, that the sense of inner emptiness diminished, and that his creative and artistic interests began to intensify again as the distance to the narcissistic object decreased.

I shall now return to Freud and his quasi analyst in order to examine the significance which the imago of Fliess may have had for Freud as narcissistic support with regard to the creative (nontherapeutic) aspects of his analysis. I am not overlooking the vast difference which separates Freud's transference experience from that of Patient E.[10] As I said before, the phenomenon under consideration is outside the realm of psychopathology and is only distantly related to such occurrences as those illustrated by Mr. E.'s trip. Nevertheless, if we shift the focus of our attention from the specific function of the narcissistic transference in psychopathology and examine instead the general psychological significance—whether in illness or in health—which the relationship to self-objects may have for people, then the previous clinical material will serve as an acceptable background for the following constructions.

It is my main thesis that during periods of intense creativity (especially during its early stages) certain creative persons require a specific relationship with another person—a transference of creativity—which is similar to that which establishes itself during the psychoanalytic treatment of one major group of narcissistic personality disorders.

In the treatment situation the endopsychic substance of this relationship is the analysand's idealizing transference to the psychoanalyst. This transference is the manifestation of a phase of normal development which, in consequence of the regression that is induced by the treatment situation, has been revived in a distorted form. During the normal phase of development which corresponds to the idealizing transference, the caretaking empathic adult is held to be omnipotent by the child, who obtains a sense of narcissistic well-being (of being whole and powerful, for example) when he is able to experience himself as part of the idealized self-object. Under

[10]I am here not alluding to the fact that Patient E.'s sublimatory activities were sustained by a *mirror* transference while Freud in the lonesome uneasiness of his voyage of discovery into the depth of the mind turned toward an omnipotent idealized figure, i.e., may be said to have established a relationship which is akin to an *idealizing* transference. These are small differences, no more than variations on a basic theme, which we may disregard in the present context. People whose self is in need of sustenance, whether because of the energic drain and the anxiety during a creative spell or for other reasons, will tend to establish narcissistic relationships to archaic self-objects—whether in the form of one of the varieties of a mirror transference (see the later remarks on p. 404 about the relationship of Picasso to Braque and the discussion on p. 411 about the relationship of the British people to Churchill) or through a merger with an idealized imago.

400 FREUD AND THE PSYCHOANALYTIC COMMUNITY

favorable conditions the adult's empathic response to the child sets up a situation in which the child's phase-appropriate need for a merger with an omnipotent object is sufficiently fulfilled to prevent traumatization. This basic fulfillment of the need, however, is the precondition for the subsequent developmental task, which involves the child's gradual recognition (1) that the adult is not omnipotent, and (2) that he, the child, is not a part of him but a separate person. In consequence of this gradual and phase-appropriate disillusionment the idealizing cathexes are withdrawn from the archaic object and set up within the psychic apparatus (e.g., idealizing the values of the superego). In other words, an archaic self-object imago has been transmuted into psychological structure. However, if this developmental task is not completed, then the personality will be lacking in sufficiently idealized psychological structures. In consequence of this defect, the person is deprived of one major endopsychic method by which he could maintain his self-esteem: the self's merging into the idealized superego by living up to the values harbored by this psychic structure. Yearning to find a substitute for the missing (or insufficiently developed) psychic structure, such persons are forever seeking, with addictionlike intensity, and often through sexual means (the clinical picture may be that of a perversion), to establish a relationship to people who serve as stand-ins for the omnipotent idealized self-object, i.e., to the archaic precursor of the missing inner structure. In everyday life and in the analytic transference the self-esteem of such persons is therefore upheld by their relationships to archaic self-objects.

Although I believe that the transference of creativity is a phenomenon which is akin to the idealizing transference, I do not claim that creative people are of necessity suffering from structural defects which drive them to seek archaic merger experiences. I suspect, however, that the psychic organization of some creative people is characterized by a fluidity of the basic narcissistic configurations,[11] i.e., that periods of nar-

[11] The metapsychological explanation of the processes of scientific and artistic creativity suggested here within the framework of the theory of narcissism (i.e., the theory of the two major narcissistic configurations and of their cathexes) should be compared with the important formulations offered by previous workers (in

cissistic equilibrium (stable self-esteem and securely idealized internal values: steady, persevering work characterized by attention to details) are followed by (precreative) periods of emptiness and restlessness (decathexis of values and low self-esteem; addictive or perverse yearnings: no work), and that these, in turn, are followed by creative periods (the unattached narcissistic cathexes which had been withdrawn from the ideals and from the self are now employed in the service of the creative activity: original thought; intense, passionate work). Translating these metapsychological formulations into behavioral terms, one might say that (1) a phase of frantic creativity (original thought) is followed by (2) a phase of quiet work (the original ideas of the preceding phase are checked, ordered, and put into a communicative form, e.g., written down), and that this phase of quiet work is in turn interrupted by (3) a fallow period of precreative narcissistic tension, which ushers in a phase of renewed creativity, and so on.

I am not prepared to decide the question whether this three-phase schema applies to the vicissitudes of Freud's work and creativity, but I can furnish some evidence in support of an affirmative answer. There is no doubt, for example, that Freud had an enormous capacity for prolonged and concen-

---

particular Sachs and Kris) within the frame of reference that is provided by the structural model of the mind.

Sachs (1942; see in particular pp. 48-49) believes, in harmony with Freud (1908), that the creative poet initially "uses his fantasy as a means of gaining narcissistic gratification for his own person." His guilt feelings, however, force him to shift his "narcissism" away from himself and onto his creation. The poet thus gives up more of his narcissism than average people "but his work wins back immeasurably more of it than others can hope for."

Kris's relevant statements (1932-1952; see in particular pp. 59-62) about the sequence of "inspiration and elaboration" in the process of artistic creation are not only psychoanalytically sophisticated behavioral descriptions, they also provide us with an account of the processes of creation in metapsychological terms. Kris sees the creative process, as does Sachs, within the metapsychological context of the functions of the structural model of the mind. In contrast to Sachs's emphasis, however, Kris does not stress the motivational importance of the superego-ego conflict, i.e., the motivational importance of guilt feelings, but the interplay between the ego and id during the collaboration of the two structures in the creative activity. To put Kris's formulation in a nutshell: during the phase of inspiration it is the id which holds sway, while during the phase of elaboration 't is the ego which predominates.

FREUD AND THE PSYCHOANALYTIC COMMUNITY

trated attention to details in the service of the completion and
perfection of his work (phase 2 of the three-phase schema) and
that he possessed high, strongly cathected, internalized values.
Furthermore, one might hypothesize that his intense oral-respiratory cravings (e.g., his increasing, unbreakable bondage
to cigar smoking)[12] were related to a depressionlike state of
precreative inner emptiness, which was the manifestation of
the decathexis of the self as the narcissistic energies detached
themselves and became available for the creative task.[13] Freud
did indeed report that a certain disturbance of his well-being
was a necessary precondition for his creativeness (Jones, 1953,
pp. 345-346). Was Freud here describing the unpleasant
feeling of tension which accompanies the precreative regression of narcissistic libido (i.e., an autoerotic tension state)?
Did he at such times feel empty and depressed, and was there
an addictionlike intensification of oral-respiratory intaking
needs—all as manifestations of the decathexis of the narcissistic structures in consequence of the fact that the narcissistic energies had to remain in uncommitted suspension,
waiting to be absorbed by the creative activity? I cannot do
more here than to raise these questions. If these hypotheses
could be confirmed, they would lend support to my interpretation of one aspect of Freud's relationship to Fliess as a
regression to the idealization of an archaic omnipotent figure.

[12]Freud himself believed that there was a connection between his addiction to
cigars and his capacity to work. He wrote (in a letter to Fliess of June 12, 1895): "I
have again begun to smoke, because I never stopped missing it (after a 14-months
abstinence) and because I have to spoil that psychic rascal in me, or else he won't
do me any work" (my translation; cf. Schur, 1972, p. 86).

[13]The feeling of estrangement which the creative person often experiences
vis-à-vis the product of his creativity, his work, is in many instances not the result of
structural conflicts (e.g., due to guilt about having produced something beautiful
or discovered something important) but the direct expression of the fact that at the
very moment of creativity the self is depleted since the narcissistic cathexes have
been shifted from the self to the work. In the productive activities of noncreative
persons, and in the phase of quiet work of creative minds, the narcissistic cathexes
are distributed between the self and the work, with the result that the self is
experienced (and later remembered) as the active initiator, the source, the shaper
of the product. During the phase of frantic creativity, however, the self is depleted
because the narcissistic cathexes are concentrated on the work, with the result that
the self is not experienced (and is later not remembered) as the initiator, source, or
shaper of the product.

As I will point out in the following, however, this inter-pretation can be adequately supported within the framework of (pre-)conscious motivations, i.e., without having recourse to an explanation of creativeness in terms of the dynamics of narcissism.

During creative periods the self is at the mercy of powerful forces which it cannot control; and its sense of enfeeblement is increased because it feels itself helplessly exposed to extreme mood swings which range from severe precreative depression to dangerous hypomanic overstimulation, the latter occurring at the moment when the creative mind stands at the threshold of creative activity. (For a summary of Freud's vivid des-cription of his emotional state during creative periods see Jones, 1953, pp. 343-345.) And when his discoveries lead the creative mind into lonely areas that had not previously been explored by others, then a situation is brought about in which the genius feels a deep sense of isolation. These are frightening experiences which repeat those overwhelmingly anxious mo-ments of early life when the child felt alone, abandoned, unsupported.[14c] Freud put it bitterly when he said (March 16, 1896), "I live in such isolation that one might suppose I had discovered the greatest truths" (1887-1902, Letter 43)—a statement to which one can add only that here a sense of humor aided Freud in confronting the fact that he had indeed discovered truths that could not but make him be alone in the newly opened territory, alone until a few courageous pupils began to follow him. Small wonder then that creative artists and scientists—the latter at times in striking contrast to their fierce rationality in the central area of their creative pursuits —often attempt to protect their creative activity by surround-

[14]See in this context Székely's perceptive contributions (1967, 1970) concerning the fear of the new and unknown in scientists. For clinical material illustrating such emotional states, see Gedo (1972b). [ᶜThe patient described in this paper fore-stalled the development of feeling states of aloneness and abandonment in consequence of his highly original discoveries by arranging to publish them only with a coauthor. The function of the collaborator in preparing the work was to listen to the patient's ideas and assure him of their pertinence and validity. Interestingly, in the small professional community qualified to judge the work, it was invariably attributed to the patient alone. In terms of Kohut's concept of the transference of creativity, this instance illustrates a variant in which the grandiose self is expressed in the form of a *twinship*.]

ing it with superstitions and rituals. But while one creative mind will have to protect himself with "a pair of tall wax candles in silver holders at the head of his manuscript" (the description of the novelist Aschenbach in Thomas Mann's *Death in Venice*) and while another (Schiller) had to work on a desk from the drawer of which the smell of rotten apples emanated (see Eckermann 1836-1848, *Conversations with Goethe,* Part 3; October 7, 1827), there are still others— among them, I believe, was Freud—who during the period of their most daring creativity will choose a person in the environment whom they can see as all-powerful, a figure with whom they can temporarily blend.

The transferences established by creative minds during periods of intense creativity are therefore much more closely related to the transferences which occur during the analysis of narcissistic personalities than to those which occur in the analysis of transference neuroses. In other words, we are dealing either (a) with the wish of a self, which feels enfeebled during a period of creativity, to retain its cohesion by expanding temporarily into the psychic structure of others, by finding itself in others, or to be confirmed by the admiration of others (resembling one of the varieties of a mirror transference), or (b) with the need to obtain strength from an idealized object (resembling an idealizing transference). Thus relationships which are established during creative periods do not predominantly involve the revival of a figure from the (Oedipal) past which derives its transference significance primarily from the fact that it is still the target of the love and hate of the great man's childhood.

It would be fascinating to pursue the investigation of the varieties of the narcissistic relationships (and of the details of the narcissistic bonds by which they are maintained) which creative people establish, especially during their creative periods. In the area of the grandiose self, for example, some evidence has already been accumulated in support of the assumption that the twinship relationship to an alter ego may provide the necessary confirmation of the reality of the self for a great man. Mary Gedo's studies (1972) show convincingly that during creative periods Picasso was in need of self-cohesion-providing relationships to alter-ego figures (e.g., to the painter Georges Braque). The presence of an alter ego, and the narcissistic relationship to it, one might speculate, protected the self of the artist from the danger of irreversible fragmentation to which it felt exposed while it was drained of narcissistic energies during periods when the genius-artist allowed the visual universe to break into meaningless pieces before he reassembled them again and, in so doing, gave Western man a new perception of the visible world.

Undoubtedly, the large areas of the relationship between homosexuality and creativity, first explored by Freud (1910b, p. 59), will also be illuminated when we investigate it by taking into account the vicissitudes of the narcissistic cathexes. Although I am not able to present empirical data concerning this relationship which were obtained through the systematic psychoanalytic investigation of a great creative artist or scientist, I will offer a substitute: the literary testimony of a great writer. The value of this evidence is enhanced by the fact that there is good reason to assume that the relevant insights contained in the artistic document under consideration were in essence derived from the writer's own experiences, in particular with regard to the vicissitudes of his own creativity. The examination of Thomas Mann's *Death in Venice* (Kohut, 1957) reveals that the essence of this beautiful novella is an almost scientifically exact portrayal of the disintegration of artistic sublimation. The artist Aschenbach, the main character of the story, had, throughout his long creative life, been able to channel the available free narcissistic cathexes toward his artistic productions.[15] While in his childhood he must still have been in severe jeopardy—his childhood self had been insufficiently sustained by his environment and had been in danger of fragmentation—he had later become capable of providing himself on his own with the needed experience of psychological perfection and wholeness—i.e., the experience of basic self-esteem—through the creation of works of art. Extensions or duplications of the self were now available which he could invest with narcissistic libido: he could give them

[15] I am here and in the following remarks expressing the conclusions reached in an early investigation (Kohut, 1957) in the terms of my more recent findings.

formal perfection. But, as the story begins, this ability is now being lost. The artist is aging, and his power to create replicas of the perfect self is waning. On the way to total disintegration, however—and here lies the focus of the novella—we see the revival of the sexualized precursor of the artistic product: the beautiful boy (though frail and already marked for destruction) who is the symbolic stand-in for the core of the still unaltered childhood self which craves love and admiration. As "the cultural structure of a lifetime . . . [is] . . . destroyed," i.e., as the writer's ability to deploy the narcissistic cathexes in the performance of the creative task is lost, the narcissistic cathexes return from the work of art to the imago of the fragmenting childhood self. There they rest briefly, delaying the ultimate destruction of the great man's personality for one more moment.

The deployment of the fluid narcissistic cathexes of creative persons toward idealized imagos seems, however, to be even more common than their search for replicas or expansions of the grandiose self—as exemplified by the case of Aschenbach. At any rate, man's need for the merger with a supporting idealized figure is more easily observable.

But we must return to Freud's self-analysis. If we accept the fact that, in its essence, Freud's self-analysis was not a self-therapeutic experience but rather the crowning achievement of his creative genius, then we will understand why Freud did not discover the clinical transference at that time. The end of Freud's self-analysis was not analogous to the termination of the usual therapeutic analysis, i.e., it did not occur in consequence of the fact that the analysand (Freud) had recognized the transference, i.e., the illusory aspects of his relationship with the analyst (Fliess), and that the transference had been worked through. It was rather the opposite: the transference—an idealizing transference of creativity—became superfluous and came to an end when the creative work done with the aid of the self-analysis had been consummated. In other words, for Freud Wilhelm Fliess was the embodiment of idealized power during Freud's most important creative spell; and Freud was able to dispense with the illusory sense of Fliess's greatness and thus with the narcissistic

relationship—in contradistinction to a resolution of transference by insight—after he had completed his great creative
task.[d]

3. CHARISMATIC AND MESSIANIC PERSONALITIES

There is one subsidiary question with regard to the transference of creativity which we must still confront. It concerns
the problem of the specificity of the choice of the narcissistically cathected self-object.

In the usual clinical circumstances, given the appropriately
neutral attitude of the analyst and his noninterference with
the unrolling of the endopsychic process that is elicited by the
psychoanalytic situation, the transference will develop in
accordance with preanalytically established endopsychic factors. The transference will portray the objects of the analysand's childhood, in particular as he loved and hated them in
the context of the crucial events which formed his personality,
especially its neurotic aspects. True, some actual features of
the analyst's personality and of his actions will become
temporarily amalgamated during the analysis with the imagos
which stem from the childhood of the analysand. But these
details of the clinical transference, while of considerable
tactical importance in clinical psychoanalysis, do not constitute its essence: their relationship to the core of the transference, i.e., to the genetic center of the psychopathology, is

---

[d] We have some evidence that a later period of Freud's creativity was marked by a
similar expansion of the grandiose self: during the creation of his work on
Leonardo da Vinci (1910b), the case histories of Little Hans (1909b), of the Rat
Man (1909d) and of D. P. Schreber (1911), and "Totem and Taboo" (1912-1913).
From the Freud-Jung correspondence (McGuire, 1974) and Jung's memoirs (1961)
it should be possible to reconstruct these vicissitudes of Freud's relationship to Jung
(J. Gedo, in preparation). The idealizing needs aroused by Freud's creativity have
been discussed in Chapters 13 and 14. Referring to Gedo's essay on the Freud-Jung
correspondence, Kohut suggested (at a meeting of the Chicago Psychoanalytic
Society, November 26, 1974) that the temporary increase of Freud's need for a
powerful figure during the time of his strongest idealization of Jung was not so
much motivated by a new creative advance as by fear vis-á-vis the consciously
wished-for but unconsciously dreaded expansion of psychoanalysis beyond the
confines of Vienna—i.e., in the language of Freud's childhood, by fear regarding a
move from a narrow (Jewish) environment into a vast (gentile) world.

the same as the relationship between the day's residue and the unconscious dream wish from childhood in dream psychology.

In the transference of creativity, on the other hand, the opposite may be held to be true. Here it is a current situation that is central, a situation in which an enfeebled self, drained of its cohesion-maintaining cathexis and engaged in the daring exploration of the moon landscapes of the unknown, will seek the temporary aid which comes to it from the relationship with an archaic self-object, in particular, for example, with an idealized parent imago. True enough, the transference of creativity repeats an archaic childhood situation: it is a reversion to that phase of development in which the self in formation had not yet separated itself from the figures in its environment — had not separated itself, in other words, from the imagos which for the social-psychological observer are the "objects" of the child. But these figures in the early environment were still experienced by the child as belonging to the self, they were still "self-objects." Now, if in the analysis of a narcissistic personality disturbance the psychoanalytic situation is established appropriately, then a narcissistic transference will develop spontaneously, and it will take on that predetermined form — or that predetermined sequence or mixture of forms — which is the outgrowth of the specific childhood history of the analysand and of the correlated specific fixation points in his development. These conditions, however, must not be expected to prevail in the creative personality — at least they are not essential.[16]

The essential ingredients of the usual clinical transference are, therefore, preanalytically established, and the personality of the analyst and other reality factors concerning him must in the main be taken into account only on the basis of the

[16]Creativity may be embedded in a great variety of personality make-ups, ranging from normal to psychotic. There are undoubtedly many creative persons who, if scrutinized with an eye to classifying them in the terms of psychopathology, would have to be counted among the narcissistic personality disorders. While, on the one hand, the fluidity of the narcissistic cathexes in the creative mind creates vulnerabilities similar to those to which (noncreative) narcissistic personalities are exposed, and, on the other hand, the favorable outcome of the psychoanalytic treatment of narcissistic personality disorders is not infrequently due to the fact that the patient succeeds in channeling some of the formerly pathogenic narcissistic energies toward creative pursuits, spontaneous creativity is, in its essence, not related to the narcissistic personality disorders.

question whether they might *interfere* with the unfolding, the maintenance, and the working through of the transference. This maxim does not hold true with regard to the transference of creativity, however—whether a twinship is sought (in which the alter ego must fit its role, i.e., it must *in fact* resemble the needy personality of the creative person) or whether it is the archaic idealized omnipotent object that is required (which must then *in fact* have certain features which make it suitable for the role that the creative person assigns to it).

But what are the characteristic features of the person who is especially suitable to become the admired omnipotent self-object for the creative person during the period when he makes his decisive steps into new territory?

There are certain types of narcissistically fixated persons (even bordering on the paranoid)—they display an apparently unshakable self-confidence and voice their opinions with absolute certainty—who are specifically suitable to be the objects of the idealizing needs of the creative person's temporarily enfeebled self during a creative spell.

The persons who fall into this psychological category are obviously not likely to offer themselves to the scrutiny of the psychoanalyst. They do not feel ill; and their self-esteem is high. What makes them specifically able to play the role of the idealized archaic object for those who are in need of it, and what makes them ready to fill it, is the fact that the maintenance of their self-esteem depends on the incessant use of certain mental functions: they are continuously judging others—usually pointing up the moral flaws in other peoples' personalities and behavior[17]—and, without shame or hesitation, they set themselves up as the guides and leaders and gods of those who are in need of guidance, of leadership, and of a target for their reverence. In many instances it appears

---

[17]The role which the function of judgment plays for most people in the psychic economy of narcissism must not be underestimated. I am not speaking here primarily of the mechanism of projection, with the aid of which our faults are assigned to others, but of the innumerable nonspecific acts of judgment with regard to the behavior, the morality, the personalities of others. For example, the pleasant glow which the participants experience in judgmental bull sessions in which those not present are taken apart is, in my opinion, not so much due to the discharge of sublimated sadism but rather to the enhanced self-esteem which the act of judging and the comparison with those who are being judged supply.

that such charismatic and messianic personalities have fully identified themselves with either their grandiose self or their idealized superego. For most of us, the herd of common mortals, the ideals[18] which we harbor are direction-setting symbols of perfection. They provide us with narcissistic pleasure when we come near to the target they have set for us, and they deprive us of narcissistic sustenance when we fall short of it by too wide a margin. The messianic leader figure, however, is done with the task of measuring himself against the ideals of his superego: his self and the idealized structure have become one.

True enough, the endopsychic arrangements which support the self-esteem of the charismatic or messianic person deprive his personality of elasticity. Mobility and the reliance on several different sources of self-esteem is in the long run a safer way of psychological survival than the maintenance of a rigid narcissistic equilibrium through the employment of a single set of restricted functions. Indeed, the endopsychic equilibrium of the charismatic leader or of the messiah seems to be of the all-or-nothing type: there are no survival potentialities between the extremes of utter firmness and strength, on the one hand, and utter destruction (psychosis; suicide) on the other. I would, nevertheless, like to stress that, in reflecting about the messianic or charismatic leader figure, the depth psychologist should not too quickly abandon his objective stance and espouse an attitude of moral judgement. Charismatic and messianic personalities come in all shades and degrees. Some among them are no doubt close to psychosis. These are dogmatic persons who lack all empathy with the inner life of others—with the notable exception of their keen grasp of even the subtlest reactions in other people which are related to their own narcissistic requirements. There are other messianic persons, however, in whom the coalescence between self and idealized superego, while chronic, is only partial, i.e., where the nonmessianic sectors of the self, although in harmony with the messianic substance of the personality, may at times even retain the freedom of displaying a sense of quite nonmessianic humor. It must be stressed in addition that the social effects of messianic and charismatic personalities are

[18]I am here fo the moment disregarding the grandiose self.

not necessarily deleterious. A figure of the kind that is required in times of grave crisis cannot be of the more modest, self-relativistic personality type to which those chosen to positions of leadership during quiescent historical periods in general belong. In a moment of crisis and profound anxiety the nation will turn to the messianic or charismatic per-sonality—not primarily because it has recognized his skills and his efficiency but because it realizes that he will satisfy its need to identify with his unquestioned righteousness or with his firmness and security.

The relationship between the British people and Winston Churchill before, during, and after the greatest danger ever faced by England (and the Western world) is a good example in this context. Churchill (a leader, by the way, whose mystique emanated, I believe, predominantly from the grand-iose self, not from the idealized superego), who was unaccept-able before the crisis, filled his role to perfection during the crisis and was the unquestioned leader of the nation. Yet he was discarded after the crisis had subsided. The British people identified themselves with him and with his unshakable belief in his and, by extension, the nation's strength, so long as their selves felt weak in the face of the serious danger. As soon as victory had been attained, however, the need for a merger with an omnipotent figure subsided and they were able to turn from him to other (noncharismatic) leaders.[19] It takes little effort to discern the parallel between the temporary needs of the enfeebled self of the creative person and the temporary needs of an endangered nation in times of crisis: in both instances the idealization of the leader, the narcissistic trans-

[19]Two relevant topics should be mentioned here which would be worthy of study by the psychoanalytic historian and sociologist. The first is the examination of the political genius of a people, i.e., its skills, its political savvy, as it manifests itself in its capacity to choose the right kind of leader in various historical situations. The second concerns the specific relationship between leader and followers, in partic-ular the question whether (1) the leader is apt to be idealized (in this case I would designate him as a messianic personality, indicating by this term that his self has largely merged with the idealized superego); whether (2) the leader is apt to become the target, in the main nonidealized, for an identification with an omni-potent object (in this case I would designate him as a charismatic personality, indicating by this term that his self has largely become the carrier of the grandiose self); or whether (3) the leader is apt to be simply the executor of certain ego functions of those who have chosen him (in this case he is neither a messianic nor a charismatic personality).

ference to him, is abandoned when the need for it has come to an end.

In contrast to the endopsychic conditions which prevail in the messianic and charismatic personality, the ego of the average person, of the man who has attained that state to which we might refer as average mental health, attempts to fulfill two tasks. On the one hand it responds to the pressure of the grandiose self in the depth of the psyche—but, when it strives for the enhancement of self-esteem through activities which fulfill the ambitions nourished by the demands of the grandiose self, it does so in a realistic way. In particular, it takes into account the needs and feelings of others, of the fellow man with whom it is in empathic contact. On the other hand, as its second task, the normal ego attempts to exert its initiative and control in order to bring about behavior which comes close to that demanded by the idealized standards of the superego. In so doing, it will compare the performance of the actual self with that demanded by the idealized standards and will acknowledge the fact that perfection cannot become reality. In consequence of this recognition, however, its sense of narcissistic pleasure when the self comes close to living up to the ideals will be a limited one. And, in particular, there will again be empathic contact with others which will prevent the development of a sense of absolute moral superiority over the fellow man. When comparing his own performance with the performance of others, the judgment of the nonmessianic person will be influenced by his empathic understanding of the fact that the others, too, experience limited failures and successes in the moral sphere, and thus no unrealistic feeling develops that the self is perfect and that the selves of other people are in essence corrupt.

But what is it that enables charismatic personalities to maintain that sense of power (as if their real self and the archaic grandiose self were one) and what bestows on messianic personalities that sense of absolute moral righteousness (as if their real self and the idealized self-object were one) that makes them so irresistibly attractive to those who need to merge with self-assured leaders and self-righteous messiahs?

Some of these personalities appear to belong to the group to which Freud first referred, in a somewhat different context, as "the exceptions" (1916, pp. 311-315). Freud thought that some people can allow themselves immoral actions all their lives because they feel they have suffered an unjust punishment in childhood and have, therefore, ahead of time, expiated for their later misdeeds which they can now commit with inner impunity.[20]

Although, as stated earlier, messianic and charismatic persons are not likely to become willing subjects of the psychoanalyst's clinical scrutiny, I have encountered a number of patients in my psychoanalytic and psychotherapeutic practice who were close to the character type that I have here in mind. My clinical experience with such patients allows me to draw some tentative conclusions about the type of personality structure which may manifest charismatic and messianic features and, especially, about the genetic matrix which seems to favor the development of such personalities.

It is true that these persons appear to have no dynamically effective guilt feelings and that they never suffer any pangs of conscience about what they are doing. They are sensitive to injustices done to them, quick to accuse others—and very persuasive in the expression of their accusations—and thus they are able to evoke guilt feelings in others who tend to respond by becoming submissive to them and by allowing themselves to be treated tyrannically by them. As far as I could discern, however, underlying this behavior and these interpersonal effects, these persons do not primarily maintain the conviction of having already expiated for their present evilness in childhood. The dynamic essence of their current behavior appears to me to lie in a stunting of their empathic capacity: they understand neither the wishes nor the frustrations and disappointments of other people. At the same time, however, their sense of the legitimacy of their own wishes and their sensitivity to their own frustrations is intense.

[20]Freud describes the psychological state of Shakespeare's King Richard III, through the medium of an imaginary soliloquy about the consequences of being congenitally deformed, in the following words: "I have the right to be an exception, to disregard the scruples by which others let themselves be held back. I may do wrong myself, since wrong has been done to me" (1916, pp. 314-315).

Genetically important is the fact, as formulated in gross approximation, that these persons suffered early severe narcissistic injuries, mainly because of the unreliability and unpredictability of the empathic responses to them from the side either of the echoing-mirroring or of the idealized self-object. To be more specific: intense feelings of self-confidence obtained through echoing-mirroring responses (e.g., the empathic mother's proud smile) and intense feelings of security obtained through the merger with the omnipotent self-object (e.g., being held and carried empathically by the adult) seem in the childhood of these persons to have been followed by abrupt and unpredictable frustrations. The specific result of this specific trauma was that the developmental process of the gradual integration and neutralization of the archaic narcissistic structures was interrupted, and the child, perhaps with the aid of certain unusually strong congenital abilities in the realm of the maintenance of self-esteem (we might here speak with Hartmann of the primary autonomy of these functions), took over, prematurely and in toto, the functions which the archaic self-objects should still have performed for him. Thus we are not dealing with persons who have escaped guilt by prior expiation. These persons do not live in accordance with the standards of an inner world which is regulated by guilt feelings—rather they live in an archaic world which, as they experience it, has inflicted the ultimate narcissistic injury to them, i.e., in a world which has withdrawn its empathic contact from them after having first, as if to tease them, given them a taste of its security and its delights. They responded to this injury by becoming superempathic with themselves and with their own needs, and they have remained enraged about a world that has tried to take from them something that they consider to be rightfully their own: the response of the self-object, i.e., a part of the archaic self. Self-righteously they are themselves performing functions which the self-object was supposed to perform; they assert their own perfection, and they demand full control over the other person, who is needed by them as regulator of their self-esteem, without regard for his rights as an independent person. In other words, the prior injustice which they suffered was the abrupt withdrawal of narcissistic sustenance, and what the world judges to be their present misdeeds is to them the expression of justified narcissistic demands.

Since mixed cases may well be encountered most frequently, I will here venture the opinion, at the risk of being over-schematic, that those personalities who manifest charismatic strength and self-certainty (often coupled with self-righteously expressed self-pitying and hypochondriacal complaints) have suffered a traumatic withdrawal of empathy from the side of those self-objects who were expected to respond to the child's mirroring needs, while those with messianic features had suffered analogous disappointments from the side of the archaic idealized object. Furthermore, if we consider the effect of these traumata from the developmental point of view of social psychology, we can say that in both instances the withdrawal of the self-object led to a severe reduction of the educational power of the environment. If the needed narcissistic sustenance is self-righteously and angrily demanded, rather than having to be earned, then the object loses his leverage as an educational factor. It cannot exert its influence any longer in leading the child toward the gradual modification of its narcissistic demands, both in the sphere of the grandiose self and in the sphere of the archaic precursor of the internalized ideals.

4. Group Psychology and the Historical Process

The elucidation of the personality of the charismatic and messianic person, and of the psychological basis of the intense relationship which the followers of such a person establish with him, is an important task for the depth psychologist who, with the tools of psychoanalysis, attempts to investigate group processes and their effect on the dynamics of history. Although, within the confines of the present essay, I cannot illuminate the details of the interplay between the personality of a specific leader, the response of his followers, and the dynamics of the course of the correlated specific historical events, the psychoanalytic historian will have no trouble finding promising subjects for study in this area. I will briefly mention two examples here in order to clarify my meaning.

One of them, Daniel Schreber, a historically insignificant figure, is surely better known to the psychoanalyst than to the student of general history, since he was the father of a man whom Freud described in one of his great case histories; by contrast, the other one, Adolf Hitler, needs no introduction since he is known to everyone as one of the most fateful historical personalities of modern times.

Daniel Gottlob Moritz Schreber, the father of the *Senatsprasident* with dementia paranoides, was the leader of a very popular health cult. Like most leaders of cults and sects, he had absolute convictions within the area of his mission — in his case convictions within the area of health morality, i.e., of the importance of physical exercise, good posture, clean living, etc. — and his teachings received an enthusiastic response not only in Germany but also in other countries, e.g., in England. So far as I know, the dynamics of his influence on the numerous devoted followers of his cult have not been investigated but (thanks to the research done by Baumeyer [1956], Niederland [1951, 1959a, 1959b, 1960a, 1963], and others) we have a good deal of information about his unempathic and tyrannical treatment of his children, which seems to have constituted a decisive genetic factor in the development of his son's famous psychosis. And there is Hitler, in essence still enigmatic in his personality and in his seemingly irresistible effect on Germany. His convictions were absolute and, in certain areas, could not be questioned or modified. After a lonesome, hypochondriacal, self-doubting period as a young adult, he emerged with that new, rigid nucleus of immovable opinions which from that time on remained untouchable, whatever his changes and vacillations might be. He knew with complete certainty what was evil and had to be eradicated in this world of ours, and what was good and worth preserving. His utter certainty that the Jews were an evil and destructive element which had infected the clean and healthy body of the godlike German race was from then on the center of his being, and not only insured the maintenance of his own heightened self-esteem but invited the participation of the German nation in this blissful self-image through the merger with him.

Schreber's father and Hitler — and perhaps in some more or

less distantly related way personalities like Wilhelm Fliess—
different as they are, what do they have in common? They
seem to combine an absolute certainty concerning the power
of their selves and an absolute conviction concerning the
validity of their ideals with an equally absolute lack of
empathic understanding for large segments of feelings, needs,
and rights of other human beings and for the values cherished
by them. They understand the environment in which they live
only as an extension of their own narcissistic universe. They
understand others only insofar—but here with the keenest
empathy!—as they can serve as tools toward their narcissistic
ends or insofar as they are in the way of their purposes. It is
not likely that depth psychology will find effective means to
influence such persons, at least not those who present themselves in the arena of history. But the historian-analyst and the
analyst-historian may well be able to make contributions
which will not only increase our psychological grasp of the
personalities of such historical figures but will also provide
answers to the following two interrelated questions: How do
the characteristic psychological features of the messianic and
charismatic person dovetail with the widespread yearning for
archaic omnipotent figures? And what are the specific historical circumstances which tend to increase this yearning?

   To repeat: there may well be a wide gap which separates the
personality of such a near-unique historical figure as Hitler
from that of a not atypical founder of a common health cult
such as Daniel G. M. Schreber. And an even wider gap may
well separate personalities of the type of Schreber's father
from those of the type of Wilhelm Fliess. But future investigations of the personalities of these and other notable figures
who, in some historically significant setting, exerted their attraction on others—whether on whole nations, or on smaller
groups, or on single susceptible individuals in times of crisis—
may well be able to demonstrate also what they have in
common. Were there similar psychological features that made
all of them so irresistible? Similar traits that were the secret of
their adamant strength, their apparently all-knowing certainty? And did the effect which they had on others lead to
similar or analogous consequences? How did those fare—their
followers, their children—who could not extricate themselves

from the bonds to the charismatic or messianic figure who was their leader, their father? These and related questions will surely prove to be a worthy challenge for the psychoanalytic historian.[e]

Unhestitatingly we will also return here to one of the central themes touched upon over and over in the preceding pages: the relationship of Freud to Fliess during the period when Freud's self was enfeebled while it undertook a daring exploratory venture. Is this need, which arose in Freud during his courageous voyage into the unknown, related, if ever so distantly, to the need which populations feel who follow a charismatic leader, or even to the need of a hypochondriac who swears by the teachings of a health messiah? I think that we should entertain the thought, without misgivings and embarrassment, that there might well be a similar set of psychological factors active in all these relationships and that the time will come when we will be able to turn toward their exploration in depth, not only with regard to Freud's relationship to Fliess but perhaps also with regard to our own relationship to the figure of Freud.

I have now come to the end. I am keenly aware of the fact — which, I am certain, has not escaped the attention of the discerning reader — that the preceding presentation is tentative and speculative to an unusual degree. Instead of adducing a sufficient number of specific data — in particular, for example, data concerning Freud's experiences during his self-analysis, or data which would illuminate the personality of Wilhelm Fliess — I have relied largely on the internal logic and consistency of my ideas and on the indirect evidence of clinical phenomena which are analogous to those for which I gave no direct empirical support. This is a regrettable shortcoming which needs to be justified.

What was the essence of the task to which I addressed myself? Why did it have to be approached so tentatively? And

[e]Confirmatory evidence for one of the basic assumptions of Kohut's essay, his reconstruction of Fliess's personality as (latently) psychotic, has recently become available. In his letters to Jung (McGuire, 1974), Freud was unequivocal in his assessment of Fliess as a paranoid person: indeed, he stated that he had gained his conviction of those dynamics of paranoia which he elucidated by means of the example of Schreber as a result of his observations of Fliess in the course of their divergences.

what is the reason for the fact that it was carried out so incompletely?

The task is the application of psychoanalytic knowledge in the investigation of group psychology, with the specific aim of making a contribution to the explanation of historical events, of the course—or, expressed more courageously, the process—of history. I suspect that the seemingly most expedient application of analysis in this area, the investigation of individuals (even as exemplified by psychoanalytically highly sophisticated biographical studies), i.e., of the personalities of men who have exerted a decisive influence on the course of historical events, can make only a limited contribution to a scientifically valid explanation of history within the framework of depth psychology. I think rather that psychoanalysis must find novel approaches if it is to provide us with those more comprehensive explanations of historical phenomena which will increase man's mastery over his historical destiny. To be specific: in addition to the study of historical figures, the psychoanalytic historian must also undertake the study of historical processes, of the dynamics of historical events.

If the study of historical sequences is to be pursued successfully, however, it will have to be coordinated with a number of basic investigations of the social field. What I have in mind here specifically is the psychoanalytic study of (more or less large) groups: their formation, cohesion, fragmentation; or, stated in more specific terms, the circumstances which favor their formation, the nature of the psychological cement which holds them together, the psychological conditions under which they begin to manifest regressive behavior and begin to crumble, etc. It will have become obvious to those who are familiar with my recent work that I am suggesting, as a potentially fruitful approach to a complex problem, that we posit the existence of a certain psychological configuration with regard to the group—let us call it the "group self"[21]

[21] I believe that here we will find a depth-psychological approach to the scientific illumination of such currently ill-defined, impressionistic concepts as national character, and the like. The notion of a nationally, ethnically, or culturally determined "identity"—a "group identity"—must also be differentiated from the concept of a "group self." The considerations which apply to the differentiation of the analogous concepts in individual psychology are also valid in the present context (see Kohut [1970b], in particular, p. 177; and Kohut [1972], in particular,

— which is analogous to the self of the individual. We are then in a position to observe the group self as it is formed, as it is held together, as it oscillates between fragmentation and re-integration, as it shows regressive behavior when it moves toward fragmentation, etc.—all in analogy to phenomena of individual psychology to which we have comparatively easy access in the clinical (psychoanalytic) situation.

It is too early to say how successful this approach will be, but not too early to suggest that it should be tried. The difficulties are great, since the relevant depth-psychological data about the group self have to be obtained with the aid of a specific instrument of observation: introspection and empathy. It is with regard to the problem concerning the accessibility of such data that I will now turn to the psychoanalytic group again. (With renewed reluctance, I am reminded once more of the concept of a "psychoanalytic movement," but I must not shrink from it in the present nonevaluative context.) The history of the psychoanalytic movement—its formation, the crystallization and sequestration of dissident groups, its continuity despite changes—should, in a certain sense, constitute an excellent study topic for the psychoanalyst who pursues the investigation of group processes. Potentially at least—and I am making this statement in full awareness of the

---

on p. 368, the comparison between the "psychopathological events of late adolescence described by Erikson" and the vicissitudes of the self). The sense of a person's identity, whether he views himself as an individual or as belonging to a particular group, pertains to his conscious or preconscious awareness of the manifestations of a psychological surface configuration—it concerns a self-representation which relates to the conscious and preconscious goals and purposes of his ego and to the conscious and preconscious idealized values of his superego. The psychoanalytic concept of a self, however—whether it refers to the self of an individual or to the self of a person as a member of a group or, as a "group self," to the self of a stable association of people—concerns a structure which dips into the deepest reaches of the psyche. Indeed, I have become convinced that the pattern of an unconscious nuclear self (the central unconscious ambitions of the grandiose self and the central unconscious values of the internalized idealized parent imago) is of crucial importance with regard to that overriding sense of fulfillment or failure which characterizes a person's outlook on his life, to some extent independent of the presence or absence of neurotic conflict, suffering, symptom, or inhibition. And I am now suggesting that these considerations concerning the influence of the basic unconscious narcissistic configurations in individual existence are valid also with regard to the life of the group, i.e., that the basic patterns of a nuclear group self (the group's central ambitions and ideals) account not only for the continuity and the cohesion of the group but also determine its most important actions.

fact that my suggestion will undoubtedly be greeted with humor or sarcasm — this is the group with the greatest insight about itself. It is the group, in other words, which should be expected to supply the researcher with the maximum number of useful data relevant to the study of the nature of group cohesion and of the causes of group disintegration. Furthermore, there is no need to be defensive about the fact that the psychoanalytic community offers to the observer a rich field for the investigation of those behavioral phenomena (including the whole spectrum of the manifestations of narcissistic rage, specifically the aggressions of the members of the group against each other) which accompany group regressions.

There are, of course, many obstacles which stand in the way of an objective assessment of the psychoanalytic community by psychoanalysts. But the fact that such a self-study is difficult does not mean that it is impossible. I rather think it likely that despite the obvious difficulties (or, perhaps, because the difficulties are obvious, i.e., that we are so much aware of them) the self-investigation of the psychoanalytic community by analysts is more promising than analogous studies which could be undertaken by other groups.

When I speak here of the self-analysis of the psychoanalytic community, I am, of course, not contemplating a group enterprise. The psychological revelations which grow out of the matrix created by group meetings are obtained in consequence of the psychological regression which the immersion into the group imposes on the individual. Group pressure diminishes individuality; it leads to a primitivization of the mental processes, in particular to a partial paralysis of the ego and to a lowering of resistances. The diminution of the influence of the ego is then followed by the cathartic expression of archaic (or at any rate undisguised) impulses, emotions, and ideation, i.e., by the revelation of material which is not accessible in normal circumstances. The insights which I have in mind, however, cannot be obtained in a regressive atmosphere. The valid self-analysis of the psychoanalytic group — or of any group — must rest not only on the clear, nonregressive perception of archaic psychological experiences which arise within the group; it also requires the intellectual and emotional mastery of this material. The validity of the insights obtained will be demonstrated by the fact that the pressure to act out (especially to act out angrily, the principal symptom of group psychopathology) will be diminished within the group. The individual who wishes to make decisive steps toward new depth-psychological insights concerning the group must therefore be able to remain deeply and directly involved in the group processes—but instead of acting them out, he must be able to tolerate the tension of seeming passivity: all his energies must be withdrawn from participating action and concentrated on participating thought. Only if he can maintain full emotional participation with the group processes of his own group yet channel all his energies toward his cognitive functions (specifically (a) the gathering of data through empathic observation and (b) the subsequent explanation of the observed data)—only then will he be able to make those decisive discoveries and obtain those crucial new insights which will deepen our understanding of the behavior of the group and its members.

Group processes are largely activated by narcissistic motives. We may therefore hope that the fact that training analysts are now paying increasing attention to the narcissistic dimensions of the personality of analytic candidates will have favorable results in the area under discussion. The strengthened ego dominance over the narcissistic sector of their personalities which future generations of analysts will obtain may, in particular, be expected to facilitate the investigation of group processes within the psychoanalytic community. And we may also assume that one or another specifically gifted individual psychoanalyst will be aided in his specific investigations concerning the influence of narcissistic motives on the behavior of the psychoanalytic community by the insights which his training analysis had given him with regard to his own narcissistic strivings.

Among the various areas which will have to be studied within the context of the psychological self-scrutiny of the psychoanalytic community, the (changing) significance of the figure of Freud for the group will prove to occupy a place of paramount importance. But the time is not quite ripe for such an undertaking. Conscious hesitations, dictated by considerations of tact and decorum, as well as unconscious inhibitions still interfere too strongly with our ability to maintain that degree of objectivity which is required if we wish through the creative act of the group's self-analysis to make a valid contribution to psychoanalytic group psychology and to the psychology of the historical process. But I also think—and here I will refrain from spelling out even some of the reasons of which I am aware on which I am basing my conclusion— that, measured by the yardstick of history, the time is not far off when psychoanalysts will indeed be able to undertake such studies with the hope of reaching objectively valid conclusions.

I am therefore justifying the presentation of this speculative and tentative essay by saying that it should be considered as a blueprint for the future. Clearly, I believe that my suggestions concerning the meaning of Freud's self-analysis and, more specifically, concerning the significance which Wilhelm Fliess had for Freud during his self-analysis, will be corroborated by the detailed work of the future analytic historian who will look upon "the origins of psychoanalysis" with a fresh eye. Although his task will remain a difficult one—i.e., he will have to reconstruct complex psychological situations across a wide gap of time on the basis of data culled from written documents[22]—his inner readiness for it will be greater than ours and the emotional atmosphere of the social circumstances in which he will perform it will be more propitious than that in which we live. The assessment of Freud's psychological state at the peak of his creative life, the scrutiny of Fliess's personality, and above all the investigation of the role which the figure of Freud played in shaping the history of the psychoanalytic community (and thus in shaping the development of the science of psychoanalysis): these are tasks which must be undertaken by future generations of analysts—perhaps already by the next one—with that favorable mixture of empathic closeness and scientific detachment that is not yet available to the psychoanalyst of our day.

[22]The collection of historical material concerning the history of psychoanalysis undertaken by the Sigmund Freud Archives will be of inestimable value for future researchers in many of the areas referred to in this essay.

In view of the fact that here, at the very end of my reflections, I have contemplated the possibility that the community of psychoanalytic scholars might someday, in a not-too-distant tomorrow, undertake, through the work of some of its creative thinkers, the task of a self-scrutiny in depth of the psychoanalytic community itself, I will close with a few remarks on the nature of scientific progress in psychoanalysis.

It is my opinion that decisive progress in man's knowledge of himself is not primarily a cognitive feat but that it is achieved mainly as a consequence of what, expressed in everyday language, must be called an act of courage. Pioneering discoveries in depth psychology require not only a keen intellect but also characterological strength, because they are in essence based on the relinquishment of infantile wishes (see in this context Freud, 1932b) and on the discarding of illusions which have protected us against anxiety. I have little doubt that, even in fields outside of the investigation of complex psychological states, pioneering discoveries require an analogous measure of courage.[23] But I would assume that his cognitive detachment toward the physical universe which he investigates protects a physicist, for example, or an astronomer, from the kind of fear which the depth psychologist experiences when he, alone, is face to face with unpleasant psychological reality. I would at least claim that this assumption is valid in our day, when scientific findings in the physical and biological sciences are not effectively opposed on moral grounds any more.

But be that as it may in these other branches of human knowledge, I am certain that decisive progress in the area of

[23] These views are in harmony with Freud's opinion (1917b) that the discoveries of Copernicus and Darwin, like his own, constituted severe blows to the narcissism of man. These discoveries, I will add, rested first and foremost on the courageous overcoming of inner resistances, because the discoverers had to deprive themselves of an illusion which had protected them against coming face to face with the painful recognition of the relative smallness and insignificance of their selves. It must not be forgotten, furthermore, that attacks on grandiose fantasies elicit dangerous narcissistic rage against the offender (see Kohut, 1972). In addition to their inner strength, therefore, the three great discoverers had to be able to muster considerable social courage when they communicated their findings to their contemporaries, whose wrath, as they undoubtedly anticipated at least preconsciously, they would now have to face.

depth psychology is tied to personal acts of courage by the investigator who suffers not only anxiety but tends to be maligned and ostracized. It is, therefore, not an accident that one of the greatest steps of individual psychology, a gigantic advance toward the scientific understanding of the inner life of the individual, was made as the result of the victorious outcome of the grueling process of one man's inner struggles, Freud's creative self-analysis. Could it be that the analogous step in group psychology, the decisive advance toward a valid depth-psychological understanding of the experiences and actions of the group, will be the result of a similarly courageous self-scrutiny of the psychoanalytic community by itself? I must leave this question open. I know that the future cannot be predicted with any degree of reliability by analogy with the past, that the success of Freud's genius in the field of individual psychology may not be repeatable with regard to the field of group psychology, despite the intense efforts of future analysts. But of one thing I am convinced: should any group ever be able to overcome its inner resistances and thus make a decisive step toward the understanding of the dynamics of its behavior, the nature and development of its group self, and the genetics of its conflicts and of the oscillations of its self— should a group ever be able to succeed in these tasks, it will have laid the foundations for a valid psychological understanding of history.

REFERENCES

Abraham, H., & Freud, E., eds. (1966), *A Psycho-Analytic Dialogue: The Letters of Sigmund Freud and Karl Abraham, 1907-1926.* New York: Basic Books.

Abraham, K. (1912), Amenhotep IV. Psycho-Analytical Contributions towards the Understanding of His Personality and of the Monotheistic Cult of Aton. *Selected Papers,* Vol. 2. New York: Basic Books, 1955, pp. 262-290.

——— (1922), Father-Murder and Father-Rescue in the Fantasies of Neurotics. In: *The Psychoanalytic Reader,* ed. R. Fliess. New York: International Universities Press, 1948, pp. 334-342.

Adams, M., & Neel, J. (1966), Study from the Institute of Human Genetics. *Med. Trib.,* June 13.

Alexander, F., Eisenstein, S., & Grotjahn, M., eds. (1966), *Psychoanalytic Pioneers.* New York: Basic Books.

Amacher, P. (1965), Freud's Neurological Education and Its Influence on Psychoanalytic Theory. *Psychol. Issues,* Monogr. No. 16. New York: International Universities Press.

Anderson, O. (1962), *Studies in the Prehistory of Psychoanalysis.* Stockholm: Norstedts.

Bakan, D. (1958), *Sigmund Freud and the Jewish Mystical Tradition.* Princeton, N.J.: Van Nostrand.

Balint, M. (1958), Letter to the Editor. *Internat. J. Psycho-Anal.,* 39:68.

Barea, I. (1966), *Vienna.* New York: Knopf.

Barry, M., & Johnson, A. (1958), The Incest Barrier. *Psychoanal. Quart.,* 27:485-500.

Baumeyer, F. (1956), The Schreber Case. *Internat. J. Psycho-Anal.,* 37:61-74.

Becker, H. K. (1963), Carl Koller and Cocaine. *Psychoanal. Quart.,* 32:309-373.

Bell, A. (1947), *Cervantes.* Norman: University of Oklahoma Press.

Bellak, L. (1961), Free Association: Conceptual and Clinical Aspects. *Internat. J. Psycho-Anal.,* 42:9-20.

Bentley, G. (1961), *Shakespeare: A Biographical Handbook.* New Haven: Yale University Press.

Beres, D. (1965), Psychoanalysis, Science and Romanticism. In: *Drives, Affects, Behavior,* Vol. 2, ed. M. Schur. New York: International Universities Press, pp. 397-417.

Berger, A. von (1896), Chirurgie der Seele. *Psychoanal. Beweg.,* 4:73-76, 1932.

Bernays, M. (1892), Zur Lehre von den Citaten und Noten. In: *Schriften zur Kritik und Litteraturgeschichte,* Vol. 4. Berlin: Behr, 1903.

Bernfeld, S. (1944), Freud's Earliest Theories and the School of Helmholtz. *Psychoanal. Quart.,* 13:341-362.

Bernfeld, S. C. (1951), Freud and Archeology. *Amer. Imago,* 8:107-127.

Blau, A. (1952), In Support of Freud's Syndrome of "Actual" Anxiety Neurosis. *Internat. J. Psycho-Anal.,* 33:363-372.

Bleuler, E. (1916), *Textbook of Psychiatry.* New York: Dover, 1951.

Blos, P. (1962), *On Adolescence.* Glencoe & New York: Free Press.

Bonaparte, M. (1934), *The Life and Works of Edgar Allan Poe; A Psychoanalytic Interpretation.* London: Imago, 1949.

Börne, L. (1823), Die Kunst, in drei Tagen ein Original-Schriftsteller zu Werden. *Gesammelte Schriften.* Hamburg: Hoffman & Kampe, 1840, pp. 231-235.

Bouillier, V. (1921), *La Renommée des Montaigne en Allemagne.* Paris.

Bowring, E. (1910), *The Poems of Schiller.* London: Bell.

Brenan, G. (1969), Cervantes. In: *Cervantes—A Collection of Critical Essays,* ed. L. Nelson. Englewood Cliffs, N.J.: Prentice-Hall, pp. 13-33.

Breuer, J. (1888-1889), Neue Versuche an den Ohrbogengängen. *Arch. Ges. Physiol.*, 44:135-152.
———— (1907), Bemerkungen zu Dr. Hans Abels Abhandlung "Über Nachempfindungen im Gebiete des Kinesthetischen und Sinnes." *Z. Psychol. Physiol. Sinnesorg.*, 45:78-84.
————, & Freud, S. (1893-1895), Studies on Hysteria. *Standard Edition*, 2. London: Hogarth Press, 1955.
Brunswick, R. (1928), A Supplement to Freud's *History of an Infantile Neurosis.* In: *The Psychoanalytic Reader,* ed. R. Fliess. New York: International Universities Press, 1948, pp. 86-128.
Büchmann, C. (1964), *Geflügelte Worte,* 31st ed. Berlin: Haude und Spenersche Verlagsbuchhandlung.
Burton, L. (1965), The Assaulted Child. *New Society,* 138:1.
Butler, E. (1935), *The Tyranny of Greece over Germany.* New York: Macmillan.
Buxbaum, E. (1951), Freud's Dream Interpretation in the Light of His Letters to Fliess. *Bull. Menninger Clin.,* 15:197-212.
Byrne, M. (1960), The Social Background. In: *A Companion to Shakespeare Studies,* ed. H. Granville-Barker & G. Harrison. New York: Doubleday Anchor Books, pp. 186-219.
Chambers, E. (1930), *William Shakespeare: A Study of Facts and Problems,* 2 vols. Oxford: Clarendon Press.
Charcot, J. (1877-1889), *Clinical Lectures on Diseases of the Nervous System,* 3 vols. London: New Sydenham Society.
Churchill, R. (1958), *Shakespeare and His Betters.* Bloomington: Indiana University Press.
Chute, M. (1949), *Shakespeare of London.* New York: Dutton.
Cranefield, P. (1958), Josef Breuer's Evaluation of His Contribution to Psycho-Analysis. *Internat. J. Psycho-Anal.,* 39:319-322.
———— (1966), Freud and the "School of Helmholtz." *Cesnerus,* 23:35-39.
Decker, H. (1971), The Medical Reception of Psychoanalysis in Germany, 1894-1907: Three Brief Studies. *Bull. Hist. Med.,* 45:468-481.
de Kleijn, A. (1926), Josef Breuer. *Acta Otolaryng.,* 10:167-171.
Demant, V. (1962), John Thomas Looney (1870-1944). *Shakespeare Authorship Rev.,* 8:8-9.
Descartes, R. (1637), Discourse on Method. In: *Modern Classical Philosophers,* 2nd ed., ed. B. Rand. Cambridge: Riverside Press, 1936.
Dickes, R. (1965), The Defensive Function of an Altered State of Consciousness: A Hypnoid State. *J. Amer. Psychoanal. Assn.,* 13:356-403.
Doryon, Y. (1940), *Lynkeus' New State.* Introductions by S. Freud & A. Einstein. Jerusalem: Rubin Mass.
———— (1946), *Ha-Isch Mosche.* Jerusalem: Masda.
Dukes, G. (1915), Ein Fall von Kryptomnesis. *Internat. Z. Psychoanal.,* 3:40-41.
Eckermann, J. P. (1836-1848), *Conversations with Goethe,* trans. J. Oxenford. London: Dent, 1930.
Edwards, P., ed. (1967), *The Encyclopedia of Philosophy,* 6:401-407. New York: Macmillan & Free Press.
Einstein, A. (1931), The World as I See It. In: *Ideas and Opinions.* New York: Crown, 1954.
Eissler, K. R. (1961), *Leonardo da Vinci: Psychoanalytic Notes on the Enigma.* New York: International Universities Press.
———— (1963), *Goethe: A Psychoanalytic Study.* Detroit: Wayne State University Press.
———— (1964), Mankind at Its Best. *J. Amer. Psychoanal. Assn.,* 12:187-222.
———— (1966a), *Medical Orthodoxy and the Future of Psychoanalysis.* New York: International Universities Press.

———— (1966b), *Sigmund Freud und die Wiener Universität.* Bern: Hans Huber.
———— (1967), Psychopathology and Creativity. *Amer. Imago,* 24:35-81.
———— (1968), The Relation of Explaining and Understanding in Psychoanalysis. *The Psychoanalytic Study of the Child,* 23:141-177. New York: International Universities Press.
———— (1971a), *Discourse on Hamlet and "Hamlet."* New York: International Universities Press.
———— (1971b), *Talent and Genius.* New York: Quadrangle.
———— (1972), To Muriel M. Gardiner on her 70th Birthday. *Bull. Phila. Assn. Psychoanal.,* 22:110-130.
———— (1974), Über Freuds Freundschaft mit Wilhelm Fliess nebst einem Anhang über Freuds Adoleszenz und einer Historischen Bemerkung über Freuds Jugendstil. *Jahrb. Psychoanal.,* 2:39-100.
Elkisch, P. (1957), The Psychological Significance of the Mirror. *J. Amer. Psychoanal. Assn.,* 5:235-244.
Ellenberger, H. (1965), Charcot and the Salpêtrière School. *Amer. J. Psychother.,* 19:243-267.
———— (1966), Review of *Bertha Pappenheim: Leben und Schriften,* by D. Edinger. *J. Hist. Behav. Sci.,* 2:94-96.
———— (1970), *The Discovery of the Unconscious.* New York: Basic Books.
Ellis, H. (1919), Psycho-Analysis in Relation to Sex. *The Philosophy of Conflict and Other Essays in Wartime,* Second Series. London: Constable.
Encyclopedia Judaica (1971), Jerusalem & New York: Encyclopedia Judaica & Macmillan.
Erasmus, D. (1487-1535), Selected Letters. In: *Erasmus and the Age of the Reformation,* by J. Huizinga. New York: Harper Torchbooks, 1957.
———— (1511), *The Praise of Folly.* New York: Modern Library, 1941.
Erikson, E. H. (1955), Freud's "The Origins of Psycho-Analysis." *Internat. J. Psycho-Anal.,* 36:1-15.
———— (1956), The Problem of Ego Identity. *J. Amer. Psychoanal. Assn.,* 4:56-121.
Federn, P. (1933), Obituary, Sándor Ferenczi. *Internat. J. Psycho-Anal.,* 14:467-485.
Feldman, A. (1953), The Confessions of William Shakespeare. *Amer. Imago,* 10:135-166.
Fenichel, O. (1945), *The Psychoanalytic Theory of Neurosis.* New York: Norton.
Ferenczi, S. (1908-1914), *Contributions to Psychoanalysis,* 2nd ed., retitled *Sex in Psychoanalysis.* New York: Basic Books, 1950.
———— (1908-1926), *Further Contributions to the Theory and Technique of Psychoanalysis,* 2nd ed. New York: Basic Books, 1952.
———— (1908-1933a), *Bausteine zur Psychoanalyse,* Vols. 1 & 2. Leipzig/Wien/Zürich: Internationaler Psychoanalytischer Verlag, 1927; Vols. 3 & 4. Bern: Hans Huber, 1939.
———— (1908-1933b), Ten Letters to Freud. *Internat. J. Psycho-Anal.,* 30:243-246, 1949.
———— (1908-1933c), *Final Contributions to the Problems and Methods of Psychoanalysis.* New York: Basic Books, 1955.
———— (1920), Supplement to "The Psychogenesis of Mechanism." *Further Contributions to the Theory and Technique of Psychoanalysis.* New York: Basic Books, 1952, pp. 393-396.
———— (1924), *Thalassa: A Theory of Genitality.* Albany: Psychoanalytic Quarterly, 1938.
———— (1927), Review of O. Rank's *Technique of Psycho-Analysis. Internat. J. Psycho-Anal.,* 8:93.
———— (1933), Confusion of Tongues between Adults and the Child. *Final Contributions to the Problems and Methods of Psychoanalysis.* New York: Basic Books, 1955, pp. 156-167.

_____, Abraham, K., Simmel, E., & Jones, E. (1919), *Psychoanalysis and the War Neuroses*. London: International Psycho-Analytic Press, 1921.

_____, & Rank, O. (1924), *The Development of Psychoanalysis*. New York & Washington: Nervous and Mental Disease Publishing Co.

Flatter, R. (1951), Sigmund Freud on Shakespeare. *Shakespeare Quart.*, 2:368-369.

Fleming, J., et al. (1958), The Influence of Parent Loss in Childhood on Personality Development. Presented at the meetings of the American Psychoanalytic Association, May.

_____, & Altschul, S. (1963), Activation of Mourning and Growth by Psychoanalysis. *Internat. J. Psycho-Anal.*, 44:419-431.

Flournoy, T. (1900), *From India to the Planet Mars: A Study of a Case of Somnambulism with Glossolalia*. New York & London: Harper.

Frame, D. (1955), *Montaigne's Discovery of Man*. New York: Columbia University Press.

Frenkel-Brunswik, E. (1940), Psychoanalysis and Personality Research. Selected Papers, ed. N. Heiman & J. Grant. *Psychol. Issues*, Monogr. No. 31:36-57. New York: International Universities Press, 1974.

Freud, A. (1936), *The Ego and the Mechanisms of Defence*. New York: International Universities Press, 1946.

Freud, E., ed. (1960), *The Letters of Sigmund Freud, 1873-1939*. New York: Basic Books.

Freud, M. (1957), *Glory Reflected*. London: Hagus & Robertson.

Freud, S. (1872-1874), Some Early Unpublished Letters of Freud. *Internat. J. Psycho-Anal.*, 50:419-427, 1969.

_____(1886), Report of My Studies in Paris and Berlin. *Standard Edition*, 1:3-17. London: Hogarth Press, 1966.

_____(1887-1902), *The Origins of Psychoanalysis: Letters to Wilhelm Fliess, Drafts and Notes, 1887-1902*. New York: Basic Books, 1954.

_____(1888a), Hysteria. *Standard Edition*, 1:41-57. London: Hogarth Press, 1966.

_____(1888b), Preface to the Translation of Bernheim's *Suggestion*. *Standard Edition*, 1:75-85. London: Hogarth Press, 1966.

_____(1892-1893), A Case of Successful Treatment by Hypnotism. *Standard Edition*, 1:115-128. London: Hogarth Press, 1966.

_____(1892-1894), Preface and Footnotes to Charcot's *Tuesday Lectures*. *Standard Edition*, 1:133-143. London: Hogarth Press, 1966.

_____(1893a), Some Points for a Comparative Study of Organic and Hysterical Motor Paralyses. *Standard Edition*, 1:157-172. London: Hogarth Press, 1966.

_____(1893b), Charcot. *Standard Edition*, 3:11-23. London: Hogarth Press, 1962.

_____(1895a), On the Grounds for Detaching a Particular Syndrome from Neurasthenia under the Description 'Anxiety Neurosis.' *Standard Edition*, 3:92-115. London: Hogarth Press, 1962.

_____(1895b), A Reply to Criticisms of My Paper on Anxiety Neurosis. *Standard Edition*, 3:123-139. London: Hogarth Press, 1962.

_____(1895c), Project for a Scientific Psychology. *The Origins of Psychoanalysis: Letters to Wilhelm Fliess, Drafts and Notes: 1887-1902*. New York: Basic Books, 1954, pp. 347-445.

_____(1896a), Further Remarks on the Neuropsychoses of Defence. *Standard Edition*, 3:163-185. London: Hogarth Press, 1962.

_____(1896b), The Aetiology of Hysteria. *Standard Edition*, 3:191-221. London: Hogarth Press, 1962.

_____(1897), Abstracts of the Scientific Writings of Dr. Sigmund Freud. *Standard Edition*, 3:225-260. London: Hogarth Press, 1962.

_____(1898a), Sexuality in the Aetiology of Neuroses. *Standard Edition*, 3:263-

285. London: Hogarth Press, 1962.

———(1898b), The Psychical Mechanism of Forgetfulness. *Standard Edition,* 3:287-297. London: Hogarth Press, 1962.

———(1899), Screen Memories. *Standard Edition,* 3:301-322. London: Hogarth Press, 1962.

———(1900), The Interpretations of Dreams. *Standard Edition,* 4 & 5. London: Hogarth Press, 1953.

———(1901), The Psychopathology of Everyday Life. *Standard Edition,* 6. London: Hogarth Press, 1960.

———(1904), Freud's Psycho-Analytic Procedure. *Standard Edition,* 7:249-256. London: Hogarth Press, 1953.

———(1905a), Psychical (or Mental) Treatment. *Standard Edition,* 7:283-304. London: Hogarth Press, 1953.

———(1905b), Jokes and Their Relation to the Unconscious. *Standard Edition,* 8. London: Hogarth Press, 1960.

———(1905c), Three Essays on the Theory of Sexuality. *Standard Edition,* 7:125-243. London: Hogarth Press, 1953.

———(1905d), Fragment of an Analysis of a Case of Hysteria. *Standard Edition,* 7:7-122. London: Hogarth Press, 1953.

———(1905-1906), Psychopathic Characters on the Stage. *Standard Edition,* 7:305-310. London: Hogarth Press, 1953.

———(1906), My Views on the Part Played by Sexuality in the Aetiology of the Neuroses. *Standard Edition,* 7:271-279. London: Hogarth Press, 1953.

———(1907), Delusions and Dreams in Jensen's *Gradiva. Standard Edition,* 9:3-98. London: Hogarth Press, 1959.

———(1908), Creative Writers and Day-Dreaming. *Standard Edition,* 9:41-153. London: Hogarth Press, 1959.

———(1909a), Some General Remarks on Hysterical Attacks. *Standard Edition,* 9:229-234. London: Hogarth Press, 1959.

———(1909b), Analysis of a Phobia in a Five-Year-Old Boy. *Standard Edition,* 10:5-149. London: Hogarth Press, 1955.

———(1909c), Family Romances. *Standard Edition,* 9:235-241. London: Hogarth Press, 1959.

———(1909d), Notes upon a Case of Obsessional Neurosis. *Standard Edition,* 10:153-250. London: Hogarth Press, 1955.

———(1910a), Five Lectures on Psycho-Analysis. *Standard Edition,* 11:9-55. London: Hogarth Press, 1957.

———(1910b), Leonardo da Vinci and a Memory of His Childhood. *Standard Edition,* 11:59-138. London: Hogarth Press, 1957.

———(1910c), A Special Type of Choice of Object Made by Men (Contributions to the Psychology of Love I). *Standard Edition,* 11:163-175. London: Hogarth Press, 1957.

———(1910d), The Psycho-Analytic View of Psychogenic Disturbance of Vision. *Standard Edition,* 11:211-218. London: Hogarth Press, 1957.

———(1910e), 'Wild' Psycho-Analysis. *Standard Edition,* 11:221-227. London: Hogarth Press, 1957.

———(1911), Psycho-Analytic Notes on an Autobiographical Account of a Case of Paranoia (Dementia Paranoides). *Standard Edition,* 12:3-84. London: Hogarth Press, 1958.

———(1911-1915), Papers on Technique. *Standard Edition,* 12:85-174. London: Hogarth Press, 1958.

———(1912), Contributions to a Discussion on Masturbation. *Standard Edition,* 12:243-254. London: Hogarth Press, 1958.

———(1912-1913), Totem and Taboo. *Standard Edition,* 13:1-164. London: Hogarth Press, 1955.

_____(1913), The Theme of the Three Caskets. *Standard Edition,* 12:289-301. London: Hogarth Press, 1958.

_____(1914a), The Moses of Michelangelo. *Standard Edition,* 13:211-236. London: Hogarth Press, 1955.

_____(1914b), On Narcissism: An Introduction. *Standard Edition,* 14:73-102. London: Hogarth Press, 1957.

_____(1914c), On the History of the Psycho-Analytic Movement. *Standard Edition,* 14:3-66. London: Hogarth Press, 1957.

_____(1914d), Some Reflections on Schoolboy Psychology. *Standard Edition,* 13:241-244. London: Hogarth Press, 1955.

_____(1915), Thoughts for the Times on War and Death. *Standard Edition,* 14:274-301. London: Hogarth Press, 1957.

_____(1916), Some Character Types Met with in Psycho-Analytic Work. *Standard Edition,* 14:310-355. London: Hogarth Press, 1957.

_____(1916-1917), Introductory Lectures on Psycho-Analysis. *Standard Edition,* 15 & 16. London: Hogarth Press, 1963.

_____(1917a), Mourning and Melancholia. *Standard Edition,* 14:243-260. London: Hogarth Press, 1957.

_____(1917b), A Difficulty in the Path of Psycho-Analysis. *Standard Edition,* 17:137-144. London: Hogarth Press, 1955.

_____(1918), From the History of an Infantile Neurosis. *Standard Edition,* 17:7-122. London: Hogarth Press, 1955.

_____(1919), The Uncanny. *Standard Edition,* 17:217-256. London: Hogarth Press, 1955.

_____(1920a), A Note on the Prehistory of the Technique of Analysis. *Standard Edition,* 18:263-265. London: Hogarth Press, 1955.

_____(1920b), Beyond the Pleasure Principle. *Standard Edition,* 18:3-66. London: Hogarth Press, 1955.

_____(1921a), Group Psychology and the Analysis of the Ego. *Standard Edition,* 18:67-144. London: Hogarth Press, 1955.

_____(1921b), Psycho-Analysis and Telepathy. *Standard Edition,* 18:175-194. London: Hogarth Press, 1955.

_____(1922), Dreams and Telepathy. *Standard Edition,* 18:196-219. London: Hogarth Press, 1955.

_____(1923a), Two Encyclopaedia Articles. *Standard Edition,* 18:234-261. London: Hogarth Press, 1955.

_____(1923b), The Ego and the Id. *Standard Edition,* 19:3-67. London: Hogarth Press, 1961.

_____(1923c), Josef Popper-Lynkeus and the Theory of Dreams. *Standard Edition,* 19:261-263. London: Hogarth Press, 1961.

_____(1923d), Letter to Señor Luis Lopez-Ballesteros y de Torres. *Standard Edition,* 19:289. London: Hogarth Press, 1961.

_____(1923e), Dr. Sàndor Ferenczi (on his 50th Birthday). *Standard Edition,* 19:266-271. London: Hogarth Press, 1961.

_____(1925a), Letter to the Editor of the Jewish Press Center in Zürich. *Standard Edition,* 19:291. London: Hogarth Press, 1961.

_____(1925b), An Autobiographical Study. *Standard Edition,* 20:3-74. London: Hogarth Press, 1959.

_____(1925c), Josef Breuer. *Standard Edition,* 19:278-282. London: Hogarth Press, 1961.

_____(1925d), The Resistances to Psycho-Analysis. *Standard Edition,* 19:213-222. London: Hogarth Press, 1961.

_____(1926a), Inhibitions, Symptoms and Anxiety. *Standard Edition,* 20:77-178. London: Hogarth Press, 1959.

_____(1926b), Psycho-Analysis. *Standard Edition,* 20:263-270. London: Hogarth

Press, 1959.
_____(1926c), Address to the Society of B'Nai Brith. *Standard Edition,* 20:272-276. London: Hogarth Press, 1959.
_____(1927a), The Future of an Illusion. *Standard Edition,* 21:3-57. London: Hogarth Press, 1961.
_____(1927b), Fetishism. *Standard Edition,* 21:149-158. London: Hogarth Press, 1961.
_____(1930a), Civilization and Its Discontents. *Standard Edition,* 21:59-147. London: Hogarth Press, 1961.
_____(1930b), The Goethe Prize. *Standard Edition,* 21:208-212. London: Hogarth Press, 1961.
_____(1932a), My Contact with Josef Popper-Lynkeus. *Standard Edition,* 22:219-224. London: Hogarth Press, 1964.
_____(1932b), The Acquisition and Control of Fire. *Standard Edition,* 22:187-193. London: Hogarth Press, 1964.
_____(1933a), New Introductory Lectures on Psycho-Analysis. *Standard Edition,* 22:3-183. London: Hogarth Press, 1964.
_____(1933b), Sàndor Ferenczi. *Standard Edition,* 22:226-232. London: Hogarth Press, 1964.
_____(1935), Postscript to An Autobiographical Study. *Standard Edition,* 20:71-74. London: Hogarth Press, 1959.
_____(1936), A Disturbance of Memory on the Acropolis. *Standard Edition,* 22:238-249. London: Hogarth Press, 1964.
_____(1937), Analysis Terminable and Interminable. *Standard Edition,* 23:211-254. London: Hogarth Press, 1964.
_____(1938), Findings, Ideas, Problems. *Standard Edition,* 23:299-300. London: Hogarth Press, 1964.
_____(1939), Moses and Monotheism. *Standard Edition,* 23:3-139. London: Hogarth Press, 1964.
_____(1940a), An Outline of Psycho-Analysis. *Standard Edition,* 23:141-207. London: Hogarth Press, 1964.
_____(1940b), Splitting of the Ego in the Process of Defence. *Standard Edition,* 23:273-278. London: Hogarth Press, 1964.
_____(1940c), Introduction to Y. Doryon, *Lynkeus' New State.* Jerusalem: Rubin Mass.
_____, & Bullitt, W. (1967), *Thomas Woodrow Wilson.* Boston: Houghton Mifflin.
Friedrich, H. (1940), *Montaigne.* Bern: Francke.
Frosch, J. (1959), Transference and Family Romance. *J. Amer. Psychoanal. Assn.,* 7:503-522.
Gedo, J. E. (1970), Thoughts on the Art in the Age of Freud. *J. Amer. Psychoanal. Assn.,* 18:219-245.
_____(1972a), The Dream of Reason Produces Monsters. *J. Amer. Psychoanal. Assn.,* 20:199-223.
_____(1972b), On the Psychology of Genius. *Internat. J. Psycho-Anal.,* 53:199-203.
_____(1972c), Caviare to the General. *Amer. Imago,* 29:293-317.
_____(1972d), Panel Report: The Methodology of Psychoanalytic Biography. *J. Amer. Psychoanal. Assn.,* 20:638-649.
_____(1973), Kant's Way: The Psychoanalytic Contribution of David Rapaport. *Psychoanal. Quart.,* 42:409-434.
_____(1974), Review of Sigmund Freud and Lou Andreas-Salomé Letters. *J. Amer. Psychoanal. Assn.,* 22:211-218.
_____(in preparation), *Magna Est Vis Veritatis Tuae et Praevalebit.*
_____, & Goldberg, A. (1973), *Models of the Mind: A Psychoanalytic Theory.* Chicago: University of Chicago Press.

_____, & Pollock, G. H. (1967), The Question of Research in Psychoanalytic Technique. In: Psychoanalytic Techniques, ed. B. Wolman. New York: Basic Books, pp. 560-581.

Gedo, M. M. (1972), Picasso's Self Image. Unpublished doctoral dissertation, Northwestern University.

_____(in preparation), Picasso: The Psychology of His Life and Art.

Gibson, H. (1962), The Shakespeare Claimants. London: Methuen.

Glauber, I. (1958), Freud's Contributions on Stuttering: Their Relation to Some Current Insights. J. Amer. Psychoanal. Assn., 6:326-347.

Goethe, J. (1780), Essay on Nature. In: Maxims and Reflections of Goethe, trans. T. Bailey. New York: Saunders, 1893, pp. 207-213.

Grene, D., & Lattimore, R., eds. (1959), Sophocles. Chicago: University of Chicago Press.

Guillain, G. (1959), J. M. Charcot, 1825-1895, His Life—His Work, ed. & trans. P. Bailey. New York: Hoeber.

Handlin, O. (1967), Jews in the Culture of Middle Europe. In: Studies of the Leo Baeck Institute, ed. M. Kreutzberger. New York: Unger, pp. 159-175.

Harrison, I. (1966), A Reconsideration of Freud's "A Disturbance of Memory on the Acropolis" in Relation to Identity Disturbance. J. Amer. Psychoanal. Assn., 14:518-527.

Hartmann, H. (1939), Ego Psychology and the Problem of Adaptation. New York: International Universities Press, 1958.

_____, Kris, E., & Loewenstein, R. (1946), Comments on the Formation of Psychic Structure. Papers on Psychoanalytic Psychology. Psychol. Issues, Monogr. No. 14:27-55. New York: International Universities Press, 1964.

Havens, L. (1966), Charcot and Hysteria. J. Nerv. Ment. Dis., 141:505-516.

Hering, E., & Breuer, J. (1868), Study of Respiratory Physiology. Sitzungsb. Akad. Wissensch. (Wien), 57:672; 58:909.

Hilgard, J. (1953), Anniversary Reactions in Parents Precipitated by Children. Psychiatry, 16:73-80.

_____(1969), Depressive and Psychotic States as Anniversaries to Sibling Death in Childhood. Internat. Psychiat. Clin., 6:197-211.

_____, & Newman, M. (1959), Anniversaries in Mental Illnesses. Psychiatry, 22:113-121.

Hoffman, C. (1955), The Man Who Was Shakespeare. New York & London.

Holland, N. (1961), Freud on Shakespeare. Publications in the Humanities, No. 47. Department of Humanities, M.I.T.

Holt, R. (1962), A Critical Examination of Freud's Concept of Bound vs. Free Cathexis. J. Amer. Psychoanal. Assn., 10:475-525.

Holzman, P. S. (1959), A Note on Breuer's Hypnoidal Theory of Neurosis. Bull. Menninger Clin., 23:144-147.

Housman, A. (1940), Collected Poems. London: Cape.

Huizinga, J. (1924), Erasmus and the Age of the Reformation. New York: Harper Torchbooks, 1957.

Hutten, E. (1962), The Origins of Science: An Inquiry into the Foundation of Western Thought. London: Allen & Unwin.

Jacobson, E. (1964), The Self and the Object World. New York: International Universities Press.

Janet, P. (1895), Charcot, J. M., son Oeuvre Psychologique. Rev. Philosophique, 39:569-605.

Jewish Encyclopedia, The (1964), 3:323-325. New York: Ktav Publishing House.

Jones, E. (1910), The Oedipus Complex as an Explanation of Hamlet's Mystery. Amer. J. Psychiat., 67:279-286.

_____(1933), Sàndor Ferenczi, 1873-1933. Internat. J. Psycho-Anal., 14:463-466.

_____(1953), The Life and Work of Sigmund Freud, Vol. 1. New York: Basic Books.

_____(1954), Freud's Early Travels. *Internat. J. Psycho-Anal.*, 35:81-84.
_____(1955), *The Life and Work of Sigmund Freud,* Vol. 2. New York: Basic Books.
_____(1957), *The Life and Work of Sigmund Freud,* Vol. 3. New York: Basic Books.
_____(1959), *Free Associations.* New York: Basic Books.
Jones, P. (1937), *French Introspectives from Montaigne to Gide.* Cambridge: Cambridge University Press.
Jung, C. (1902), On the Psychology and Pathology of So-Called Occult Phenomena. *Collected Works,* 1:3-92. New York: Pantheon, 1957.
_____(1905), Cryptomnesia. *Collected Works,* 1:95-106. New York: Pantheon, 1957.
_____(1961), *Memories, Dreams, Reflections.* New York: Pantheon.
Kahler, E. (1967), The Jews and the Germans. In: *Studies of the Leo Baeck Institute,* ed. M. Kreutzberger. New York: Unger, pp. 19-43.
Kant, I. (1781), The Critique of Pure Reason. In: *Modern Classical Philosophers,* 2nd ed., ed. B. Rand. Cambridge: Riverside Press, 1936.
Kardiner, A. (1957), Freud—The Man I Knew, the Scientist, and His Influence. In: *Freud and the 20th Century,* ed. B. Nelson. New York: Meridian, pp. 46-58.
Karpe, R. (1961), The Rescue Complex in Anna O.'s Final Identity. *Psychoanal. Quart.,* 30:1-27.
Klein, G. S. (1966), The Several Grades of Memory. In: *Psychoanalysis—A General Psychology,* ed. R. Loewenstein, L. Newman, M. Schur, & A. Solnit. New York: International Universities Press, pp. 377-389.
Koestler, A. (1964), *The Act of Creation.* New York: Macmillan.
Kohut, H. (1957), "Death in Venice" by T. Mann; A Story about the Disintegration of Artistic Sublimation. *Psychoanal. Quart.,* 26:206-228.
_____(1959), Introspection, Empathy and Psychoanalysis. *J. Amer. Psychoanal. Assn.,* 7:459-483.
_____(1960), Beyond the Bounds of the Basic Rule. *J. Amer. Psychoanal. Assn.,* 8:567-586.
_____(1966), Forms and Transformations of Narcissism. *J. Amer. Psychoanal. Assn.,* 14:243-272.
_____(1968), The Psychoanalytic Treatment of Narcissistic Personality Disorders. *The Psychoanalytic Study of the Child,* 23:86-113. New York: International Universities Press.
_____(1970a), Scientific Activities of the American Psychoanalytic Association: An Inquiry. *J. Amer. Psychoanal. Assn.,* 18:462-484.
_____(1970b), Discussion of D. Levin's "The Self: A Contribution to Its Place in Theory and Technique." *Internat. J. Psycho-Anal.,* 51:176-181.
_____(1971), *The Analysis of the Self.* New York: International Universities Press.
_____(1972), Thoughts on Narcissism and Narcissistic Rage. *The Psychoanalytic Study of the Child,* 27:360-400. New York: Quadrangle.
_____(1973), Psychoanalysis in a Troubled World. *The Annual of Psychoanalysis,* 1:3-25. New York: Quadrangle.
Kris, E. (1932-1952), *Psychoanalytic Explorations in Art.* New York: International Universities Press.
_____(1939), On Inspiration. *Psychoanalytic Explorations in Art.* New York: International Universities Press, pp. 291-302, 1952.
_____(1950a), On Preconscious Mental Processes. *Psychoanalytic Explorations in Art.* New York: International Universities Press, 1952, pp. 303-320.
_____(1950b), Introduction to *The Origins of Psychoanalysis,* ed. M. Bonaparte, E. Freud, & E. Kris. New York: Basic Books, 1954.
_____(1956), On Some Vicissitudes of Insight in Psycho-Analysis. *Internat. J. Psycho-Anal.,* 37:445-455.

Kristeller, P. (1961), *Renaissance Thought*. New York: Harper Torchbooks.
———(1965), *Renaissance Thought II*. New York: Harper Torchbooks.
Kupper, H., & Rollman-Branch, H. (1959), Freud and Schnitzler—(*Doppelgänger*). *J. Amer. Psychoanal. Assn.*, 7:109-126.
Leavy, S. (1964), *The Freud Journal of Lou Andreas-Salomé*. New York: Basic Books.
Loewald, H. (1955), Hypnoid State, Repression, Abreaction and Recollection. *J. Amer. Psychoanal. Assn.*, 3:201-210.
Looney, J. (1920), *"Shakespeare" Identified*. New York: Stokes.
Lorand, S. (1966), Pioneer of Pioneers. In: *Psychoanalytic Pioneers*, ed. F. Alexander, S. Eisenstein, & M. Grotjahn. New York: Basic Books, pp. 14-35.
Lowenfeld, H. (1956), Sigmund Freud. *J. Amer. Psychoanal. Assn.*, 4:682-691.
Mach, E. (1900), *Die Analyse der Empfindungen*, 2nd ed. Jena.
Machiavelli, N. (1512-1527), Discourses on the First Ten Books of Titus Livius. In: *The Prince and the Discourses*. New York: Modern Library, 1950.
McGrath, W. (1967), Student Radicalism in Vienna. *J. Contemp. Hist.*, 2:183-201.
McGuire, W., ed. (1974), *The Freud/Jung Letters*. Princeton: Princeton University Press.
McManaway, J. (1962), *The Authorship of Shakespeare*. Washington: Folger Shakespeare Library.
Meng, H., & Freud, E., eds. (1963), *Psychoanalysis and Faith*. New York: Basic Books.
Merlan, P. (1945), Brentano and Freud. *J. Hist. Ideas*, 6:375-377.
———(1949), Brentano and Freud—A Sequel. *J. Hist. Ideas*, 10:451.
Meyer, H. H. (1928), Josef Breuer 1842-1925. *Neue Oester Reichische Biographien*, 5:30-47. Wien: Amalthea.
Michelangelo (1496-1563), *Complete Poems and Selected Letters*, ed. R. Linscott. New York: Modern Library, 1965.
Montaigne, M. (1580-1592), *The Complete Essays of Montaigne*, trans. D. Frame. Palo Alto: Stanford University Press, 1965.
Moruzzi, G., & Magoun, H. (1949), Brain Stem Reticular Formation and Activation of the EEG. *EEG Clin. Neurophysiol.*, 7:455-473.
Nagera, H., ed. (1969-1970), *Basic Psychoanalytic Concepts*, 4 vols. New York: Basic Books.
Niederland, W. (1951), Three Notes on the Schreber Case. *Psychoanal. Quart.*, 20:579-591.
———(1959a), Schreber, Father and Son. *Psychoanal. Quart.*, 28:151-160.
———(1959b), The "Miracled-Up" World of Schreber's Childhood. *The Psychoanalytic Study of the Child*, 14:383-413. New York: International Universities Press.
———(1960a), Schreber's Father. *J. Amer. Psychoanal. Assn.*, 8:492-499.
———(1960b), The First Application of Psychoanalysis to a Literary Work. *Psychoanal. Quart.*, 29:228-235.
———(1963), Further Data and Memorabilia Pertaining to the Schreber Case. *Internat. J. Psycho-Anal.*, 44:201-207.
———(1965), Panel Report: Memory and Repression. *J. Amer. Psychoanal Assn.*, 13:619-633.
———(1971), Freud's Literary Style: Some Observations. *Amer. Imago*, 28:17-23.
Nunberg, H., & Federn, E., eds. (1962-1974), *Minutes of the Vienna Psychoanalytic Society*, 4 vols. New York: International Universities Press.
Oberndorf, C. P., ed. (1953), Autobiography of Josef Breuer (1842-1925). *Internat. J. Psycho-Anal.*, 34:64-67.
Paquet, A. (1930), Brief an S. Freud. In: *Gesammelte Werke*, 14:545(fn). London: Imago, 1948.
Pauncz, A. (1952), Psychopathology of Shakespeare's King Lear. *Amer. Imago*, 9:57-78.

Pico della Mirandola, G. (1494), Oration on the Dignity of Man. In: *Renaissance Philosophy I—The Italian Philosophers*, ed. A. Fallico & H. Shapiro. New York: Modern Library, 1967.

Pfeiffer, E., ed. (1966), *Sigmund Freud and Lou Andreas-Salomé Letters*. New York: Harcourt Brace Jovanovich, 1972.

Platt, J. (1964), Strong Inference. *Science*, 146(No. 3642): October 16.

Pollock, G. H. (1961), Mourning and Adaptation. *Internat. J. Psycho-Anal.*, 42:341-361.

———(1962), Childhood Parent and Sibling Loss in Adult Patients. *Arch. Gen. Psychiat.*, 7:295-305.

———(1971), Glückel von Hameln: Bertha Pappenheim's Idealized Ancestor. *Amer. Imago*, 28:216-227.

———(1972), Bertha Pappenheim's Pathological Mourning: Possible Effects of Childhood Sibling Loss. *J. Amer. Psychoanal. Assn.*, 20:478-493.

———(1973), Bertha Pappenheim: Addenda to Her Case History. *J. Amer. Psychoanal. Assn.*, 21:328-332.

Popper-Lynkeus, J. (1878), *Das Recht zu Leben und die Pflicht zu Sterben, Sozialphilosophische Betrachungen, anknüpfend an die Bedeutung Voltaires für die neuere Zeit*.

———(1899a), *Phantasien eines Realisten*. Dresden: Reissner, 1922.

———(1899b), Dreaming like Waking. *Psychoanal. Rev.*, 34:184-197, 1947.

———(1912), *Die Allgemeine Nährpflicht*. Dresden: Reissner.

Putnam, S. (1952), Introduction to *Cervantes: Three Exemplary Novels*, trans. S. Putnam. London: Cassel.

Rabelais, F. (1532), Pantagruel. In: *The Portable Rabelais*, ed. S. Putnam. New York: Viking, 1946.

Rado, S. (1933), Obituary, Sàndor Ferenczi. *Psychoanal. Quart.*, 2:356-358.

Rank, O. (1925), *Der Doppelgänger*. Wien: Internationaler Psychoanalytischer Verlag.

———(1941), *Beyond Psychology*. New York: Dover, 1958.

Rapaport, D. (1947), Dynamic Psychology and Kantian Epistemology. *J. Hist. Behav. Sci.*, 2:192-199, 1966.

———, ed. (1951), *Organization and Pathology of Thought*. New York: Columbia University Press.

———(1952), Review of Edwin G. Boring, *A History of Experimental Psychology*. *Psychoanal. Quart.*, 21:123-126.

———(1959), The Structure of Psychoanalytic Theory. *Psychol. Issues*, Monogr. No. 6. New York: International Universities Press, 1960.

Reich, W. (1933), *Character Analysis*, 3rd ed. New York: Orgone Institute Press, 1949.

Reichert, S. (1956), A Re-examination of "Studies in Hysteria." *Psychoanal. Quart.*, 25:155-177.

Reik, T. (1956), *The Search Within*. New York: Funk & Wagnalls, 1968.

Ribot, T. (1881), *Maladies de la Mémoire*. Paris: Alcan.

Rieff, P. (1959), *Freud: The Mind of the Moralist*. New York: Viking.

Rogawski, A. (1970), Young Freud as Poet. *Celebration of Laughter*. Los Angeles: Mara Books, pp. 99-117.

Rose, H. (1936), *A Handbook of Latin Literature*. New York: Dutton, 1960.

Rosenzweig, S. (1958), The Idiocultural Dimension of Psychotherapy. *Psychoanalysis and the Social Sciences*, 5:9-49. New York: International Universities Press.

Sachs, H. (1942), *The Creative Unconscious*. Cambridge, Mass.: Sci-Art.

———(1944), *Freud, Master and Friend*. Cambridge: Harvard University Press.

Sayce, R. (1972), *The Essays of Montaigne: A Critical Exploration*. London: Weidenfeld & Nicolson.

Schick, A. (1968-1969), The Vienna of Sigmund Freud. *Psychoanal. Rev.*, 55: 529-551.

Schlessinger, N. (1965), On Faust's Descent to "the Mothers." Manuscript.
Schönau, W. (1968), *Sigmund Freuds Prosa.* Stuttgart: Metzlersche Verlagsbuchhandlung.
Scnorske, C. (1967), Politics in a New Key: An Austrian Triptych. *J. Mod. Hist.,* 39:343-386.
Schur, M. (1966a), Some Additional "Day Residues" of "The Specimen Dream of Psychoanalysis." In: *Psychoanalysis—A General Psychology,* ed. R. Loewenstein, L. Newman, M. Schur, & A. Solnit. New York: International Universities Press, pp. 45-85.
———(1966b), The Background of Freud's "Disturbance" on the Acropolis. *Amer. Imago,* 16:303-324.
———(1972), *Freud: Living and Dying.* New York: International Universities Press.
Schusdek, A. (1966), Freud's "Seduction Theory": A Reconstruction. *J. Hist. Behav. Sci.,* 2:159-166.
Sharpe, E. F. (1946), From "King Lear" to "The Tempest." *Internat. J. Psycho-Anal.,* 27:19-30.
Shengold, L. (1971), Freud and Joseph. In: *The Unconscious Today,* ed. M. Kanzer. New York: International Universities Press, pp. 473-494.
———(1972), A Parapraxis of Freud's in Relation to Karl Abraham. *Amer. Imago,* 29:123-159.
Slochower, H. (1970), Freud's Déjà Vu on the Acropolis; A Symbolic Relic of "Mater Nuda." *Psychoanal. Quart.,* 29:90-102.
Spiegel, L. (1959), The Self, the Sense of Self, and Perception. *The Psychoanalytic Study of the Child,* 14:81-112. New York: International Universities Press.
Spitzer, L. (1969), On the Significance of Don Quijote. In: *Cervantes—A Collection of Critical Essays,* ed. L. Nelson. Englewood Cliffs, N. J.: Prentice-Hall, pp. 82-97.
Stanescu, H. (1965), Unbekannte Briefe des Jungen Sigmund Freud an Einen Rumanischen Freund. *Neue Literatur,* 16(3):123-129.
———(1967), Ein Gellgenheitsgedicht des Jungen Sigmund Freud. *Deutsch für Ausländer,* Jan.:13-18.
———(1971), Young Freud's Letters to his Rumanian Friend, Silberstein. *Israel Ann. Psychiat.,* 9:195-207.
Starkie, W. (1964), Introduction to *Cervantes: Don Quixote de la Mancha.* New York: Signet Classic.
Stekel, W. (1922), *Peculiarities of Behavior.* New York: Liveright, 1924.
Sterba, R. (1969), The Psychoanalyst in a World of Change. *Psychoanal. Quart.,* 38:432-454.
———, & Sterba, E. (1960), *Beethoven and His Nephew.* New York: Pantheon.
Stewart, W. (1968), *Psychoanalysis: The First Ten Years.* New York: Macmillan.
Strachey, J. (1953), Editor's Note to Three Essays on the Theory of Sexuality. *Standard Edition,* 7:125-129. London: Hogarth Press.
———(1955a), Editor's Introduction to Studies on Hysteria. *Standard Edition,* 2:ix-xxviii. London: Hogarth Press.
———(1955b), Editor's Note to Beyond the Pleasure Principle. *Standard Edition,* 18:3-6. London: Hogarth Press.
———(1957), Editor's Introduction to Papers on Metapsychology. *Standard Edition,* 14:105-107. London: Hogarth Press.
———(1959), Editor's Note to Delusions and Dreams in Jensen's *Gradiva. Standard Edition,* 9:3-6. London: Hogarth Press.
———(1961), Editor's Note to Fetishism. *Standard Edition,* 21:149-151. London: Hogarth Press.
Sullivan, J. (1959), From Breuer to Freud. *Psychoanal. & Psychoanal. Rev.,* 46:69-90.
Székely, L. (1967), The Creative Pause. *Internat. J. Psycho-Anal.,* 48:353-367.

438   REFERENCES

————(1970), Über den Beginn des Maschinenzeitalters: Psychoanalytische Be-
merkungen uber das Erfinden. *Schweiz. Z. Psychol.*, 29:273-282.
Taylor, F. (1965), Cryptomnesia and Plagiarism. *Brit. J. Psychiat.*, 111:1111-1118.
Telle, E. (1968), A Propos du Mot "Essai" chez Montaigne. *Bibliotheque d'Hu-
manisme et Renaissance*, 30:228.
Thompson, C. (1944), Ferenczi's Contribution to Psychoanalysis. *Psychiatry*,
7:245-255.
————(1950), Introduction to S. Ferenczi, *Sex in Psychoanalysis*. New York:
Basic Books.
Titherley, A. W. (1952), *Shakespeare's Identity: William Stanley, Sixth Earl of
Derby*. Winchester, Eng.
Trilling, L. (1950), *The Liberal Imagination*. New York: Viking.
Trosman, H., & Simmons, R. (1972), The Freud Library. *J. Amer. Psychoanal.
Assn.*, 21:646-687.
Universal Jewish Encyclopedia, The (1939-1943), 2:474-476. New York: The Uni-
versal Jewish Encyclopedia.
Veith, I. (1965), *Hysteria: The History of a Disease*. Chicago: University of Chi-
cago Press.
Wadsworth, F. (1958), *The Poacher from Stratford*. Berkeley: The University of
California Press.
Waelder, R. (1956), Freud and the History of Science. *J. Amer. Psychoanal.
Assn.*, 4:602-613.
————(1962), Psychoanalysis, Scientific Method, and Philosophy. *J. Amer. Psy-
choanal. Assn.*, 10:617-637.
————(1965), *Psychoanalytic Avenues to Art*. New York: International Univer-
sities Press.
Weiss, E. (1970), *Sigmund Freud as a Consultant*. New York: Intercontinental
Medical Book Corp.
Whyte, L. (1960), *The Unconscious before Freud*. New York: Basic Books.
Winnicott, D. W. (1931-1956), *Collected Papers*. New York: Basic Books, 1958.
————(1957-1963), *The Maturational Process and the Facilitating Environment*.
New York: International Universities Press, 1965.
Wittels, F. (1924), *Sigm. Freud: Der Mann, die Lehre, die Schule*. Leipzig: Tal.
————(1947), Freud's Correlation with Josef Popper-Lynkeus. *Psychoanal. Rev.*,
34:492-497.
Wolf, E. S. (1971), Sigmund Freud: Some Adolescent Transformations of a Future
Genius. In: *Adolescent Psychiatry*, Vol. 1: *Developmental and Clinical
Studies*. New York: Basic Books, pp. 51-60.
————(1973a), Minister to a Mind Diseased: Freud at the Allgemeine Kranken-
haus. *The Annual of Psychoanalysis*, 1:336-344. New York: Quadrangle.
————(1973b), The Debunker Debunked. Review of K. R. Eissler's *Talent and
Genius*. *Contemp. Psychol.*, 18:56-57.
————, Gedo, J. E., & Terman, D. (1972), On the Adolescent Process as a Trans-
formation of the Self. *J. Youth Adolesc.*, 1:257-272.
Wolman, B. (1964), Psychoanalysis and Applied Science. *Amer. Imago*, 21:
153-164.
Wortis, J. (1954), *Fragment of an Analysis with Freud*. New York: Simon &
Schuster.
Wright, B. (1941), *A History of Modern Philosophy*. New York: Macmillan.
Zeller, E. (1883), *Outlines of the History of Greek Philosophy*. Cleveland: World,
1955.
Zilboorg, G. (1952), Some Sidelights on Free Association. *Internat. J. Psycho-
Anal.*, 33:489-495.
————, & Henry, G. (1941), *A History of Medical Psychology*. New York:
Norton.
Zweig, S. (1943), *The World of Yesterday*. New York: Viking.

INDEX

439

Dukes, G., 235, 247
Dumreicher, J. von, 145
Dürer, A., 210
Durning-Lawrence, E., 315

Ebner-Eschenbach, M. von, 153
Eckermann, J. P., 404
Education, Montaigne on, 27
Edwards, P., 339, 340, 342
Ego psychology, Ferenczi and, 366-369
Einstein, A., 207, 228, 337, 339, 340, 346
Eisenstein, S., 357
Eissler, K. R., 11, 63, 64, 72, 73, 75-77, 92, 94, 127, 145, 170, 182, 218, 223, 224, 245, 249, 309, 345, 378, 380, 388
Elkisch, P., 352
Ellenberger, H., 50, 62, 96, 118, 139, 168, 170, 198, 226, 339, 351, 394
Ellis, H., 226, 233, 240
Empedocles, 238
Erasmus, 16, 34, 89, 97, 99
Erikson, E. H., 249, 270, 288, 294-295, 297, 420
Euclid, 43
Exner, S., 145

Faust, 140, 150-152
Federn, E., 170, 231
Federn, P., 369, 377
Feldman, A., 309
Fenichel, O., 275
Ferenczi, S., 5, 235, 236, 273, 280, 290, 292, 293, 302, 303, 308, 357
  conflicting views on, 359-360
  contributions of to psychoanalysis, 361-375, 377-378
  Freud's analysis of, 358-359, 365-366, 372
  technical experiments of, 369, 371-376
  terminal illness of, 376
  Thalassa, 376-377
Feuerbach, L. A., 47, 350
Flatter, R., 312
Flaubert, G., 18, 39
Fleischl, E. von, 145j
Fleming, J., 136, 137
Fliess, W., 4, 13, 53, 57, 74, 92, 109, 154, 161, 169, 171, 182, 200, 204, 212, 213, 218, 242, 269, 270, 273, 279, 288, 295, 300, 305, 331, 417
  Breuer's relationship with, 135, 142, 149, 155
  Freud's relationship with, 5, 132,

135, 155-156, 184, 190, 221-224, 245-247, 250, 264, 287, 294, 296-298, 308, 333, 345-346, 358, 380, 392-394, 398, 402, 406, 418, 423
  theories of, 223, 246, 308, 376
Florio, J., 41
Flournoy, T., 234
Fluss, E., 71-86, 108, 170, 227, 245
Fluss, G., 71-72, 75, 76, 82, 83, 107-110, 351
Fonk, —, 233, 253
Forel, A., 147
Frame, D., 19, 39
Francis, St., 31
Franz Josef, Emperor, 83
Free association, development of technique of, 229-253
Frenkel-Brunswick, E., 236, 247, 250
Freud, Alexander, 290
Freud, Amalia, 287, 295
Freud, Anna (daughter), 143, 169, 290, 292, 293, 302, 371, 375
Freud, Anna (sister), 330-331
Freud, Emmanuel, 292, 295, 302, 330-331
Freud, Ernst, 57, 63, 74-76, 89, 90, 92, 93, 125, 127, 129, 140, 157, 161, 169, 170, 220, 227, 231, 237, 244-245, 272, 277, 280, 281, 292, 293, 296, 302, 310, 336-338, 346, 360, 366, 367
Freud, Jakob, 55, 109-111, 287
Freud, Jean Martin, 127
Freud, John, 155
Freud, Julius, 109, 155, 280, 295
Freud, Martha; see Bernays, Martha
Freud, Martin, 295
Freud, Matilde, 143
Freud, Pauline, 155
Freud, Philipp, 295, 330-331
Freud, Sigmund
  Acropolis, experience of on, 111, 287, 289, 292, 293, 296-297, 299-300, 334, 352
  anxiety theory of, 274-276, 278-279, 283, 285
  applied psychoanalytic studies of, 212
  archaeology, interest of in, 12, 69, 216-217, 224-225, 298, 301
  Breuer, J , and, 133-135, 138, 141, 142, 146-149, 154-158, 160-162, 173, 188-190, 200-201, 203-206
  career choice of, 52, 55, 57, 72-73, 75, 77, 84

442

INDEX

Cervantes, M. de, and, 87-94, 96, 98, 99, 102, 103, 105, 108, 110
Charcot, J. M., and, 115-119, 121, 125-132
classical education of, 46, 66-70, 73, 83-84
creativity of, 394, 401-404, 406-407
cryptomnesia of, 229, 232-233, 236-238, 242, 245-246, 248-251, 341, 349
cultural background of, 46-70
defense concept of, 201-203, 262-264, 283, 284
"doubles" of, 250-251, 333, 347-348, 350-353
on "the exceptions," 413
family of, 162
family-romance interpretations of, 308, 309, 327, 329-331
Fliess, W., and, 221-224, 287
Fluss, E., and, 71-72, 74-75, 79, 81-82, 86, 108
Fluss, G., adolescent love for, 71-72, 75-76, 82, 83, 107-110
free association, discovery of, 229-251
hypnosis, disillusionment with, 205
hypothesis changes of, 257-285
idealizations of, 190, 264, 287, 308, 333, 346-347, 353, 358; see also Freud, identification figures of; transferences of
identification figures of, 90, 128, 129, 131-132, 224-225, 243, 248, 296, 299, 301, 303-305; see also Freud, idealizations of; transferences of
influence of on immediate followers, 357-358
Jewish tradition and, 46-47, 61-66, 70
Josef, significance of name for, 350-351
on King Lear, 158-159
library of, 18, 64, 69
literary style of, 73, 77-85, 92, 110, 193-194, 213-224, 226-228
Montaigne compared to, 38-40
nanny of, relationship to, 294-295, 305
narcissistic vulnerability of in adolescence, 109
as an orator, 214
philosophy and, 12-13, 47, 239, 245
political interests of, 47, 49, 54-55, 57-59
Popper-Lynkeus, J., and, 332-353

psychoanalysts' attitude toward, 379-381, 383-391
Romantic view of nature of, 47-54, 59
scientific style of, 137, 167-174, 181, 185, 187-188, 190-191, 199, 201, 203, 206; see also Freud, hypothesis changes of
self-analysis of, 171, 204, 205, 211, 238, 258, 264, 270, 272-274, 285-306, 380-384, 391-394, 398-399, 406, 418, 423-425
self-observation of, in adolescence, 78
Shakespearean controversy and, 307-313, 315, 327-331
Silberstein, E., and, 92-93
transferences of, 296-298, 300, 305, 345; see also Freud, idealizations of; identification figures of
travels of, 290-299, 305
Freud, Sophie, 280, 281, 304
Freund, A. von, 280
Friedrich, H., 18
Frisch, —, 145
Frosch, J., 327

Gable, L., 6, 252
Galton, F., 240
Gedo, J. E., 1, 3-6, 11-45, 71-132, 167-207, 210, 229, 239, 245, 257-307, 332, 334, 357-378, 382, 383, 403, 407
Gedo, M., 225, 404
Gersuny, —, 145
Gibson, H., 315, 320, 321
Glauber, I., 185
Goethe, J. W. von, 18, 39, 49, 50, 52-53, 58, 59, 65, 69, 72, 77, 80, 83-86, 110, 150-153, 210, 220, 224, 227, 233, 253, 308, 340
Goldberg, A., 288, 368
Goltz, F., 195
Great men
  ambivalence toward, 359, 377, 382
  identification with, 131, 384
  see also Charismatic/messianic personalities
Greece, introspective psychology in, 11-12, 15
Grene, D., 299
Groddeck, G., 90, 237
Grotjahn, M., 357
Group psychology, 419-423, 425; see also Self, group
Guillain, G., 118, 125, 126, 130

ABOUT THE AUTHORS

All of the authors represented in this volume obtained their psychoanalytic training at the Chicago Institute for Psychoanalysis. Drs. Sabshin and Trosman hold full-time academic appointments; the others have been principally engaged in the private practice of analysis.

JOHN E. GEDO obtained his M.D. at New York University and his psychiatric training with the Associated Psychiatric Faculties of Chicago. He is currently Clinical Professor of Psychiatry at the Abraham Lincoln School of Medicine of the University of Illinois, and a Training Analyst of the Chicago Institute for Psychoanalysis. He is co-author of *Models of the Mind: A Psychoanalytic Theory* (1973).

HEINZ KOHUT received his M.D. from the University of Vienna; he was trained in neurology and psychiatry at the University of Chicago, where he is now Professorial Lecturer in Psychiatry. He has also been appointed Visiting Professor of Psychoanalysis at the University of Cincinnati. At the Chicago Institute for Psychoanalysis, he serves as Training Analyst. He was President of the American Psychoanalytic Association (1964-65) and has been Vice-President of the International Psycho-Analytical Association since 1965. His book *The Analysis of the Self* (1971) is being translated into German and French.

The late JULIAN MILLER had his medical and psychiatric training from the University of Chicago. At the time of his death at age 38, he was Director of Residency Training in the Department of Psychiatry at the University of Illinois College of Medicine.

GEORGE H. POLLOCK obtained his doctorates in medicine and physiology, as well as his psychiatric training, at the University of Illinois. He is Director of the Chicago Institute for Psychoanalysis; before assuming this post in 1971, he was for many years a Training Analyst and its Director of Research. He is also Professor of Psychiatry at Northwestern University Medical School. In 1974-75 he was President of the American Psychoanalytic Association. He is the principal author of *Psychosomatic Specificity* (1968).

MELVIN SABSHIN received his M.D. from the University of Florida and his psychiatric training at Tulane University. He is Medical Director of the American Psychiatric Association and was formerly Professor and Head of the Department of Psychiatry at the Abraham Lincoln School of Medicine of the University of Illinois. He has been co-author of a number of books and during 1973-74 he was President of the American College of Psychiatrists.

LEO SADOW had his medical and psychiatric training at the University of Chicago. He is currently Clinical Associate Professor of Psychiatry at the Abraham Lincoln School of Medicine of the University of Illinois. He is a Training Analyst of the Chicago Institute for Psychoanalysis.

NATHAN SCHLESSINGER obtained his M.D. from the University of Cincinnati and his psychiatric training at the Associated Psychiatric Faculties of Chicago. He is currently Clinical Associate Professor of Psychiatry at the Abraham Lincoln School of Medicine of the University of Illinois and Attending Physician at Michael Reese Hospital. He is a Training Analyst of the Chicago Institute for Psychoanalysis.

HARRY TROSMAN received his M.D. from the University of Toronto and his psychiatric training at the Universities of Iowa and Cincinnati. He is Associate Professor of Psychiatry at the Pritzker School of Medicine of the University of Chicago. He is also a Training Analyst of the Chicago Institute for Psychoanalysis.

ERNEST WOLF had his medical training at the University of Maryland and his psychiatric residency at the University of Cincinnati. He is currently Associate Director of the Center for Psychosocial Studies, Chicago, and Assistant Professor of Psychiatry at Northwestern Medical School. He is a Training Analyst of the Chicago Institute for Psychoanalysis.

PSYCHOLOGICAL ISSUES